Apple Pro Training Series
Final Cut Pro 5

Diana Weynand

Apple
Certified

Apple Pro Training Series: Final Cut Pro 5
Diana Weynand
Copyright © 2006 by Diana Weynand and Shirley Craig

Published by Peachpit Press. For information on Peachpit Press books, contact:

Peachpit Press
1249 Eighth Street
Berkeley, CA 94710
(510) 524-2178
Fax: (510) 524-2221
http://www.peachpit.com
To report errors, please send a note to errata@peachpit.com
Peachpit Press is a division of Pearson Education

Project Director: Shirley Craig
Series Editor: Serena Herr
Managing Editor: Kristin Kalning
Editor: Nancy Peterson, Alchemy Editing
Production Coordinator: Laurie Stewart, Happenstance Type-O-Rama
Technical Editor: Nathan Haggard
Technical Reviewers: Brendan Boykin and Stephen Kanter
Copy Editors: Darren Meiss and Emily K. Wolman
Compositor: Robin Kibby, Happenstance Type-O-Rama
Indexer: Valerie Perry
Cover and Interior Designs: Frances Baca Design
Cover Illustration: Alicia Buelow
Cover Production: George Mattingly / GMD
Front cover photos: Claudio Miranda

Notice of Rights

All rights reserved. No part of this book may be reproduced or transmitted in any form by any means, electronic, mechanical, photocopying, recording, or otherwise, without the prior written permission of the publisher. For information on getting permission for reprints and excerpts, contact permissions@peachpit.com.
Footage from *A Thousand Roads* was provided by the Smithsonian's National Museum of the American Indian, www.americanindian.si.edu; all rights reserved.
The Motocross footage was provided by Michael Bryant and Perry Karidis of State of Mind Productions; all rights reserved.
"Box Office Stud" performed by the "All Hours" band (The Midnight Radio, LLC), written by Gilly Leads, used courtesy of Hybrid Recordings, LLC, and BMG Film and TV Music. "Box Office Stud" music video produced and provided by Weynand Training International, Inc., www.weynand.com. All rights reserved.
Additional music tracks provided with permission from Megatrax, Production Music and Original Scoring, www.megatrax.com.

Notice of Liability

The information in this book is distributed on an "As Is" basis, without warranty. While every precaution has been taken in the preparation of the book, neither the authors nor Peachpit Press shall have any liability to any person or entity with respect to any loss or damage caused or alleged to be caused directly or indirectly by the instructions contained in this book or by the computer software and hardware products described in it.

Trademarks

Throughout this book trademarked names are used. Rather than put a trademark symbol in every occurrence of a trademarked name, we state we are using the names only in an editorial fashion and to the benefit of the trademark owner with no intention of infringement of the trademark
ISBN 0-321-33481-7
9 8 7 6 5 4
Printed and bound in the United States of America

To Barry Clark, thank you for saying yes—twice.

Acknowledgments First and foremost, I'd like to thank my business partner, Shirley Craig, for supporting our ongoing training programs at our company, Weynand Training International, while I was busy writing.

To those who provided the exceptional footage for this book, you have my deepest gratitude. A huge thank you to Barry Clark and Scott Garen for letting me use the actual media files from their dramatic film, *A Thousand Roads*, and to Elizabeth Duggal at the Smithsonian's National Museum of the American Indian for supporting their decision. Their footage brings extraordinary beauty to the exercises in this book. Thank you as well to Michael Bryant and Perry Karidis for the use of their daring and adventurous motocross documentary footage, and last but certainly not least, many thanks to the All Hours band— Gilly Leads, Dean Moore, Nick Burns, and Amit LeRon—for their hard work at The Viper Room during the shooting of the music video; their manager, Jodi Chall; Al Cafaro of Hybrid Recordings; and Lauren Haber at BMG for allowing me to use an excerpt from "Box Office Stud" for the multicam lesson.

A big debt of gratitude goes to my excellent editorial team, headed by Nancy Peterson of Alchemy Editing; to Nathan Haggard for his technical editing; Mary Plummer and Adam Green for their Apple-wise input; Darren Meiss for copyediting; and Brendan Boykin and Steve Kanter for the quality control.

At Apple, thanks to Patty Montesion for her generous enthusiasm and for creating the Apple Pro Training Series, and to Kirk Paulsen, Brian Meaney, Paul Saccone, and Erin Skitt for their support in all things Final Cut Pro. Thanks to the Peachpit team who guided this book along its way: Nancy Ruenzel, Serena Herr, Kristin Kalning, Laurie Stewart, Maureen Forys, and Eric Geoffroy.

To Claudio Miranda for the book cover image; Karen Jossel at Lucky Dog Graphic Design for her graphics; Roger Mabon at G-Technology, Inc., for the use of a G-RAID drive, which performed flawlessly; Ted Shilowitz and Gerard Tassone at AJA for the use of the Io board; Manny Gaudierat at Sony for the use of the PDW-1 deck to capture XDCAM optical disk material; and Andrew Robbins of Megatrax.

Finally, it's always valuable to have other eyes looking over my shoulder. Thanks to Christian Dangaard, Jeff Morse, David Heimann, and especially Susan Merzbach for their work and feedback on the sequences.

Xsanadmin (XSAN) > paths
Paths (File System XSAN)
ACFS Disk Volumes:
<000393000006B88>
            Controller: <5000393000006B88
device: rdisk1 hba id: 2 lu
            LUN1 on device: rdisk1 h
       Available LUN1 on device
<0393000006CC4>
            Controller: <5000393000006CC4
    rdisk2 hba id: 1 lun
          LUN2 on device: rdisk2 h
       Available

Contents at a Glance

Table of Contents

Xsanadmin (XSAN) > paths
Paths (File System XSAN)
ACFS Disk Volumes:
    Controller: <5000393000006B88
device: rdisk1 hba id: 2 lun.
    LUN1 on device: rdisk1 h
    Available LUN1 on device
<0393000006CC4>
    Controller: <5000393000006CC4
    rdisk2 hba id: 1 lun:
umes: LUN2 on device: rdisk2 h
    Available
<5000393000

Getting Started

Welcome to the official Apple Pro Training Series course for Final Cut Pro 5, Apple's dynamic and powerful nonlinear editing package. This book is a comprehensive guide to the Final Cut Pro application and uses real-world footage in both NTSC and PAL to show the many uses of the application.

In addition to the lessons contained in this book, the accompanying DVD contains an introduction to LiveType, the 32-bit animated titling application that comes bundled with Final Cut Pro along with Cinema Tools and Compressor.

Whether you're a seasoned veteran or just getting started in the editing field, Final Cut Pro 5 can serve all your editing needs. So let's get started.

The Methodology

This book is first and foremost a hands-on course. Every exercise in this book is designed to help you begin editing in Final Cut Pro at a professional level as quickly as possible. Each lesson builds on the previous lesson and continues to step you up through the program's functions and capabilities. If you are new to Final Cut Pro, start at the beginning, and progress through each lesson in order. If you are familiar with an earlier version of Final Cut Pro, you can pop into a specific section and focus on that topic, since every lesson is self-contained.

Course Structure

This book is designed to get you up and running with the basic Final Cut Pro editing and trimming functions first, then give you a broader understanding of how to customize and use the program for your own purposes, and finally to immerse you in the more advanced features of Final Cut Pro effects, titling, and output. The lessons fall into the following categories:

▶   Lessons 1–7   Basic editing and trimming

▶   Lessons 8–9   Customizing and capturing

▶   Lessons 10–13   Video and audio effects and audio mixing

▶   Lesson 14   Multicam editing

▶   Lessons 15–16   Titling and final outputting

Each lesson begins with a "Preparing the Project" section, which shows you what you will create in that lesson. In addition to the exercises contained within each lesson, most lessons include a section called "Project Practice," which gives you an opportunity to stop and practice what you've learned before moving on to new material.

Using the DVD Book Files

Apple Pro Training Series: Final Cut Pro 5 comes with a DVD containing the files you will use for each lesson (called project files) as well as files containing sound and visual media (called media files). Each lesson has its own project file. In the Media folder, you will find three primary audio/video media file folders titled A Thousand Roads, Motocross, and Music Video. (You can read more detail about this footage in the next section.) The Exports and Graphics folders are used for specific lessons only. Once you load the files onto your hard drive, each lesson in the book will guide you in the use of all of the project and media files.

To Install the Final Cut Pro 5 Lesson Files

The *Apple Pro Training Series: Final Cut Pro 5* DVD-ROM includes a folder titled FCP5 Book Files, which contains two subfolders: Lessons and Media. These folders hold the lessons and media files you will need for this course. Make sure you keep these two folders together in the FCP 5 Book Files folder. If you keep them together on your hard drive, you should be able to maintain the original link between the lessons and media files.

1   Insert the *Apple Pro Training Series: Final Cut Pro 5* DVD into your CD-DVD drive.

2   Drag the FCP5 Book Files folder from the DVD to your hard drive to copy it. The Media folder contains about 7.75 GB of media.

To begin the course, you will open a project file after you have launched Final Cut Pro.

Reconnecting Media

In the process of copying the media from the DVD in this book, you may break a link between the project file and the media file. If this happens, a window appears asking you to reconnect the project files. Reconnecting the project files is a simple process that's covered in more depth in Lesson 16, in the section on reconnecting media. But should this happen when opening a lesson, just follow these steps:

1   If an Offline Files window appears, click the Reconnect button.

A Reconnect Files window appears. Under the Files To Connect portion of the window, the offline file is listed along with its expected location.

2   In the Reconnect Files window, click Search.

Final Cut Pro will search for the missing file. If you know where the file is located, you can click the Locate button to find the file manually.

3   After the file is found and displayed in the Files Located section of the Reconnect Files window, click Connect.

With the link reestablished between the project file and the media file, Final Cut Pro will be able to play the media within the project.

Changing System Preferences

A few editing functions within Final Cut Pro use the same function keys used by other programs, such as Exposé and the Dashboard. If you think you would like to use the FCP editing shortcuts, you will need to reassign these functions keys.

1   From your Desktop, launch System Preferences.

2   Under the Personal section, click the Dashboard & Exposé icon.

3   Reassign the shortcuts for these functions to keys other than F9, F10, F11, and F12, which will be used during the course of these lessons.

As you begin to work with Final Cut Pro and discover the different approaches you can use for each function, you can always come back and change these options in your System Preferences.

About the Footage

There are three sets of footage used throughout this book, each representing a very different type of project.

Smithsonian's National Museum of the American Indian: *A Thousand Roads* (NTSC)

The first set of footage with which you will work is from the film, *A Thousand Roads*, the signature film of the Smithsonian's National Museum of the American Indian. This film was brought to life by executive producer W. Richard West, Jr. (Southern Cheyenne), producers Barry Clark and Scott Garen, director Chris Eyre (Cheyenne/Arapaho), writers Scott Garen and Joy Harjo (Muscogee), director of photography Claudio Miranda, editor Harry Miller, III, and

American Indian poet, activist, and performer John Trudell, who provided the voice-over narration.

This dramatic film was shot on super 35mm, transferred to HD, and then to DV for offline editing. The footage in this book is the original DV media that was used in the actual offline editing process. As with many film projects, you will see numbers burned into the offline images for reference. All editing decisions were then applied to the super 35mm film, and the final film was digitized. *A Thousand Roads* represents the first U.S. public exhibition of a motion picture that has been produced and displayed in accordance with the newly established guidelines of the Digital Cinema Initiative (DCI), a consortium of seven major Hollywood studios that established standards for the digital display of motion pictures.

Motocross Footage (NTSC)   The second set of media is motocross racing footage, produced and directed by Michael Bryant and Perry Karidis of State of Mind Productions. This footage is being used for a behind-the-scenes documentary sports series on motocross racing.

The production crew followed the Yamaha of Troy racing team, based in Dayton, Ohio, to several motocross races and shot the action using Sony PDW-530 XDCAM cameras, which record to an optical disk rather than videotape. These cameras can record at different speeds, each yielding a different quality, such as DVCAM (25 megabits per second, or Mbps), and MPEG IMX quality at 30, 40, and 50 Mbps. For this project, the producers chose to shoot in the highest quality (50 Mbps), but did their preliminary editing in the DV format, which is the format included in this book. Final Cut Pro 5 captured the media directly from the Sony PDW-V1 optical disk player using the AJA Io capture card via the SDI input.

All Hours Music Video (PAL)   The third set of media is from a music video of the song, "Box Office Stud," written by Gilly Leads and performed by his Los Angeles–based band, All Hours. The song is from their premiere CD, In Flagrante Delicto (Hybrid Recordings), available from the iTunes Apple Music Store. This video was shot at The Viper Room in Los Angeles with band members Gilly Leads (lead singer and guitar), Dean Moore (bass), Nick Burns (drums), and Amit LeRon (lead guitar). The music video was shot using the

HDV format by Perry Karidis and Mike Pescasio. It was directed by Diana Weynand and produced by Weynand Training International. For the purposes of this book, some of the footage was transferred to DV-PAL Anamorphic to be used in Lesson 14.

System Requirements

Before beginning to use *Apple Pro Training Series: Final Cut Pro 5,* you should have a working knowledge of your computer and its operating system. Make sure that you know how to use the mouse and standard menus and commands and also how to open, save, and close files. If you need to review these techniques, see the printed or online documentation included with your system. For the basic system requirements for Final Cut Pro 5, please refer to the Final Cut Pro documentation.

About the Apple Pro Training Series

Apple Pro Training Series: Final Cut Pro 5 is part of the official training series for Apple Pro applications developed by experts in the field. The lessons are designed to let you learn at your own pace. If you're new to Final Cut Pro, you'll learn the fundamental concepts and features you'll need to master the program. If you've been using Final Cut Pro for a while, you'll find that this book covers most of the new features found in Final Cut Pro 5.

Although each lesson provides step-by-step instructions for creating specific projects, there's room for exploration and experimentation. However, try to follow the book from start to finish, or at least complete the first seven chapters before jumping around. Each lesson concludes with a review section summarizing what you've covered.

Apple Pro Certification Program

The Apple Pro Training and Certification Programs are designed to keep you at the forefront of Apple's digital media technology while giving you a competitive edge in today's ever-changing job market. Whether you're an editor, graphic designer, sound designer, special effects artist, or teacher, these training tools are meant to help you expand your skills.

Upon completing the course material in this book, you can become an Apple Pro by taking the certification exam at an Apple Authorized Training Center. Certification is offered in Final Cut Pro 5, DVD Studio Pro 4, Shake 4, and Logic Pro 7. Certification as an Apple Pro gives you official recognition of your knowledge of Apple's professional applications while allowing you to market yourself to employers and clients as a skilled, pro-level user of Apple products.

To find an Authorized Training Center near you, go to www.apple.com/ software/pro/training.

For those who prefer to learn in an instructor-led setting, Apple also offers training courses at Apple Authorized Training Centers worldwide. These courses, which use the Apple Pro Training Series books as their curriculum, are taught by Apple Certified Trainers and balance concepts and lectures with hands-on labs and exercises. Apple Authorized Training Centers for Pro products have been carefully selected and have met Apple's highest standards in all areas, including facilities, instructors, course delivery, and infrastructure. The goal of the program is to offer Apple customers, from beginners to the most seasoned professionals, the highest quality training experience.

Resources

Apple Pro Training Series: Final Cut Pro 5 is not intended as a comprehensive reference manual, nor does it replace the documentation that comes with the application. For comprehensive information about program features, refer to these resources:

▶   The Reference Guide. Accessed through the Final Cut Pro Help menu, the Reference Guide contains a complete description of all features.

▶   Apple's Web site: www.apple.com

1

Lesson 1
Working with the Interface

The Final Cut Pro 5 interface is flexible and dynamic. It offers not only a place to edit your masterpiece but a place to view your source material and to organize your project elements as well.

In this lesson, you will work with the Final Cut Pro interface, learn about the workflow of a project, organize project elements, work with the transport controls in the interface, and zoom and adjust the Timeline. You will also learn about Final Cut Pro menus and shortcuts, as well as added features available using a two-button mouse.

Preparing the Project

Before you get started, you will need to install the Final Cut Pro application onto your hard drive. You will also need to copy the lessons and media from the DVD in this book onto your hard drive as well. There are steps for doing this in the Getting Started chapter of this book. Once those two tasks are complete, you can move forward with this lesson.

You will open Final Cut Pro by opening, or *launching*, the program, which you can do in one of three ways:

▶   In the Applications folder on the hard drive, double-click the Final Cut Pro application icon.

▶   In the Dock, click the Final Cut Pro icon once.

▶   Double-click a Final Cut Pro project file.

> **NOTE ▶**   Placing the Final Cut Pro icon in the Dock will make it easier to launch the program in future lessons.

1   If the Final Cut Pro icon does not already appear on your Dock, find the icon in your hard drive Applications folder, drag it into the Dock, and release the mouse.

2 In the Dock, click the Final Cut Pro icon once to launch the program.

NOTE ▶ The first time you launch Final Cut Pro, a Choose Setup window will appear, where you select the type of footage you are editing. The default is DV-NTSC, which represents the majority of footage you will use in these lessons. Choosing setups is discussed in a later lesson. For now, you can click OK to bypass this dialog. If an External A/V window appears with a warning that it can't locate the external video device, click Continue. You do not need an external video device for these lessons.

The program interface opens with a default project titled *Untitled Project 1* in the Browser window. The Browser is located in the upper-left corner of the interface. If you have already worked on other projects, they may appear here as well.

Name	Duration	In	Out
Sequence 1	00:00:00;00	Not Set	Not Set

Final Cut Pro Interface

Four primary windows make up the Final Cut Pro interface: the Browser, Viewer, Canvas, and Timeline. The most basic functions of these windows can be broken down into two areas. The Browser and Viewer windows are where you organize and view your *unedited* material, and the Canvas and Timeline are where you view your *edited* material.

There are two secondary windows: The Tool palette contains an assortment of editing tools, and the audio meters allow you to monitor audio levels.

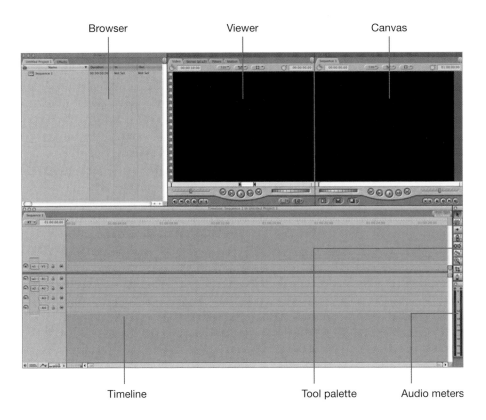

Browser   Viewer   Canvas

Timeline   Tool palette   Audio meters

Each window fulfills a unique purpose in the editing process.

Browser

The Browser is where you organize all of the project elements you use when editing. You can view the different elements as a list or as icons.

Viewer

The Viewer is where you view your source material and choose edit points. But you can also edit audio, modify transitions and effects, and build titles here.

Timeline

The Timeline is a graphical representation of all the editing decisions you make. This is your workbench area, where you edit your material, trim it, move it, stack it, and adjust it. Here you can see all your edits at a glance.

Canvas

The Canvas and Timeline windows are different sides of the same coin. Both display your edited project, but whereas the Timeline shows your editing choices graphically, the Canvas displays those edits visually like a movie.

Tool Palette

The Tool palette is a collection of Final Cut Pro editing tools. Each tool has a shortcut key, so you can access each one directly from the keyboard.

Audio Meters

The audio meters window displays two audio meters that reflect the volume level of whatever audio is playing. It could be a source clip in the Viewer you screen before editing or the final edited piece you view in the Canvas.

Project tab   Browser   Shuttle control   Viewer

Track   Sequence   Editing and   Timeline
controls area   tab   marking controls

Scrubber bar   Jog control

Timecode
Duration field

Sequence tab

Canvas

Current
Timecode field

Timeline
ruler area

Generator
pop-up menu

Playhead

Editing
controls

Transport
controls

Audio meters

Tool palette

Window Properties

Final Cut Pro's interface windows share similar properties with other OS X windows. They can be opened, closed, minimized, and repositioned using the OS X Close, Minimize, and Zoom buttons in the upper-left corner of the window. Each window displays its name in the title bar area.

1 Click the Browser to make it the active window.

Active Browser window when selected

Inactive Browser window when another window is selected

An active window has a lighter title bar, and you can easily read the window name. An inactive window has a dark gray title bar that blends in with the name. Only one window can be active at a time. Making a window active in the interface is an important part of the editing process because some editing functions will only be available to you if a specific window is active.

2   Click the Viewer window to make it active, and then click the Close button in the upper-left corner.

In most OS X windows, this button is red. In Final Cut Pro, this set of buttons takes on the gray of the interface. But these buttons still perform the same functions as they do in other OS X windows.

3   To restore the Viewer window, choose Window > Viewer, or press Cmd-1.

You can open and close each interface window by choosing the window name in the Window menu or with a keyboard shortcut.

NOTE ▶ Because of the small size of the Tool palette and audio meters, they have just one button to close the window.

4   Drag the Browser window title bar to move this window away from its current position. Drag it again and allow it to snap back into its original position.

All Final Cut Pro interface windows snap together, even though they are separate windows.

Menus, Shortcuts, and the Mouse

Final Cut Pro's editing functions can be selected in three ways: by choosing a menu selection, pressing a keyboard shortcut, or clicking a button. Most functions have keyboard shortcuts, but you can easily assign one to those that don't by using the customizable keyboard, which will be covered in a later lesson.

Final Cut Pro's menu bar organizes editing functions by category, such as View, Modify, Effects, and so on. Within each menu, specific functions are grouped together if they share a similar purpose or topic.

1   Choose the File menu in the menu bar of the interface.

File	
New	▶
New Project	⇧⌘N
Open...	⌘O
Open Recent	▶
Close Window	⌘W
Close Tab	^W
Close Project	
Save	⌘S
Save As...	⇧⌘S
Save All	⌥⌘S
Revert Project	
Restore Project...	
Import	▶
Export	▶
Send To	▶
Batch Export	
Batch Capture...	^C
Log and Capture...	⌘8
Media Manager...	
Reconnect Media...	
Set Logging Bin	
Print to Video...	^M
Edit to Tape...	

The New and Open functions are grouped together, as are the Save functions, Import, and so on. Like in all Apple menus, black menu options can be selected, but dimmed options cannot.

2   Click the Window menu and choose Arrange.

A submenu appears.

3   Place the cursor over Standard in the submenu, but don't release the mouse.

Keyboard shortcuts appear in menus and submenus to the right of the listed function. Similar functions often share the same shortcut letter.

The shortcuts in this submenu all use the letter *U* with one or more modifier keys. There are four modifier keys: Shift, Control, Option, and Command (the Apple key).

4   Click elsewhere in the interface to close the Window menu.

5   In the Tool palette, move the pointer over the icon that looks like a magnifying glass.

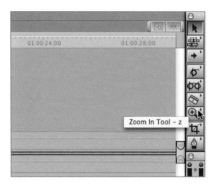

A *tooltip* appears with the tool name and keyboard shortcut. Tooltips also appear when you hold the mouse pointer over buttons and other areas in the interface.

NOTE ▶ You can turn tooltips off and on in the User Preferences window (Option-Q), which we will cover in a later lesson.

6   Move the pointer over the first tool in the Tool palette.

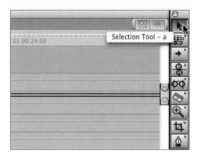

The Selection tool is the default tool you use most frequently. Its shortcut is the letter *A*.

TIP ▶ You will use different tools throughout the editing process, but it's a good habit to return to your Selection tool after you've used another tool.

7   Move the pointer over the horizontal double line in the Timeline. This is the audio/video dividing line.

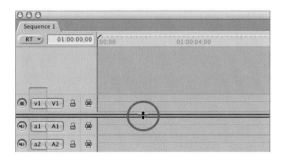

Final Cut Pro has a position-sensitive mouse pointer. When you move it over certain parts of the interface, the pointer will automatically change to allow you to perform a specific function in that location. Here you can drag the audio/video dividing line up or down to allow more room for either audio or video tracks in the Timeline.

8   Hold down the Control key and click in the gray area of the Name column in the Browser window.

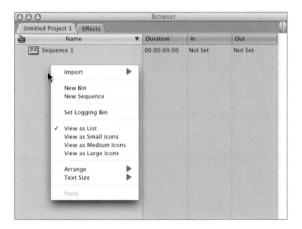

A *shortcut* menu appears with a list of options for that specific area. Ctrl-clicking in different areas of the Final Cut Pro interface will produce different shortcut menus from which you can choose or change your editing options.

> **TIP** ➤ You can also access this shortcut menu by clicking in the same area with the right button of a two-button mouse.

Following a Workflow

Before you work with projects, which you'll do in the next section, let's take a minute to review the non-linear editing process and some of the terminology you'll need to know. Final Cut Pro follows the normal conventions of the non-linear editing process. That process usually begins with *capturing* material from the original source tape, thereby converting it into digital media files. The media files are actually QuickTime movies that play like any other QuickTime movie on your computer. One file is created for each portion of source footage you choose to capture. Each media file may be a different length, as measured in minutes, seconds, and frames.

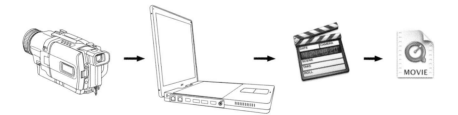

The Final Cut Pro editing process is nondestructive, which means that you never make changes to the actual media files. Instead, you work with clips that represent these media files. For example, you can change the audio level or add an effect to a clip inside Final Cut Pro, which causes the media file to be played back with those changes. But the actual media file itself is still unchanged.

You choose edit points on clips and combine clips with other edited clips to form a sequence. When you edit the sequence of shots together, you are not actually making changes to your original media. You are only specifying what portions and in what order you want Final Cut Pro to show you the original media. You can change your mind over and over again about the placement or length of a shot without affecting the original captured media clips.

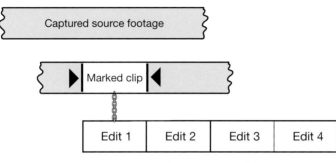

Edited sequence of clips

You can also save the initial captured media files to a separate hard drive connected through FireWire, or to a CD or DVD. The material in the accompanying DVD in this book has already been captured for the purposes of preparing these lessons. You will learn to capture your own source footage and export it in different ways in later lessons.

Working with Projects

Every time you begin editing a new body of material, you create a new *project file* to contain that material. Each project may have several kinds of elements, such as QuickTime clips, music, sound effects, narration, and graphics, which you will combine to form an edited version of the material. Project elements are displayed in the Browser window under a project tab.

Opening and Closing Projects

When you launch Final Cut Pro, it will open the last project you worked on or a new untitled project. In the Browser, there is a tab with the project name on it. To work with the project file created for this lesson, you will open it from the files you transferred from the DVD in this book.

1   Choose File > Open.

2   In the first column of the Choose a File window, click the Macintosh HD icon; in the second column, click the FCP5 Book Files folder; and in the third column, click the Lessons folder.

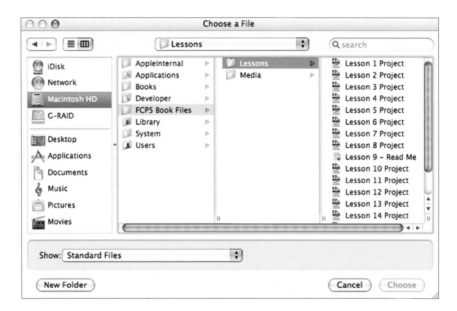

NOTE ► If you copied the FCP5 Book Files folder to a FireWire drive, select that drive in the first column.

3   Select the **Lesson 1 Project** file, and click Choose.

In the Browser window, Lesson 1 Project appears as a separate tab next to the Effects tab. (If you already worked on another project before starting these lessons, that project's tab may appear here as well.)

4   In the Browser window, click the Effects tab.

This is where you select effects such as video and audio transitions and filters. Effects will be covered in a later lesson.

NOTE ▶ The use of tabs throughout Final Cut Pro helps maximize space in the interface while keeping windows organized.

5   If any projects other than **Lesson 1 Project** are open, click the project's tab to make it the active project.

6   To close that project, choose File > Close Project.

Identifying Project Elements

Lesson 1 Project has four different types of project elements. Each is represented by a unique icon, which can appear larger or smaller depending on what view you select. You'll learn about views in the next exercise, but in the following examples you can see two views for each icon. The first image represents the view you see in the current project, which is a list view. The second image represents an icon or picture view.

Clip

Each clip in your project represents some portion of your original captured source footage. It links back to a digital media file on your hard drive. This type of clip icon can represent video-only or video and audio combined.

When viewed as a list, such as the current display in the Browser, the clip icon resembles a piece of film.

Audio Clip

An audio clip represents sound clips or files such as music, sound effects, narration, and so on. Like the video clips, these audio clips link back to the original audio files stored on your hard drive. Audio clips contain no video. The icon is an audio speaker.

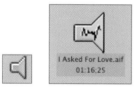

Sequence

A sequence is a group of audio and video clips that have been edited together. A sequence might also contain effects and transitions you may have applied to the edited clips. When you view a sequence in the Canvas or work with it in the Timeline, Final Cut Pro links back to the media clips on the hard drive and plays just the selected portions of the clips you have identified and marked. The sequence icon resembles two pieces of overlapping film.

Bin

A bin is a folder used to organize clips and sequences in the project. The term *bin* comes from the days of film editing when pieces of cut film hung on hooks over large canvas containers called bins. These pieces of film, or film clips, would hang in a bin until the film editor selected them to use in a sequence.

Viewing Project Elements

You can view project elements in the Browser several different ways. You can view elements as image icons or as an alphabetized list. With a View As Icons option, you see a visual reference or thumbnail image of each video clip. Seeing a clip's thumbnail image can be a helpful reminder of your material. With the View As List option, you can see and have access to more clips in a smaller space.

1   To see what view is currently selected, hold down the Control key and click in the empty gray space of the Name column in the Browser window. (Or, if you use a two-button mouse, right-click in the same area.)

This shortcut menu contains three View As Icons options, each with a different-sized icon or image, and a View As List option. The check next to View As List indicates that it is the current view.

2   Choose View As Medium Icons from the shortcut menu.

Each video clip is now represented by a medium-sized thumbnail image of the first frame of that clip. The name and duration of the clip appear under the thumbnail image. In this view, you may have to drag the blue vertical scroll bar in the Browser to see all of the elements.

3   Click the Browser Zoom button to see all the clips in this view. Click the Zoom button again to return to the default window size.

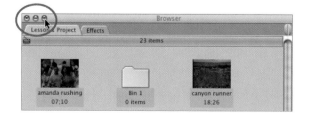

Like other Mac OS X window Zoom buttons, this one expands the Browser to display as many elements as possible.

4   Ctrl-click again in the Browser gray area and this time choose Text Size > Medium from the shortcut menu.

This option enlarges the type identifying the project elements in the Browser and Timeline.

5   Ctrl-click again and choose View As List and whatever text size you prefer.

In this view, elements are sorted and listed by name, making it easier to see and organize a larger group of project elements.

NOTE ▶ The lessons in this book were prepared with the View As List option for this reason. You may choose whichever view you prefer for your own editing.

Working with Bins

The key to organizing a Final Cut Pro project is to sort clips and elements into bins, just as you would organize computer documents by placing them in folders. You can also place bins within bins, just as you would place folders within folders. Organizing your material into bins will streamline your editing process, making it easier to find and access project elements.

Creating and Naming Bins

The first step to organizing your project is to create new bins to sort your elements. You will create three new bins to organize the current project, one each for clips, audio, and sequences. Typically with Final Cut Pro, you can accomplish the same task several ways. You will create three bins using three different methods.

1   Click in the Browser window to make it active.

2   Choose File > New > Bin.

A new bin appears in the Browser with the default name Bin 2.

NOTE ▶ A default sequential number always appears in the name of new bins, sequences, and projects. Since this project already has a Bin 1, the new bin is named Bin 2.

3   If the bin name is already highlighted, type *Clips*.

4   Press Return or the Tab key to accept the name. If you need to correct it, click the text of the name itself, not the bin icon, to highlight the name again.

When you press Return, the newly named bin is placed in its appropriate alphabetical order.

TIP ▶ If you want to change a bin name, but the bin is not highlighted, click once to select the bin, and once again on the name to highlight the text. Pressing the Enter key is another way of highlighting the name of a selected item.

5   To create another bin folder, press the keyboard shortcut Cmd-B.

6   Name the bin *Audio*, and press Return to accept the name.

7   To create the third bin, Ctrl-click the Browser gray area under the Name column and choose New Bin from the shortcut menu. You can also right-click using a two-button mouse.

8 Name this bin *Sequences*.

9 To remove the bin labeled Bin 1, click once to select it and press Delete.

Organizing Clips in Bins

You've created three bins to organize the different elements in this project. Now you will select the elements and drag them into their appropriate bins.

1 Drag the **I Asked For Love.aif** audio clip (speaker icon) to the Audio bin. When the Audio bin becomes highlighted, release the mouse button. Do the same with **intro narration.aif** and **lightness bells.aif** clips.

> **NOTE ▶** Whenever you drag and drop an item in Final Cut Pro, make sure the tip of the Selection tool pointer touches the target destination, in this case the bin icon or name.

2   To select items next to each other (contiguous), such as the three sequences, click the first sequence, *Intro – Audio Only*, and Shift-click the third sequence, *Intro – Starting*.

3   Drag one of the selected sequences to the Sequences bin.

plowing fields	00:00:13;27	Not Set	Not Set
ruin steps	00:00:15;17	Not Set	Not Set
▼ Sequences			
sunrise	00:00:22;14	Not Set	Not Set
tall buildings	00:00:13;24	Not Set	Not Set
truck on road	00:00:10;25	Not Set	Not Set

As you drag these sequences together, the name of only the sequence you clicked shows, as well as the number of other items you're dragging.

4   When the Sequences bin becomes highlighted, release the mouse.

5   Select the largest group of remaining contiguous clips by clicking to the left of the first clip and dragging diagonally until the pointer touches all the clips you want to select. Then, drag these clips into the Clips bin.

city street	00:00:13;03	Not Set	Not Set
▶ Clips			
girl on plane	00:00:16;10	Not Set	Not Set
healer at ruins	00:00:30;02	Not Set	Not Set
healer cu	00:00:15;09	Not Set	Not Set
healer walking	00:00:18;12	Not Set	Not Set
ice fishers	00:00:12;07	Not Set	Not Set
ice floes	00:00:12;07	Not Set	Not Set
johnny runs	00:00:12;11	Not Set	Not Set
plowing fields	00:00:13;27	Not Set	Not Set
ruin steps	00:00:15;17	Not Set	Not Set
▶ Sequences			
sunrise	00:00:22;14	Not Set	Not Set
tall buildings	00:00:13;24	Not Set	Not Set

NOTE ▶ Dragging diagonally to select clips is often referred to as *marqueeing*, as in "drag a marquee around these clips."

6   Select the group of four clips on the bottom of the list, then hold down the Command key and click each of the remaining clips once to add them to the current selection. Drag them as a group into the Clips bin.

NOTE ▶ You can select any number of noncontiguous clips by holding down the Command key and clicking a clip to select or deselect it.

All the project elements are now neatly tucked away in their bins.

7   To save these organizational changes, press Cmd-S.

TIP ▶ How you organize your project is a personal choice. When others will be working on the same project, make sure the organizational structure is clearly defined.

Viewing Bin Contents

Although this arrangement looks neat and organized, you can't see your clips or sequences to access them. Let's look at different ways to display the contents of a bin so you can get to your material easily.

1   Click the disclosure triangle next to the Audio bin to display its contents. Click the disclosure triangle next to the Sequences bin to display the sequences in that bin.

2   Click the disclosure triangle next to the Audio bin to hide the contents of that bin. Hide the contents of the Sequences bin.

3   Double-click the Clips bin.

This opens the bin as a separate window, which you can move anywhere in the interface.

4   Drag the window by its title bar and position it away from the Browser.

In the Browser, the Clips bin icon changes to an open folder, indicating that the bin is open as a separate window or tab.

5   In the Clips bin window, click the Close button in the upper-left corner to close this bin window, or press Cmd-W.

In the Browser, the Clips bin icon changes back to a closed folder.

6   To view the contents of the Clips bin a different way, hold down the Option key and double-click the Clips bin.

This opens the bin as a separate tab next to the Lesson 1 Project tab.

TIP ▸ Opening a bin as a separate tab is a helpful way to view and access clips without placing an additional window in the interface.

7   To change the view of the Clips bin, Ctrl-click in the gray area under the Name column and choose View As Medium Icons. Click the Clips bin tab and then the Lesson 1 Project tab.

Each bin can be set to a different view option.

8   Ctrl-click the Clips tab, or right-click it with a two-button mouse. Choose Close Tab from the shortcut menu.

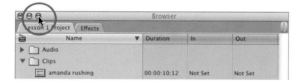

This returns the Clips bin to its closed bin configuration in the Lesson 1 Project tab area.

9   Now display the contents of the Clips bin by clicking the disclosure triangle next to it.

10   In the upper-left corner of the Browser window, click the Zoom button.

When viewing bin contents as a list, you have access to over 60 columns of information in the Browser window. This may include information Final Cut Pro knows about an item (number of audio tracks, frame size, frame rate, and so on) or descriptive information you enter for further clarification, such as scene and take numbers. These columns will be covered in a later lesson.

11 Click the Browser Zoom button again to return to the default Browser layout.

> **NOTE** ▶ If you resize an OS X window manually after clicking the Zoom button, clicking that button again will take you back to the most recent size, not the original window size.

12 To resize the Browser dynamically, move the pointer between the Browser and Viewer windows until you see the vertical resize arrow. Drag right to expand the Browser.

Browser   Viewer

As the Browser expands, the Viewer and Canvas become smaller to allow for the change in Browser size. The windows in the interface can all be dynamically resized by dragging the resize arrow left and right or up or down (between the Timeline and upper windows).

> **TIP** ▶ To get back to your standard layout, choose Window > Arrange > Standard, or press Ctrl-U.

Working with the Timeline and Canvas

Before you begin the editing process, let's focus on playing a sequence already in the Timeline and viewing it in the Canvas to get to know these windows. Whereas the Browser is a container for *all* your project elements, the Timeline is a container for only the specific items that make up a sequence. The Canvas is where you see the sequence in the Timeline play. The name of the current sequence appears on a tab and also at the top of both the Timeline and Canvas windows.

Clicking and Dragging the Playhead

In the Timeline, blue video and green audio clips sit on horizontal tracks. These tracks are a linear representation of time proceeding from left to right. In the middle of the current sequence is a thin vertical bar with a yellow triangle at the top. This is the *playhead*.

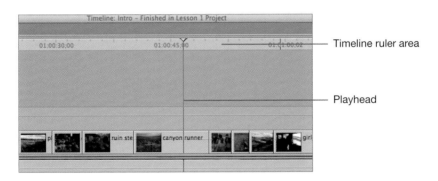

Timeline ruler area

Playhead

When the playhead is still, the frame at that location is displayed in the Canvas. When the playhead is moving, you see that portion of the sequence playing in the Canvas. You can reposition the playhead several different ways:

1   Click in several different places in the number, or ruler, area of the Timeline.

The playhead jumps to where you click, and you see that frame in the sequence displayed in the Canvas image area.

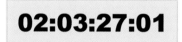

Hours : Minutes : Seconds : Frames

NOTE ▶ The Timeline ruler numbers identify the location of clips in the sequence. This number is called *timecode*, which is a video labeling system that records a unique eight-digit number—representing hours, minutes, seconds, and frames—onto each frame of a clip or sequence.

2   Drag the yellow triangle of the playhead across the Timeline ruler area.

Dragging through the sequence this way is called *scrubbing*. You are viewing your sequence, but not at normal play speed.

NOTE ▶ As you drag the playhead through the clips in the Timeline, notice how it snaps like a magnet to the beginning of each clip in the sequence.

3 Drag the playhead through the last clip in the sequence, the **healer cu** clip, and watch in the Canvas until the healer looks towards the camera.

Under the Canvas image area is a *scrubber bar*. This bar represents the length of the entire sequence. A tiny playhead in the Canvas scrubber bar tracks with the movement of the Timeline playhead.

NOTE ▸ The small timecode numbers in the image are part of the video. They were used to coordinate the film-to-tape transfer and edit the original sequence for the Smithsonian's National Museum of the American Indian film, *A Thousand Roads.* You can read more about this special project in the Getting Started section of this book.

Canvas playhead

Scrubber bar

4 In the Timeline, click several times in the ruler area, and watch the playhead in the Canvas scrubber bar track with the Timeline playhead.

5 Click in several places in the Canvas scrubber bar to view other frames of the sequence. Notice that the playhead in the Timeline now tracks with the movement of the Canvas playhead.

6   Drag the playhead through the Canvas scrubber bar backward and forward through the sequence.

In both situations, you are viewing frames from your edited sequence.

Using Shortcuts and Visual Clues

Moving the playhead to precise locations in the Timeline is an important part
of the screening and editing process. You can use a variety of shortcuts to do
this, and you can use visual clues that help you identify specific frames within
the sequence. These visual clues appear in the Canvas as an overlay on top
of the image area.

1   With the Timeline window active, press the End key to position the playhead at the end of the sequence.

NOTE ▶ If you are working on a laptop, the End key may share a position
with the right arrow key and require an additional key to access it, such as
the fn (function) key in the lower left of the keyboard.

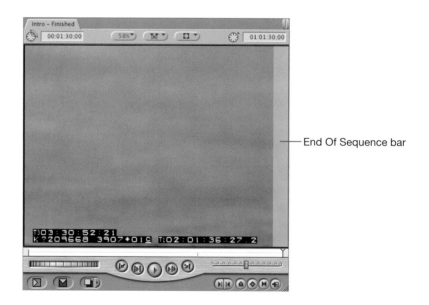

End Of Sequence bar

A blue vertical bar appears on the right side of the Canvas window, indicating that you are looking at the end or very last frame of the sequence.

2   Drag the playhead to the **ruin steps** clip, and press the down arrow key to move the playhead to the start of the next clip in the Timeline, **canyon runner**.

An L-shaped mark appears in the lower-left corner of the Canvas image area, indicating that the playhead is positioned on the first frame of a clip in the sequence.

TIP ▶ The visual clues appear by default, but if you don't see them, choose View > Show Overlays. Make sure the Timeline or Canvas window is active.

3   Press the down arrow key four times, and look for the L-shaped first-frame indicators on each clip in the Canvas window until you reach the **girl on plane** clip.

4 Press the up arrow key to move the playhead *backward* to the first frame of the **truck on road** clip.

NOTE ▶ The up and down arrow keys always move the playhead forward or backward to the first frame of a clip.

Under the sequence name tab in the Timeline is a Current Timecode field that displays the exact timecode location of the playhead in the sequence. The default starting time for sequences is 01:00:00;00.

NOTE ▶ The semicolon between seconds and frames in this timecode number indicates that drop-frame timecode is being used for this sequence. The glossary explains drop-frame and non-drop-frame time-code in more depth.

The Canvas also has a Current Timecode field, which displays the same timecode number, identifying the playhead location in the sequence.

5 To move the playhead to a specific timecode location in the sequence, such as 01:00:23;10, click in the Current Timecode field in either the Canvas or

Timeline window, and type that number. Press Return. You don't have to type the colons or semicolons.

NOTE ▶ You can also just type the number anywhere in the Timeline or in the Canvas image area, press Return, and the number will be entered into the Current Timecode field.

6 Press the down arrow key.

7 Press the left arrow key to move one frame backward.

In the Canvas, the reverse L in the lower-right corner of the image area indicates that you are on the last frame of that clip. Look at the Current Timecode field to note the current sequence location.

8 Press the right arrow key to move the playhead forward one frame to the first frame of the following clip.

Look at the Current Timecode field again. It has changed by one frame.

9 Press Shift-left arrow or Shift-right arrow to move the playhead 1 second (30 frames) in either direction. Repeat this as you look at the Current Timecode fields to see the timecode location change.

NOTE ▸ In the upper left of the Canvas is a Timecode Duration field. This field displays the duration or length of the entire sequence and does not change as you move the playhead.

10 Press the Home key to position the playhead at the beginning of the sequence.

Playing a Sequence

There are two approaches to playing a sequence: either using specific buttons and controls on the interface or using keyboard shortcuts. Three keys in particular—J, K, and L—provide a very convenient way to play your sequence. By using combinations of these keys, you can play a sequence slow or fast, forward or backward, and view it frame by frame.

1 Make the Timeline window active, and press the spacebar to begin playing the sequence.

In the Timeline, the playhead moves across the clips and ruler area as the sequence images and sounds play in the Canvas.

2 Press the spacebar again to stop playing the sequence. Press it again to play and again to stop. Press Home to return to the beginning of the sequence.

3 Position your first three fingers over the J, K, and L keys. Press the L key to play forward, then press J to reverse and play backward. Press K to stop.

4 To double the forward play speed, press L twice. Press it again to play even faster. Press J, and the speed slows down a notch. Press K to stop. Press J twice to play in reverse 2x speed. Press K to stop.

TIP ▸ Using the J, K, and L keys when editing will help you build speed as an editor. You can also use them in the Canvas and Viewer.

5   Hold down the K and L keys together to play forward in slow motion. Release the L key to stop. Hold down the K key, then tap the L key to move forward one frame at a time. Repeat these actions using the K and J keys.

6   Click in the Canvas window, and press L to play the sequence. Press L again to increase the play speed. Press K to stop.

> **NOTE** ► You can also use the Home and End keys, and up, down, left, and right arrows in the Canvas.

7   Under the Canvas image area, click the Play button once to play the sequence. Click it again to stop the sequence. These and other transport controls will be used in later lessons.

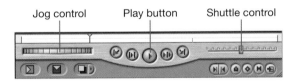

Jog control   Play button   Shuttle control

8   Drag the jog control to the left to move backward a frame at a time or right to move forward. Drag the shuttle control left or right to move through the sequence at a variable speed.

Project Practice

To practice playing a sequence, moving the playhead to specific locations, and utilizing visual indicators, use the key combinations you've learned so far to move the playhead to these exact locations in the sequence:

► skyscrapers with two flags on the right center of the frame

► the sun half way over the horizon

► the walk symbol turning green in the city street

► last frame of the ice floes clip

► the canyon runner jumping on a rock

Magnifying Timeline Tracks

During the editing process, you often need to take a closer look at a clip in the Timeline. You can magnify or zoom into your clips in two ways: vertically to appear taller, or horizontally to appear wider. Magnifying tracks does not in any way change the length of the clips in the sequence, only their appearance in the Timeline.

1 In the bottom of the Timeline, move the pointer over the fourth control from the left, the Track Height control. Click different columns to see the track height options. Press Shift-T repeatedly to toggle through these options.

2 Click the second track height column to return to that option.

3 Choose Sequence > Settings, or press Cmd-0 (zero). Click the Timeline Options tab.

4 Click the Thumbnail Display pop-up menu, and make sure Name Plus Thumbnail is selected.

In this pop-up menu, you can choose whether you want to view the clips in your Timeline with thumbnail images, just by name, or as a visual filmstrip. When the track height is at its smallest, the clip icons will not be displayed.

NOTE ▶ This tab is also where you can enter a different starting timecode for your sequence.

5   Click OK to close the window.

6   Look at the bottom of the Timeline next to the Track Height control.

Directly beneath the tracks of the Timeline are a zoom control and zoom slider used to adjust the horizontal scale of the tracks and the position of the sequence within the Timeline.

Zoom control   Zoom slider

7   Drag the zoom control to the left to magnify or zoom into the sequence.

Notice in the ruler area that the timecode numbers also expand and contract to reflect the zoom change.

TIP ▶ You can also zoom into the Timeline by pressing Option-+ and zoom out by pressing Option--(minus sign).

8   Drag the zoom slider left and right to change the portion of the sequence that is in view.

TIP ▶ If the playhead is not visible in the current zoom, click the tiny purple line in the zoom slider area. This line represents the playhead location. Clicking it repeatedly will bring that area of the sequence into view.

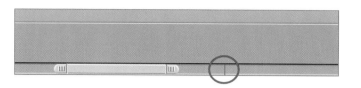

9   In the Tool palette, click the Zoom In tool (magnifying glass), or press Z, and click in the Timeline track area to zoom into that area.

NOTE ► You can also use the Zoom In tool to enlarge a specific area of the sequence by dragging a marquee around that area.

10   Click the first tool in the Tool palette, or press the A key, to return to the default Selection tool. Then press Shift-Z to view the entire sequence.

Quitting and Hiding Final Cut Pro

You quit Final Cut Pro just as you would any Apple application from the menu or using the keyboard shortcut. You can also hide the interface if you want to work on your Desktop or in another program.

1   To hide the interface, choose Final Cut Pro > Hide Final Cut Pro, or press Cmd-H.

The interface disappears, and you see your Desktop or any other programs you may have open in the background.

2   Restore the Final Cut Pro interface by going to the Dock and clicking the program icon.

NOTE ► The small black arrow or triangle next to the program icon in the Dock is a reminder that a program is still open, even if it's not showing.

3   If you are finished working, quit the program altogether by choosing Final Cut Pro > Quit Final Cut Pro, or by pressing Cmd-Q. If you are not finished working, leave the program open, and continue with the next lesson.

Lesson Review

1. Name three ways to launch Final Cut Pro.

2. To open and close projects, you select the appropriate option from which menu?

3. What are the four modifier keys that are often used in conjunction with keyboard shortcuts to initiate functions or commands?

4. How do you access a shortcut menu?

5. Name three ways to create a bin.

6. Besides using the Canvas Play button, what keys on your keyboard can you press to play a sequence?

7. What is the visual indicator in the Canvas window that lets you know the playhead is on the first or last frame of a clip?

8. How do you adjust the height of the audio and video tracks?

9. How do you zoom in or out of a sequence?

10. How do you hide Final Cut Pro? How do you restore it? And how do you quit the program?

Answers

1. Double-click the application in the Applications folder, click once on the icon in the Dock, or double-click a Final Cut Pro project file.

2. The File menu.

3. Shift, Control, Option, and Command.

4. Ctrl-click, or right-click with a two-button mouse.

5. Choose File > New Bin, press Cmd-B, or Ctrl-click in the gray area of the Browser.

6. The spacebar, and the J and L keys.

7. An L in the lower left means you're on the first frame of a clip, and an L in the lower right means you're on the last frame.

8. Click the Track Height control, or press Shift-T repeatedly.

9. Use the Zoom control in the Timeline, the Zoom In or Zoom Out tool, or shortcuts Option-+ or Option-–. Press Shift-Z to see the entire sequence in full view.

10. Press Cmd-H to hide the application. To restore it, click the application icon in the Dock. To quit, press Cmd-Q.

Keyboard Shortcuts

Organizing Project Elements

Cmd-B	Creates a new bin
Ctrl-click	Brings up different shortcut menus throughout Final Cut Pro

Navigating the Interface

Ctrl-U	Selects the standard window layout
Ctrl-Option-W	Shows overlays
Shift-T	Toggles through track height options
Z	Selects the Zoom tool
A	Selects the default Selection tool
Cmd-H	Hides the Final Cut Pro interface
Cmd-Q	Quits Final Cut Pro

Moving the Playhead and Playing a Sequence

Home	Takes playhead to head of the sequence
End	Takes playhead to end of the sequence
Up arrow	Moves playhead backward to the first frame of the current clip, or previous clip if currently on the first frame of a clip in the Timeline

Keyboard Shortcuts

Moving the Playhead and Playing a Sequence

Down arrow	Moves playhead forward to the first frame of the next clip in the Timeline
Left arrow	Moves playhead one frame to the left
Right arrow	Moves playhead one frame to the right
L	Plays sequence forward in Timeline or Canvas
K	Stops playing the sequence in Timeline or Canvas
J	Plays sequence backward in Timeline or Canvas
K + L	Plays forward in slow motion
K + J	Plays backward in slow motion
K + tap L	Moves playhead one frame to the right
K + tap J	Moves playhead one frame to the left

2

Lesson Files	Lesson 2 Project
Media	A Thousand Roads > Amanda and Sound Effects folders
Time	This lesson takes approximately 90 minutes to complete.
Goals	Open source clips in the Viewer
	Play clips in the Viewer
	Set edit points in the Viewer
	View and remove edit points
	Create a new sequence
	Make Overwrite edits
	Edit audio clips
	Back up a sequence
	Make Insert edits

Lesson 2
Marking and Editing

In the simplest terms, editing consists of screening clips, deciding exactly what portion of a clip you will use, and placing it in a sequence in a specific order. In this lesson, you will screen your clips in the Viewer window. You will then mark the portion of the clip you want to use. Finally, you will edit the marked selections to the Timeline using two types of edits, *Overwrites* and *Inserts*. In addition, you will open, close, and duplicate sequences.

The Overwrite button in the Canvas window

Preparing the Project

You will begin by opening the **Lesson 2 Project** file and playing a finished sequence.

1   In the Dock, click the Final Cut Pro icon once.

2   Choose File > Open, and navigate to the Lessons folder, as you did in Lesson 1.

3   Select the **Lesson 2 Project** file, and click Choose.

In the Browser, the project elements are already organized into bins, the way you organized the elements in the previous lesson.

4   If you have another project open (as shown in the following figure), Ctrl-click its tab in the Browser and choose Close Tab from the shortcut menu.

5   In the Timeline, play the current sequence titled *Amanda – Finished*.

Remember to press Shift-Z whenever you want to see the entire sequence in full view.

> **TIP**   You will be working with audio in this lesson, so make sure you take a moment to adjust your computer's sound levels.

This sequence is from another section of the Smithsonian's National Museum of the American Indian film, *A Thousand Roads*. You can read more about this project in the Getting Started section of this book.

6   To hear the sequence without the narration, or *voice-over*, click the green
Audible control button for the A4 track to temporarily toggle off the sound
of that track.

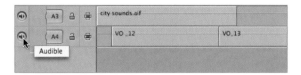

Each track has a green Visible (video) or Audible (audio) control in the
Timeline track control area. When clicked, that track turns dark and will
not be seen or heard as you play the sequence.

7   Play the sequence again, and listen to it without the voice-over narration.

In this lesson, you will edit Scenes 97 and 98. You will also edit one of the
voice-over clips. The others will be added in the next lesson.

8   Click the A4 Audible control once again to toggle on the audio for that
track.

9   In the Timeline, drag the playhead across the ruler area until it snaps to
the green *marker*. Look at the marker name displayed in the Canvas.

TIP ▶ If the playhead doesn't appear to snap, press N on your keyboard
to turn on snapping. We'll discuss snapping in Lesson 3.

Markers are used throughout Final Cut Pro to help locate or identify a
specific frame in a clip or sequence. Here it is identifying where Scene 98
begins. This is the scene you will edit first. You will create your own markers in later lessons.

Playing Clips in the Viewer

The Viewer window is where you play and mark your source clips in preparation for editing. The Viewer has four tabs. The default is the first tab, Video, where you can see, hear, and mark your clips. When you first open Final Cut Pro, the Video tab displays a black *slug*, or placeholder. The audio tab is where you'll work more closely with the audio of a clip. If no audio is present in the clip, no audio tab will appear. The Filters and Motion tabs will be used when you start to create effects in later lessons. In this exercise, you will learn different ways to open and play clips in the Viewer.

Tabs — Timecode Duration field — Image area — Scrubber bar — Shuttle control — Editing and marking controls — Play button — Jog control — Transport controls — Current Timecode field

1   In the Browser window, click the disclosure triangle next to the Clips bin.

Generally, with scripted material, scene numbers are included in the name of the clip. The letters that follow the scene number represent a different camera setup. The clips in this bin represent the original Scene 97 and 98 from the *A Thousand Roads* script. Since you don't have this script, the names of the clips have a descriptive note.

2 Double-click the **97F-man cu** clip to open it in the Viewer.

In the Viewer title bar, the clip name and project appear. Like the Canvas, the Viewer has an image area and a scrubber bar beneath it with a small playhead. It also has transport, shuttle, and jog controls.

3 To play this clip, click the Viewer Play button.

As the clip plays, the playhead moves forward through the scrubber bar, as it did in the Canvas when you played a sequence.

4 Double-click the **98C-wide** clip to open it in the Viewer. Play this clip by pressing the spacebar to start and stop it.

The Viewer also has a Timecode Duration field. But unlike in the Canvas where the length of the sequence is displayed, here the length, or duration, of the current clip is displayed.

> **NOTE** ► You see a boom microphone in this image hanging above the man's head. The microphone will not be visible in the final version of this film because the upper and lower portions of the image will be cropped, or matted, creating a widescreen image effect.

5 Now drag the **98B-man** clip from the Browser into the Viewer, and release the mouse anywhere in the image area.

Dragging a clip from the Browser to the Viewer also opens the clip in the Viewer and replaces the previous clip.

6 Press the L key to play this clip. Press it again to double the play speed. Press K to stop. Press J to go backward. Press J again to play at 2x reverse speed.

The same J, K, and L play options you used in Lesson 1 to play a sequence in the Canvas or Timeline can also be used to play a clip in the Viewer.

7   Drag the **97B-walking slo-mo** clip into the Viewer. Press End to go to the end, or *tail*, of the clip, and Home to go to the beginning, or *head*, of the clip.

NOTE ▶ If you are using a laptop, press the fn (function) key and the left arrow for Home, and the fn key and the right arrow for End.

First frame of clip

Last frame of clip

The film strips that appear at the head and tail of the clip are overlays that represent the first frame and last frame of the entire clip.

8   This time, single-click the **98A-amanda** clip in the Browser to select it, and then press Return to open it in the Viewer. Use the shuttle and jog controls to move through this clip.

NOTE ▶ The Enter key is not used interchangeably with Return to open a clip. If you select a clip, bin, or sequence and press Enter, the name will become highlighted allowing you to rename it.

9   In the Browser, select the **97C-back slo-mo** clip, and press Return to open it. Press the right arrow key repeatedly, and look at the Current Timecode field.

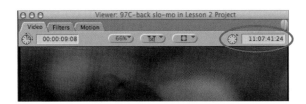

Like the Canvas and Timeline, the Viewer also has a Current Timecode field that indicates where the playhead is located within that clip.

10   To access a clip that has recently been opened in the Viewer, click the Recent Clips pop-up menu button in the lower-right corner of the Viewer window. In the pop-up menu, choose the **98A-amanda** clip.

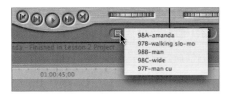

NOTE ▶ The Recent Clips window stores a default of 10 recent clips, but you can change that in the User Preferences window (Option-Q) to save up to 20 clips.

11   Click the Stereo (a1a2) tab in the Viewer to see the audio portion of the **98A-amanda** clip.

When you open a clip with audio, either a Stereo or Mono audio tab appears in the Viewer, depending on how the clip was captured or exported. If you have two channels of audio, they may be shown together as a stereo pair, or as two separate Mono tabs. In any one of these tabs, audio is displayed in the form of waves and peaks that represent the sound signal. This display is referred to as a *waveform*.

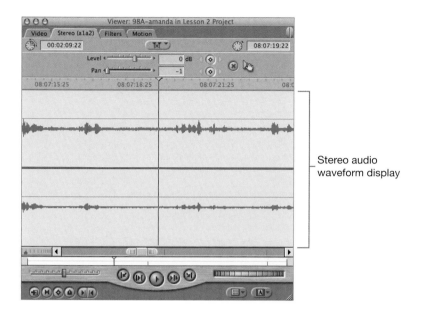

Stereo audio
waveform display

NOTE ▶ Notice that the Current Timecode and Duration fields are still
visible when you select the audio tab. You'll learn more about the functions in this tab later in this lesson.

12 Open the **97C-back slo-mo** clip again using any of the previous methods.

This clip was created using a slow-motion video effect, and no audio tab
appears in the Viewer.

Marking Clips

Now that you've screened your clips, you're ready to identify the portion you
want to edit into the sequence. Once you determine what portion of a clip to
use, you mark the starting and stopping points of the desired action or sound.
These marks define the edit points of the clip. Later in this lesson, you will edit
the marked clips into a sequence. But for now, you will practice different ways
to mark a clip before editing it to the Timeline.

NOTE ▶ You will be marking clips and building a sequence similar to the one in the Timeline. You can always play the *Amanda – Finished* sequence as a reminder of what you're creating.

Marking with Buttons

One way to mark edit points in a clip is to use the Viewer marking controls, also referred to as buttons. These controls are located beneath the shuttle control in the Viewer.

Mark In button ⌐ ⌐ Mark Out button

The Mark In button sets a starting point, or *In point*, in the clip. The Mark Out button sets a stopping point, or *Out point*, in the clip.

1   From the Browser menu, open the **98A-amanda** clip into the Viewer. Look at the Timecode Duration field.

   The Timecode Duration field reflects the full length of the clip when there are no edit points. When you mark this clip, this duration will change to reflect the marked portion only.

2   Press Home, and play the clip from the beginning. Stop when you see Amanda's face fully in the frame. You can adjust a few frames either way to account for background action.

   TIP ▶ To find a specific edit point, you can either drag the playhead in the scrubber bar, press the J or L key, or press K and J or K and L together to play slowly. To move a frame at a time, you can hold down K and tap the J or L key, or press the left or right arrow. If you work with a scrolling mouse, you can move the pointer over the image area or the scrubber bar and scroll to jog frame by frame.

3 In the Viewer, click the Mark In button to set an In point at this location.

A new In point appears in the scrubber bar where the playhead is located. Notice the In point overlay in the upper-left corner of the image area.

4 Play the clip and stop after the man on the street says, "Thank you, sister."

5 Click the Mark Out button to set an Out point at this location.

A new Out point appears in the scrubber bar where the playhead is located and in the upper-right corner of the image area. The Timecode

Duration field reflects the length of the marked portion of the clip, and the scrubber bar becomes gray outside of the marked area.

6   Click the Play In To Out button to see just the marked portion of your clip.

This is the portion of the clip that will be edited into the sequence in a later exercise.

7   In the Browser, click the disclosure triangle next to the Audio bin. Open the **VO_16** clip, and play it.

This clip has just one channel of audio, which is displayed as a single waveform image on the Mono (a1) tab. You will learn more about this tab later in this lesson.

8   To mark the full length of the **VO_16** clip, click the Mark Clip button.

Marking the entire clip places an In point on the first frame of the clip and an Out point on the last frame of the clip.

Marking with Keyboard Shortcuts

For some, working with keyboard shortcuts is a preferred way to edit, whereas others prefer clicking buttons on the interface. In Final Cut Pro, shortcuts are often created from the first letter of the functions. This is true for the Mark In and Mark Out shortcuts. All the keyboard shortcuts that relate to the In point use the letter *I* with or without a modifier key. All the shortcuts that relate to the Out point use the letter *O*.

1   From the Clips bin, open the **98B-man** clip in the Viewer. Play it, and stop after you hear the man say, "Thank you, sister."

Since you heard him say, "Thank you, sister," in the previous clip, you will cut to this camera angle for his next line.

2   Press the I key to set an In point at this location.

An In point is placed in the scrubber bar at this location, as well as over the image area, just as it did when you clicked the Mark In button.

NOTE ▶ You can also mark clips while they're playing, with either the shortcut keys or the mark buttons. This is called *marking on the fly*.

3   Play from the In point, and without stopping, press O to set an Out point after the man says, "Nice suit. Armani?" Notice the duration in the Timecode Duration field because it will change in the next step.

4   To move the playhead back to the In point, press Shift-I. Play from the In point, and this time set a new Out point after Amanda says, "Yeah," to allow time for the man to look up at her.

When you set a new In or Out point when one already exists, the new mark replaces the previous mark, and a new duration appears.

5   Click the Play In To Out button to play the new marked portion of this clip.

6   From the Browser, open the **98A-amanda** clip again, or you can click the Recent Clips pop-up menu and select it.

Once you set edit points on a clip, those edit points stay with the clip until you remove them or remark the clip.

7   From the Audio bin in the Browser, open the **VO_17** clip, and play it. You will use this clip in its entirety.

8   To apply the Mark Clip command using a shortcut, press the X key.

Just as when you used the Mark Clip button, an In point is placed on the first frame of this clip, and an Out point is placed on the last frame.

9   Choose File > Save Project, or press Cmd-S, to save the edit points you've created.

> **TIP** ▶ Choose Mark > Go To to see the shortcuts for going to edit points. You can also choose other mark options here, or use this menu to remind yourself of the keyboard shortcuts.

Marking Single Edit Points and Durations

When you spend a lot of time editing, saving a few keystrokes here and there can be very useful. As you continue marking clips, it may be helpful to know you can use just one edit point or sometimes no edit points at all. And sometimes, when working with sound effects, or static video shots, you may choose to enter a duration to define the length of an edit, rather than find a specific In or Out point.

1   Open the **97F-man cu** clip and play it until you hear the man say, "Hey, Bro, how're ya doin'?"

2   Set an In point at the beginning of this line, and click the Play In To Out button.

With no Out point, the clip plays from the In point to the end of the clip.

3   Open the **97C-back slo-mo** clip, and play it.

You will use this clip from the beginning, so you will not need to set an In point.

NOTE ▶ This clip, along with the **97B-walking slo-mo** clip, has had a slow-motion effect applied to it. You will learn to change the speed of a clip in a later lesson.

4   Play the clip, and stop a beat after the woman with blonde hair leaves the right side of the frame. Set an Out point at this location. Click the Play In To Out button to view the marked portion of the clip.

Without an In point, this clip automatically starts at the beginning and plays to the Out point.

5   From the Audio bin in the Browser, open the **city sounds.aif** clip, and play a few seconds of this sound effect.

In this clip, an In or Out point isn't as important as the length of time you will use the sound effect.

NOTE ▶ Audio clips created using Apple's Audio Interchange File Format have an aif suffix. However, many AIFF audio clips do not have the suffix attached to their names.

6   To create a 4-second duration, click the Timecode Duration field in the upper left portion of the Viewer, and type *4:00*. Press Return to enter this duration.

An Out point is automatically created in the scrubber bar 4 seconds from the head of the clip. Having an In point at a different location would create a duration from that point. In this situation, it doesn't matter where the playhead is located when you enter the duration.

> **TIP** ▶ You can also type this number without a colon (400), or with a period following the 4, such as *4.*, to represent zero frames. Substituting a period for double zeros is used throughout Final Cut Pro.

7   Let's change the duration to 7 seconds. Enter *7.* (number seven followed by a period) in the Timecode Duration field, and press Return.

The Out point adjusts automatically to create a 7-second duration.

> **TIP** ▶ If you change your mind, Cmd-Z, or Edit > Undo, removes the mark or returns you to a previous mark. The default number of undos is 10, but you can change that number in the User Preferences window (Option-Q).

Marking Timecode Numbers

You can also screen and log timecode numbers for each clip and go to those numbers to set In and Out points. This procedure is used in many interview and reality television shows, where there is no shooting script. A screener views and logs source tapes, then a writer or producer creates what is sometimes called a *paper cut*, a list of timecode references to shots they want included in the show. In this situation, an editor cuts together a rough cut by entering selected timecode numbers and marking those points.

1   Open the **97B-walking slo-mo** clip, and *scrub* through it by dragging the playhead through the scrubber bar.

Although this clip does not have any dialogue, it has portions that are not as usable because the man walking behind Amanda becomes too prominent in the frame. The best portion has been noted for you.

2   Click in the Current Timecode field, type *11:06:34:00*, and press Return.

In the scrubber bar, the playhead jumps to the timecode location labeled 11 hours, 6 minutes, 34 seconds, and 0 frames.

NOTE ▶ When typing a timecode number, you don't need to type the zeros before the first digit if it's a single-digit hour, or the colons or semicolons that separate the values. Final Cut Pro will add those automatically. However, the text of this book uses colons to make the timecode numbers easier to read.

3   Set an In point at this location.

4   This time, don't click in the Current Timecode field. Just type *11:06:42:08*, and press Return.

When the Viewer window is active, any number you type is automatically entered into the Current Timecode field as a timecode number.

TIP ▶ You can move the playhead to specific timecode locations in the Canvas and Timeline by using this same approach. Make sure the appropriate window is active before typing a number.

5   Set an Out point at this location, and click the Play In To Out button to view the marked portion of this clip.

6   Open the **98C-wide** clip, and play it until you see Amanda start to walk away. To find the exact frame, type *13:02:10:23*, and press Return. Set an In point at this location.

7   Type *13:02:19:19*, and press Return. Set an Out point at this location, and play from the In to the Out.

TIP ▶ Entering a timecode number for a clip is a great timesaver when marking clips, especially when others have taken the time to find a specific location for you.

Viewing and Removing Marks

During the editing process, you will often need to review or change your edit points. In this exercise, you will learn additional ways to view, go to, and remove your marks using the Viewer transport buttons and keyboard shortcuts. These methods utilize the same keys you've been using for marking Ins and Outs—I and O. For now, let's practice viewing and removing marks on a single clip.

1   Open the **97B-walking slo-mo** clip from the Browser, and press Shift-I to move the playhead to the In point. Press Shift-O to move it to the Out point.

2   In the Viewer transport button area, click the Previous Edit button and then the Next Edit button. Click each several times in a row.

These buttons move the playhead backward or forward to an edit point and then to the head or tail of the clip.

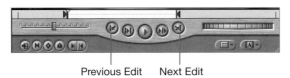

Previous Edit   Next Edit

NOTE ▶ The straight vertical line in the transport controls represents an edit point. The arrows represent the direction the playhead will move to go to the next edit point, backward or forward—that is, previous or next.

3   With the playhead at the head of the clip, press the down arrow several times, then the up arrow several times.

When edit points are present, the up and down arrows stop at each edit point, just as the Previous Edit and Next Edit buttons do.

TIP ▶ You can also press the : (colon) and ' (apostrophe) keys to perform this function. Since they're close to the J, K, and L keys, they may be more convenient.

4 To view the clip from the playhead to the Out point, drag the playhead to a point between the In and Out marks, and press Shift-P.

In a clip with a longer marked duration, this is a helpful way to review material up to the Out point.

5 Move the playhead to the middle of the clip, and click the Play Around Current Frame button to play a little before the playhead location and a little after. You can also use the keyboard shortcut, which is the \ (back-slash) key.

The Play Around Current Frame function is not tied to a mark. It will play around the current location of the playhead, wherever that is in the clip or sequence. There are many uses for this function. For instance, you can use it to move the playhead back a few seconds and give youself a running start to set a new edit point.

TIP ▶ You can set the distance the playhead moves back from its location to begin to play in the Preview Pre-roll entry in the User Preferences.

6 To remove the In point for this clip, press Option-I. Press Option-O to remove the Out point.

7 To undo those steps and return the marks, press Cmd-Z twice.

8 Press Option-X to remove both marks at the same time. Press Cmd-Z to return the marks.

9 Press Cmd-S to save your project changes.

NOTE ▶ You can loop the playback of a clip or marked area by choosing View > Loop Playback, or pressing Ctrl-L. When this option is checked or active, the clip will automatically play again from the head of the clip after it reaches the end, or play from the In to Out repeatedly. When Loop Playback is active, it applies to any play activity in the Viewer, Canvas, and Timeline windows.

Working with Audio Clips

As you've seen, you mark audio clips the same way you mark video clips. However, audio is displayed differently in the Viewer and utilizes audio meters to reference audio volume levels. Working with audio is an important part of the editorial process and is covered in more detail throughout this book.

1   In the Audio bin in the Browser, open the **VO_13** clip, and play it.

2   Look beneath the waveform area, and find the zoom control and zoom slider.

Zoom control ⌐   ⌐ Zoom slider

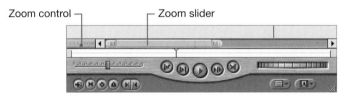

These controls zoom and magnify the waveform display in the Viewer just as they magnified the sequence in the Timeline.

3   Drag the zoom control all the way to the left, and watch the playhead as you drag.

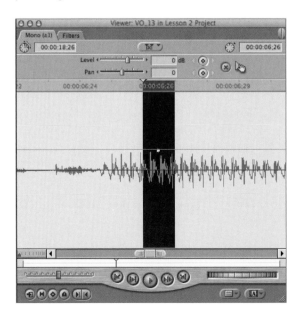

When you zoom into a clip or a sequence as far as possible, the representation of time is expanded. The black bar next to the playhead indicates the width of a single frame.

4 Click in the middle of the zoom control, and drag the zoom slider left and right to see another area of this clip.

5 Press Shift-Z to see the entire audio clip in full view.

6 Above the waveform display is a ruler area, like the one that appears in the Timeline. Click and drag the playhead in this area.

The playhead here and the one in the scrubber bar move in tandem as you scrub through the audio.

7 Play this clip again, and look at the audio meters in your interface.

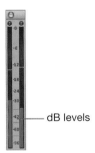

dB levels

> **TIP** Depending on your computer, the audio meters may appear beneath the Tool palette or to the side. If you don't see this window in your interface, choose Window > Audio Meters, or press Option-4 to open it.

The tiny numbers between the two audio meters represent dB, or decibels. That is the unit of measurement for audio. A good rule of thumb is to have the narration average around −12 dB on the audio meters. However, depending on the level of the original media file, this may mean raising or lowering the audio level on the clip in the Viewer.

8   From the Audio bin, open the **city sounds.aif** clip. Play a few seconds, and look at the volume level for this clip in the audio meters.

This sound effect should fall much lower in volume to blend under the dialogue and voice-over clips.

9   Drag the Level slider to the left until you see −15 in the Level field. You can also enter −15 directly in the Level field, and press Return.

When you change the audio level, you see the pink volume line move in the waveform display. If you entered a new number in the Level field, you won't see the volume line change until you press Return.

NOTE ▸ These dB numbers represent a change of volume up or down relative to the original sound level of this clip. You will work with other sound options in later lessons.

Preparing to Edit

Before you edit marked clips into a new sequence in the Timeline, you need to do a little preparation. First, you need to create the new, empty sequence in the Browser, name it, and open it in the Timeline. Then you have to position the playhead to indicate where you want the clip to be placed. And finally, you must make sure the clip will be edited to the correct audio or video track.

1   In the Browser, click the disclosure triangle to display the contents of the Sequences bin.

2   Ctrl-click in the empty gray area of the Browser under the Name column. Choose New Sequence from the shortcut menu.

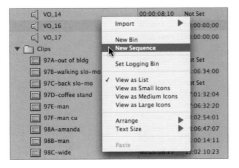

NOTE ▶ You can also create a new sequence by choosing File > New > Sequence or by pressing Cmd-N in the Browser.

In the Browser, a new sequence icon appears with *Sequence 2* (or other sequential number) in the name area. This sequence will have the correct default settings for this footage unless you have changed the settings to accommodate your personal projects. You'll learn about project settings in Lesson 8.

3   In the sequence name area, type *Amanda – Starting*, and press Return.

4   To keep the elements in your Browser organized, drag the new sequence into the Sequences bin.

5   Double-click this sequence to open it in the Timeline.

> **NOTE ▶** You can also select the sequence and press Return to open it.

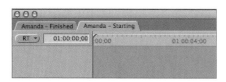

The Timeline now contains two sequence tabs identifying the two open sequences. The same two sequence tabs appear in the Canvas as well.

6   From the Clips bin in the Browser, open the **98A-amanda** clip in the Viewer. Click Play In To Out to view the previously marked portion of the clip.

7   To prepare to edit this clip, make sure the playhead is parked at the head of the sequence in the Timeline. To do this, click in the ruler area and drag the playhead to the beginning of the sequence, or click in the Timeline and press the Home key.

The playhead position determines the placement of the edit in the sequence, and the clip's marked duration determines how much of the clip is used.

On the far left of the Timeline is the track control area. Each track you use in a sequence is given a different number, such as V1 for the video track, and A1, A2, A3, and A4 for the audio tracks. These are referred to as *destination* tracks.

When you open a clip in the Viewer, source controls appear in the Timeline. These represent the video and audio tracks of the clip.

Although the order of the destination tracks is fixed, you can move and connect source controls, or *patch* them, to any destination. This determines the placement in the Timeline of the audio and video tracks of the source clip.

8   Look at the source controls for the current clip. Open the **97B-walking slo-mo** clip, and view the source controls in the Timeline for that clip.

When you open a video-only clip, just a video source control appears in the Timeline.

9   Open the **VO_13** clip in the Viewer.

This clip has only one track of audio, so only one audio source control appears.

10 Click the Recent Clips pop-up menu, and choose **98A-amanda** to reopen that clip. Before you edit this clip, make sure the v1 source control is connected, or patched, to the V1 destination track, and that a1 and a2 are connected to the A1 and A2 destination tracks. If they are not, drag the source control into place.

> **NOTE ▶** If a source control is not connected to a destination track, click either the source or destination control to connect them.

Making Overwrite Edits

You can make different types of edits in Final Cut Pro, and each type places a clip in a sequence a little differently. In this lesson, you will work with two types of edits: Overwrites and Inserts. An Overwrite edit places a clip over whatever is on a Timeline track. The Timeline may be empty at that point, or another clip may be present. Either way, the new clip simply overwrites whatever is there. An Insert edit positions a clip between other clips currently on a track. However, the *method* of making edits is similar for all edit types.

Dragging to the Edit Overlay

As with most functions in Final Cut Pro, you can use different methods to make an edit. In this exercise, you will use the Edit Overlay in the Canvas to place the edits into the *Amanda – Starting* sequence in the Timeline.

> **NOTE ▸** You will begin by editing the dialogue between Amanda and the man on the street in Scene 98. Later in this lesson, you will go back and add clips from Scene 97.

1   In the Viewer, click and hold your pointer in the image area of the **98A-amanda** clip.

A thumbnail of your edit attaches to the pointer.

2 Drag the thumbnail image into the Canvas window, but don't release the mouse.

The Edit Overlay appears in the Canvas window with a palette of seven sections. These sections represent seven different types of edits. The red Overwrite section has a brighter border around it, indicating that it is the default edit option.

Notice that the icon on the Overwrite section has a downward-facing triangle or arrow. This is a visual clue that you will be covering, or *overwriting*, anything in its place in the Timeline.

3   Drag the **98A-amanda** thumbnail image onto the Overwrite section in the Edit Overlay, and release the mouse.

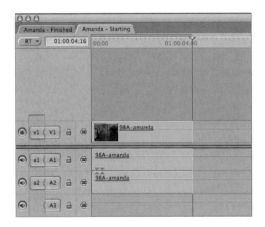

The marked clip is placed in the Timeline at the playhead position. Because the audio has stereo tracks, the clip occupies two audio tracks in the Timeline. The playhead jumps to the end of the clip, or more specifically, the first frame of the space following the clip, awaiting the next edit.

4   Open the **98B-man** clip, and play from the In to the Out. The marks should include the man saying, "Nice suit. Armani?"

In the Timeline, the playhead is positioned where you want this edit to be placed, after the first clip in the sequence. The source controls should be patched to the appropriate destination tracks. You are ready to make another Overwrite edit.

5   Drag this marked clip to the Overwrite section in the Canvas Edit Overlay.

NOTE ▶ If the Overwrite section is highlighted in the overlay, you can drop the clip anywhere in the Canvas image area to make an Overwrite edit.

6   Open the **98A-amanda** clip again. Play from the previous Out mark, and
     set a new In and Out point around her saying, "My traditional outfit." You
     can include his head nod and reaction. Drag this clip to the Overwrite
     option in the Edit Overlay.

7   Play this group of clips from the beginning of the Timeline.

     Remember, this is a first cut, or rough cut. You will learn to trim and
     adjust these clips in a later lesson.

8   Press Cmd-S to save your work.

Using the Edit Button and Keyboard Shortcut

To make an Overwrite edit, you can also click the Overwrite button in the
Canvas, or press a keyboard shortcut. These methods will produce the same
result as dragging to the Edit Overlay. You will continue editing clips in this
dialogue scene. As always, be aware of playhead placement as well as the source
to destination track controls.

1   Press End to position the playhead at the end of the current clips in the
     Timeline. This is where you will edit the next video clip. You can also
     drag the playhead to this location and let it *snap* to the end of the second
     98A-amanda clip.

2   Open the **98B-man** clip in the Viewer. Play from the current Out point,
     and set a new In and Out to include the man saying, "Mine, too. Where
     are you from?"

3 To edit this clip, click the red Overwrite button in the Canvas.

The clip is automatically placed at the end of the video clips, at the playhead position, just as the other video edits were.

4 Open the **98A-amanda** clip, and set an In and Out to include Amanda saying where she is from and the man's first response that sounds like, "Waynah-zee." Click the Overwrite button.

NOTE ▶ The actual Mohawk term is "We' ne tsi."

5 In the Timeline, drag the playhead to the beginning of this clip, and play it.

After you've edited a clip to the Timeline, you may find that it's too long. You can easily overwrite the tail end of a clip, or an entire clip, as you make your next Overwrite edit.

6 In the Timeline, move the playhead back to before the man says "We' ne tsi."

TIP ▶ If Audio Scrubbing is not on in the View menu, turn it on so you can hear the audio even in reverse when you're dragging the playhead.

The next edit will begin at the playhead location and overwrite the remainder of this clip, erasing it from the sequence.

7 Open the **98B-man** clip and mark the portion beginning with "We' ne tsi" and ending before Amanda speaks again. Click the Overwrite button again.

The previous **98A-amanda** clip is shorter in the Timeline than it was before.

8 Hold the pointer over the red Overwrite button in the Canvas.

When you move the pointer over the Overwrite button, a tooltip appears displaying its shortcut, F10.

9 Open the **98A-amanda** clip, and set an In point when she begins to speak. Set an Out when she has finished speaking in her native tongue. This time press F10 to edit this clip into the sequence.

NOTE ▶ OS X assigns functions to F9, F10, F11, and F12 that will override the FCP functions unless you change them in System Preferences. If you need help setting Preferences, go to the "Getting Started" chapter.

TIP ▶ As you edit more clips to the Timeline, some of the earlier clips may move out of sight. You can always press Shift-Z to bring all the clips back into view.

10 From the Audio bin, open the **VO_14** clip. Drag the playhead toward the end of this clip, and set an Out point when the narration stops.

You want this clip to be placed on the A4 track in the Timeline, so you need to patch the source control to that track.

11 In the Timeline, drag the a1 source control down to the A4 destination track.

12 Make sure the playhead in the Timeline is at the end of the last clip, and press F10 to edit this voice-over clip.

13 Press Home, and play the sequence. Then press Cmd-S to save your work.

Project Practice

Continue to practice making Overwrite edits by adding the following clips to the end of the current *Amanda – Starting* sequence. You can follow the marking and setup directions that follow for each clip, or you can simply refer back to the end of the *Amanda – Finished* sequence as a guide.

> **TIP** To make the clips smaller in the Timeline and allow more editing space at the end of your sequence, press Option-–(minus), drag the zoom control, or drag the zoom slider tabs.

98B-man   Set an In point at 11:00:38:09 and an Out point at 11:0046:12. Lower the sound level for this clip to –14dB so the voice-over clip can be heard above it. Make sure the source controls are patched to the A1 and A2 audio tracks. Move the playhead back to the end of the last video clip.

98B-man   Set an In point at 11:01:15:20 and an Out point at 11:01:31:06. These two edits of the man will jump slightly when you play them, but later you will cover this with a shot of Amanda.

98A-amanda   Set an In point at 8:08:38:16 and an Out point at 8:08:44:10.

98C-wide   Set an In point at 13:02:10:26 and an Out point at 13:02:22:04.

VO_16 Edit this clip onto the A4 track after the man sings a verse of the song.

VO_17 Edit this clip in line with the first frame of the last clip in the sequence.

Backing Up Sequences

In the next exercise, you will insert clips from Scene 97 before the dialogue clips from Scene 98. Before making major changes to a sequence, it's a good idea to back up the sequence by duplicating it. This way, if you don't like the new changes, you can go back to the previous version and start again. Duplicating a sequence makes an exact copy of the edit information. It does not duplicate the source media.

1   In the Browser, Ctrl-click the *Amanda – Starting* sequence icon.

A shortcut menu appears with different options.

2   Choose Duplicate.

A duplicate sequence is created and placed under the original sequence in the Browser. The word *Copy* is added to the sequence name.

3   To rename this sequence, click in the name area, and type *Amanda – Starting backup*. Press Tab or Return to accept it.

TIP ▸ If you're not making a major change to your sequence but just want to back up the current version, you can add a date or version number in the sequence name.

4   In the Browser, double-click the *Amanda – Starting backup* sequence to open it in the Timeline.

5   Click alternately the *Amanda – Starting* and *Amanda – Starting backup* sequence tabs.

At this point, the two sequences should be identical.

6   To close the *Amanda – Starting backup* sequence, Ctrl-click its tab in the Timeline or Canvas and choose Close Tab. You will continue working in the *Amanda – Starting* sequence.

7   Take a moment to save the work you've done in the project by pressing Cmd-S.

NOTE ▸ As you edit, you can have multiple sequences open at the same time. Keep sequences open if you are using them or referring to them. If you create a sequence as a backup, you don't have to keep it open.

Inserting Clips

The beauty of the nonlinear editing process is that you don't have to make all of your editorial decisions in a linear fashion, editing one clip after the other in the sequence. For example, if you are editing an interview, you might edit all the questions from the interviewer into the sequence and then go back and insert the answers from the person being interviewed. When you insert a clip into the sequence, all clips *in all tracks* following the new clip are moved forward the length of the clip. Inserting a clip lengthens the sequence by the length of the clip.

As in Overwrite editing, you will use the same three methods of making an edit, and you will use the location of the playhead to determine where a clip will be inserted.

1 From the Browser, open the **97A-out of bldg** clip, and play it.

You will use the clip as marked. Since the marked portion does not include the musical group playing, you will edit just the video portion of this clip.

2 In the Timeline, move the playhead to the beginning of the sequence, where you will insert the new edit.

3 Click the a1 source control to disconnect it from any destination track. Repeat this with the a2 source control.

When the source controls are disconnected from the destination tracks, no source audio will be used in the edit.

4   As you did with the first Overwrite edit, click and drag the Viewer image to the Canvas Edit Overlay, but don't release the mouse.

The Insert section is yellow, and its icon is an arrow pointing to the right. This indicates that all the following clips in the sequence will be moved forward to allow room for the new clip you are editing.

5   Drag the clip to the yellow Insert section, and when the section becomes highlighted, release the mouse.

In the Timeline, just the video portion of the clip is inserted *before* the first clip in the sequence. All the other clips are moved down to allow room for the new clip.

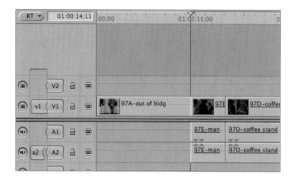

6   Open the **97E-man** clip, and play from the In to the Out.

You will edit the audio and video of this clip as marked at the current playhead location.

7   Click the a1 and a2 source controls to reconnect them to the A1 and A2 destination tracks. You may need to drag the a1 source control to the A1 destination track.

8   Click the yellow Insert button in the Canvas.

The clip is inserted at the playhead location, and all the remaining clips in the sequence are moved down, including the voice-over clip on A4.

9   Open the **97D-coffee stand** clip. Edit this clip as an Insert edit at the current playhead location.

10 Open the **97F-man cu** clip. Insert the marked portion into the sequence by using the F9 keyboard shortcut.

11 If necessary, press Shift-Z to see the entire sequence. Press Home to go to the head of the sequence and play it.

This completes the dialogue portion of this sequence. You can follow the steps in the next section to continue adding the voice-over and sound effect clips to this sequence.

Project Practice

To complete this sequence, edit the remaining clips using the following steps or by referring to the *Amanda – Finished* sequence.

1 Open the **city sounds.aif** clip from the Audio bin, and create a 20-second duration. Edit this clip to the A3 track at the head of the sequence as an Overwrite edit. Remember to bring the audio level down to about –15 before you edit it into the sequence.

2 Open the **VO _12** clip, and set an In and Out around the narration. Edit this clip as an Overwrite edit to the A4 track about 2 seconds in from the head of the sequence.

3 Open the **VO_13** clip, and set an In and Out around the narration. Edit this clip as an Overwrite edit to the A4 track at the end of the previous voice-over clip.

4 Open the **98A-Amanda** clip, and mark about a 3-second duration to use as a cutaway. Edit it as an Overwrite edit at the edit point between the two **98B-man** clips.

> **TIP** ▶ If you want to continue practicing marking and editing, create a new sequence and open it in the Timeline. Use different clips, such as the two slo-mo clips or different dialogue selections, to build a new sequence.

Saving and Quitting

Save frequently throughout your editing process, and again at the end of your session, whether the sequence is complete or not. You may have made only minor organizational changes or marked a few clips. Saving your project ensures these decisions are included the next time you open that project.

1 Press Cmd-S to save the current project.

2 Choose File > Close Project if you want to close this project.

> **NOTE** ▶ When you close a project or quit Final Cut Pro, a prompt to save appears if you have made any changes since the last time you saved the project. If this window appears, click Yes to ensure that you are saving the most recent changes.

> If you want to keep working on this project the next time you open Final Cut Pro, you don't have to close the project prior to quitting the program. If you quit with that project open, it will open along with the program the next time you launch Final Cut Pro.

3 Press Cmd-Q to quit Final Cut Pro, or continue to the next lesson.

Lesson Review

1. Name three ways to open a clip.

2. How do you mark a clip?

3. How do you set a specific duration from the In point or head of the clip?

4. How do you readjust an edit point using In or Out marks?

5. When viewing an audio clip, what do you see instead of a video image?

6. Which keyboard shortcuts can be used to move the playhead directly to an edit point? Which do you use to remove edit points?

7. Name three ways to create a new sequence.

8. When you open a clip in the Viewer, what do you see in the Timeline track area?

9. Before making an edit, what two things should you do to ensure proper placement of the clip?

10. List three ways to edit a marked clip as an Overwrite edit.

11. List three ways to insert a clip into a sequence.

12. How do you edit a sound clip into a sequence?

13. How do you duplicate a sequence?

Answers

1. Double-click the clip in the Browser, drag it to the Viewer, or select it and press Return.

2. Use the Mark In and Mark Out buttons in the Viewer, or the keyboard shortcuts, I and O.

3. Enter the amount in the Timecode Duration field.

4. Drag an In or Out mark in the Viewer.

5. You see a waveform display of the sound. All marking functions are the same.

6. Press Shift-I or Shift-O to go to an In or Out point. Press Option-I or Option-O to remove an In or Out point. Press Option-X to remove both marks at the same time.

7. Choose that option from the File menu, press Cmd-N, or Ctrl-click in the Browser and choose New Sequence.

8. The representative source tracks from the clip appear as source controls in the Timeline track area.

9. Position the playhead where you want to place the clip in the sequence, and patch the source controls to the desired destination track.

10. You can drag the marked clip into the Canvas and drop it into the Overwrite section of the Edit Overlay, click the red Overwrite button, or press F10.

11. You can drag the clip into the Insert section of the Edit Overlay, click the yellow Insert button, or press F9.

12. Click the appropriate edit button or shortcut.

13. Ctrl-click in the Browser and choose Duplicate from the shortcut menu.

Keyboard Shortcuts

Marking

I	Sets an In point
O	Sets an Out point
X	Marks the entire clip length
Shift-I	Moves the playhead to the In point
Shift-O	Moves the playhead to the Out point
Option-I	Removes an In point
Option-O	Removes an Out point
Option-X	Removes both In and Out points together
Shift-P	Plays the clip from the playhead to the Out point
Shift-	Plays from the In to the Out point
****	Plays around the current playhead location
Cmd-Z	Undoes the last action

Playing and Viewing

Shift-Z	Shows the entire sequence in the Timeline
Ctrl-L	Enables Loop Playback

About Projects

Cmd-O	Opens a project
Ctrl-click	Brings up a shortcut menu
Cmd-S	Saves the current status of a project

Keyboard Shortcuts

Editing

F10	Makes an Overwrite edit
F9	Makes an Insert edit

3

Lesson **3**
Drag-and-Drop Editing

Final Cut Pro's flexibility allows an editor to work with different styles of editing. You can drag a clip to the Edit Overlay in the Canvas, click an edit button, or use the keyboard shortcuts F9 and F10 to make Insert and Overwrite edits. But there's another editing style that's easy yet extremely powerful at the same time: drag-and-drop editing. This method involves dragging a clip directly to the Timeline to make an edit. Once a clip is in the Timeline, you can select it, move it, or copy and paste it. You can really speed up the editing process since you can do just about anything you need to do to manipulate the clip or sequence using this method. Some editors cut or edit their entire sequence using only drag-and-drop editing.

Preparing the Project

To get started in Lesson 3, you will launch Final Cut Pro and open the project for this lesson. You will also create a new sequence to begin editing.

1 Launch Final Cut Pro.

2 Close all open projects by Ctrl-clicking their tabs and choosing Close Tab from the shortcut menu.

The Canvas and Timeline windows close when there are no sequences to display, and the Effects tab is the only tab in the Browser.

3 Choose File > Open, or press Cmd-O, and choose the **Lesson 3 Project** file from the FCP5 Book Files > Lessons folder on your hard drive.

This project has three bins: Canoe Club Audio, Canoe Club Video, and Sequences.

NOTE ▶ When you save a project with all sequences closed, neither the Canvas nor Timeline window appears when you open the project again. This is because the sole purpose of these windows is to display open sequences.

4 Display the contents of each bin. In the Sequences bin, double-click the *Canoe Club – Finished* sequence to open it. You may have to scroll down to see that sequence.

pan to totem	00:00:11;27	07:47:05;29
tilt down canoe	00:00:09;28	07:44:10:00
▼ 🗀 Sequences		
Canoe Club – Finished	00:01:06;00	Not Set
Moving Clips	00:00:59;13	Not Set

The Canvas and Timeline windows open to display the open sequence.

5 Play this sequence to see what you will create in this lesson.

This sequence has five audio tracks. On A1 and A2 is a stereo sound effect, which was recorded on a separate system at the original film shoot. This clip has been duplicated several times to continue the sound effect under the other video-only clips. Track A3 contains mono (single-channel) narration or *voice-over* clips, and Tracks A4 and A5 have a stereo music track.

6   In the Sequences bin, double-click the *Moving Clips* sequence to open it. Then click each two sequence tab in the Timeline.

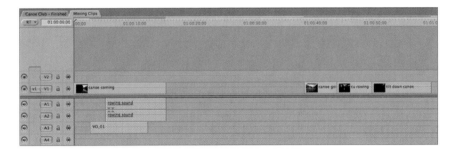

The *Moving Clips* sequence contains six clips that are part of the *Canoe Club – Finished* sequence you viewed in the previous step. The first three clips are positioned in the same place in each sequence. The other three video clips have been moved down in the Timeline away from their original position. You will work with all these clips to learn the basics of moving and selecting clips in the Timeline. Also, this sequence has only four tracks of audio. You will add the other track later in this lesson.

7   Play the first three clips.

Notice that the **rowing sound** clip does not appear at the head of the sequence because the canoe is still at a distance. Instead, it is aligned to the end of the video clip. The narration, or voice-over clip, **VO_01**, does not have a restriction about placement. It could be positioned at the beginning of the video clip, at the end, or in the middle.

Manipulating Clips in the Timeline

One aspect of drag-and-drop editing includes dragging or moving clips in the Timeline. Moving clips is helpful when you want to change the location of a clip, such as moving a sound effect or voice-over narration to coincide with a specific video cue. You can move one clip's position in the sequence or move a group of clips on one or more tracks. You can also copy and paste a clip or a group of clips to another point in the sequence or to a different sequence altogether. Before you work with multiple clips in the Timeline, you'll start by working with a single clip.

> **NOTE ▶** The more facility you have moving and dragging clips within the Timeline, the easier it will be to drag clips directly to the Timeline as you edit.

Selecting and Deselecting a Clip

Learning to correctly select a clip in the Timeline is very important. You select a clip during the editing process when you want to move it, delete it, add an effect to it, view its properties, or make other changes to it. To select a clip in the Timeline, you follow the general Apple selection principles. Clicking a clip just once selects it. Clicking off the clip deselects it. The key is learning to click the correct portion of the clip for the desired function.

1   In the Timeline, click the *Moving Clips* sequence tab, and select the **canoe coming** clip by clicking once in the middle of the clip.

The clip turns brown to indicate that it is the selected or highlighted clip.

2   To deselect this clip, click in the blank Timeline area above the clip.

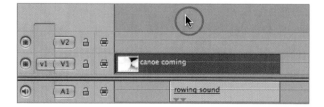

3   Select the **canoe coming** clip again, and then select the **VO_01** clip.

When you select a different clip, any other selected clip becomes deselected.

4   Move the mouse pointer to the tail of the **canoe coming** clip. Note that the pointer changes to a vertical resize arrow. Click once to select the Out point of this clip.

5   In the **VO_01** clip, move the pointer to the In point. When you see the resize arrow, click once to select the In point.

Selecting the In or Out edit point of a clip will be useful when you begin trimming and adjusting clips in later lessons.

6   On the A1 track, click in the middle of the **rowing sound** clip.

When you click one track of a stereo audio clip, both tracks become high-lighted together.

NOTE ▶ Although a pointer is present in many applications, in Final Cut Pro it is the default Selection tool.

7   To delete this clip, press the Delete key.

Deleting a clip removes it from the sequence but does not delete the media file or the original *master* clip in the Browser.

8   Press Cmd-Z to undo the delete.

9   To deselect the clip using the keyboard shortcut, press Shift-Cmd-A.

Dragging and Moving a Clip

You can drag clips left or right and up or down in the Timeline. Dragging clips left or right repositions them in the sequence. Dragging clips up or down repositions them vertically onto another track in the sequence. You can also move a clip by typing an offset amount directly in the Timeline and using shortcut keys.

1   In the Timeline, click the **canoe coming** clip again to select it. Then move the mouse pointer through the clip *without clicking or dragging it.*

The pointer changes to a move tool. Like the resize arrow that indicates a possible size adjustment, this indicates that you can move a clip. However, it's not a tool you select from the Tool palette.

2   Click and drag the **canoe coming** clip to the right, but *don't release it.*

Several things happen. A small duration box appears that displays a + sign and a number. This is how far in time you have moved the clip forward from its original position. Also, the pointer changes to a downward arrow. (You'll learn about the two small viewing frames in the Canvas in the next exercise.)

3   Release the clip. Then drag it to the left and then right past its most recent position.

A minus or plus sign appears to indicate how far the clip is being moved from its current position. If you move the clip again, the distance is measured from the new location.

4   Drag the clip up to the V2 track and release it. Drag it above the V2 track where the V3 track would appear and release it.

When you drag a clip to an empty track area, a new track will automatically be created.

5   Press Cmd-Z to return the clip to its previous location and to remove the added track.

You can also move a clip vertically and horizontally at the same time.

6   Drag the clip back down to the V1 track, dragging left horizontally as you go.

7   With the clip selected, type *300* (for 3 seconds and zero frames) in the Timeline track area.

> **NOTE ▶** It may seem strange to just start typing a number without typing it somewhere specific, but with the clip selected, Final Cut Pro anticipates what you want to do.

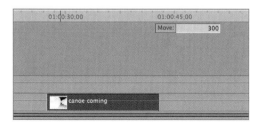

In the center of the Timeline, a Move box appears with the number you typed.

8 Press Return to enter the amount and move the clip.

9 To move the clip to the left 4 seconds, type –4. (minus 4 followed by a period) and press Return.

As in the Timecode Duration field, a period here also represents two zeros.

10 Drag the **VO_01** clip until its In point aligns, or *snaps*, to the beginning of the **canoe coming** clip.

When a clip snaps to another clip's In or Out point, brown snapping arrows appear, just as they do when you snap the playhead to the same location.

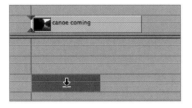

NOTE ▶ Snapping is a magnet-like function that allows you to easily align clips to each other, or to the playhead location. Snapping is discussed in more detail later in this lesson.

11 Drag the **rowing sound** clip, and snap its Out point to the Out point of the **canoe coming** clip. Play these three clips to see if you like the new placement of the voice-over.

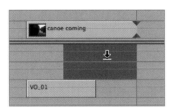

When you selected one track of a stereo pair in the previous exercise, both tracks became selected. When you drag or move one track of a stereo pair, they both move in tandem. Notice the green arrows, indicating a stereo pair, on the **rowing sound** clip.

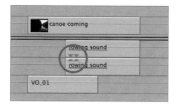

Selecting and Moving Multiple Clips

Just as you may need to select a single clip during the editing process, you will at times need to select a group of clips together. For example, you may have a series of voice-over clips, such as in the A3 track of the *Canoe Club – Finished* sequence, and decide you want to move them all farther down in the Timeline to start later in the sequence. You can use several methods to select a group of clips. Some follow the normal selection process you used to select clips and put them in bins in Lesson 1. In this exercise, you will practice different methods of selecting and moving a group of clips.

> **TIP** You may need to adjust the zoom control or zoom slider to create more space around the clips for these steps.

1 Select all the clips in this sequence by choosing Edit > Select All, or by using the keyboard shortcut, Cmd-A.

2   Click any one of the selected clips, and drag right. Release the clips when you've moved them about 5 seconds forward in the Timeline.

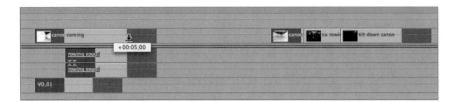

As you drag, the dark, shadow clips represent the new clip location. The distance you move the clips appears in the duration box.

TIP ▶ As you drag clips in the Timeline, make sure to keep the pointer on the same track you were on when you started dragging. Otherwise, the clips will follow the pointer to a different track.

3   With the clips still selected, type –5. (minus 5 followed by a period) in the Timeline, and press Return.

This moves the group of clips 5 seconds back to the left.

4   Deselect these clips in one of three ways:

   ▶   Choose Edit > Deselect All.

   ▶   Press Shift-Cmd-A.

   ▶   Click in an empty track or Timeline area.

5   There are several ways to select a group of clips. After trying each method, deselect the clips using one of the options in step 4.

   ▶   Click the first clip in the V1 track, and Shift-click the last clip.
   All video clips in-between become selected, even if there is a space or gap separating them.

   ▶   Click the first V1 clip, and Cmd-click the last clip.
   Just those two clips become selected.

   ▶   Drag a marquee around the first video clip and the two audio clips in the sequence.

As you start to drag down, a dotted box outlines the area you have selected. Every clip that the tip of the pointer touches becomes selected. Do not deselect.

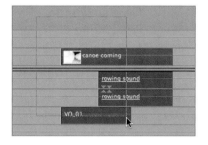

TIP To marquee clips in the Timeline, click above the first clip and drag down and across to select the clip or clips. When you've completed the selection, release the mouse.

6   Click any one of the selected clips, drag to the head of the sequence, and deselect them.

7   Select and drag the second and third V1 clips left until they snap to the end of the first clip.

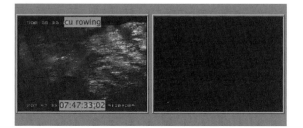

8   Drag the fourth clip to the end of the third clip, but *don't release the mouse.*

In the Canvas window, two edit frames appear. This is referred to as a *two-up display*. The left frame displays the last frame of the clip before the clip you're dragging. The overlay identifies the clip name and source time-code number. The right frame displays the clip frame that follows the clip you're dragging. In this case, no clip follows this one in the sequence, so the right frame is black.

TIP ▶ If you accidentally release a clip over another one, it will overwrite the clip beneath it. To undo this action, press Cmd-Z.

9   Now continue to drag the fourth clip left, *into* the other clips, but *don't release the mouse*.

As you drag a clip over other clips in the Timeline, the Canvas two-up display updates to display the frame before and frame after the clip that's being dragged or repositioned. In this example, you can use these frames to match the rowing actions.

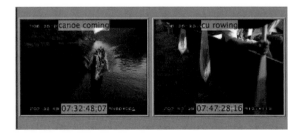

10   Move the clip to snap to the end of the last clip, the **cu rowing** clip, and release it. Deselect the clip, and click each sequence tab to compare the sequences.

The video clips should be back in their original order once again.

Copying and Pasting Clips

In the previous exercise, you heard the **rowing sound** clip under the first video clip. The other video-only rowing clips would also benefit from having this sound effect play under them. To continue the sound effect under all the rowing clips, you could edit the rowing sound clip to the sequence several times. Or you could copy and paste the clip in the sequence multiple times.

Copying and pasting in the Final Cut Pro Timeline is similar to copying and pasting in a word-processing program. First you select a clip. Next you copy it. Then you move the playhead to where you want to paste the clip, and you paste it. You use the same Apple shortcut commands for copy and paste: Cmd-C and Cmd-V.

1   Click the *Canoe Club - Finished* sequence tab, and count the number of **rowing sound** clips on the A1 and A2 tracks.

   There are six **rowing sound** clips in this sequence. To create six clips in the *Moving Clips* sequence, you will copy the first one and paste it five times.

2   Click the *Moving Clips* sequence tab.

3   Click the **rowing sound** clip to select it. Choose Edit > Copy, or press Cmd-C.

4   Use the up or down arrow to position the playhead at the end of the first **rowing sound** clip.

5 Choose Edit > Paste, or press Cmd-V.

A copy of the **rowing sound** clip is placed at the playhead position in the Timeline, and the playhead moves to the end of that new clip.

6 With the playhead at its current position at the end of the second **rowing sound** clip, press Cmd-V again, and then three more times, for a total of six **rowing sound** clips. Deselect all clips and play the sequence.

NOTE ▶ You can keep pasting the clip again and again because it remains on the computer Clipboard until something else replaces it.

7 Save your project by pressing Cmd-S.

Preparing for Drag-and-Drop Editing

You have just completed the first step in learning about drag-and-drop editing by manipulating clips already in the Timeline. Now it's time to learn to edit clips by dragging them to the Timeline. This method goes hand in hand with the drag-and-drop approach you've been using to manipulate the current clips.

But before you start making edits directly to the Timeline, let's focus on some of the *automatic* functions in the drag-and-drop editing process.

Positioning the Pointer

When you edit to the Timeline, the position of your pointer in a track will determine the type of edit—Overwrite or Insert—you make. Properly positioning your pointer is the key to drag-and-drop editing.

If you look at any empty area of an audio or video Timeline track, you see a thin gray line running across the upper-third area of the track. This is the line you focus on when you drag and drop clips to the Timeline.

1 Move the tip of your pointer up and down over the thin gray line.

Nothing happens now, but this is the point on each track where edit options will change when you have a clip in hand.

TIP For this exercise, make your track height taller so that you clearly see this line.

2 From the Browser, open the **daryl cu** clip into the Viewer. You will use the clip as it's marked. Press Shift-\, or click the Play In To Out button, to see the marked portion of this clip.

NOTE ► All the Canoe Club clips have been marked so that each clip begins wiht the same downward stroke in the rowing action. This approach helps to maintain the sync of the rowing sound effect to the video clips.

3 Click in the Viewer image area, and drag the **daryl cu** clip thumbnail to the middle of the empty V2 track in the Timeline, but *don't release the mouse.*

NOTE ► If you accidentally released the mouse, press Cmd-Z to undo that action. Then repeat step 3.

4   With clip thumbnail in hand, focus on the tip of your pointer, and drag it up and down over the thin gray line in the V1 track just as you did before.

When the tip of the pointer is positioned below the thin gray line, an Overwrite edit is indicated with a downward arrow and solid box representing clip length.

When the tip of the pointer is positioned above the thin gray line, an Insert edit is indicated with a forward arrow and hollow box representing clip length.

NOTE ▶ In both situations, the thumbnail image remains the same.

5   While still holding the mouse button down, drag the clip back to the Viewer, and release the mouse.

TIP ▶ You can always drag a clip back into the Viewer if you change your mind about using it in the sequence.

Snapping to the Playhead

When you made Overwrite and Insert edits in the previous lesson, you moved the playhead in the Timeline to where you wanted to place the new clip. This is not required when you drag a clip into the Timeline. You can place a new clip wherever you choose to drop it, regardless of the playhead position.

However, a clip *will* snap to the playhead when you move past it as long as snapping is active. Using the snapping function to snap a clip to the playhead will ensure that you position your clip exactly where you want. The Snapping button is located in the upper-right corner of the Timeline button bar and can be toggled off or on any time during the editing process.

NOTE ▶ Every window has its own button bar that you can customize with a unique set of functions, tools, or commands. The two default functions that appear in the Timeline window are snapping and linked selection. You will learn to customize these button bars in a later lesson.

1   In the Timeline, click the Snapping button several times.

Snapping on   Snapping off

When snapping is on, or active, the icon design is green and looks concave. When the function is toggled off, the design is gray and appears flatter.

2   Make sure snapping is toggled on.

3   To position the playhead free of other video clips, drag it to the beginning of the fifth **rowing sound** clip.

4   Drag the **daryl cu** clip from the Viewer to the Timeline V2 track again and drag the clip across the playhead as an Overwrite downward arrow—but *don't release it.*

TIP ▶ Make sure you focus on snapping the shaded clip box on the track and not the clip thumbnail image.

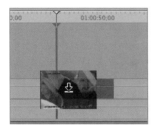

The head or tail of the dark, square portion of the clip beneath the thumbnail snaps to the playhead. In the Timeline ruler area, brown snapping arrows appear just beneath the yellow playhead, and the playhead stem in the track area is thicker.

NOTE ▶ As in previous editing exercises, when you drag a clip from the Viewer, you are dragging only the marked portion to the Timeline.

5   Return the clip to the Viewer, and release the mouse.

Returning the clip to the Viewer is a good way to pause and rethink your edit before releasing a clip in the Timeline.

6   In the Timeline button bar, turn off snapping by clicking the Snapping button.

7   Now drag the **daryl cu** clip from the Viewer to the Timeline V2 track, and drag it over the playhead, but *don't release it.*

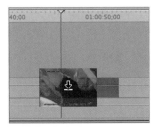

The clip passes over the playhead without snapping to it. With snapping off, it is difficult to tell whether the clip is lined up at the playhead position or not.

TIP▶ Snapping a clip to the playhead is a great way to move a clip to a specific location.

8   As you drag, press N to toggle snapping back on again.

You can toggle snapping on and off even while you're moving a clip.

9   Return the clip to the Viewer, and release the mouse.

Dragging Clips to the Timeline

Let's complete the video to this sequence by making some additional edits. You will edit two video clips as Overwrite edits and two more as Insert edits. You will edit these clips using the drag-and-drop method.

NOTE ▶ Make sure Snapping is on for these steps.

1   Drag the **daryl cu** clip from the Viewer down to the V1 track, and snap it to the end of the **tilt down canoe** clip. Make sure the downward, Overwrite edit arrow is showing, and release the clip.

The playhead jumps to the end of the newly placed clip, just as it did when you made Overwrite edits in the previous lesson.

TIP ▶ If you release the clip in the Timeline before placing it where you want it to go, you can drag the clip into place as a separate step, as you did earlier in this lesson. If you release it over an existing clip, press Cmd-Z to undo and try again.

2   Open the **pan to totem** clip from the Browser, and play the marked portion. You will use this clip as marked.

If you look closely at the visual timecode and film key frame numbers in the image portion of this clip, you will see that they are reversed. In order for these two clips to match direction, the **pan to totem** clip had to be flopped or turned around to face the opposite direction. Also, the black area at the top of the image is a shade attached to the camera. Because the final version of this film screens as a widescreen format, the black area won't show. You will learn to flop clips and add mattes in a later lesson.

3   Drag the clip from the Viewer to the Timeline as an Overwrite edit, and snap it to the end of the **daryl cu** clip. Remember, it doesn't matter where the playhead is located for this edit.

Let's say you want to add a few more video clips to cover the sound effects on A1 and A2. But after reviewing the **pan to totem** clip, you decide you would like for that to be the last clip in the sequence. In this case, you will need to insert any additional clips before the **pan to totem** clip.

When you make Insert edits, no matter what method you use, all clips from the insert point on are moved forward the length of the new clip. In the previous lesson, you wanted all the clips to move forward to allow room for the new clip. In this lesson, you want just the video clips to move forward, but not the audio clips. First, you'll try the edit without locking the tracks to see what happens. Then, you'll lock the audio tracks so they won't be affected by the video Insert edit.

> **TIP** ▶ Snapping should always be active when inserting clips between other clips for the most accurate placement.

4   Open the **canoe from left** clip, and play the marked portion. Drag this clip into the Timeline, and snap it to the edit point at the head of the **pan to totem** clip. Position the tip of the pointer above the thin gray line in the V1 track. Make sure you see the Insert edit visual clues—the forward pointing arrow and the hollow clip—and then release the clip.

Inserting this clip at this location moves all clips on all audio and video tracks forward by the clip duration. This is not what you want in this case.

5 Press Cmd-Z to undo the last action—in this case, the Insert edit.

Another track control in the Timeline is the Track Lock control. Locking a track keeps it from being affected by an editing function, such as inserting the clip in step 4.

6 In the Timeline, click the Track Lock controls for the A1 and A2 tracks.

Diagonal lines appear on these audio tracks, indicating that they are locked and cannot be changed.

> **TIP** You can also press Shift-F5 to toggle the locks off or on for all audio tracks.

7 Now repeat step 4, and play this area of the sequence.

The clip is inserted after the **daryl cu** clip, and only the **pan to totem** video clip is moved down the length of the new clip. The playhead has repositioned itself after the new clip. This is where you will insert the next edit.

8   Open the **daryl slo-mo** clip, and play the marked portion.

The speed of this clip has been slowed to half its normal rate. You will learn to change the speed of a clip in a later lesson.

NOTE ▶ This footage was originally shot on super 35mm film and transferred to tape. You may see some film artifacts, such as frame duplication, in this clip.

9   Drag the **daryl slo-mo** clip to the V1 track, and insert it after the **canoe from left** clip.

NOTE ▶ You can also insert a clip right in the middle of another clip. For example, you might decide to break up the action of a long clip by inserting a different image for a few seconds in the middle. The long clip will be split into two parts, and the second part will be pushed down the length of the newly inserted clip.

10 Play the sequence from the beginning.

In later lessons, you will learn to trim and adjust clips already in the Timeline.

> **TIP** ▶ Don't forget to press Shift-Z to see the entire sequence in full view, or Option-+ or Option-− (Option-minus sign) to zoom in or out of the Timeline.

Dragging Audio to the Timeline

When you edit directly to the Timeline, you drag from the image area of a clip in the Viewer. But when you open an audio-only clip, there is no video display. Instead, you drag an icon from the audio tab in the Viewer called a Drag Hand icon.

1 Since you don't need to protect the A1 and A2 tracks anymore, you can click their Track Lock controls to unlock them, or press Shift-F5.

2 From the Canoe Club Audio bin, open the **VO_02** clip, and play it. Set an Out point where the narrator stops talking.

3 Play the clip again, and watch the audio level on the audio meters. The audio level of this clip is a little low. Raise it to 6 dB by entering that amount in the Level field, or by dragging the Level slider.

4 To drag this clip to the Timeline, drag the Drag Hand icon to the A3 track. Release it on the A3 track as an Overwrite (downward arrow, solid clip) somewhere under the **cu rowing** video clip.

If you were using the edit button, Edit Overlay, or keyboard shortcut to edit this clip, you would have to change the destination for this voice-over clip to the A3 track. But when you drag edits to the Timeline, you can simply drag them to the specific track where you want to place them.

5   Play this part of the sequence.

6   From the Audio bin in the Browser, open the **VO_03** clip, and play it. You will use this entire clip, and you'll also need to raise the volume to 6 dB.

7   Drag this clip to the A3 track under the **daryl cu** video clip. Play this area of the sequence.

> **TIP** ▶ If you're trying to place a clip in the Timeline, but you don't want to snap to another edit point or the playhead, press N to turn off snapping, and place the clip. Once you've positioned the clip where you want it, you can press N again to turn snapping back on.

8   From the Audio bin in the Browser, open the **battlesong** clip into the Viewer, and play until the singing begins. You will use this clip as marked.

Although the drumming may be soft enough not to overpower the narration, singing at this volume could be distracting.

9   Drag the Level slider to the left to –15 dB, or enter –15 dB in the Level field, and play the singing portion again.

10   This time, drag the clip icon from the Browser to the Timeline. Position the first track on the A4 track at the head of the sequence, and release the clip as an Overwrite edit.

You can drag clips directly from the Browser to the Timeline, and like other methods of editing, only the marked portion is edited. Notice here that the name of the clip appears next to the pointer. Also, when you release the clip, the A5 track is automatically added to accommodate the stereo music tracks.

> **TIP** ▶ Don't forget to save (Cmd-S) frequently throughout your editing session.

Changing a Clip in the Timeline

After you edit a clip to the Timeline, it becomes part of the sequence and is referred to as a *sequence clip*. There are times you will need to change certain aspects of a sequence clip, after it's already been edited. For example, in the steps in the preceding section, you changed the audio level for the voice-over narration clips before you edited them into the sequence. You also changed the volume of the music track. But when you listen to them together in the Timeline, you may find that the voice-over needs to be louder, or the music or sound effect needs to be softer. Let's look at how you change a sequence clip.

1   Play the sequence again, and listen to the **battlesong** music track. It plays very softly between the voice-over clips, perhaps too softly.

2   To make a change to this sequence clip, double-click the clip in the Timeline.

When you double-click a sequence clip in the Timeline, that clip opens up in the Viewer. There are two indications that this is not the original source clip from the Browser, but rather the clip that is from the sequence. Look at the title bar of the Viewer.

When you open a source clip from the Browser, the name of the clip appears in the Viewer along with the project name. Here the clip name appears along with the name of the sequence it is in.

Now look at the scrubber bar. The two rows of dots that appear throughout the scrubber bar is another indication that this is a sequence clip. It is not the original source clip from the Browser.

Whatever marks or settings you originally made to the clip prior to editing it are exactly the same. In this case, the sound level is –15 dB, which is what you set prior to editing.

3 Raise the volume of this clip to –10 dB. Click the Timeline to make it the active window, and play the sequence to see if you like the audio level change.

4 Double-click the first **rowing sound** clip to see what the audio level is.

This clip was already in this sequence when you opened the project. When you made a copy and pasted this clip, the copies all had the same sound level.

5 Raise the volume of the **rowing sound** sequence clip in the Viewer to –15 dB. Play this clip in the Timeline to see if you like the new level.

Just as you copied and pasted the **rowing sound** clip earlier in this lesson to create a continuous background sound of rowing, you can also copy and paste a single attribute from one clip to another.

6 Select the first **rowing sound** clip in the sequence, and press Cmd-C to copy it.

This copies everything about this clip—the audio content and even the audio levels.

7 To paste just the audio level attribute of this clip to the next **rowing sound** clip, Ctrl-click the second **rowing sound** clip. From the shortcut menu, choose Paste Attributes.

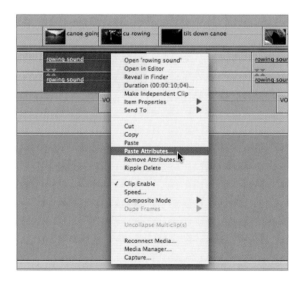

The Paste Attributes window appears. Here you can select any available attributes from the copied clip that you want to paste to another clip.

8   Click the Levels check box, and then click OK.

9   Double-click the second **rowing sound** clip to see the audio level, which is –15 dB, just like the first **rowing sound** clip.

10 To paste this same level to the remaining **rowing sound** clips at one time, click the third **rowing sound** clip and Shift-click the sixth, or last, one.

NOTE ▶ This is a good example of when you need to select multiple clips in the Timeline.

11 Ctrl-click any one of the selected clips and choose Paste Attributes from the shortcut menu.

12 In the Paste Attributes dialog, click the Levels check box, and click OK.

13 Double-click one of these **rowing sound** clips to see the new audio level.

Project Practice

In the *Moving Clips* sequence, reposition each voice-over clip in the A3 track by dragging it left or right. You may find you prefer the first voice-over to come in later, or the last one to start earlier.

> **TIP** ▶ Remember to press N to turn off snapping if you don't want the clip to snap to another clip's edit point.

Saving and Quitting

Always save your project frequently throughout your editing session and again before you close the project or quit Final Cut Pro.

1 Save the current project one last time by pressing Cmd-S.

2 If you are finished working in Final Cut Pro, quit the program by pressing Cmd-Q. If not, continue with the next lesson.

Lesson Review

1. To select a clip in the Timeline, you click it once. Name two ways to deselect it.
2. How do you change a clip's location in the Timeline?
3. What are the keyboard shortcuts you use to copy and paste a clip in the Timeline?
4. What are two ways to turn snapping off or on?
5. When dragging clips directly to the Timeline, your pointer changes as you position the clip depending on the type of edit you're making. When you're making an Overwrite edit, what type of arrow does your pointer change into? What is it for an Insert edit?

6. When you edit a video clip directly to the Timeline, you drag from the image area of the clip. How do you edit directly to the Timeline using an audio-only edit?

Answers

1. Click in the gray empty space above the track, or press Shift-Cmd-A.

2. Drag the clip, or select it and enter a move amount.

3. Cmd-C copies a selected clip, and Cmd-V pastes the copy.

4. Press N, or click the Snapping button in the Timeline.

5. The downward arrow is for an Overwrite edit. The forward arrow is for an Insert edit.

6. In the Audio tab, drag the Drag Hand icon onto the desired track, and release the clip as an Overwrite or Insert edit.

Keyboard Shortcuts

Cmd-A	Selects all clips in the sequence
Shift-Cmd-A	Deselects all clips in the sequence
Cmd-C	Copies
Cmd-V	Pastes
N	Toggles snapping off and on
Shift-F5	Toggles locks off and on for all audio tracks

4

Lesson Files	Lesson 4 Project
Media	A Thousand Roads > Amanda, Canoe Club, Intro, and Sound Effects folders
Time	This lesson takes approximately 60 minutes to complete.
Goals	Set edit points in the Timeline
	Select tracks in the Timeline
	Delete clips and gaps in a sequence
	Edit to a narration track
	Import clips into the project
	Edit sound effects to video clips
	Link separate clips together
	Add cutaways

Marking in the Timeline

Overwrite and Insert edits are the basic building blocks of the editing process; you will use these editing options in almost every project. There are, however, ways you can set up an edit other than by marking a clip in the Viewer. How and where you mark an edit depends on your material and your editing approach. For example, you can mark portions of a narration or voice-over track, or even music, directly in the Timeline, to determine the length and placement of new material.

In this lesson, you will explore marking in the Timeline and other ways to make changes to your sequence, such as deleting clips and gaps, adding sound effects, editing from the Browser, and linking separate audio and video clips together.

As in all projects, editing functions follow purpose. As you explore these different editing options, think about how you might apply them to your own projects.

Preparing the Project

To prepare for this lesson, you will launch Final Cut Pro, open the project for this lesson, and play one of the finished sequences.

1   In the Dock, click the Final Cut Pro icon.

2   Choose File > Open, or press Cmd-O.

3   Choose the **Lesson 4 Project** file from the FCP5 Book Files > Lessons folder on your hard drive.

4   Close any other projects that may be open from a previous session by Ctrl-clicking the project name tab in the Browser and choosing Close Tab from the shortcut menu.

> **NOTE** ▶ Final Cut Pro allows you to work with multiple projects open at one time. Closing a project here is just a matter of simplifying what you're looking at in the interface as you move through the lesson.

5   In the Timeline, click the *Canoe Club* sequence tab and then the *Intro – Finished* tab to compare the two sequences.

The elements in this project link back to the same set of source media on your hard drive as you used in Lesson 1 and Lesson 3. Only the links back to the media have been duplicated for this lesson, not the media itself.

6 In the Timeline, Ctrl-click the *Intro – Finished* sequence tab and choose Close Tab from the shortcut menu.

You will work with this sequence later in this lesson.

Marking in the Timeline

You follow the same general procedures for marking in the Timeline as you did with marking in the Viewer. You position the playhead where you want to set an edit point and then use the shortcut keys, I and O, to set an In or Out point. You can also use the Mark In and Mark Out buttons in the Canvas window to set marks in the Timeline.

Mark In button   Mark Out button

1 In the Timeline, move the playhead to snap to the beginning of the **canoe from left** clip. You will see the first frame overlay in the lower left of the Canvas. Press I to set an In point at this location.

An In point appears in the ruler area of the Timeline, in the Canvas scrubber bar, and in the Canvas image area. In the Timeline, all the clips that follow the In point become lighter, or *highlighted*, to indicate they are part of the selected area.

2 Move the playhead to the last frame of this clip. In the Canvas, click the Mark Out button to set an Out point at this location.

> **TIP** With snapping on, the playhead will snap to the first frame of the following clip. Look in the Canvas for the overlay (which looks like a reverse L) in the lower-right corner that indicates the last frame. If necessary, click the left arrow once to move back one frame to the last frame of this clip.

Now, only the material that falls between the marked portion appears highlighted. This color shade difference helps you to see at a glance what portion of the sequence and what specific clips will be affected as you move forward in your editing process.

3   Before you remove these marks, which you will do in the next step, look closely at the duration of the marked clip in the Canvas Timecode Duration field. It is 7:18.

4   Press Option-X to remove the edit points in the Timeline.

When you remove the In and Out marks from the Timeline, the Canvas Timecode Duration field again displays the length of the entire sequence.

Another useful way to mark in the Timeline is to use the Mark Clip function, which marks an In and Out for a specific clip. This is helpful because it identifies the exact duration and location for a clip in the Timeline. The Mark Clip button also appears in the Canvas; its shortcut is the *X* key.

Mark Clip button

5   Position the playhead in the middle of the **canoe from left** clip, and press X, or click the Mark Clip button in the Canvas. Look at the Canvas Timecode Duration field.

Notice that the duration for this clip is the same as in the previous step. Using the Mark Clip function marks the entire clip in a single step without having to position your playhead at an exact location.

6 Press Shift-I and then Shift-O to go to the In and Out points in this clip.

These shortcuts work just as they did in the Viewer. Notice that the In and Out marks also appear in the Canvas scrubber bar and in the image area.

7 Move the playhead to several clips in the sequence, and press X, or click the Mark Clip button in the Canvas, to find its duration.

Notice as you press X to mark a different clip, those marks replace the previous marks. If you want to remove all marks from the Timeline, you can press Option-X.

TIP To find the length of a group of clips in the sequence, set an In point on the first frame of the first clip in the group, and set an Out point on the last frame of the last clip in the group.

Selecting Tracks in the Timeline

In the previous exercise, you positioned the playhead over a video clip and pressed X to find its duration. But what if your producer turns to you and says, "How long is the **VO_01** narration clip?" To find a specific point, you need a vertical and horizontal reference. The playhead provides the *vertical* reference point in the Timeline, and you can use a track selection control to identify the specific track, or *horizontal* reference.

1   Move the playhead over the middle of the **canoe coming** clip, and press X.

   In this case, the playhead is actually over one video and three audio clips. The Canvas Timecode Duration field displays the duration of the video clip on the V1 track. The V1 track has the highest priority when it comes to track selection. Since you are looking for the length of the clip on A3, you must deselect the other tracks and *point to* the A3 track.

2   In the Timeline track control area, click the V1 Auto Select control.

   The video clip within the marked selection becomes deselected, and the highlighted area now includes only the audio clips.

3   Make sure the playhead is over the first **rowing sound** clip, and press X to mark this clip.

   With the V1 track deselected, and with no clips on the V2 track, Final Cut Pro defers to the first audio track—A1—marks that clip, and displays its duration in the Canvas Timecode Duration field.

4   Toggle off the Auto Select controls for the A1 and A2 tracks.

   In the Timeline, the **rowing sound** clip is no longer highlighted.

5 Press X.

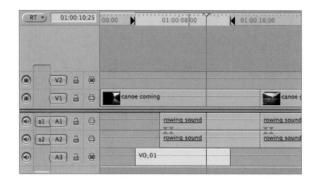

Now the **VO_01** clip is marked, and its duration is displayed. The track selection priority always begins with V1 and continues upward through the other video tracks, then defers to A1 and continues downward through the remaining audio tracks.

6 Toggle on the Auto Select control for all the video and audio tracks, and press Option-X to remove all marks from the sequence.

TIP To toggle off or on all video or audio tracks but one, Option-click that track's Auto Select control.

Deleting Clips and Gaps

You may have created a perfect sequence, but if it's a minute and a half too long, you're in trouble. Deleting material from your sequence is another reason to mark a clip or area in the Timeline. You can mark and delete an entire clip, a portion of a clip, or a portion of the entire sequence, which might include several clips. You can delete a clip and leave a *gap* the length of the clip behind. Or you can delete a clip and the gap at the same time, shortening the sequence in the process. Before you get started, look at the Canvas Timecode Duration field to determine the current length of the sequence.

This sequence's duration is 1:10:00 (1 minute and 10 seconds). Let's say your producer wants the sequence cut down to 1 minute. You must cut 10 seconds out of this sequence by either deleting one or more clips in their entirety, or by shaving a few seconds from several different clips. As always before making major changes, it's a good idea to create a backup of this sequence.

1 In the Browser, Ctrl-click the *Canoe Club* sequence and choose Duplicate from the shortcut menu. Name the new sequence *Canoe Club Short*, and double-click it to open it in the Timeline.

2 Move the playhead to the head of the sequence, and set an In point at this location.

You will begin by deleting the portion of the **canoe coming** clip that has no audio under it.

3 Position the playhead on the frame just before the **VO_01** clip begins, and press O to set an Out point.

NOTE ▶ Remember that when you drag the playhead with snapping on, it will snap to the first frame of the **VO_01** clip. You must then back up one frame. Use the overlays in the Canvas to guide you.

In the Canvas Timecode Duration field, a 3:18 duration appears. In the lower right of the Canvas image area, the last frame overlay appears. In this case, the last frame is the last frame of the gap area before the **VO_01** clip.

NOTE ► When the playhead is over a first or last frame of any clip in the Timeline, that overlay will appear in the Canvas image area even if the overlay is not related to the current image.

4   To remove this portion of the **canoe coming** clip, press the Delete key on your keyboard.

TIP ► If you have a clip selected in the Timeline and press Delete, the selected clip will override the In and Out marks. You can deselect all clips by pressing Cmd-Shift-A.

Removing a portion of the clip also removes, or *lifts*, all material between the In and Out marks in the Timeline and leaves a *gap*. This would be helpful if you wanted to edit other material to this location. However, it did not actually shorten the sequence.

NOTE ▶ If you get an "Operation not allowed" dialog, make sure that you've turned on the Auto Select controls for all tracks. If you pressed the wrong delete key, you can press Cmd-Z to undo your action.

5 Play from the beginning of the sequence through this gap.

Whenever a gap in the sequence occurs, Final Cut Pro will continue to play through it, acting as if it were a black clip. Gaps are not clips, but you can select and delete them like clips.

6 Click in the gap before the first video clip, and press Delete. You can also choose Sequence > Lift.

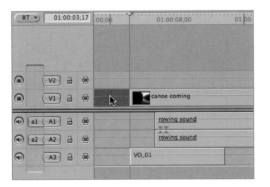

Selecting and deleting a gap will remove the gap from the sequence. But you can delete material *and* the gap in one step.

7 Press Cmd-Z twice to return the deleted portion of the clip and the Timeline marks. Now choose Sequence > Ripple Delete, or press Shift-Delete. If you are using an extended keyboard, you can also press the Forward Delete key.

The clip, along with the gap, is removed, and all the clips that follow are moved up in its place, creating a *ripple* effect in the Timeline. Check the Canvas Timecode Duration field to see the new duration.

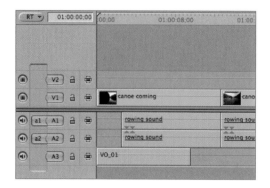

8   Move the playhead over the **canoe going** clip, and press X to mark this clip's length.

This clip's duration is 6:12, which is the amount you need to cut to bring the sequence down to 1 minute.

9   To delete the video clip and the audio sound effect under it, press Shift-Delete.

All selected clips between the In and Out points are deleted, along with the space they occupied. The duration in the Canvas Timecode Duration field displays 59;28 (59 seconds and 28 frames), which gets you very close to a 1-minute duration.

NOTE ▶ The Auto Select controls determine which tracks are included in certain Timeline operations. If the V1 Auto Select control were toggled off, for example, only the audio would be deleted in step 9, and the video would be left alone.

Project Practice

To continue practicing marking and deleting in the Timeline, press Cmd-Z to undo the last delete. Then mark and delete portions of the sequence as you like, to bring the sequence down to 1 minute. When you're finished, close this sequence by Ctrl-clicking the *Canoe Club Short* sequence tab and choosing Close Tab from the shortcut menu. Close the *Canoe Club* sequence the same way.

Editing to an Audio Track

Another reason to mark in the Timeline is if you want to edit new material on top of existing clips. For example, if you are cutting picture to an audio track, such as music or narration, you will need to mark certain portions of the audio track in order to know where the video clip should go. Whenever you mark in the Timeline and use a new source clip from the Viewer, the theory of *three-point editing* comes into play.

Three-point editing is the term used when you edit a clip to the Timeline using any combination of three edit points to determine the duration, location, and content of a clip. When you made edits to the Timeline in previous lessons, you identified the edit duration and content by setting In and Out points in the Viewer, and you identified the location of the edit by moving the playhead to a specific point in the Timeline. These three points—Source In, Source Out, and playhead position—determined the duration, location, and content of this edit. This is one example of three-point editing. But you can also use Timeline In and Out points to determine duration and location of a new edit.

Marking a Narration Track

Often when you edit to narration, the script or narration takes priority. So instead of opening a source clip in the Viewer and setting edit points on the video clip, you first need to know what the narrator is saying in order to pick the appropriate video clip and content. In this exercise, you will mark the narration track in the Timeline to determine the duration and location for each new video clip. Then you will open a source clip in the Viewer and mark it to determine the content, or what part of it you will use in the edit.

1   In the Timeline, close all open sequences. From the Browser, open the *Intro – Finished* and *Intro – Starting* sequences.

2   To preserve a copy of the *Intro – Starting* sequence to work with later, duplicate it in the Browser, and name the copy *Intro – Starting backup.*

3   In the Timeline, click between the two sequence tabs to compare the sequences, then play the *Intro – Finished* sequence.

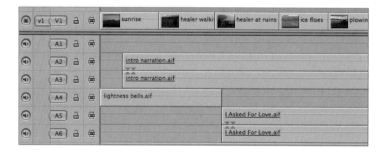

You worked with a version of the *Intro – Finished* sequence in Lesson 1. This version has one stereo narration clip on A2 and A3. It has a music sound effect on A4 and a stereo music track on A5 and A6. The *Intro – Starting* sequence has only audio clips. You will add the video clips to this sequence, and later in this lesson, you will add sound effects to the A1 track.

4   Click the *Intro – Starting* sequence tab to make it the active sequence.

5   Move the playhead to the beginning of the sequence, and press I to set an In point. Play the sequence, and stop a beat after the narrator says, "…wake up and shine." Press the O key to set an Out point at this location.

> **NOTE ▶** An In mark at the head of the sequence may be difficult to see. When you move the playhead away from the In point, it's easier to see the edge of the mark. You can also see the edit points in the Canvas.

The duration from the In point to the Out point is displayed in the Canvas Timecode Duration field. This is the duration you will need for the first video clip.

6 In the Browser, display the contents of the Intro Clips bin, and open the **sunrise** clip. Scrub through this clip.

Since you have already defined the duration and location for this clip in the Timeline, you only need an In point to determine where you will begin using the source content.

7 Set an In point in the **sunrise** clip somewhere between the beginning of the clip and where the sun is halfway over the mountain's edge.

8 In the Timeline, make sure the v1 source control is patched to the V1 destination control.

NOTE ▶ In this situation, you don't need to position the playhead because Timeline marks take priority over the playhead location.

9   Edit this clip as an Overwrite edit, using any of the methods you've used before.

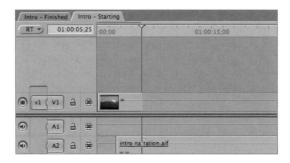

In the Timeline, the clip is edited to the V1 track. The edit points have been removed, and the playhead is aligned to the first frame after this clip, where you will edit the next video clip.

10   While the playhead is in its current position, set an In point in preparation for the next clip. Play from the beginning of the sequence, and set an Out point after the narrator says, "Breathe it all in."

TIP ▶ You can also set In and Out points on the fly as the sequence is playing, just as you did in the Viewer.

11   In the Browser, open the **healer walking** clip, and set an In point when the healer begins to walk. Edit this clip as an Overwrite edit, and play the new clip in the sequence.

Backtiming a Clip

When you have an Out point in the Timeline, you can take advantage of another approach to three-point editing called *backtiming*. You can use this approach when the placement of the last frame of a source clip is more important than the first frame. In this case, you set In and Out points in the Timeline to create the edit location and duration, and set an Out point in the Viewer on what is to be the last frame of the clip content.

1   Snap the playhead to the first empty video frame after the **healer walking** clip. Set an In point at this location as the beginning of the next clip. Play

the sequence, and set an Out point *before* the narrator says, "We have met along the way."

TIP ▶ This is a good time to use the J and L keys to play backward or forward to find this edit point.

2   In the Browser, open the **healer at ruins** clip, and scrub down toward the end of the clip. Set an Out point where the healer bows down.

The Out point in this source clip is more important than the In point.

NOTE ▶ This type of edit is referred to as *backtiming* because Final Cut Pro starts from the end of the clip and measures the duration backward to determine where the clip begins.

3   Edit the clip as an Overwrite edit, and play the clip.

The source Out point was aligned to the Timeline Out point. The source In point was determined by *backtiming* the clip, or filling in the distance back to the Timeline In point.

4   Press the up or down arrow to move the playhead to the first empty frame in the video track, and set an In point at this location. Play from this point, and set an Out after the narrator says, "hunting on the ice floes of Alaska."

> **TIP** ▶ Just as you viewed audio waveforms in the Viewer, you can also view audio waveforms in sequence clips in the Timeline. It can be helpful for focusing on where specific audio references occur. To see the audio waveforms appear in the Timeline, press Option-Cmd-W. You will work more with this feature in a later lesson.

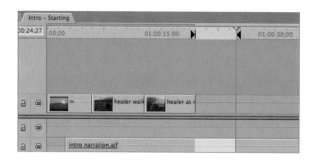

5   In the Browser, open the **ice floes** clip, and play the middle portion where the snowmobile goes over a few bumps. Set an Out point after the second bump, around 5:16:22:00.

In this situation, as in the previous source clip, the action where the clip stops is more important than where it begins.

> **TIP** ▶ To change or adjust an existing Out point, drag the mark left or right in the Viewer scrubber bar. As you drag, you see the new frame in the Viewer image area. When you stop dragging, the image in the Viewer reverts to the playhead location. Be sure to drag from the black triangle of the Out point, otherwise you will move the playhead instead.

6   Edit this clip as an Overwrite edit, and play the clip.

As before, the source clip's Out point is aligned to the Timeline Out point, and the rest of the source clip is backtimed into position.

TIP ▶ When backtiming clips, make sure there is no In point in the Viewer. Otherwise, the clip's In point will line up with the Timeline In point instead of lining up Out point to Out point.

Using a Source Duration

A third way to use three-point editing is to set an In and Out point in the Viewer and set just an In point in the Timeline. In this situation, you are giving priority to the source clip duration.

> **NOTE** ▶ If you have In and Out points in both the Viewer source clip and the Timeline, and they represent different durations, the Timeline edit points will always take priority, and the Out point in the Viewer will be ignored.

1   Use the up or down arrow to move the playhead to the first empty frame in the video track, and set an In point at this location.

Without an Out point in the Timeline, the edit duration will default to the source duration in the Viewer.

2   In the Browser, open the **plowing fields** clip, and play it. Set an In point when the man plowing is fully in the frame. Set an Out point when the man is directly in front of the animal in the middle of the image.

> **NOTE** ▶ This is another image where a camera shade was used to block the sun's glare from the lens. The final version of this film was output in widescreen format, and this shade is not visible in that format.

3 Edit this clip as an Overwrite edit, and play the clip.

Although the clip covers this portion of the narration nicely, it might go a little too long. This is easily corrected by overwriting the tail of the clip when you make the next edit.

4 Play this clip in the sequence again, and stop the playhead *before* the narrator says, "Trekking through the streets of Manhattan." Set an In point at this location.

TIP Editing is a subjective process. When editing to audio in these exercises, set the edit points based on what feels and looks right to you as an editor.

5 In the Browser, open the **city street** clip, and play it. Set an In point after the man in the white shirt lowers his arm, and set an Out point when the image goes blurry.

6 Edit this clip as an Overwrite edit, and play the clip.

The marked source clip is edited into the Timeline at the In point. Again, when you listen to the narration, the clip seems to play a little too long.

7 Play this clip in the Timeline again, and set a new In point just as the voice in the music track begins to sing. You may have to turn up the volume on your audio monitor to hear this clearly.

8 In the Browser, open the **ruin steps** clip, and play it. Set an In point before the tilt up begins, and set an Out point where the tilt ends. Edit this clip as an Overwrite edit, and play the new clip in the sequence.

NOTE ▸ You can also set an In point in the Timeline and enter a duration in the Canvas Timecode Duration field to determine the Out point.

Project Practice

Continue setting In and Out points in the Timeline and editing the following clips to complete the video for this sequence. Use your own sense of timing and the narration that follows as a reference for where you set the marks for each clip. You can also review the *Intro – Finished* sequence to see how that version was edited. The two clips with asterisks in the following list could easily be backtimed in order to make the Out point a priority.

TIP ▸ Remember, you can set an In point in the Timeline and overwrite the end of a clip if you think that will improve the timing. And you can always press Cmd-Z to undo an edit. You will learn to trim and adjust these edits in the next two lessons.

canyon runner	"The first peoples of this great land. We Indians, we're always going home, no matter how far from the birthing grounds we've traveled."
amanda rushing	"We always go back…"
johnny runs	"By foot…"
truck on road	"By road…"
girl on plane	"By plane or by spirit, we migrate by heart."
walking in fields	"So as you walk out into the fields to plant or gather…"

tall buildings*	"Into steel and glass towers to trade…"
ice fishers	"To the ocean or woods to hunt…"
healer cu**	"Remember, we're all on this journey together, down a thousand roads."

---

* Backtime this clip from where the two U.S. flags are framed in the center of the image.

** Backtime this clip just after the healer leaves the frame.

Importing Clips into a Project

Now that you've edited all the video clips into the V1 track, you can focus on other ways to improve the sequence. One way to do this is to add a sound effect to each video clip to give the audio track more depth. The FCP5 Book Files > Media folder contains some sound effects, but they have not been included in this project. You will have to import them into this project to use them in editing. You can import a single file or an entire folder at one time.

You import a file in one of three ways:

▶   Choose File > Import > Files.

▶   Press Cmd-I.

▶   Ctrl-click in the Browser and choose Import > Files from the shortcut menu.

1   Ctrl-click in the Browser and choose Import > Files from the shortcut menu.

2   When the Choose A File window opens, navigate to the FCP5 Book Files > Media > A Thousand Roads > Sound Effects folder. Click the **bird sounds.aif** clip once to select it.

An icon appears in the column to the right of the sound effect clip you selected. Depending on how this clip was created, it may display a QuickTime icon or the Final Cut Pro slate icon. Notice the information about the clip under the slate icon. The kind of file is listed as a Final Cut Pro Media File. You will learn more about different export options in a later lesson.

3   Click Choose.

The new **bird sounds.aif** clip appears in the Browser.

4   To import a few clips at a time, Ctrl-click in the Browser and choose
Import > Files from the shortcut menu.

5   In the Media > A Thousand Roads > Sound Effects folder, select **light
wind.aif**, and then Cmd-click **car passes by.aif**. Click Choose.

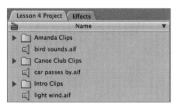

The new files appear in alphabetical order in the Browser.

TIP   You can select or deselect a file by using Cmd-click. You can also
select a group of contiguous files by clicking the first file and then Shift-
clicking the last file in the group.

6 This time, Ctrl-click in the Browser and choose Import > Folder. In the Choose A Folder window, navigate to the Media > A Thousand Roads folder, and select the Sound Effects folder.

When you choose this option, individual files are dimmed and cannot be selected.

7 Click Choose.

The entire Sound Effects folder is imported into the project as a bin.

8 Click the disclosure triangle to display the contents of the Sound Effects bin.

9 To remove the redundant individual clips you imported in the earlier steps of this exercise, Cmd-click each one, and press Delete.

When you delete clips from a project, you are not deleting any media from your hard drive. You are only deleting that specific link in your project back to those clips. In this case, you still have the complete set of sound effects in the Sound Effects bin, which are the links you will use to edit this media.

TIP You can also use the drag-and-drop approach to import clips into a Final Cut Pro project. To do this, arrange your interface windows so you can see the Browser and a Finder window on your Desktop. Navigate to the location of the desired clip or folder in the Finder window. Drag the file or folder into the Browser and release it.

Editing Sound Effects to Video Clips

For this exercise, you will add sound effects on the A1 track to cover the length of each video clip on V1. To begin, you will mark the duration of a video clip, as you did earlier in this lesson, and then edit a sound effect at that location. This is another example of marking in the Timeline, but this time you are using the existing video clips as a reference.

NOTE ▶ You can continue working with the *Intro – Starting* sequence, or you can duplicate the *Intro – Finished* sequence in the Browser, which represents all the work done in this lesson up to this point.

1   In the Timeline, make sure the Auto Select controls on all tracks are selected. Move the playhead over the first video clip, and press X to mark its duration.

2   In the Browser, open the **bird sounds.aif** clip from the Sound Effects bin, and set an In point at the head of this clip.

TIP Don't forget to check the volume of each sound effect and adjust it to blend with the narration and music tracks. You'll learn more about adjusting audio levels and mixing audio in upcoming lessons.

3   In the Timeline, make sure the a1 source control is connected to the A1 destination control.

4   Edit this clip as an Overwrite edit, and play the clip in the Timeline.

5   Park the playhead over the second video clip, **healer walking**, and press X to mark this clip's duration.

6   From the Sound Effects bin in the Browser, open the **light wind.aif** clip, and set an In point somewhere at the beginning of this clip.

7   Edit this clip into the Timeline as an Overwrite edit.

8   Move the playhead down in the sequence to the **truck on road** clip, and press X to mark this clip.

Toward the end of this clip, the truck comes around the bend. Having the sound match this action would make it more believable.

9   Open the **car passes by.aif** clip, and find the place where the sound of the car passing by is the loudest. You can use the height of the waveform display as a guide. You may have to use the zoom slider, or press Shift-Z, to see this area.

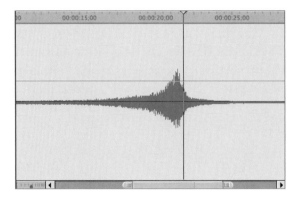

In this situation, setting an Out point as the car passes by in the sound effect might help to create a better match to the video than setting an In point.

10   To align the end of the sound effect with the end of the clip in the Timeline, set an Out point just after the peak of the drive-by sound. Edit this clip as an Overwrite edit, and play the clip.

The sound of the car passing by is now closely aligned to the image in the Timeline. You can press Cmd-Z to undo this clip if you want to improve the timing.

Project Practice

Continue adding sound effects to match the video clips in the Timeline. Don't forget to set the audio levels for the sound effects in the Viewer before editing them so they don't overpower the narration and music tracks. If you want a reference to the completed sound effects sequence, you can view the *Intro with SFX* sequence in the Sequences bin.

> **TIP** ▶ To change the audio level of a sound effects clip you've already edited, double-click the clip in the Timeline to open it into the Viewer. When you change the volume, it will only change the sequence clip in the Timeline, not the original clip in the Browser.

Linking Clips Together

Now that you have an audio sound effect positioned with each video clip, you may want to go one step further and link these clips together. When clips are originally captured with the audio and video together, they are automatically linked. But you can also join unlinked clips together if you want to make changes to both the audio and the video at the same time. When a clip's audio and video tracks are linked, you can move the clip or adjust its length by adjusting just one track, and all tracks in the linked clip will be adjusted equally. In the next lesson, you will learn to adjust the length of a clip. Here you will link the V1 video clips together with the A1 audio clips in preparation for the next lesson.

> **NOTE** ▶ For these steps, you may want to press Option-+ to zoom into the clips you will be linking.

1   In the Timeline, look at the second video clip in the V1 track, the **healer walking** clip.

Notice that the clip name has no underline. An underlined name in a video clip tells you that the clip is linked to audio that's presently in the sequence.

2   Click the **healer walking** video clip.

When you select this clip, only the video is selected because there is currently no audio attached to this video clip.

3   Now Cmd-click the **light wind.aif** sound effect clip beneath the **healer walking** video clip so that both are selected together.

4   Choose Modify > Link, or press Cmd-L, to link the video and audio clips together.

When you link these clips, the link line appears under the video clip name, indicating it's linked to audio in the sequence.

5   Deselect this clip, then click the video portion of the clip again.

Both clips become selected because they are linked together.

6   Use the methods in steps 2 through 4 to select and link each set of V1 and A1 clips.

NOTE ▶ Although you can link multiple audio clips together, you can only have one video clip as part of a linked clip.

Adding Cutaways or B-Roll Material

Often when editing material, you may want to use only a portion of what someone is saying, then jump ahead to something else that person is saying. This jump from one part of a clip to a different part of the same material is referred to as a *jump cut*. Jump cuts are jarring to the viewer, going from one talking head shot to another. These cuts are generally covered up by editing a new shot of something else over the actual edit point. These replacement shots are referred to as *cutaways*, and can be selected from another area in the clip, or completely different material, often referred to as B-roll because it is not the primary footage.

The first step in covering a jump cut is to mark the location in the Timeline where you want the cutaway to go. Then you choose the source you want to use for the cutaway and set an In point. In the *Amanda* sequence you edited in Lesson 2, you edited two shots (of the man) next to each other in order to create the correct soundtrack of him talking and then singing. To cover that jump cut, you will edit a cutaway of Amanda listening to the man.

1   In the Sequences bin in the Browser, double-click to open the *Amanda Cutaways* sequence.

This sequence should look familiar to you from Lesson 2.

2   In the Timeline, drag the playhead to the second green marker.

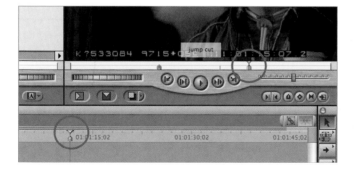

This marker identifies the edit point that jumps from one image of the man to a similar image of the man. In the Canvas image area, notice that the name of the marker is displayed. In the Canvas scrubber bar, the marker appears yellow when the playhead is positioned directly over it.

3   Play around this edit point.

The audio track is good, but the video needs to be improved by adding a cutaway to cover this jump cut.

4   Set an In point in the Timeline somewhere before the edit point that jumps, and set an Out point just after the edit point.

This identifies the area you will cover up with a shot of Amanda.

5   Open the **98A-amanda** clip, and find a nice facial reaction that you can use for the cutaway. Set an In point at that location.

6   To edit only the video, make sure the a1 and a2 source controls are disconnected from the audio destination tracks.

7   Edit the cutaway as an Overwrite edit, and play the new edit.

Now the adjacent placement of the two **98B-man** clips is not distracting because you cut *away* to Amanda, in between them. You can also use a cutaway to break up a longer action in one clip, such as when the man is singing.

8   Play past this new edit into the following clip of the man singing. Set an In point around 1:01:18:08.

9   In the **98A-amanda** clip in the Viewer, find the place where Amanda mouths the words to this song. Set an In point at that location. Set an Out point when she stops mouthing.

10   Edit the clip as a video-only Overwrite edit, and play the new clip.

NOTE ▶ In another lesson, you will learn how to adjust the placement of these two cutaways.

Project Practice

To continue practicing what you've learned in this lesson, open the *Intro – Starting Backup* sequence, and mark the narration in the Timeline. These marks will be for video clip length and placement. You will then mark the source video clips for content. Use clips from all three clips bins to edit a different version of this sequence.

Remember to save your project before you close it or quit Final Cut Pro.

Lesson Review

1.   What are the shortcuts for setting In and Out points in the Timeline?

2.   What is the shortcut for marking the duration of a clip in the Timeline?

3.   What does the Auto Select control in the Timeline track area determine?

4.   What track priority do the Auto Select controls follow?

5.   When you mark an area of the Timeline and press Delete, will you leave a gap? What is the name of this type of delete?

6. What happens to the marked area of the Timeline when you press Shift-Delete or the Forward Delete key?

7. On what menu do the Lift and Ripple Delete functions appear?

8. When the playhead moves through a gap in the Timeline, what do you see in the Canvas?

9. What mark is necessary in the Viewer when backtiming a source clip into a marked area in the Timeline?

10. Name two ways to change the volume of a clip.

11. What are three ways to access the Import Files command?

12. How do you link a video clip to a separate audio clip?

Answers

1. Press I to set an In point and O to set an Out point.

2. You can press X to mark the duration of a clip in the Timeline.

3. If the Auto Select control is toggled on for a track, the clips between the edit points on that track will be highlighted and will be included in the selection.

4. They follow the priority of V1 through V99, and then A1 through A99.

5. Pressing Delete alone leaves a gap where the material was edited. This type of delete is referred to as a lift.

6. Pressing Shift-Delete or Forward-Delete removes both clips and gap within the marked area. This type of delete is referred to as Ripple Delete.

7. The Lift and Ripple Delete functions appear on the Sequence menu.

8. When you play through gaps between clips in the Timeline, they look like black clips.

9. The Out point of a source clip in the Viewer is neccessary to backtime it into the Timeline edit points.

10. You can change the volume of a clip in the Viewer before you edit it into the Timeline, or you can double-click the clip in the Timeline to open the sequence clip in the Viewer and change the volume there.

11. You can import a clip by choosing File > Import > Files, pressing Cmd-I, or Ctrl-clicking in the Browser and choosing Import > Files from the shortcut menu. Importing a folder does not have a keyboard shortcut.

12. You select the clips in the Timeline and choose Modify > Link, or press Cmd-L.

Keyboard Shortcuts

Delete	Lifts an item or section from the Timeline and leaves a gap
Shift-Delete (or Forward Delete)	Removes an item or section from the Timeline and ripples the following edits up the duration of the gap
X	Marks the full length of a clip
Cmd-L	Links together the audio and video tracks of clips in the Timeline

5

Lesson Files	Lesson 5 Project
Media	A Thousand Roads > Amanda folder; Motocross > Team Story folder
Time	This lesson takes approximately 60 minutes to complete.
Goals	Trim overview
	Trim an edit point by dragging
	Trim clips in the V2 track
	Trim one track of a linked clip
	Trim using the Ripple tool
	Trim clips in the Viewer
	Trim using the Razor Blade tool
	Extend an edit point

Lesson **5**

Trimming Edit Points

No matter how you edit clips into a sequence, once they're there, you will want to refine. The refining process is based on the concept of trimming. There are several ways to trim in Final Cut Pro. You can drag an edit point in the Timeline, use a Razor Blade tool to *cut off* a portion of a clip, or use the Ripple tool to trim an edit point. You can even trim a clip in the Viewer window. Trimming clips often changes the length of a sequence, making it longer or shorter. In this lesson, you will practice trimming clips in different ways.

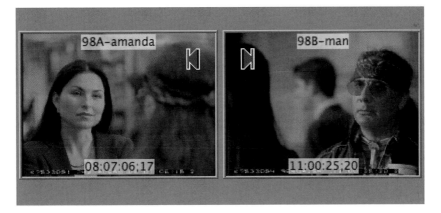

Trimming two-up display in Canvas

Preparing the Project

To get started in Lesson 5, you will launch Final Cut Pro and then open the project for this lesson.

1   Launch Final Cut Pro, and choose File > Open, or press Cmd-O. Select the **Lesson 5 Project** file from the Lessons folder on your hard drive.

2   Close any other projects that may be open from a previous session by Ctrl-clicking their name tabs in the Browser and choosing Close Tab from the shortcut menu.

3   In the Timeline, play the *Amanda – Starting* sequence.

This is a different version of the Amanda street scene you edited in Lesson 2. In this version, the edit points are very loose and obviously need trimming. To apply different methods of trimming to this sequence, you will duplicate this sequence and work with the duplicate.

4   In the Sequences bin in the Browser, Ctrl-click the *Amanda – Starting* sequence and choose Duplicate from the shortcut menu. Name the new sequence *Dragging*, and double-click to open it in the Timeline. Dragging edit points will be the first method you will use to trim clips.

Trimming Overview

Trimming an edit point is a way of changing your mind about where you want a clip to start or stop *after* you've placed it in the Timeline. When you trim an edit point, you are lengthening or shortening the clip either at the head or the tail. Lengthening or shortening a clip in the Timeline often affects the length of the entire sequence.

Consider the In point at the head of the clip:

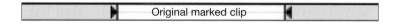

▶   Trim the In point to the left, and the clip will begin on an earlier frame. The clip will be longer.

▶ Trim the In point to the right, and the clip will begin on a later frame. The clip will be shorter.

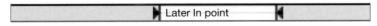

Consider the Out point at the tail of the clip:

▶ Trim the Out point to the left, and the clip will end on an earlier frame. The clip will be shorter.

Earlier Out point

▶ Trim the Out point to the right, and the clip will end on a later frame. The clip will be longer.

Later Out point

Remember that the maximum amount you can trim in an outer direction (head or tail) to lengthen a clip depends on how much material is available in the original media file. Even though you are seeing only the marked portion in the Timeline, you have access to all the frames from the original media file. These additional frames are referred to as *handles*.

Dragging to Trim

Dragging edit points to trim a clip is a direct and easy way to change the length of a clip in the Timeline. It works much like dragging a whole clip, but when you drag an edit point, the clip itself remains stationary; just the In or Out point moves, and the length of the clip is changed.

Dragging Edit Points

In this exercise, you will work with the *Dragging* sequence you duplicated earlier. You will drag an edit point to trim a clip. To shorten a clip, you will trim inward toward the center of the clip. To lengthen a clip by dragging, you drag away from the center of the clip.

1 In the Timeline, play the *Dragging* sequence to review how the clips are currently cut together.

These clips were loosely edited to create what is called a *rough cut* sequence.

NOTE ▶ If you want to review how this sequence was originally edited in Lesson 2, you can open and view the *Amanda – Finished* sequence from the Browser.

2   In the Timeline, play the last clip in the sequence, **98C-wide**.

When this clip was edited, the narration had not yet been included. Now that the narration clip is present, you can see that this clip is too short. It needs to be lengthened to cover the narration.

3   Click the Out point of this clip once to select just the edit point.

The Out point becomes selected on all tracks because the video and audio portions of this clip are linked together. The line under the clip name indicates this link.

NOTE ▶ Just the edge of the clip is selected, not the body of the clip. If the entire clip were selected, you would end up moving the clip, not trimming it.

4   Hold the pointer over the edit point until it becomes the resize arrow, then click the edit point and drag right as far as you can, but don't release the mouse. As you drag, look at the trim amount and the new clip duration as they are being updated in the information box.

As you drag, all linked tracks are dragged together.

TIP ▶ When you are trimming, adjust the zoom control in the Timeline so the clips you are working with appear a little larger.

In the Canvas image area, the end-of-clip filmstrip overlay appears on the right side of the image, indicating you have reached the last available frame of the clip's media. You cannot trim the clip any further in that direction.

5   Release the mouse, and play the clip to see the new edit point.

In this situation, trimming the Out point as far as possible does not make the best-looking edit because people start to move in front of the man.

6   Play this clip again, and stop the playhead just as the man finishes singing his song, which is just before the camera moves near the end of the clip.

7   Drag the Out point to snap to the playhead location.

TIP ▶ Positioning the playhead to where you want to trim an edit point is an effective way of trimming.

Dragging Edit Points Between Clips

When two clips are side by side, Final Cut Pro won't allow you to drag the edit point of one clip into its neighboring clip. You can drag away from the neighboring clip but not into it. Trimming or shortening a clip by dragging it away from a neighboring clip will leave a gap in the sequence. If you leave the gap, the sequence length will be the same as it was before you trimmed the clip. If you delete the gap, the sequence length is changed. You delete gaps just as you did in the previous lesson.

1   Play through the edit point between the last two clips in the sequence.

Amanda starts to leave in the **98A-amanda** clip. In the **98C-wide** clip, you need to pick her up later, and match the action as she's starting to leave.

NOTE ▶ When working with dramatic scenes, you match the visual action first, and then finesse the audio as needed. In this situation, you will hear Amanda repeat her farewell greeting in the final clip. You can trim this away in a later exercise.

2   In the **98C-wide** clip, position the playhead after Amanda has finished speaking and has started to walk away. This will be the new In point.

3   Click and drag the In point of the **98C-wide** clip to snap to the playhead. Release the mouse.

TIP ▶ If snapping is off, toggle it on by pressing N. You can toggle snapping off and on even as you drag the mouse.

As you drag, a brown outline appears around the clip, indicating the new clip length. The new clip duration appears in the information box. When you release the mouse, a gap appears in the sequence the length of the trim.

4   To remove the gap between the clips, click in the gap area, and press Delete.

When you delete the gap, the following clip is pulled up. As mentioned in Lesson 4, this is called *ripple deleting* because deleting the gap ripples the location of the following clip or clips earlier in the Timeline.

5 Play the last **98A-amanda** clip in the sequence from the head of the clip. Position the playhead after the man stops singing off-camera and just *before* Amanda nods her head.

6 Drag the In point of this clip to snap to the playhead location. Click the gap to select it, and press Delete to delete the gap.

7 Try dragging the Out point of this **98A-amanda** clip to the right to make it longer.

Nothing happens because you cannot drag a clip into a neighboring clip to make it longer without a special trim tool you will use later in this lesson.

8 Press Cmd-S to save your changes.

NOTE ▶ This method of deleting gaps works only on gaps without clips above or below the gap on other tracks.

Dragging Edit Points on V2

Dragging an edit point is an easy approach to trimming a clip except for the fact that you can't lengthen a clip when it sits next to another clip. But there is a way around this problem. It involves placing a clip onto the V2 track where, with no neighbors, you have the freedom to trim it in either direction.

1   To find the next clip to trim in the *Dragging* sequence, move the playhead to the head of the sequence. Press Shift-M to move the playhead to the green marker in the ruler area of the Timeline.

When the playhead is on a sequence marker, the name of the marker appears in the Canvas image area. You will learn to create markers in a later lesson.

2   Press Option-+ to zoom into this area so you can see the clips on either side of this cutaway more clearly. Play these clips.

This is a cutaway of Amanda that was edited to help break up the long clip of the man singing. To make this clip shorter, you can use the dragging approach and drag inward on the clip. But to make it longer, you have to place it on the V2 track to drag its edit points outward.

3   Drag the **98A-amanda** cutaway clip up onto the V2 track. Make sure you have not moved the clip left or right, but straight up. Deselect the clip after you release it.

TIP ▶ To ensure you don't move the clip any frames left or right, you can hold down Shift as you move a clip to another track. This locks the movement to just a vertical move.

4   Drag the In point to the left about 1 second to lengthen this cutaway. Play
    these clips in the sequence.

When video clips are stacked on top of each other, the clip on the highest
track takes precedence and will be seen. In this situation, the **98B-man**
clip will be seen from the beginning of the clip to the point where the cutaway appears on the V2 track. At that point, the only video you see will
be the video clip on the V2 track until it stops. When the V2 clip ends,
whatever video is beneath it on the V1 track will be seen.

5   Drag the Out point of the **98A-amanda** cutaway clip on the V2 track to
    lengthen it slightly.

    When a clip stands alone on a separate track, both the head and tail of the
    clip can be trimmed to make the clip longer or shorter without being
    restricted by the other sequence clips.

6   Click the center of the **98A-amanda** cutaway clip, and drag the entire clip
    left until its Out point snaps to the In point of the following **98B-man** clip.
    Play this area of the sequence again.

With the cutaway on a separate track, you can move the clip to reposition
it, trim it by dragging its edit points, or even turn off the track visibility to
see what the sequence looks like without it. Make sure that when you
reposition the V2 clip, it covers the V1 gap in its entirety. Any uncovered
areas of the gap will play as black frames.

7   Press Cmd-S to save your work.

Trimming One Track of a Linked Clip

When you capture the audio and video of a clip together, Final Cut Pro links those tracks together. You can click one edit point, such as the video Out point, to select all Out points on all tracks of that clip. This can be very helpful when you want to change the Out point of the clip the same amount on all tracks. But sometimes when editing, you may want to trim just the video track of a clip to be shorter or longer than the audio and vice versa.

The function that determines whether or not you can select a single track or all tracks of a linked clip is the linked selection function. As with snapping, you can toggle this function off and on by clicking its button in the Timeline button bar. When linked selection is off, you can select a clip's audio or video tracks individually, even if the tracks are linked together. When linked selection is on, however, when you trim one track, all other tracks that are part of that linked clip will also be trimmed the same amount.

1 In the current *Dragging* sequence, move the playhead to the sixth clip in the sequence, which is the first **98B-man** clip, and play the clip.

So far, you have been trimming both the audio and video tracks at the same time. In this clip, you want the video to continue to where the man looks up to Amanda. But when you extend the video to that location, you hear Amanda say, "Yeah," off-camera. In this exercise, you will trim the audio tracks to remove Amanda saying, "Yeah," but not the video.

2 In the Timeline, click once on either the video or audio track of the **98B-man** clip to select it.

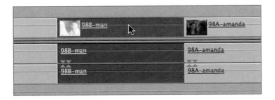

All tracks in this clip become selected. This is because the linked selection function is on. Notice the link line under the clip names in all tracks of this clip.

3   Deselect this clip. Click the Linked Selection button in the Timeline button bar to toggle it off. You can also use the shortcut, Shift-L.

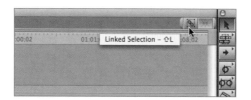

Like snapping, linked selection is on, or active, when the button is green, and it's off when it is gray.

4   Click once on the first **98B-man** clip in the Timeline to select it again.

With linked selection toggled off, only the track you click is selected.

NOTE ▶ Clicking one track of a stereo pair will select both audio tracks.

5   Position the playhead just before Amanda says, "Yeah."

6   Drag the Out point on either audio track of the **98B-man** clip to snap to the playhead location.

The audio tracks are trimmed back, and the video track is left alone.

7 Move the playhead to the last clip in the sequence, the **98C-wide** clip, and play it.

In a previous exercise, you matched the visual action of this clip but ended up with Amanda repeating her farewell greeting.

8 Park the playhead after Amanda says her farewell greeting in the **98C-wide** clip. Drag the audio In point to snap to the playhead location. Play the last two clips in the sequence.

You have corrected the audio by removing her line from this clip. Later, in the audio mixing stage, you can add some ambient sound to fill this gap.

9 In the Timeline, click the Linked Selection button to toggle that function back on.

You can choose to edit with linked selection on or off. For now, and for the purposes of these lessons, keep linked selection on, in its default state.

TIP To temporarily override linked selection to trim a single track, press Option and then drag the edit point. You will drag just the audio or video edit point you select.

Project Practice

For practice, you can trim each clip in the *Dragging* sequence by using the dragging approach. In most cases, you will trim away the redundant sounds of the actors saying their lines off-camera. If you need a reference, open and view the *Amanda – Finished* sequence from the Browser.

Trimming and Rippling Edits

Dragging edit points is one way to trim in the Timeline. You can also drag an edit point and ripple the remaining edits in the sequence at the same time *without* having to delete a gap or use an additional track. You do this with the Ripple tool. The Ripple tool is the fourth tool from the top in the Tool palette.

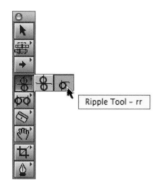

When you use the Ripple tool to trim an edit point, you can drag an In or Out point of one clip into its neighboring clip. All the clips that follow are automatically pushed down or pulled up the length of the trim. You can also use shortcuts along with the Ripple tool to trim and ripple specific amounts.

Using the Ripple Tool

Using the Ripple tool, like dragging an edit point, adjusts either the head or tail of a clip in a sequence in either a forward or backward direction, making the clip longer or shorter. Any change you make with the Ripple tool will cause a change in the overall length of the sequence.

1   In the Browser, duplicate the *Amanda – Starting* sequence, as you did earlier in this lesson. Name the new sequence *Ripple Trimming*, and double-click to open it in the Timeline.

    This is the same sequence that was loosely cut. This time, you will trim the edit points using the Ripple tool.

2   In the Tool palette, click and hold the Roll tool (fourth from the top). When you see the Ripple tool icon, which looks like a single roller, click it. You can also press the keyboard shortcut RR to select this tool.

3   Don't click or drag, but just move your pointer over the middle of the **97F-man cu** clip.

    The Ripple tool has an X on it, indicating that the tool can't be applied to this area. You can only use the Ripple tool on an edit point.

4   Move the Ripple tool toward the clip's Out point.

When the Ripple tool gets close to the Out point, the X disappears, and the tail of the Ripple icon points toward the inside of the clip you will be trimming.

5   Move the Ripple tool to the clip's In point, and click the inside edge of the In point.

When the Ripple tool is positioned over the In point, the tail points inward toward the body of the clip you are trimming. This is a visual clue so you know which clip you are adjusting. When the In point is correctly selected, just the In point of this clip is highlighted.

6   Play this clip and stop the playhead just before the man says, "Hey, bro." Now drag this edit point right to snap to the playhead location.

As you drag with the Ripple tool, an information box appears with just the trim amount. There is no gap left over, and all the clips in the sequence are pulled up by the amount of the trim.

NOTE ▶ Both the audio and video of a linked clip are trimmed together, just the same as when you dragged the edit point with the default Selection tool.

7   Play the previous clip in the sequence, the **97D-coffee stand** clip.

This clip stops early before Amanda settles on watching the man. You will need to trim the Out point to lengthen this clip. Since you need to add more of this clip into the sequence, using the playhead for placement will not be helpful here.

8   Click the Out point of the **97D-coffee stand** clip.

Now the tail of the Ripple icon points inward to this clip, not to the **97F-man cu** clip.

9   Drag this Out point to the right about 4 seconds, but don't release the mouse.

As you drag, the clip boundary box in the Timeline expands to indicate the new length of the clip.

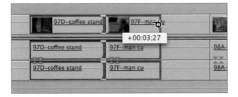

In the Canvas image area, you see a two-up display. The image on the left updates the new Out point as you drag. The image on the right displays the first frame of the clip that follows in the sequence.

NOTE ▶ When you drag an edit point to the end of the original source clip's limits, a note will appear in the information box, indicating you've reached the media limit on that clip.

10 Release the mouse.

The following clips in the sequence are pushed down the Timeline toward the right the length of the trim.

11 Move the playhead back to the **97E-man** clip, and play this clip. Park the playhead just before the man says, "Thank you, bro."

Notice that even though you have the Ripple tool selected, when you move the playhead in the ruler area of the Timeline, the default pointer appears.

12 Using the Ripple tool, drag the In point of the **97E-man** clip to the right to snap to the playhead location.

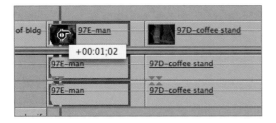

When you drag a clip's edit point to make it shorter using the Ripple tool, the boundary box of the clip shortens to display a representative clip length. When you release the mouse, all the clips that follow are pulled up toward the left by the trim amount.

TIP If you don't want the Ripple tool to snap to the playhead, press N to turn off snapping as you trim a clip.

Rippling with Durations and Shortcuts

Sometimes you may have a fixed trim amount in mind. It could be a few frames, or 10, or 30. Just as you typed a move duration in the Timeline to move a clip, you can also type a trim amount to trim a clip. You can also use a few keyboard shortcuts to trim an edit point.

1   Play the first clip in the sequence, the **97A-out of bldg** clip.

     This clip has a lot of pad at the head of the clip. You will trim 5 seconds off the head of this clip, which will start the clip 5 seconds later.

2   Use the Ripple tool to click the inner edge of that clip's In point.

3   Type *5.00*, or *5.* (5 followed by a period).

     A Ripple information box appears in the center of the Timeline with the amount of the trim.

4   Press Return to enter that trim amount.

     The selected In point is trimmed forward by that amount, and no gap is created.

5 To find the next clip to trim, you will use a Find command. Press Shift-Z to see the sequence in full view. Move the playhead to the head of the sequence, and press Cmd-F. In the Find dialog, enter **98B-man** in the Find field. Click the Find All button (not the Find button).

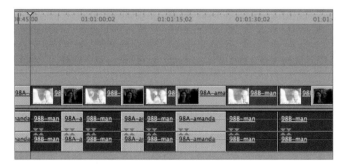

In the Timeline, the playhead jumps forward to the first **98B-man** clip and highlights all clips named **98B-man** in this sequence.

6 Move the playhead to the third highlighted **98B-man** clip. Deselect the highlighted clips, and press Option-+ to zoom into the playhead location. Play this clip.

At the end of this clip, you hear Amanda say, "Ahh." She says it again on camera in the following clip so you can trim it from this clip.

7 To ripple using a keyboard shortcut, click the Out point of this **98B-man** clip, and press the [(left bracket) key.

Pressing the left bracket key trims the selected Out point one frame to the left, or one frame earlier. The following clips in the sequence are pulled up by one frame. You can press the bracket key repeatedly to trim additional frames. However, you will need more than a few frames to trim off Amanda's "Ahh."

8   To trim by a slightly larger amount, press Shift-[(left bracket).

The Out point jumps a default number of frames.

NOTE ▶ Using Shift with a bracket key applies a multi-frame trim size to the trim. You can change this amount (from 1 frame up to 99 frames) in the Editing tab of the User Preferences window.

9   If necessary, press Shift-[a few times to remove Amanda's "Ahh." You can also add frames back by pressing] (right bracket) or Shift-].

Any change you make using these keyboard shortcuts ripples the following clips in the sequence.

TIP ▶ You can also press the < or > keys to trim the selected edit point one frame backward or forward. You can use Shift with these keys to trim the multi-frame trim amount.

10   Press A to restore the default Selection tool.

Trimming in the Viewer

You have used the Viewer to screen and mark your clips before editing them into the Timeline, and you have opened a sequence clip in earlier lessons to change the audio level. You can also use the Viewer to trim sequence clips in the Timeline. One advantage of trimming a sequence clip in the Viewer is that you can easily see the media outside your edit points and not just the media in-between. To trim a clip in the Viewer, you can drag edit points in the scrubber bar, or you can apply the Ripple tool to an edit point. Let's begin by trimming a clip in the Viewer using the Selection tool to drag an edit point.

1   In the Timeline, play the first clip in the sequence, the **97A-out of bldg** clip.

You trimmed the head of this clip in a previous exercise. When you look at the end of this clip, you may consider extending or trimming the Out point to include additional material. But the material is not available to view in the Timeline.

2   With the default Selection tool, double-click the **97A-out of bldg** clip in the Timeline. You can also select the clip and press Return to open it.

The clip opens in the Viewer, and the In and Out points used for this clip in the sequence appear in the scrubber bar. The scrubber bar displays two lines of dots, as it did when you opened clips to change audio levels in previous lessons. These dots are the visual indication that you are working with a sequence clip, that is, a clip that has already been edited into a sequence.

3   In the Viewer, click the Play In To Out button, or press Shift-\ (backslash), to play from the current In to Out. To see what material is beyond the current Out point, just continue playing beyond the Out point.

4   Move the pointer over the Out point in the scrubber bar, and look for the pointer to change to the resize arrow you saw when you dragged the edit point in the Timeline.

5   Drag the Out point to the left to shorten the clip.

In the Timeline, the clip is shorter, but there is a gap. This gives you the same result as earlier in this lesson when you dragged edit points.

6   In the Viewer scrubber bar, drag the Out point of this clip back to its original location, until you see the Media Limit On V1 message appear.

If you can't drag a clip any farther using the current tool, a note will appear letting you know you're bumping up against another clip on the same track. Notice that the change you made in the Viewer also updates the Out point in the Timeline.

7   Now position the playhead in the Viewer past the current Out point, just after Amanda leaves the frame.

8   In the Tool palette, select the Ripple tool, or press RR.

9   Move the pointer into the Viewer scrubber bar and then over the Out point.

The cursor changes to the Ripple tool when it's over an edit point.

10 Drag the Out point to the right to snap to the playhead location.

As you drag, all the remaining clips in the Timeline are pushed back to allow for the length of the trim, just as they were when you used the Ripple tool in previous exercises.

11 Press Cmd-S to save your project.

Project Practice

For practice, you can trim each clip in the *Ripple Trimming* sequence by using the Ripple tool. You can match the edits you made in the *Dragging* sequence, or try cutting a different version of this sequence. As a reference, open and view the *Amanda – Finished* sequence from the Browser as a reference. You can also open and work with the *Intro w_sfx* sequence. In the previous lesson, you linked the video clips to the sound effects so they could be trimmed together.

Using the Razor Blade Tool

Another way to trim a clip is to simply cut off the portion of the clip in the Timeline you don't want to use. You can do this with the Razor Blade tool. The Razor Blade tool will literally slice through all the tracks associated with a clip and make a separate clip out of that portion. You can then select and delete the portion you no longer want. Using the Razor Blade tool is a good way to shape clips in a sequence, and especially to pull out "ums" and "ahhs" from non-professional talent.

1   In the Browser, open the *Razor Blade* sequence, and play the two clips in the sequence.

> **NOTE ▶** This is Jeff Montgomery, the team manager for the Boost Yamaha Motocross Racing Team. This clip is part of footage from a documentary series on motocross racing, which you can read more about in the Getting Started section of this book.

> You will use a tightly edited version of these clips in a later lesson. For now, you will remove a few unwanted portions of these clips.

2   Play the beginning of the **JM stakes rise** clip, and park the playhead after Jeff says, "…interesting to say the least."

> You will not need the remaining portion of the clip after the playhead location.

3   In the Tool palette, select the Razor Blade tool, or press the keyboard shortcut, B.

4   With the pointer inside the clip area in the Timeline, move the Razor
    Blade tool toward the playhead until it snaps.

When the Razor Blade snaps to the playhead, the playhead stem becomes
lighter over the tracks that will be cut. In this case, the razor blade will cut
through all three tracks.

5   Click the Razor Blade on the playhead in any of this clip's tracks.

NOTE ▶ When a clip's tracks are linked together, you can click in any one
of the tracks with the Razor Blade tool.

A new edit point is created where you clicked the Razor Blade tool, and
the original clip is now divided into two separate clips. Red *through edit*
indicators appear on each track to indicate that this material currently
plays continuously from the first clip to the next.

TIP ▶ When you want to slice through all clips in all tracks of the Timeline, even clips that aren't linked together, select the second Razor Blade option, Razor Blade All tool, or press BB.

6   Press A to return to the default Selection tool, and then select the unwanted second portion of this clip.

7   To delete this unwanted clip, as well as the gap, press Shift-Delete.

The through edit indicators no longer appear because the material is no longer contiguous from one clip to the next.

Extending an Edit Point

Another way to trim a clip is to extend a selected edit point to a new location either backward or forward. Extending an edit always works in conjunction with the playhead location and the default Selection tool. The selected edit point snaps to the location of the playhead in the sequence. As with all trim options, extending an edit can make a clip longer or shorter.

1   Press A to select the default Selection tool.

2   In the current sequence, play the second half of the **JM what you see** clip. Position the playhead after he says, "…who and what they are."

You will shorten this clip by moving its Out point to the playhead location.

3   Select the Out point on the second **JM what you see** clip.

Both sides of the edit point are selected.

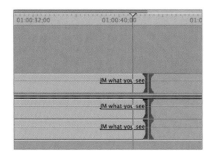

4   Press E, or choose Sequence > Extend Edit.

The Out point is moved backward to the playhead location.

NOTE ▶ You can only extend an edit if you have enough clip material to support the move. If you have placed the playhead out of the clip's range of material, you can't extend the clip to the new location, and no change will be made to that clip.

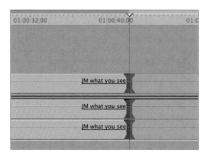

5   To extend an edit point to lengthen a clip, open the *Extend Edit* sequence from the Browser, and play some of this sequence.

Music has been added to these Amanda clips, and the last clips in the sequence do not end together. You will change this using the Extend function.

6   Move the playhead to the end of the last narration clip in the A4 track. Select the Out point of the **98C-wide** clip.

7   Press E to lengthen this clip to the playhead location, at the end of the narration clip.

This lengthens the clip to match the narration. However, the music clip also needs to be adjusted. These two clips can be changed at the same time.

8   Press Cmd-Z to undo the last step. With the Out point of the **98C-wide** clip still selected, Cmd-click the Out point of the music track on the A5 and A6 tracks.

9   Press E to extend both clips to the playhead location.

TIP ▶ Extending an edit point is a great way to even up clips at the end of a sequence because you can extend the edit points of more than one clip on different tracks simultaneously and in different directions.

Lesson Review

1. What tools can you use to drag an edit point in the Timeline?
2. How do you drag a clip vertically in the Timeline without moving it horizontally?
3. What is the advantage of editing on the V2 track?
4. What does toggling off linked selection in the Timeline do?
5. What does the Ripple tool do when you use it for trimming?
6. What keys can you use as shortcuts to ripple a clip's edit point by a few frames?
7. What is one advantage of trimming a clip in the Viewer?
8. What tracks does the Razor Blade tool cut through when you click a clip?
9. What is the keyboard shortcut for extending an edit?

Answers

1. Use the default Selection tool and the Ripple tool.
2. Hold down the Shift key as you drag.
3. It allows you to lengthen a clip without bumping into a bordering clip on either side.
4. It allows you to select and trim one track of a linked clip.
5. It ripples the trim amount through the unlocked tracks in the sequence.
6. Use the left and right bracket keys ([and]) and the < and > keys.
7. You can view the material outside the marked area.
8. It cuts through all the tracks of a linked clip when linked selection is on.
9. The *E* key extends an edit.

Keyboard Shortcuts

Shift-L	Toggles linked selection off and on
E	Extends an edit
RR	Selects the Ripple tool
B	Selects the Razor Blade tool
BB	Selects the Razor Blade All tool

6

Lesson 6
Adjusting Edit Points

The trimming process often involves paring down a sequence to fit time requirements. But there are several ways to adjust clips in the Timeline without changing clip or sequence length. Once your sequence duration is set, you can use several Final Cut Pro tools—the Slip, Roll, and Slide tools—to finesse the actual content of each clip.

Clip being slipped in the Viewer and Canvas windows

Preparing the Project

To get started in Lesson 6, you will launch Final Cut Pro and open the project for this lesson.

1 Choose File > Open, or press Cmd-O, then select the **Lesson 6 Project** file from the Lessons folder on your hard drive.

2 Close any other projects that may be open from a previous session by Ctrl-clicking their name tabs in the Browser and choosing Close Tab from the shortcut menu.

There are three open sequences in the Timeline, similar to ones you built in earlier lessons. In each case, adjusting the edit points will improve or polish the sequence.

Adjusting Two Edit Points

There are three ways to adjust or trim two edit points at the same time without changing sequence length. The three methods are rolling, slipping, and sliding. In each method, the length of a sequence is not changed, because you are trimming both edit points simultaneously by equal amounts. Each of these trimming methods uses a tool from the Tool palette.

> **NOTE** ▶ The term *edit point* can refer to a single clip's In or Out point, but it can also refer to the juncture between adjoining clips.

Rolling

Rolling an edit point trims the Out point of one clip and the In point of the following clip simultaneously. You can *roll* the edit point left or right. If you roll left, the first clip will be shorter, and the second clip will be longer. The opposite is true when you roll to the right: the first clip becomes longer, and the adjacent clip becomes shorter. Rolling edit points left or right does not change the overall sequence duration because as one edit point changes, its neighbor compensates for the change.

Edit point selected

Rolling edit point left

Rolling edit point right

Slipping

Slipping adjusts both the In and Out points in a *single* clip at the same time. You can *slip* the contents of a clip left or right of its edit points. Clip and sequence durations remain the same, but you will be showing a different selection of clip content.

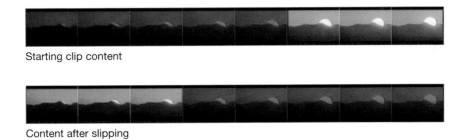

Starting clip content

Content after slipping

Sliding

Sliding adjusts two edit points but involves *three contiguous clips*. You can shift, or *slide*, the middle clip into the one on the left, making the first clip shorter; but the In point of the third clip adjusts to compensate, and the third clip becomes longer. The opposite holds true if you slide the middle clip to the right. The middle clip content remains unchanged though its position shifts slightly right or left in the Timeline.

Starting center clip position

Sliding center clip left

Sliding center clip right

Rolling Edit Points

The Roll tool adjusts both sides of an edit point at the same time. It will adjust the Out point of one clip the same amount it adjusts the In point of the following clip. This allows you to move the edit point earlier or later without changing the overall sequence duration. There are many valuable uses for rolling edit points. For example, if you are cutting a sequence of two people talking, rolling the *video* edit point of the clips left or right can make the dialogue seem more natural. You can also roll video edit points to change their timing against a narration track.

> **TIP** ▶ In each example, zoom into that area of the Timeline in order to see the clip names more clearly.

1   In the Timeline, click the *Intro Rolling* sequence tab to make it active. Play the two clips, **johnny runs** and **truck on road**.

    The clips' timing against the narration track in this sequence seems to be a little off. The **truck on road** clip should really start sooner, where the narrator says, "By road." But the length of the sequence is correct.

2   Move the playhead to just *before* the narrator says, "By road." Make sure snapping is on so you can snap to the playhead location.

3   In the Tool palette, select the Roll tool, or press R.

Roll Tool – r

The Roll tool shares the same tool area as the Ripple tool. The Roll icon looks like two rollers because it trims or adjusts two sides of an edit point.

4   Click the edit point between the **johnny runs** and **truck on road** clips.

Both sides of the edit point become highlighted.

5   Drag the edit point left until it snaps to the playhead location, and note the following *before* you release the mouse:

▶   In the Timeline, a brown outline box surrounds both clips. This indicates that these two clips are involved in this adjustment. The outer edges of these boxes will not change, only the edit point in the middle.

▶   The amount or duration of the roll appears in the information box.

▶   In the Canvas two-up display, the left frame displays the outgoing clip's new Out point along with an Out mark in the frame's upper-right corner. The right frame displays the incoming clip's new In point along with an In mark in its upper-left corner. The clip name and source time-code locations also appear on the Canvas frames.

NOTE ▶ When the Caps Lock key is engaged, the two-up display is disabled in the Canvas.

6   Release the mouse, and play the edit.

The timing between the video and narration is improved, and the length of the sequence remains the same.

NOTE ▶ You can come back to this sequence later to continue practicing rolling edit points to improve the timing.

7   In the Timeline, click the *Canoe Club Rolling* sequence tab to make it active. Play through the edit point between the **tilt down canoe** clip and the **daryl cu** clip.

In this sequence, each clip begins with a downward rowing stroke. This was one way to maintain sync with the other video clips and the rowing sound effects. But let's say you want to give the **daryl cu** clip an extra stroke at the head of the clip without changing the sequence length or upsetting the sync between the clips.

8   With the Roll tool selected, drag the edit point between the **tilt down canoe** and **daryl cu** clips to the left. In the Canvas, look at the new edit points as you drag, and release the mouse when you see the frames you like. Play through the new edit point.

> **TIP** ▶ In this situation, you may want to press N to toggle off snapping so you have greater control as you roll the edit point.

These two clips remain in sync with the rowing action because the amount that was added to the head of the **daryl cu** clip was taken away from the end of the **tilt down canoe** clip.

9   Click the *Amanda Rolling* sequence tab in the Timeline, and play the third **98B-man** clip.

> **TIP** ▶ You can always press Cmd-F to find a clip in the Timeline. Make sure the playhead is at the head of the sequence before you begin your search.

This clip includes the man speaking, so you don't want to adjust the audio portion of this clip. But this edit might appear smoother if you stay on Amanda's video a little longer and slightly delay going to the man's video.

10   Move the playhead to after the man says, "We' ne tsi." To adjust just the video portion of these linked clips, toggle off linked selection by pressing Shift-L or clicking the Linked Selection button in the Timeline (so it is gray).

11   With the Roll tool, drag the edit point to the right to snap to the playhead. Play through the new edit point.

Rolling this video edit point creates a smoother transition between these two video clips but maintains the consistency in the audio.

NOTE ▶ If a clip has no additional frames to use in the adjustment, an end-of-clip filmstrip will appear on one of the Canvas frames, and you won't be able to roll the edit point any farther.

Other Rolling Options

You can enter the amount of a roll adjustment in the Timeline or use shortcut keys, just like you did with the Ripple tool. You can also use the Extend Edit function, which will extend the selected Out point of one clip and the In point of the adjacent clip to the playhead location.

1   In the Amanda Rolling sequence, play the next two clips, where Amanda and the man speak together in their native tongue.

The edit point between these two clips might be improved if you stay longer on Amanda's video before cutting back to the man. But, as in the previous example, you don't want to change the audio portion of these clips, just the video.

2   With the Roll tool, select the video edit point between the **98A-amanda** clip and **98B-man** clip.

3   In the Timeline, type *1.00* to roll this edit point to the right 1 second.

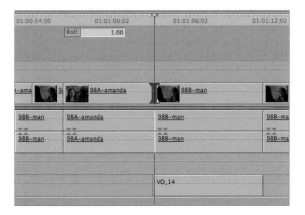

4   Press Return, and play the edit.

As with any new edit, the playhead jumps to the edit point after completing the adjustment.

NOTE ▸ If the clip handle is not long enough to cover the duration you entered, it will roll as many frames as it can in that direction.

5   To further finesse this selected edit point, press the left or right bracket keys to roll one frame left or right. To roll the multi-frame trim amount, press Shift-[(left bracket) or Shift-] (right bracket).

TIP ▸ Pressing the Shift key with the Roll tool on the pointer will temporarily change the pointer to the Ripple tool. Then you can make a change on both edit points at the same time (Roll tool) or just one edit point (Ripple).

6 Play the last **98A-amanda** clip in this sequence.

To roll the beginning of this clip into the previous clip so that it begins earlier, you can also use the extend function. Again, this will extend the Out point of the outgoing clip and the In point of the incoming clip the same amount in the same direction. This is essentially what the Roll tool does, but you can perform this function with the default Selection tool.

7 Press A to return to the default Selection tool.

8 Move the playhead toward the end of the previous **98B-man** clip, and select the edit point between this and the **98A-amanda** clip. This time use the Extend Edit shortcut key, E, to extend the edit point to the playhead location.

Since the playhead was parked where you wanted the new edit point to be, pressing E extends, or rolls, the selected edit point to that location.

TIP You can also use the bracket keys and Shift-bracket to extend or roll edit points selected with the default Selection tool.

9 Play the new edit, and press Cmd-S to save your work.

Project Practice

To practice rolling edits, continue working in these *Rolling* sequences. Remember to toggle linked selection off or on depending on whether or not you want to roll *both* the audio and video of a linked clip at the same time.

Slipping Clip Content

Slipping a clip shifts both the In and Out points of a single clip the same amount as you select slightly different content for that clip. Slipping is a good option to choose when the clip is placed correctly in the sequence and is the correct length, but the clip content is not ideal. Perhaps an earlier or later action would improve the sequence. You can slip a clip only if there is additional source material or if there are handles on either side of the current edit points. If you used the entire clip length when you made the edit, you won't have any additional frames to slip the clip.

Working with the Slip Tool

When you apply the Slip tool to a clip in the Timeline, you drag right to see earlier clip material before the In point and left to see later material after the Out point. Think of the clip as your windshield, and the additional material to the left or right outside your windshield view makes up your handles. The Slip tool is the fifth tool from the top in the Tool palette.

1   In the Timeline, close all the open *Rolling* sequences, and open the *Intro Slipping* sequence from the Browser.

     This is the first version of the *Intro* sequence without sound effects. The placement and duration of each clip is correct. However, the selection of clip content is not the best it could be in all cases.

2   Move the playhead to the **tall buildings** clip, which is the third clip from the end of the sequence. Press Option-+ to zoom into this clip, and play the clip.

     From other screenings of this clip and sequence, you may remember that two U.S. flags appear later in this clip.

3   In the Tool palette, click the Slip tool, or press S.

4   With the Slip tool, click and hold the **tall buildings** clip in the Timeline.

One brown outline appears around the video clip box, and another one appears past the clip box. This outer outline indicates graphically how much original source materia is available for you to draw from on either side while making a slip adjustment.

5   With the Slip tool, drag left until you see both U.S. flags appear in the center of the right frame of the Canvas, but don't release the mouse.

TIP ▶ If you want greater control as you slip a clip, press N to turn off snapping.

In the Canvas two-up display, the new In and Out points of this clip are updated.

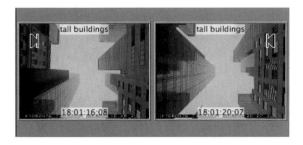

In the Timeline, an information box appears, showing the amount you have adjusted the clip forward or backward.

6   Release the mouse, and play the new clip content.

7   Press Shift-Z to zoom back to the full sequence, and play the first clip, the **sunrise** clip. With the Slip tool, click and drag the clip right as far as you can.

In the Canvas, the end-of-clip filmstrip overlay appears in the left frame to indicate that you are currently on the first frame of the clip. You cannot move any farther to the right. If you drag all the way to the left, you will see the end-of-clip overlay on the right frame.

8   Slip the **sunrise** clip however you like.

Other Slipping Options

Another way to slip a clip is by typing in the number of frames, or even seconds, you want to slip, just as you did with the Roll tool in the previous exercise. In order to use numbers or other shortcuts to slip a clip, the clip must first be selected in the Timeline. Also, once a clip is in the sequence, you can double-click it and make slip adjustments in the Viewer.

1   In the Timeline, play the **ruin steps** clip.

    This clip should start a few seconds later where the camera starts to tilt up. To slip this clip by entering a slip amount, the clip first has to be selected.

2   Try to select the **ruin steps** clip with the Slip tool.

    The Slip tool and other adjustment tools are for specific editing functions and do not allow you to simply select a clip. You could press A to return to the default Selection tool, select the clip, then return to the Slip tool. But there is a shortcut.

3   To select this clip, hold down the Shift key. When the pointer reverts to the default Selection tool, select the **ruin steps** clip, then release the Shift key to revert the pointer back to the Slip tool.

    TIP ▶ You can also use the Shift key to temporarily revert to the default Selection tool when you are working with other tools, such as Ripple or Roll.

4   Type *–2.* (minus 2 followed by a period) in the Timeline, and press Return.

    NOTE ▶ Unlike other uses of plus or minus in adjusting a sequence clip, when you slip a clip using numbers, the direction may seem reversed. Adding a minus sign to a number is the same as dragging the clip left with the Slip tool, and therefore choosing *later* clip content. A plus sign is the equivalent of dragging the clip to the right, or slipping earlier content into the clip.

5 Play the new clip content.

6 Press A to return to the default Selection tool, and double-click the **ice floes** clip. In the Viewer, move the pointer over one of the edit points in the scrubber bar.

The two rows of dots appear in the scrubber bar to indicate that this clip is already in the sequence. Also, the pointer changes to the resize arrow when you move it over an edit point.

7 In the Viewer scrubber bar, press Shift, and click and hold either the In or Out point.

The first frame of the clip appears in the Viewer, and the last frame appears in the Canvas.

8 Now drag left until you see the sled first appear in the left side of the frame. Release the mouse when you see the new In and Out points you like.

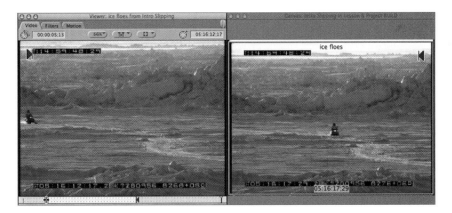

As you drag, both edit points move simultaneously.

> **NOTE** ▶ When slipping in the Viewer, you drag left to move earlier in time, and right to move later in time. This is the opposite of working with the Slip tool in the Timeline. You can also use the Slip tool to slip a clip's edit points in the Viewer.

Project Practice

Continue practicing the different methods of slipping clips in the *Intro Slipping* sequence. Remember, slip adjustments do not change clip duration. Don't forget to watch the Canvas two-up display to capture a specific action in the clip.

Adjusting and Changing Clip Placement

The third method of adjusting two edit points is to slide a clip that sits between two others. Sliding the middle clip maintains its content and duration but adjusts its placement between its bordering clips, altering the duration of its two neighbors but not the overall sequence. To slide a clip, you use the Slide tool. You can also reposition a clip or a copy of a clip to an entirely different location in the sequence. To do this does not require a tool, only a modifier key.

Using the Slide Tool

The Slide tool is used when you want to adjust a clip slightly to the left or right. The clip you are moving does not change duration or content. But the previous clip's Out point and following clip's In point do change. In this respect, sliding a clip is like rolling an edit point, except that you are rolling both of a clip's edit points at once as you slide the clip in one direction or another. The Slide tool shares the same location as the Slip Item tool in the Tool palette.

1 For this exercise, make sure linked selection is toggled on.

2 In the Browser, open the *Amanda Sliding* sequence, and play the first three clips.

If you want to reposition the middle clip, **97E-man**, slide it into the clip on either the left or the right. For this exercise, you will slide it left to start earlier in the sequence, just after the narrator says, "…steep fall markets."

3   To select the Slide tool in the Tool palette, click and hold the Slip tool until the Slide icon appears; then select it, or press SS.

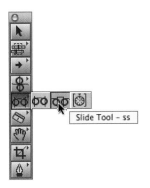

4   With the Slide tool, click and hold the **97E-man** clip.

The brown outline boxes appear, this time around the three clips involved with this adjustment.

5   Press N to turn off snapping, and drag the **97E-man** clip to the left. Don't release the mouse until you look at both the clip in the sequence and the two-up display in the Canvas image area.

As you slide the middle clip, the outside edges of the outer two clips do not move; only the inner edges that border the middle clip move to show how the clips are compensating for the adjustment.

In the Canvas two-up display, the two frames show the new Out point of the first clip and the new In point of the third clip. You can watch these frames as you drag to determine the best position for the clip you are sliding.

6   Release the mouse, and play these three clips again.

> **NOTE ▸** The length of the sequence does not change when you slide clips.

7   Press Shift-M to move the playhead to the marker. Press Option-+ to zoom into this part of the sequence, and play the area around this cutaway of Amanda.

This cutaway might appear smoother if it were positioned a little earlier, into the previous clip, just before the man speaks again toward the end of the clip.

8   With the Slide tool, drag the **98A-amanda** cutaway clip to the left. Watch the left Canvas frame to see where the man begins talking. Position the **98A-amanda** clip where the man begins talking, and position the 98A-amanda clip just before this point. Then, release the mouse.

9   Play the cutaway in its new position. If it needs to be readjusted, slide it left or right.

TIP ▶ You can also press Shift to select the clip and then enter an amount for a slide, or use the left or right bracket keys to make slide adjustments, just as you did with the Slip tool.

Dragging to Reposition a Clip

In addition to sliding a clip left or right between its bordering clips, you may want to reposition a clip, or a copy of a clip, to an entirely different location in the Timeline. Since no new clips are added to the sequence, and you've only made a location change, the overall sequence length remains the same. Repositioning a clip to a new location in your sequence does not require any editing tool other than the default Selection tool.

1   In the Browser, open the *Intro Repo* sequence, and play it. Then snap the playhead to one or more markers and look at the marker names in the Canvas. (Press N if snapping is not on.)

This sequence contains video clips of people in motion from the Intro and Canoe Club bins. The sequence begins with city shots and ends with nature shots. You will rearrange the order of these clips in this exercise.

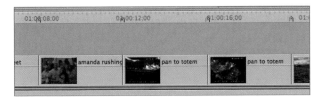

There is a green marker for every four strong beats of music. The video clips were edited using these markers as a guide. You will learn to do this in the next lesson.

2   Press A to choose the default Selection tool.

NOTE ▶ To successfully reposition a clip, you must use precise key combinations at specific times. Follow steps 3–5 carefully, and release the mouse only when instructed to do so.

3 Drag the **canyon runner** clip to the left between the **healer walking** and **johnny runs** clips, but *don't release the mouse*.

As you drag, the Overwrite downward arrow appears. If you were to let go at this point, you would overwrite the material beneath the clip you are dragging and also leave a gap at the end of the sequence, where it was originally positioned.

In the Canvas, look at the names of the clips in the two-up display. These are the frames that would appear on either side of this clip if you released it as an Overwrite edit.

4 Drag the **canyon runner** clip to its final destination at the head of the sequence, but don't release the mouse. This time, press and hold the Option key.

When you press Option, the pointer changes to a hooked downward arrow, indicating that you will be inserting the clip at this point.

The two Canvas frames now display a new image in the right frame. This is the first frame of the **tall buildings** clip. This clip will be pushed down to allow room for the **canyon runner** clip to be inserted here. The left frame of the Canvas is black, because you are at the head of the sequence.

The next step is important to successfully reposition this clip.

5   First release the mouse, and then release the Option key.

The **canyon runner** clip is now the first clip in the sequence, and the following clips have moved down to allow room for it.

6   Drag the **johnny runs** clip left from the end of the sequence, and snap its In point to the In of the **tall buildings** clip. Make sure you're snapping to the edit point and not to the markers in the ruler area.

TIP   Look for the snapping triangles around the edit point to ensure you are at the correct location.

7   Press and hold Option key. Release the mouse, and then release the Option key.

8   Play the first few clips in the sequence.

TIP   In one step, you can create and drag a copy of a clip by selecting the clip, holding down Option, and then dragging. Whether you release this clip as an Overwrite or Insert edit depends on whether you continue to hold the Option key when you release the clip.

Project Practice

Continue to reposition the clips in the *Intro Repo* sequence, reversing the original order to begin with the nature shots and end with the city shots. You can reposition a clip earlier or later by dragging it forward or backward in the sequence. You can also drag a copy of a clip and delete any clip you don't want in this sequence. Although these clips are similar in length, they do not share the exact duration. Once the clips are in the correct position, you may want to use the Slide tool to slide the clips into position with the music beats. You can use the markers as a guide to snap the clip to the music beat locations.

Using the Trim Edit Window

One more feature in Final Cut Pro can help you refine your edits—a separate window called the Trim Edit window. Working in the Trim Edit window is a way to preview edit points and apply either the Ripple tool to trim one or both clips, or the Roll tool to adjust the relationship between the outgoing and incoming clips' edit points. Rippling will, of course, change the sequence length.

Working in the Trim Edit Window

Before you make trims or adjust any clips, let's look at how the Trim Edit window works.

1   From the Browser, open the *Amanda Trim Edit* sequence.

   This is the rough sequence you used in the previous lesson to practice trimming. But in this sequence, the narration clips have been removed so you can concentrate on the dialogue clips.

2   Make sure you have the default Selection tool selected and that linked selection is toggled on.

3   To open the Trim Edit window, double-click the edit point between the first two clips in the Timeline: **97A-out of bldg** and **97E-man**.

> **NOTE** ▶ Clicking the Timeline will automatically close the Trim Edit window. To reopen an edit point in the Trim Edit window, simply double-click the edit point in the Timeline.

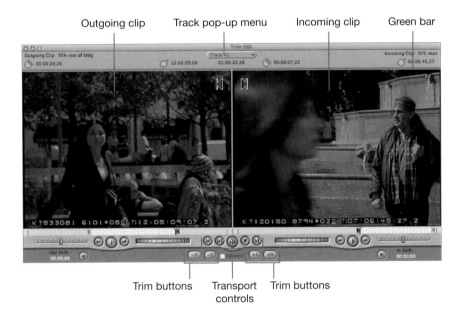

Outgoing clip   Track pop-up menu   Incoming clip   Green bar

Trim buttons   Transport controls   Trim buttons

A large window opens that covers the Viewer and Canvas windows. The image area on the left displays the *outgoing* **97A-out of bldg** clip. The image on the right displays the *incoming* **97E-man** clip.

> **NOTE** ▶ You can reposition the Trim Edit window in the interface by dragging from its title bar.

In the outgoing clip's scrubber bar is an Out point, and in the incoming clip's scrubber bar is an In point. These are the two edit points that can be adjusted in the Trim Edit window, either separately with the Ripple tool, or together with the Roll tool.

Beneath and between the two image areas are transport controls and trim buttons. The clip name, duration, and timecode location appear above each clip in the window. The sequence location of the edit point appears beneath the window name between the two image areas.

4   Move the pointer into the outgoing clip area on the left.

The pointer changes to the Ripple tool, which will adjust only the Out portion of this edit.

5   Click the outgoing clip's image in the Trim Edit window.

In the Timeline, the outgoing clip's Out point is highlighted. In the Trim Edit window, the green bar appears above just this image.

6   Move the pointer into the incoming clip on the right, and the pointer changes, but not the edit point selection in the Timeline or the green bar over the image. Click the incoming image to change the edit point selection in the Timeline.

The green bar now appears over the incoming clip.

NOTE ▶ The green bar is a good visual clue as to which side of the edit is currently selected. That is the side that will be changed.

7   Move the pointer to the middle area between the two image frames, and a Roll tool appears. Click here, and both edit points are selected in the Timeline, and a green bar appears over both image areas.

Using the Roll tool here will change both clips' edit points by the same amount and will not change the length of the sequence.

8   Click the Play Around Edit Loop button, or press the spacebar, to play around the edit point. The edit point plays in the right image area; the left image area is dimmed during the preview.

The preview is looped and will continue until you stop it by clicking the Stop button or pressing the spacebar again.

9   To change the length of time the clip plays before the edit point (pre-roll) and after it (post-roll), press Option-Q to open the User Preferences window. Click the Editing tab and change the Preview Pre-roll and Preview Post-roll to 3 seconds, then click OK.

10 In the Trim Edit window, position the pointer over the outgoing clip and press J to move the playhead earlier, toward the dimmed In point. Press L to play forward from this location, or click the outgoing clip's Play button.

Even though you can't change the In point of the outgoing clip in the Trim Edit window, it still appears as a reference.

Editing in the Trim Edit Window

There are different ways you can edit using the Trim Edit window. Some of these methods use the Ripple and Roll tool, and others use the J, K, and L keys to play a clip forward and backward.

1 In the Trim Edit window, make sure the Dynamic box under the two images is *unchecked* at this point.

2 Press the spacebar to see the loop of the current edit point. Then press it again to stop the preview.

You will trim this edit point so the outgoing clip stops before Amanda goes down the steps, and the incoming clip begins *just before* the man says, "Thank you, bro."

3 To change just the outgoing clip, click the left image area.

The green bar appears over just that image.

NOTE ▶ You can also press the U key to toggle the highlight and selection of each side of the selected edit point in the Timeline. In the Trim Edit window, the green bar changes to reflect the active edit point.

4   Use the J key to play the outgoing clip backward to locate the place before Amanda goes down the steps on the sidewalk. Press the K key to stop the playhead at this location, and press O to set a new Out point for this clip.

TIP ▶ Use the J and L keys to rock the playhead back and forth until you find the best location for the new edit point.

In the Trim Edit window, the Out point is updated to the new mark. In the Timeline, the clip is trimmed to this new edit point.

5   Click the incoming clip side of the Trim Edit window. Use the L key to play this clip forward to locate where the man says, "Thank you, bro." Press K to stop the playhead just before the man says, "Thank you, bro."

As before, the In point in the Trim Edit window is updated to the new mark. In the Timeline, the clip is trimmed to the new edit point.

6   Press the spacebar to see a preview of this edit point.

7   To make minor adjustments as you preview this edit point, click the trim buttons beneath the transport controls in the Trim Edit window.

If you click a positive trim amount, you will move the edit point forward by that amount. If you click a negative amount, you will move the edit point backward by that amount. You can adjust the outgoing clip, the incoming clip, or both at the same time.

NOTE ▸ The button with the larger number of frames is the Multi-Frame Trim Size and can be set from 1-99 frames in the Editing tab of the User Preferences window (Option-Q).

User Preferences

General | Editing | Labels | Timeline Options | Render Control | Audio Outputs

Still/Freeze Duration: 00:00:10:00   ☐ Dynamic Trimming
Preview Pre-roll: 00:00:03:00   ☑ Trim with Sequence Audio
Preview Post-roll: 00:00:03:00   ☐ Trim with Edit Selection Audio (Mute Others)
                                             Multi-Frame Trim Size: 5 frames

8   Double-click the edit point between the first **98A-amanda** clip and the **98B-man** clip. Press the spacebar to see a preview of this edit.

To tighten this edit point, you will trim the tail of the outgoing clip of Amanda to after the man says, "Thank you, sister." You will trim the head of the incoming clip to where the man says, "Nice suit. Armani?" But this time, you will work with the Dynamic check box selected to be able to trim *on the fly*.

9   Under the transport controls, click the Dynamic check box to enable dynamic trimming.

With the Dynamic option active, simply pressing the K key will set the new edit point on the fly.

10   Click the outgoing image on the left to make it the active trim side. Press the J key to move the playhead backward between the edit points. Press the L key to play forward. After the man says, "Thank you, sister," press K.

A new Out point is created when you press the K key.

TIP ▶ To stop a clip without setting a new edit point, press the spacebar.

11 Now click the incoming clip image on the right. Apply the methods in the preceding steps to tighten this clip so it begins when the man says, "Nice suit. Armani?"

12 To adjust the two edit points at the same time, click between the two images in the Trim Edit window, and use the trim buttons to roll both the Out and the In point at the same time.

Project Practice

Continue trimming and adjusting the edit points in the *Amanda Trim Edit* sequence by opening each edit point into the Trim Edit window and making the necessary adjustments. You can use the following keyboard shortcuts with the Trim Edit window as you practice:

▶ Press V to select the edit point closest to the playhead location.

▶ Press Cmd-7 to open the selected edit point into the Trim Edit window.

▶ When an edit point is selected in the Timeline, and the Trim Edit window is already open, press the up or down arrow keys to open the previous or next edit point into the Trim Edit window.

▶ With an edit point selected, press U to toggle between the outgoing clip's Out point, the incoming clip's In point, and both edit points together.

▶ As with previous exercises, you can also use the bracket and Shift-bracket keys while in the Trim Edit window to change an edit point.

Lesson Review

1. What two edit points does the Roll tool adjust?

2. What two edit points does the Slip tool adjust?

3. How many clips are affected when you apply the Slide tool?

4. Extending two edit points is a lot like rolling, slipping, or sliding edit points?

5. What modifier key is essential to reposition a clip in a sequence without overwriting any other material?

6. What does Option-dragging a clip do?

7. How do you open the Trim Edit window?

Answers

1. The Roll tool adjusts one clip's Out point and the adjacent clip's In point.

2. The Slip tool adjusts the In and Out point of the same clip.

3. The Slide tool affects three clips.

4. Extending changes an edit point in the same way rolling does.

5. The Option key is used to reposition a clip and move all other clips down in the sequence.

6. Option-dragging creates a copy of a sequence clip and repositions the copy to a different location, leaving the original sequence clip in place.

7. Double-click an edit point in the Timeline to open it in the Trim Edit window.

Keyboard Shortcuts

S	Selects the Slip Item tool
R	Selects the Roll tool
SS	Selects the Slide tool
E	Extends selected edit points to the playhead location
Drag then Option	Inserts a clip in a new location
Spacebar	Plays around the edit point in the Trim Edit window
Option-drag	Drags a copy of a clip to a new sequence location
Option-Q	Selects the User Preferences window
V	Selects the edit point closest to the playhead

Keyboard Shortcuts

Cmd-7	Opens the selected edit point into the Trim Edit window
Up and down arrow keys	Changes the highlighted edit point to the previous or next edit point
U	Toggles between the outgoing clip's Out point, incoming clip's In point, and both edit points together
[(left bracket)	Adjusts the selected edit point or points left in single-frame increments
] (right bracket)	Adjusts the selected edit point or points right in single-frame increments
Shift-[	Adjusts the selected edit point or points backward the length of the multi-frame duration
Shift-]	Adjusts the selected edit point or points forward the length of the multi-frame duration

7

Lesson Files Lesson 7 Project

Media A Thousand Roads > Amanda, Canoe Club, and Intro folders

Time This lesson takes approximately 60 minutes to complete.

Goals Create subclips

Create markers

Edit with markers

Create subclips using markers

Copy and arrange clips in the Browser

Replace edits

Maintain sync in linked clips

Lesson 7
Other Editing Options

Overwrite and Insert edits are the basic building blocks of the editing process, but there are additional editing options that will broaden the scope of what you've learned. These options include taking one clip and making mini-clips, or *subclips*, from it; creating markers and using them in the editing process; copying, pasting, and storyboarding clips; and working with a third type of edit, the Replace edit. In addition, there is an audio option that allows you to maintain sync during the editing process.

The Replace edit option in the Canvas Edit Overlay

Preparing the Project

To prepare for this lesson, you will launch Final Cut Pro and open the project for this lesson.

1 In the Dock, click the Final Cut Pro icon to launch the application. Press Cmd-O, and then choose the **Lesson 7 Project** file from the Lessons folder on your hard drive.

Lesson 7 Project contains bins of clips and sequences you will work with in this lesson. You will work with the open sequence later in this lesson.

2 In the Browser, click the disclosure triangle next to the Sequences bin to reveal its contents.

NOTE ▶ If you changed the Easy Setup preset in Final Cut Pro to edit formats other than DV-NTSC, change it back to DV-NTSC before you perform the next step. You will work with Easy Setup options in the next lesson.

3 To create a sequence directly in the Sequences bin, Ctrl-click the Sequences bin icon and choose New Sequence from the shortcut menu. Name this sequence *Amanda Subclips*.

You can use this sequence later in the lesson.

Making Subclips

When you capture source material, which you will do in Lesson 9, you determine the duration of each clip. You might start and stop your tape and capture several short clips, or you might let the tape run and capture longer clips. During editing, if it's a challenge to find what you're looking for in a longer clip, you can create shorter *subclips* of just the sections you want to edit. Making a subclip begins with setting In and Out points on a clip in the Viewer to identify the material you want to use.

1   In the Browser, reveal the contents of the Canoe Club bin, and double-click the **pan to totem** clip to open it in the Viewer. Drag the playhead through this clip to review it.

The duration of this clip is 1:16:20. During that time, the cameraman captured shots of the boat totem, water splashing against the boat, close-ups of paddles on the water, and camera pans of the paddlers. You could break this clip into subclips for more direct access to these specific shots.

2   Set an In point at the beginning of the clip. Then play the clip, and set an Out point when the camera starts to pan down to the splashing water. This should be about a 5- or 6-second duration.

TIP ▶ Since subclips stand alone when you edit them, you might want to allow a little extra space, or *handles*, on either side of the desired action to be able to make editing adjustments.

3 Choose Modify > Make Subclip, or press Cmd-U.

daryl slo-mo	00:00:12:16	Not Set	Not Set
pan to totem	00:00:05:28	07:46:27:03	07:46:33:00
pan to totem Subclip	00:00:05:28	Not Set	Not Set
rowing sound	00:00:32:18	Not Set	Not Set
tilt down canoe	00:00:18:24	Not Set	Not Set

The Browser window becomes active, and a new icon appears under the original clip in the Canoe Club bin. The subclip icon has jagged edges as if it had been torn or cut from the original clip. It also shares the original clip's name for the moment, but the text box is highlighted, awaiting a name change.

NOTE ▶ If the Make Subclip option is not available from the Modify menu, make sure the Viewer window is active.

4 Rename the subclip *totem against mtns*, and press Return.

When you press Return, this clip is sorted alphabetically among the other Canoe Club clips.

5 Double-click the new **totem against mtns** clip to open it in the Viewer, and play it.

In the Viewer duration, you see that the clip is only as long as the distance between the In and Out points you marked previously.

6 Open the **pan to totem** clip again, and set an In point when the camera begins to pan right to include the paddlers. Set an Out point when the camera starts to zoom into the paddles, about an 8- to 10-second duration.

7 Choose Modify > Make Subclip, or press Cmd-U. In the Browser, enter *pan to paddlers* as the new subclip name.

8   To organize these subclips, Ctrl-click the Canoe Club bin and choose New
Bin from the shortcut menu. Name the new bin *Pan to Totem Subclips,* and
drag the original **pan to totem** clip and the **totem against mtns** and **pan to
paddlers** subclips into this new bin. Then display the contents of this bin.

▼ 📁 Canoe Club			
🔊 battlesong	00:04:37:02	Not Set	Not Set
🎞 canoe coming	00:00:32:18	Not Set	Not Set
🎞 canoe from left	00:01:08:20	Not Set	Not Set
🎞 canoe going	00:00:33:24	Not Set	Not Set
🎞 cu rowing	00:01:16:20	Not Set	Not Set
🎞 daryl cu	00:00:11:27	Not Set	Not Set
🎞 daryl slo-mo	00:00:12:16	Not Set	Not Set
▼ 📁 Pan to Totem Subclips			
🎞 pan to paddlers	00:00:09:29	Not Set	Not Set
🎞 pan to totem	00:00:11:17	07:47:32:06	07:47:43:22
🎞 totem against mtns	00:00:05:28	Not Set	Not Set

Just as you created a new sequence inside the Sequences bin earlier in this
lesson, you can create a new bin inside a specific bin. Notice how this new
bin is indented in line with the Canoe Club clips, and the clips within the
new subclips bin are indented further. Any new subclips created from the
pan to totem master clip will be placed in this bin.

TIP ▶ After you edit a subclip into a sequence, you cannot lengthen the
subclip. You can, however, remove the subclip restrictions you placed on it
by selecting the sequence clip and choosing Modify > Remove Subclip
Limits. This reverts the clip back to the original clip length but retains the
subclip name.

Project Practice

You can continue to practice making subclips by finding the following areas in
the **pan to totem** master clip, marking them, and creating subclips:

▶   water splashing on bow of boat

▶   sun reflecting off totem

▶   cu paddles on shimmering water

NOTE ▶ It's okay if one subclip overlaps another. They will each be individual clips.

Working with Markers

You have used markers in previous lessons to find a specific location in a sequence, such as where Scene 98 began, where Amanda's cutaway was located, and where music beats occurred in a sequence. You can use markers to identify any location in any sequence *or* clip. When editing, you can also use markers as snapping points.

Creating and Naming Markers

When you create a marker, it is added at the playhead location, whether the playhead is stopped over a specific frame or moving in real time. In this exercise, you will create markers at strong beats in a music track. Later you will use those markers to help identify where to place video clips. There are several ways to create a marker once the playhead is correctly positioned:

▶   Press the M key.

▶   Choose Mark > Markers > Add.

▶   In the Viewer or Canvas, click the Add Marker button.

▶   Press the grave key (`). It's located to the left of the number 1 key and above the Tab key; it shares the tilde key and looks like a backward accent.

NOTE ▶ You will also use this key to delete markers later in this lesson.

1 In the Timeline, play the *Intro – Markers* sequence.

This is a similar sequence to the *Intro Repo* sequence you worked with in Lesson 6. Notice that the audio tracks are a different height than the video tracks. You will learn to customize your tracks in the next lesson. Also, even though the name of the music track in this sequence is different than it was in the previous lesson, it still links back to the same music file.

2 Drag the playhead to snap to the first marker in the sequence, *beat 1*. Then play from this point to the second marker, *beat 2*.

The bass line riff repeats every four beats (about 3:22) in this music track, the distance between the two markers. Having a marker in the Timeline where these strong beats occur can be helpful when you edit your video clips to this sequence.

3 Play from the second marker, and stop after the next four beats, somewhere around 1:00:11;18.

4 To set a marker in the Timeline at this location, press M.

A green marker appears in the ruler area of the Timeline and also in the Canvas scrubber bar. Remember, when the playhead is directly over a marker in the Canvas, that marker appears yellow.

5 To name this marker, press M again to open the Edit Marker window. Type *beat 3* in the Name field. Take a look at the Edit Marker window before you click OK to close it.

Edit Marker
Name: beat 3
Comment:
Start: 01:00:11;18   Delete
Duration: 00:00:00;00
Add Chapter Marker
Add Compression Marker
Add Scoring Marker
Cancel   OK

The Edit Marker window has options to set a marker at a specific time-code location, to create a duration for a marker, or to delete a marker. You can also add other types of markers here, such as scoring markers to use with Apple's Soundtrack Pro application, or you can add compression and chapter markers if your Final Cut Pro sequence will be used in a DVD Studio Pro project.

NOTE ▶ Naming markers to use them in editing isn't necessary. However, naming them is helpful if you're working with several markers in your sequence.

6 Continue playing the music track for another four beats, and stop the playhead at this location. This time, click the Marker button in the Canvas window to set a marker. Press M again to open the Edit Marker window. Name this marker *beat 4*.

7   Play the music from the *beat 4* marker, and this time, without stopping, press M every time you here the strong beat of music until the music stops.

> **TIP** ▶ To delete a marker, move the playhead to the marker, and press Cmd-` (grave key). If you want to reposition a marker you've already created, move the playhead forward to a new location and press Shift-`.

8   Press Option-M to move the playhead backward to the previous sequence marker in the ruler area. Press Option-M repeatedly until you reach the first marker.

9   Press Shift-M to move forward to the second marker.

> **TIP** ▶ Just as you use the up or down arrow to move backward or forward to the next clip, you can use Shift with the up or down arrow to move backward or forward to a marker.

10 In the ruler area, Ctrl-click the second marker.

All of the markers in the sequence appear at the bottom of the shortcut menu.

11 Choose *beat 4* from the shortcut menu, and release the mouse.

The playhead jumps ahead to the *beat 4* marker in the Timeline. Another way to move to markers is to choose Mark > Next > Marker and Mark > Previous > Marker.

12 Move the playhead to each of the markers with a default name, and rename each one with a sequential beat number (rename *Marker 5* to *beat 5*, and so on).

> **TIP** ▶ To delete all the markers in the Timeline ruler area, press Ctrl-`. You can access these and other marker commands by choosing Mark > Markers.

Adding Markers to Clips

You can also place a marker directly on a clip in the Viewer or in the Timeline when the clip is selected. When attached to a clip, a marker will always mark the same point of reference on that clip no matter where the clip is positioned in the sequence.

1 In the Timeline, play the **canyon runner** clip.

Although the runner in this clip is very small, you can see him jump onto a rock toward the end of this clip. If you place a marker on the clip at this location, you can use it later to sync this action to a beat of music.

2 Park the playhead where the runner lands after jumping, and select the clip.

> **NOTE** ▶ If a clip is not selected when you press M, the marker will appear in the ruler area as a sequence marker. If this happens, press Cmd-Z to undo the step.

3 Press M to place a marker on the **canyon runner** clip.

4 Press M to open the Edit Marker window, and enter *runner jumps* as the marker name.

With this clip selected, the marker appears on the clip and not in the Timeline ruler area.

5 Drag this clip to the right, and snap its Out point to the end of the sequence, then deselect the clip.

Clip markers stay with the clip wherever it's positioned in the sequence. Notice that the clip marker is pink, not green.

6   From the Pan to Totem Subclips bin in the Browser, open the subclip **pan to paddlers**, which you created earlier in this lesson.

7   In the Viewer, park the playhead where the paddlers begin their second complete stroke. Press M to add a marker at this location. Press M again to open the Edit Marker window. Name this marker *2nd stroke*.

Like the Canvas marker, the Viewer marker is yellow when the playhead is over it. If you move the playhead away, the Viewer marker is pink.

NOTE ▶ You can apply the same shortcuts that you used for a sequence marker to delete or go to a clip marker in the Viewer. To apply these shortcuts to a clip in the Timeline, you must first select the clip.

8   In the Browser, click the triangle next to the **pan to paddlers** subclip.

When you add a marker to a clip (or a subclip) in the Viewer, it is attached to the clip and appears as an entry in the Browser.

NOTE ▶ You can rename or delete a marker in the Browser just as you do a clip or sequence.

Editing with Markers

There is real power in using markers to edit. You can set edit points to markers; you can also align a clip marker to a sequence marker. In the following steps, you will set edit points and align the canyon runner jumping to a beat of music.

> **TIP** ▸ Make sure snapping is on whenever you want to snap to markers as reference points.

1   In the Timeline, position the playhead on the *beat 4* marker. Press I to set an In point at this location. Press Shift-M to move the playhead to the *beat 5* marker, and press O to set an Out point.

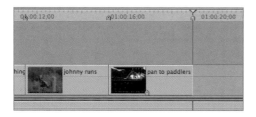

2   With the **pan to paddlers** subclip still loaded in the Viewer, drag the play-head earlier to include the first paddlers' stroke. Press I to set an In point. Click the Overwrite button to edit this clip to the Timeline. Play this clip.

The clip now fills the exact distance between the two music markers. The marker you added in the previous exercise is still attached to the **pan to paddlers** clip, although it may be difficult to see if it's close to the thumb-nail image.

3   Repeat steps 1 and 2 to make the next edit, and use the **totem against mtns** subclip as your source.

4   To use a marker as a sync point, click and hold your pointer directly above the marker in the **canyon runner** clip, but don't move the clip just yet.

Dragging a clip from a marker makes that the active sync point when you snap it to other markers in the Timeline.

5   Drag this clip from its marker over the last sequence marker in the ruler area, which would be *beat 7*, and release it when the markers snap to each other.

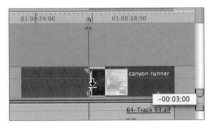

When snapping is on, a snapping line appears that connects the two markers.

6   Play this part of the sequence to see the alignment between the runner jumping and the strong music beat.

7   To complete this sequence, drag the In point of the **canyon runner** clip to fill the gap before it, and drag its Out point to the end of the music. Play the finished sequence.

> **TIP** ▶ You can use markers to slip a clip by selecting the Slip tool and dragging the clip marker left or right to snap to a sequence marker. You can also use markers as reference points when you roll or slide a clip.

Using Markers to Create Subclips

You previously created subclips from In and Out points in a source clip. But you can also use a marker to create a subclip since it too identifies a specific location in a clip. In this exercise, you will add markers to the Amanda dialogue clips and create subclips from those markers.

1   In the Browser, hide the contents of the Canoe Club bin, and reveal the contents of the Amanda bin. Open the **98A-amanda** clip in the Viewer, and review the clip.

    In previous lessons, you marked this clip at different locations to edit the scene. Here you will set markers where Amanda speaks, and use those markers to create subclips. Since this material follows a script that you don't have, you will number these markers for clarity of order.

2   Play the clip from the beginning, and stop where you first see Amanda enter the frame. Add a marker at this location, and name it *1-approaches man*.

    TIP ▶ When you add a marker as a reference for making a subclip, as you're doing here, remember to give yourself some extra pad before the action or sound you want to use in editing.

3   Play the clip from this marker, and stop the playhead just before Amanda responds to the "Nice suit. Armani?" question. Add a second marker here, and name it *2-armani suit*.

4   Add a third marker just before Amanda says where she is from. Name that marker *3-where you from*.

5   Add one more marker just before Amanda speaks in her native tongue, and name that marker *4-native tongue*.

    You should now have four markers in the Viewer scrubber bar. Each marker represents a start point for a portion of this longer clip.

6   In the Browser, click the disclosure triangle next to the **98A-amanda** master clip to see the markers attached to this clip.

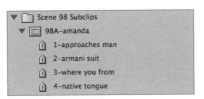

7   To organize all of the subclips you will be creating, Ctrl-click the Amanda bin and choose New Bin from the shortcut menu. Name this bin *Scene 98 Subclips*. Drag the **98A-amanda** clip into this bin and reveal the bin contents.

▼ 🗀 Scene 98 Subclips	
▼ 🎞 98A-amanda	
🔖 1–approaches man	
🔖 2–armani suit	
🔖 3–where you from	
🔖 4–native tongue	

Now when you create subclips from this clip, they will appear in this bin, as they did when you organized subclips earlier in this lesson.

8   To create a subclip from the first to second marker, select the *1-approaches man* marker in the Browser, then choose Modify > Make Subclip.

In the Scene 98 Subclips bin, a new subclip has been created using the marker name followed by the master clip name as a reference.

TIP To see the full name of the new subclip, move the pointer between the Name and Duration column heads. When you see the resize arrow, drag right.

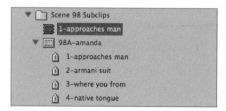

9   To shorten this subclip name, click its name area and delete the portion after the word *man*. Double-click this new subclip to open it in the Viewer. Play the clip.

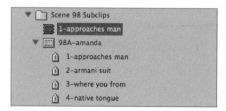

The length of this subclip is from the first marker to the second marker. If you set a marker duration in the Edit Marker window, the subclip would be created starting at the marker for the length of the marker duration. If there are no markers following the one you selected, the subclip will be created from that marker to the end of the clip.

10   Select the other markers in the Scene 98 Subclips bin, and choose Modify > Make Subclip. Then shorten the remaining **98A-amanda** subclip names.

When you create subclips from markers, you can select a group of markers and convert them all to subclips at the same time.

TIP ▶ You can drag a marker icon into the Viewer and it opens as a sub-clip. You can also double-click a marker icon in the Browser to open it in the Viewer. In fact, when you edit with markers, they *are* subclips.

Project Practice

Open the **98B-man** clip and add four or so markers at places before the man delivers his lines, similar to the way you marked the **98A-amanda** clip. Convert all of those markers into subclips as you did in step 10 in the preceding exer-cise. You can use the *Amanda Subclips* sequence if you want to edit together just the subclips from these two master clips.

Copying Clips in the Browser

Before moving on to the next type of editing function, let's take a moment to prepare your project. In the following steps, you will duplicate a sequence, delete markers, work with clips in icon view, copy a bin of clips, and remove edit points from a group of clips. You will also arrange clips in a bin using the icon view, and change the representative frame for a clip.

Having a duplicate set of clips allows you to organize the same clips in differ-ent ways. For example, in this exercise, you will duplicate the set of marked Intro clips and remove the edit points from the duplicate set. Remember, copy-ing clips in the Browser doesn't duplicate media files, just the links to those files.

1 In the Browser, duplicate the *Intro – Markers* sequence, and rename the new sequence *Replace Edit*. Double-click it to open it in the Timeline. Close all other open sequences.

   In the next exercise, you will learn to replace edits in the Timeline and will not need the markers in the ruler area.

2 Make sure no clips are selected in the Timeline, and press Ctrl-` (grave) to delete all the markers in the ruler area.

3   In the Browser, double-click the Intro Clips – Marked bin to open it as a separate window.

Name		Duration	In	Out
64–Track 93.aif		00:00:33;14	Not Set	Not Set
amanda rushing		00:00:03;23	13:04:18;27	13:04:22;19
canyon runner		00:00:03;23	19:03:29;26	19:03:33;18
city street		00:00:03;23	12:07:45;21	12:07:49;13
girl on plane		00:00:03;23	04:36:25;12	04:36:29;04
healer at ruins		00:00:03;23	05:06:58;03	05:07:01;27
healer cu		00:00:03;23	02:01:28;01	02:01:31;23

In the Duration column, you see that all the video clips have the same marked duration. These durations match the music beats in the sequence. For the next exercise, you will want to work with unmarked clips. However, you may want to use the edit points on these clips again at a later time.

4   Close the open Intro Clips – Marked bin. In the Browser, with this bin still selected, press Cmd-C to copy the bin. Press Cmd-V to paste it back into the project.

- Amanda
- Canoe Club
- Intro Clips – Marked
- Intro Clips – Marked

A duplicate bin is created in the Browser. You can copy any clip, sequence, or bin in a project and paste it within that project, or in a different project. Final Cut Pro will still link back to the original media.

5   Name the lower bin *Intro Clips – NOT Marked*. Double-click this bin to open it as a separate window.

NOTE ▶ You can perform the following steps in the Browser without opening the bin. Opening the bin in a separate window here just helps focus on this set of clips.

Since this is a duplicated set of clips, we can remove the In and Out points for these clips without affecting the clips in the Intro Clips – Marked bin.

6   Ctrl-click the first video clip's timecode number under the In column. In
the shortcut menu, choose Clear In.

The In point for this clip is removed, and Not Set appears under the In
column. You generally remove In and Out points for a clip in the Viewer,
but you can also remove an In or Out point in an opened bin or Browser
column. But in the bin or Browser, you can remove edit points for a group
of clips.

7   To remove all of the In points on all of the clips in this bin at one time,
select the clips by pressing Cmd-A. Ctrl-click any timecode number in the
In column and choose Clear In from the shortcut menu.

Not Set appears in the In column for all the selected clips, and the clip
durations are extended accordingly.

8   To remove all of the clips' Out points, Ctrl-click any timecode number in
the Out column and choose Clear Out from the shortcut menu.

Not Set appears in the Out column for all the selected clips, and the durations revert to the full length of the clip.

NOTE ▶ You will learn more about organizing and customizing Browser columns in the next lesson.

9   Drag the lower-right corner of this bin to the right to make it wider. Ctrl-click under the Name column of this bin and choose View As Medium Icons from the shortcut menu.

In the icon view, you can drag a clip or group of clips to arrange them however you like.

10   Group the clip icons in this bin according to content, such as city clips, nature clips, healer clips, Alaskan clips, and so on.

Notice that the clip icons in the bin display the first captured frame of each clip. This frame is called a *poster frame*, just as a movie poster is a visual representation of a film. In some cases, the poster frame does not represent the clip content. You can choose any frame within this clip to use as its poster frame.

11   Double-click the **healer cu** clip to open it in the Viewer. In the Viewer, position the playhead when you see the healer in the middle of the frame. Choose Mark > Set Poster Frame, or press Ctrl-P.

Now the poster frame for the `healer cu` clip makes the clip content easier to identify in this view.

12 In the Browser window, Option-double-click the Intro Clips – NOT Marked bin to simultaneously close that bin's window and open it as a tab in the project. Ctrl-click in the gray area and choose Arrange > By Name from the shortcut menu.

You will use this view of these clips in the next exercise. To see the other clips in this bin, you can either use the scroll bar or use a scrolling mouse.

TIP You can change the bin views in these lesson projects at any time according to your preference.

Replacing Edits

In Lesson 6, you rearranged clips by dragging to reposition them in the sequence. But if you want to use a different clip in the sequence, other than the current clip, you can simply replace it. The Replace edit function in Final Cut Pro appears as an option in the Canvas Edit Overlay and in the edit button area as well. Using it places a new clip into the sequence the same length and position as the previous clip. An important consideration when making Replace edits is where the playhead is located in both the source clip in the Viewer and in the sequence clip in the Timeline.

1   In the Timeline, move the playhead to the first frame of the fourth clip, **johnny runs**.

Unlike other types of edits where you marked an In and Out point in the sequence, here you don't have to use In or Out points to identify clip duration. Identifying the clip with the playhead and using the Replace edit function saves these steps for you. Since the clip has a specific length, only that portion of the sequence will be affected.

2   From the Intro Clips – NOT Marked tab in the Browser, open the **girl on plane** clip, and play it. Scrub through the clip to where the girl is looking back over her shoulder. Park the playhead just *before* she turns her head forward.

You will begin using this clip from the playhead location. Imagine the playhead as an In point for the edit. With Replace edits, you just use the playhead; you don't use edit points.

3   Drag the source clip from the Viewer to the Canvas into the blue Replace section in the Edit Overlay. Release the mouse, and play the edit.

The entire video portion of the Timeline sequence clip is replaced by source content starting at the Viewer playhead position.

4   To replace the **tall buildings** clip, place the playhead on the first frame of
    that clip.

5   From the Intro Clips – NOT Marked bin, open the **ruin steps** clip, and
    park the playhead where the camera starts to tilt up. This time, click the
    blue Replace edit button. Play the clip in the sequence.

> **TIP** ▶ If you don't like the edit you made, you can press Cmd-Z to
> undo the edit, readjust your playhead positions, and perform another
> Replace edit.

    You can also use the two playhead positions to backtime a clip into place.

6   From the Browser, open the **healer cu** clip. Move the playhead toward the
    end of the clip where the healer is walking out of the frame.

    This is the frame you want the clip to end on in the sequence. Since the
    Replace function works off of synchronized playhead positions, you will
    need to position the Timeline playhead at the end of the target clip.

7   In the Timeline, move the playhead to the last frame of the **totem against
    mtn** clip. Look for the lower-right last frame indicator in the Canvas. Click
    the Replace edit button, or press the shortcut key, F11.

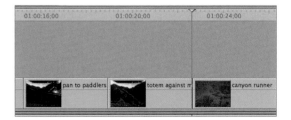

In this case, rather than replacing from first frame forward, the sequence clip is replaced from the last frame backward from the playhead location to fill the existing clip duration. You can also use this function to sync an action to a music beat.

8 In the Timeline, move the playhead to 1:00:26;10.

This is the final music beat where the runner currently jumps. You will choose an action point in a source clip and use the Replace edit to sync it to this location.

9 From the Browser, open the **ice floes** clip, and position the playhead where the snowmobile goes over the first big bump. Press F11, and play the clip in the Timeline.

Although not a dramatic action, you see that the bump in the source clip is aligned to the music beat in the sequence.

10 Press Cmd-S to save project changes.

NOTE ▶ If you try to replace the sequence clip with a shorter source clip, or position the playhead in the Viewer too close to the head or tail of the clip, a message will appear saying "Insufficient content for edit."

Storyboard Editing

Storyboards are used to explain the flow of a story with pictures or drawings. For example, to explain how a scene will look when it's cut together, an artist sketches intended camera shots and places them side by side as individual frames. This allows the director to imagine more clearly what the film will look like or anticipate what problems may arise during the shoot.

In the previous exercises, you arranged, or storyboarded, clips in the bin window. You can edit those clips to the Timeline in a few simple steps. However, where you place the images in the bin will determine how they eventually line up in the Timeline sequence. Final Cut Pro starts with the first clip at the top-left corner of the bin and *reads* across the line. It then drops down to the next row, and so on, like reading a book. Follow these general guidelines to create your own storybook edit.

1 Ctrl-click the Sequences bin in the Browser, and choose New Sequence from the shortcut menu. Name the new sequence *Storyboard Edit* and double-click to open it.

2 From the Browser, double-click the Intro Clips – Marked bin. Ctrl-click in the gray area under the name column and choose View As Medium Icons from the shortcut menu.

3 Make the window wider to show all the clips. If necessary, Ctrl-click in the gray area and choose Arrange > By Name from the shortcut menu.

4 Arrange the video clips in rows according to how you want to see them in the sequence. Make sure the rows slant down from left to right. Higher clips, even though they are on the same row, will actually go first when you edit the group to the Timeline. Higher-to-lower order overrides left-to-right order.

5 In the Intro Clips – Marked bin, select all the video clips.

> **NOTE ▶** You can also press Cmd-A to select all the clips in this bin, and then Cmd-click on each of the audio clips to deselect them.

6   Drag one of the selected clip icons down into the Timeline and snap them
    to the head of the sequence. When you see the Overwrite downward
    arrow, release the mouse.

NOTE ▶ Depending on the size of your Timeline, you may not see all of
the clips in full view. If not, continue with the edit and then press Shift-Z
to bring the sequence into full view.

All the clips are positioned in the Timeline just as they were in the
Storyboard bin. Only the marked portions are edited.

7   To complete the sequence, drag the music, and then the narration clip to
    the sequence and position them to your liking.

Keeping Linked Clips in Sync

Maintaining sync between the audio and video tracks of a clip is one more
useful editing option. So far in these lessons, you haven't encountered a situation where the audio and video of a clip have gotten out of sync. But it can
happen.

When you work with linked selection on, the video and audio portions of a
clip can be moved, trimmed, or slipped together. But if linked selection is toggled off, or you have locked one of the tracks in the clip, making an editing
adjustment to just one track may throw it out of sync with the other tracks.

1   In the Browser, open the *Sync Clip* sequence, and play the clip.

    This representative clip has linked audio and video. The **98A-amanda** clip
    was captured with sync sound.

2   Click the Linked Selection button to toggle it off, or press Shift-L. Drag the
    98A-amanda video clip to the left about 2 seconds. Play this clip.

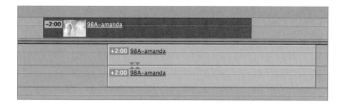

With linked selection off, when you change the location of one track of a clip, red out-of-sync indicators appear on each linked track, indicating the amount you are out of sync. If moving just the video track alone was an oversight, you can simply press Cmd-Z to undo the move, turn linked selection back on, and move the entire clip at one time. However, you have other choices as well:

▶   Leave the audio where it is, and it will remain out of sync.

▶   Move the audio's position in the Timeline to be in position with the video again and back into sync.

▶   Slip the audio so the portion that overlaps with the video clip is in its original sync.

▶   Move or slip the video back to the audio.

3   Ctrl-click the red out-of-sync indicator in the A1 track of this clip and choose Move Into Sync from the shortcut menu. Make sure you click the red out-of-sync indicator, and not the clip itself.

The audio tracks are moved in the Timeline to be in sync under the video clip.

NOTE ► You can choose to move either the video or audio portion of a clip that is out of sync.

4   To view another sync option, press Cmd-Z to return the tracks to their out-of-sync state. This time, Ctrl-click one of the out-of-sync indicators on the audio tracks and choose Slip Into Sync from the shortcut menu. Play the clip.

Now the tracks remain in their current positions, but the audio tracks have been slipped so that they match the video.

TIP ► If you want to synchronize a sound effect with a video action, turn off linked selection, and slip or position the clips so they look or sound the way you want them to. Choose Modify > Mark in Sync to reset the sync to this state. The out-of-sync indicators are removed.

Lesson Review

1.   How do you create a subclip?

2.   Where are markers named?

3.   Where can you place a marker?

4.   Does snapping affect markers?

5.   How do you create a subclip from a marker?

6.   How do you copy and paste a clip or bin in the Browser?

7.   What modifier key is used to create a new poster frame?

8.   What does the Replace edit function do?

9.   How should clips be organized in a bin before making a storyboard-type edit?

10. What two methods can bring out-of-sync video and audio tracks back into sync?

Answers

1.   Set an In and Out in the clip, and choose Modify > Make Subclip.

2.   You name a marker in the Edit Marker window.

3. Place markers in the Timeline ruler area or to a selected clip in the Timeline. You can also add markers to a clip in the Viewer.

4. Yes. When snapping is on, you can snap the playhead to markers, and snap a clip marker to a sequence marker or other clip marker.

5. Select the marker under the clip in the Browser, and choose Modify > Make Subclip.

6. Select it, and press Cmd-C to copy it. Press Cmd-V to paste it back into the current project.

7. The Control key is used to create a new poster frame (Ctrl-P).

8. It replaces a sequence clip with a source clip aligning the two playhead positions.

9. In rows, with each clip in the row appearing slightly lower than the previous clip.

10. Slip or move either the video or audio track.

Keyboard Shortcuts

Cmd-U	Makes a subclip
M	Adds a marker
Shift-M	Moves forward between markers
Shift-down arrow	Moves forward between markers
Option-M	Moves backward between markers
Shift-up arrow	Moves backward between markers
Cmd-`	When playhead is over the marker, deletes marker in sequence or selected clip
Ctrl-`	Deletes all markers in sequence or selected clip
Shift-`	Moves a marker forward to playhead position
Ctrl-P	Resets the poster frame in a clip

8

Lesson Files Lesson 8 Project and Sample Project

Media A Thousand Roads > Amanda and Intro folders

Time This lesson takes approximately 45 minutes to complete.

Goals Customize Browser columns

Find items in Browser

Work with master clips

Organize project elements

Customize and save interface layouts

Change keyboard layout

Create shortcut buttons

Choose Easy Setup presets

Select user preferences

View clip properties and change sequence settings

Browser Basics and Project Customization

Although production practices follow similar guidelines, every production is unique. The beauty of Final Cut Pro is that you might use DV for one project, HD for another, and HDV for yet another. One project might use on-camera slates to identify clip content, while another might include notes entered in the Browser.

No matter what type of footage you use in your project or how the material was originally labeled, two things remain certain. Every project will require appropriate Final Cut Pro settings that support the originating format; and every project will benefit from some kind of organizational structure within the Browser.

In this lesson, you will learn more about the Browser columns and how to use them to organize your clips and material in different ways. Also in this lesson you will make changes to your Final Cut Pro interface by customizing and saving your keyboard, window, Timeline, and track layouts. And finally, you will select the appropriate settings and preferences to make the system fully complement your project.

Preparing the Project

For this project, you will save custom layouts and change user preferences. Before launching Final Cut Pro, let's see where these files will be saved.

1 Open a Finder window on your Desktop and navigate this path: Macintosh HD > Users > [user name] > Library > Preferences > Final Cut Pro User Data.

This is where all Final Cut Pro customized layouts, preferences, and even plug-ins for the current user are saved. If another user has been set up on this computer, that user's preferences and layouts would appear when they log in and launch the application.

2 Launch Final Cut Pro, and choose File > Open, or press Cmd-O. Select the **Lesson 8 Project** file from the Lessons folder on your hard drive.

3 Close any other projects that may be open from a previous session by Ctrl-clicking their name tabs in the Browser and choosing Close Tab from the shortcut menu.

There are no open sequences in **Lesson 8 Project**, so the Timeline and Canvas windows do not appear when other projects are closed.

Customizing Browser Columns

Final Cut Pro knows everything there is to know about all the clips and other items in your project. It knows the length, start and stop timecode, number of audio tracks or whether it's video-only, the In to Out duration, and so on. This information is made available to you through the 65 Browser columns available in the View As List mode. Although it's not necessary to view these columns continuously during the editing process, referring to them when you need to review or add additional clip information can be a great help.

Viewing and Sorting Browser Columns

In the Browser, clips are sorted alphabetically according to their names because the Name column is the default sort mode. If you need to identify clips based on specific criteria—for example, according to their scene numbers—clicking once on that column heading will reorder the clips accordingly.

1   Reveal the contents of all the bins in the Browser, but don't change the size of the Browser window yet.

2   To enlarge the window to show the contents of the open bins, click the Browser Zoom button.

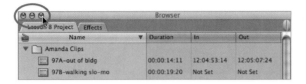

When you click this button, the Browser expands to display all contents, or as many items as possible, in the window. In the Name column, all clips and sequences are arranged alphabetically by name within a bin, and all bins are arranged alphabetically as well.

> **TIP ▶** Another way to open and close bins and navigate through items in the Browser is to use the up, down, left, and right arrows. When a bin is highlighted, the up and down arrows move the highlight from one bin to the next. The right arrow will reveal contents of the highlighted bin. Clicking the right arrow again will step into those contents, and clicking the left arrow will step back up and out.

3   At the bottom of the Browser window, drag the blue horizontal scroll bar to the right to see the other column headings. Then drag the scroll bar left, back to the Name column.

When the Name column heading is selected, the title bar is lighter than the others. This indicates that it is the primary sort column. There is a downward arrow indicating that sorting is from low to high, or from A to Z.

Name	▼	Duration	In	Out
▼ Amanda Clips				
97A–out of bldg		00:00:14:11	12:04:53:14	12:05:07:24
97B–walking slo-mo		00:00:19:20	Not Set	Not Set
97C–back slo-mo		00:00:09:08	Not Set	Not Set
97D–coffee stand		00:00:08:15	07:01:35:07	07:01:43:21
97E–man		00:00:05:07	07:06:46:12	07:06:51:18
97F–man cu		00:00:21:21	Not Set	Not Set

4   Click the Name column heading to reverse the current sort order so the elements go from high to low, or from Z to A.

Name	▲	Duration	In	Out
▼ Sequences				
Amanda		00:01:44:21	Not Set	Not Set
▼ Intro Clips				
walking in fields		00:00:15:20	Not Set	Not Set
truck on road		00:00:10:25	Not Set	Not Set
tall buildings		00:00:13:24	Not Set	Not Set

The arrow in the Name heading now points upward, and all the elements in the window reverse order, including the bins themselves.

5   Click the Duration column heading to sort the clips by duration. Click it again to reverse the sort order.

The default sort order is always from low to high, or in this case, low durations to high durations.

6   Drag the blue scroll bar to the right until you see the Reel column. Click this column head to sort the clips by reel number.

7   Drag the scroll bar to the left, and click the Name column heading.

 To widen any column, drag its right boundary line to the right.

Moving, Showing, and Hiding Columns

You may not need to refer to many of the Browser columns during editing, but there may be times when you want quick and easy access to specific information, such as clip scene and shot/take numbers. Although the Name column is a fixed column, all other columns can be repositioned. In addition, there are two preset column layouts you can use: standard columns and logging columns. And you can choose to hide or show a variety of other columns that do not appear as part of the default Browser layout.

1   Drag the Duration column to the right and release it just after the Out column.

When you drag a column heading, a faint bounding box appears representing that column. Surrounding columns shift to make room for the column you are moving.

2   Drag the Good column to the left to follow the Duration column, then drag the Log Note column to follow the Good column.

These are currently empty, but in the next exercise you will add clip information to these columns.

3   Ctrl-click the Good column heading and look at the different column options that appear on the shortcut menu.

You can hide a column, save or load a column layout, or choose a preset layout. And there are several column headings you can choose to show or add to the current Browser layout.

4   Choose Show Length from the shortcut menu.

The Length column appears to the left of the Good column.

5   In the Name column, select the **97D-coffee stand** clip, and look at the In, Out, Duration, and Length columns.

Name	In	Out	Duration	Length
▼ 🗀 Amanda Clips				
97A–out of bldg	12:04:53:14	12:05:07:24	00:00:14:11	00:00:49:11
97B–walking slo-mo	Not Set	Not Set	00:00:19:20	00:00:19:20
97C–back slo-mo	Not Set	Not Set	00:00:09:08	00:00:09:08
97D-coffee stand	07:01:35:07	07:01:43:21	00:00:08:15	00:00:13:22
97E–man	07:06:46:12	07:06:51:18	00:00:05:07	00:00:21:17
97F–man cu	Not Set	Not Set	00:00:21:21	00:00:21:21

If a clip has marked In and Out points, the marked duration appears in the Duration column. The Length column always displays the full length of the media.

6   Ctrl-click the In column heading and choose Show Thumbnail from the shortcut menu. Scroll down to see the clips in the Intro Clips bin.

A thumbnail appears next to each clip name, giving you a visual reference to the clip's contents.

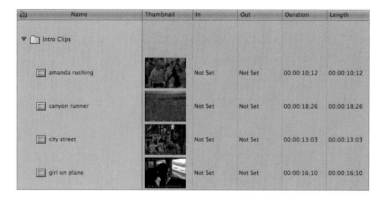

Name	Thumbnail	In	Out	Duration	Length
▼ 🗀 Intro Clips					
amanda rushing		Not Set	Not Set	00:00:10;12	00:00:10;12
canyon runner		Not Set	Not Set	00:00:18;26	00:00:18;26
city street		Not Set	Not Set	00:00:13:03	00:00:13:03
girl on plane		Not Set	Not Set	00:00:16;10	00:00:16;10

7   Find the **healer cu** clip. To scrub through the clip, click the thumbnail image and drag right, then left. To reset a clip's poster frame in this column, drag to a new frame, hold down Control, release the mouse, and then release the Control key.

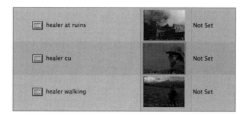

8 Ctrl-click the Show Thumbnail column heading and choose Logging Columns from the shortcut menu to display a different layout.

This layout places columns that reflect logged information—such as Scene, Shot/Take, and Reel—closer to the Name column for easier access.

9 To return to the previous layout, Ctrl-click any column heading and choose Standard Columns from the shortcut menu.

The changes you make in one preset layout do not affect the other preset layout.

NOTE ▶ Changes you make to Browser or bin columns in a project remain until you change them again or load a previously saved layout. If you create a new project, it will have the default Standard Columns layout.

10 To save this column layout, Ctrl-click any column head and choose Save Column Layout from the shortcut menu. In the Save window, enter *thumbnails* for the layout name, and click Save.

The automatic destination for the saved layout is a folder named Column Layouts in the Final Cut Pro User Data folder, discussed earlier in this lesson. If you want to transfer this layout to another computer station, go to the Column Layouts folder, copy the appropriate file, and place it in the same location on the other computer.

TIP ▶ To recall a saved layout, Ctrl-click a column head and choose the layout from the shortcut menu.

11 To hide a column, Ctrl-click that column heading and choose Hide Column from the shortcut menu. Hide the Thumbnail and Length columns.

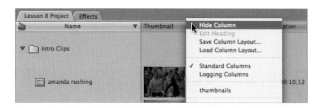

These columns are removed from the current Browser layout but can be chosen again from the shortcut menu by Ctrl-clicking any active column heading. Notice in the image above that the saved layout, thumbnails, appears as an option to recall.

Adding Column Information

As you can see, Browser columns can contain a lot of information that could be helpful when you want to find a clip or group of clips using specific criteria. Yet some of the columns in **Lesson 8 Project** appear blank. When these clips were captured from tape, this clip information was not entered. However, most clip information can be entered any time after capturing. For larger projects, being able to search for clips that have been checked "Good," or more specifically given a log note such as "great sunset" or "very smooth pan," can make a big difference in how quickly you find a certain clip. Let's add some information about the clips in this project.

1 Find the **VO_12** clip in the Amanda Clips bin under the Name column, move the pointer toward the right to the Good column, and click. A checkmark appears, identifying this narration clip as "good."

When you move the pointer over a clip or line of information, a dark, faint highlight appears across the entire Browser window. This acts as a guide to ensure you are making changes to the correct clip.

2   Click in the Good column for these clips: **97A-out of bldg**, **97F-man cu**, and **98C-wide**.

3   Now click the Good column heading to sort and display the clips checked Good. Click again to reverse the sort order so the clips appear at the top of the column.

The clips that have a check in the Good column appear together.

4   Click the Name column to sort by name once again. Select the **healer at ruins** clip, and click in the Log Note column on the clip's highlighted line.

A text box appears with a flashing cursor.

5   In the Log Note text box, type *Peru*, and press Return.

NOTE ▶ Each vignette of this film was shot at a different location. The material with the healer was shot in Peru.

6   Select the **girl on plane** clip, and enter *Alaska* in the Log Note text box.

7   Move to the row where the **healer cu** clip sits. This time, Ctrl-click in the Log Note area and choose Peru from the shortcut menu of previously entered options. Add Peru as a log note for the **healer walking** clip as well. In this option, you don't have to preselect the clip before bringing up the Log Note options.

Once a note has been added, it can easily be deleted.

8   Double-click the **girl on plane** log note, and press Delete.

Log notes are one way to further identify a clip. Another way is to use the Final Cut Pro set of labels, which color the clip in the Browser and Timeline. There are two ways you can choose a label, in the Label column or by Ctrl-clicking the clip icon in the Name column.

9   Find the Label column, and Ctrl-click the word *None* for any one of the clips in the Amanda Clips bin. Now Ctrl-click the **97A-out of bldg** clip under the Name column. Choose Label > Best Take from the shortcut menu.

In the latter option, you can see the colors assigned to each label category. When you choose Best Take, the selected clip icon becomes red.

NOTE ▶ You can also select a group of clips and choose a label for the entire group.

10 Open the *Amanda* sequence.

In the Timeline, the **97A-out of bldg** clip name is red to indicate it is labeled "Best Take."

Labeling clips in this way can be helpful when you want to organize your material by type or be able to quickly identify it in the Timeline.

TIP ▶ To remove a label, Ctrl-click the clip or group of selected items and choose Label > None from the shortcut menu. For the moment, leave these labels attached for the next exercise.

Finding Items in the Browser

In an earlier lesson, you used the Find function in the Timeline to locate a clip by name. You can also use this function to locate clips based on specific criteria found in the Browser columns. In conjunction with a rational naming and labeling convention, the Find function allows you to call up a clip instantly when you want it or when someone else on the production team requests it.

1 Click the disclosure triangle next to each bin to hide its contents.

This is not a required step for finding items, but it's helpful to demonstrate how the Find function works.

2   Click an empty space in the Browser to deselect everything, then choose Edit > Find, or press Cmd-F.

A Find window appears in which you can enter the name of the clip or item you wish to locate and the name of the project where you want to look for it.

3   In the Search pop-up menu, choose Project: Lesson 8 Project, if it's not already selected, and in the field with the blinking cursor enter *city street.* Click Find Next, or press Return, to find this clip in this project.

After clicking the Find Next button, the clips in the Intro Clips bin are revealed, and the appropriate clip is highlighted.

4   Let's say you don't know the clip name but remember entering a log note for it referring to where the footage was shot, in Peru. Press Cmd-F to bring up the Find window again, and type *Peru* in the lower-right search field.

5   In the lower left, click the pop-up menu and look through the list of column headings to find Log Note.

6   Click the Find All button to find *all* the clips that have *Peru* entered as part of their log notes.

When you click Find All, a Find Results window opens, listing the clips having the specified criteria, in this case, a log note that included the word *Peru*.

7   Reposition the Find Results window so you can also see the other clips in the Browser. Now press Cmd-A to select all the clips in the Find Results window.

    As soon as you select clips in this window, the same clips are also selected in the Browser window. You can either determine which clip is the one you were looking for in the Find Results window and select it by itself, or take a closer look at the selected clips in the Browser. You can also make changes, such as choose a different label, to the selected clips at one time.

8   Close the Find Results window.

Working with Master Clips

In Final Cut Pro, the first time a clip is either captured or imported into a project, it is given master clip status. If a clip is copied within the project, say for organizational purposes, the copied clip becomes an *affiliate* of the master clip. The main purpose of a master clip is to *supervise* the naming of the clip. If you rename a master clip, all other uses of that clip—for example, a copy of the master clip placed in a different bin or a sequence clip edited in the Timeline—will change names to follow the master clip name. Final Cut Pro uses this master clip naming convention to help track clips if they become disconnected from their original media files.

1   Display the contents of the Amanda Clips bin once again. Drag the blue scroll bar in the Browser to the far right until you see the Master Clip column.

Comment A	Comment B	Master Clip	Offline	Last Modified
		✓		Today, 10:20 AM
		✓		Today, 10:20 AM
		✓		Today, 10:20 AM
		✓		Wed, Apr 20, 2005, 9:13 AM
		✓		Wed, Apr 13, 2005, 11:50 AM

A check in the Master Clip column means a clip is a master clip—it is the first use of that clip in this project.

2   In the Name column, select the first clip in the Amanda Clips bin, **97A-out of bldg**. Press Cmd-C to copy it, and press Cmd-V to paste it back into the project. Look again at the Master Clip column

The copied clip is the second use of the **97A-out of bldg** clip in this project, and therefore is not considered a master clip.

3   Scroll left as far as possible to return to the default column display. Make sure you can see the clips in the *Amanda* sequence that's open in the Timeline. Expand the Timeline so it's easier to see the full name on the clips.

The clips in this sequence have been edited using master clips in this project originally named **98A-amanda** and **98B-man**.

4 In the Browser, find the clip named **98A-amanda,** and change its name to just *amanda*, without the scene number information.

In the Timeline, each sequence clip that was edited from the original **98A-amanda** master clip is now renamed **amanda**.

NOTE ▶ When you create a subclip, it becomes a master clip because it is the first use of that new clip in the project. If you rename the master clip used to create the subclip, the subclip name would remain unchanged.

Another time you use master clips is when you want to locate the original frame in a source clip that you used in a sequence clip, or vice versa. This is called finding a *match frame*. For example, you may want to know whether a specific frame from a master clip was used in the sequence. You can open the master clip in the Viewer, then ask Final Cut Pro to search for its match in the sequence.

5 From the Browser, open the **amanda** clip, and move the playhead to 8:07:10:07. Play from this point to hear Amanda's brief dialogue in her native tongue, then reposition the playhead back to the specific timecode number.

To determine whether or not this section of the master clip has been used in the sequence, you can search for its matching frame.

6 Choose View > Match Frame > Master Clip, or press F.

This function automatically moves the playhead in the Timeline to the exact frame that matches the master clip frame in the Viewer.

7   Click in the Viewer, and press Shift-left arrow two times to move the playhead back 2 seconds. Press F to search for a matching frame in the sequence that matches this master clip frame.

You hear a computer beep, indicating there is no frame in the current sequence that matches this frame of the master clip. Now you know that you have not used this frame in the sequence.

TIP ▶ When you want to find a match frame from the Timeline, the Auto Select controls determine what track you will match. To find a match to tracks other than the V1 track, turn off all Auto Select controls for all tracks but the one you want to match.

You can also extend this process to search for a master clip in the Browser that matches a particular frame.

8   Move the Timeline playhead to the first frame of the previous clip in the sequence, the **98B-man** clip. To find the master clip frame that matches this sequence frame, press F. To locate that master clip in the Browser, choose View > Reveal Master Clip, or press Shift-F.

In the Browser, the master clip is automatically selected to identify itself. Even if the bin is closed, this function opens the bin to display the master clip.

9   Choose the Modify menu and look at the option regarding master clips.

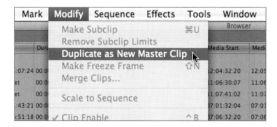

The Modify menu offers an option to duplicate a master clip. This option allows you to work with the same media but use different names for each clip. However, each clip would link back to the original media file, and the media file name itself would not change. If you select a clip in the Timeline and choose Modify, you can choose an option to make that sequence clip independent, so it won't follow the master clip naming conventions.

NOTE ▶ Although you can easily rename a clip in the Browser, it's not a good idea to do so once you've used the clip in the project. It may be more difficult for Final Cut Pro to relink it later.

10 In the Browser, select the newly named **amanda** clip, and press Delete.

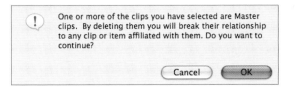

If you try to delete a master clip from a project, and that clip has been used in a sequence, a warning will appear reminding you that you will break the relationship to any clip associated with that master clip.

TIP ▶ If you delete a master clip, the clips that were affiliated with it in the project will simply become their own master or independent clips. You will, however, lose the ability to match frame to the deleted clip in the project. But you can select a clip in the sequence and choose View > Match Frame > Source File to load the original source file directly into the Viewer.

11 Click Cancel to keep this master clip in the project.

NOTE ▶ Breaking the relationship to a master clip will have an impact on reconnecting clips if you transfer media from one computer or FireWire drive to another. When clips are affiliated with a master clip, you have to reconnect to the master clips only. All affiliated clips will automatically become reconnected.

Organizing Project Elements

Thinking about your project and creating a specific organizational system for it can save hours of time during the editing process. How an editor organizes a project can vary according to the size of the project, whether other editors and assistants might be working on the same project, whether the project is based within a larger system or facility, and of course, personal preference. You have been working with footage from the Smithsonian's National Museum of the American Indian film, *A Thousand Roads*. As an example of project organization, let's take a closer look at how this film's editor, Harry Miller III, organized his project.

1   Press Cmd-O to bring up the Choose A File window. From the Lessons folder, select **Sample Project**, and click Choose to open this project. This project has a lot of clips in it, so it may take a while to open.

> **NOTE** ▶ If a Reconnect window appears, click Continue.

This project includes several bins that organize elements according to type, such as dramatic scenes, stock footage, narration, music, sound effects, and so on.

2   Click the disclosure triangles for the Edit and Backup bins to display their contents.

These bins contain the sequences for this project. Notice that each sequence name includes a date. Only the sequence with the most recent date is in the Edit bin. This would be used as the current sequence. The Backup bin contains all previous versions of sequences.

3   Hide the contents of the Edit and Backup bins. Then display the contents of the Scenes bin.

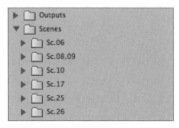

Most of the scenes have separate bins containing clips used in them. Single-digit scene numbers contain leading zeros. Without a leading zero—as in the Sc.06 bin—that bin would appear after the Sc.55 bin.

4   Display the contents of the Sc.06 bin.

The naming convention for these clips follows typical dramatic or narrative-type shows, using the scene and take numbers in the name.

NOTE ▶ Each of the clips in this project has a red line through it, indicating they are not linked to any media files. You will not be viewing any clips or sequences from this project, only examining its organizational structure.

5   Scroll down to see the Sc.36 bin.

This bin has a colored label that makes it easy to identify, just like the bin you labeled earlier in this lesson.

6   Close all the open bins, and look at the bottom of the list to see the bins whose names begin with an underscore.

If you want a bin to appear at the top of the alphabetized Name column, enter a space before the first letter of the name. If you want a bin to appear at the bottom of the list, such as in this project, use an underscore before the first letter.

7   To close this project, Ctrl-click the **Sample Project** project tab and choose Close Tab from the shortcut menu.

Customizing the Interface

Whether you need to mix audio, add transitions, or color correct your clips, you can change Final Cut Pro's interface to accommodate any particular aspect of your project and then change it again when you move on to something else. Each part of the interface can be customized. And just like the Browser columns, those customized changes can be saved and used in different projects or loaded onto another computer station.

Rearranging Windows in the Interface

Final Cut Pro has made it easy to reposition the interface windows to any configuration you like. Maybe you like working with the Browser on the right side of the screen and not in its default position on the left. And what about the size of a window? If you have a lot of tracks in your Timeline, you might want to make the Timeline taller so more tracks are visible. And you can always work with a preset window layout.

1   Choose Window > Arrange > Color Correction.

This preset layout rearranges the windows to allow for a set of video scopes to appear in the Tool Bench window. This is a good layout to use when color correcting clips or any time you want to monitor the luminance and chroma values of your video.

2   Choose Window > Arrange > Audio Mixing.

The Audio Mixer appears, which you can use when you're mixing audio tracks.

3   Choose Window > Arrange > Standard, or press Ctrl-U, to return to the default layout.

4   Rearrange the top three windows, placing the Viewer on the far left, the Canvas in the middle, and the Browser on the far right. Remember to drag each window from the title bar at the top.

As you drag a window into place, it seems to *snap* to that location.

5   Move the cursor over the Canvas and Browser boundary line. When you see the resize arrow, drag to the right.

This dynamically shrinks the Browser, and the Canvas grows to fill the space.

6   Move the pointer between the Timeline and Canvas or any upper window. When you see the resize arrow, drag up. Move the pointer to the corner where the Viewer, Canvas, and Timeline boundaries converge. Drag diagonally.

Depending on where you position the pointer over one of the interface boundary lines, you can drag left or right, up or down, or diagonally.

7   To add a tool to your layout, choose Tools > Video Scopes. Position the video scopes over the Viewer on the left. In the next exercise, you will save this layout.

Saving and Recalling Window Layouts

If you prefer your own personal window layout over the Final Cut Pro preset window layouts, you can save these layouts and return to them at any time without having to create them again manually. You can also start with a preset layout, make changes to that, and then save the layout. Window layouts apply to all open projects.

1   To save the existing layout, hold down the Option key and choose Window > Arrange > Set Custom Layout 1. Release the mouse and then release the Option key.

2   To create a second arrangement of the windows, scroll left and then click the Browser Zoom button to see it in the expanded column view.

NOTE ▶ This is a helpful layout to save if you need a wider view of Browser columns on a regular basis.

3   Hold down the Option key and choose Window > Arrange > Set Custom Layout 2. Release the mouse button and then the Option key.

NOTE ▶ You can also choose Window > Arrange > Save Window Layout to save additional named layouts in your Final Cut Pro User Data folder.

4   To recall the first layout of the rearranged windows (Custom Layout 1), choose Window > Arrange > Custom Layout 1, or press Shift-U.

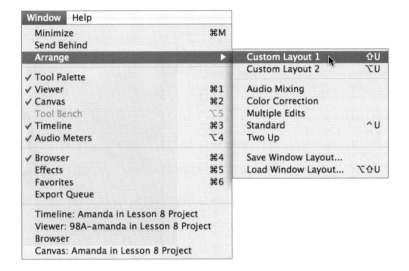

5   Choose Window > Arrange > Custom Layout 2, or press Option-U, to return to the wide Browser layout.

> **TIP** The Browser window is so wide, it may come up behind one of the other interface windows. Click any portion of the Browser window you see to bring it to the front. Or press Cmd-4 to make the Browser the active window.

6   Choose Window > Arrange > Standard, or press Ctrl-U, to return to the default window layout.

Customizing and Saving Timeline Tracks

The Timeline tracks can also be customized to your project's needs. For example, you can minimize or reduce the height of just the audio tracks in your Timeline as you work with your video tracks, or vice versa.

1   In the Timeline, move the cursor over the line between A1 and A2 in the far left area of the Timeline track control area. Click and drag up.

The A1 track becomes shorter while all the other tracks remain the same height.

2   To make all the audio tracks this same height, hold down the Option key and resize the A2 track to the shortest height possible.

All audio tracks are now the same height.

TIP ▶ To customize both video and audio tracks to the same height, hold down the Shift key while you resize either a video or audio track.

3   To save this small audio track configuration, click the Track Layout pop-up menu.

A pop-up menu appears with different track layout choices.

4   Choose Save Track Layout, and a Save window appears. Enter the name *small audio*, and click Save.

5   Toggle through the Track Height controls to restore the tracks to a default height, and then click the Track Layout pop-up menu again.

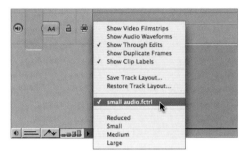

Small audio has been saved as a track layout. To restore that layout, just select it.

Final Cut Pro will store up to 40 track layouts. To choose another of your saved layouts, one that isn't listed in the shortcut menu, click the Track Layout pop-up menu again and choose Restore Track Layout. A window will appear listing all of your saved layouts. You can choose the track layout you want from this list.

Customizing Shortcut Keys and Buttons

Like all good tools, Final Cut Pro can be customized to fit an individual's needs. Do you want to use the J, K, and L playback keys on the default right side of the keyboard or shift those functions to keys on the left? Do you prefer clicking a button to select a function or using a keyboard shortcut? Once you become familiar with FCP's basic functions, taking the time to create the most efficient layout of your keyboard and buttons will help you accomplish your editing tasks more efficiently.

Changing the Keyboard Layout

Using keyboard shortcuts allows you to access any Final Cut Pro function by pressing a combination of keystrokes. Sometimes these keystrokes require one or more modifier keys.

1   To open the keyboard layout map, choose Tools > Keyboard Layout > Customize.

The tabs across the top of the window organize the keyboard shortcuts according to modifier keys—cmd, shift, opt, ctrl, or a combination of these.

2   In the lower left of this window, click the lock to allow changes to the current keyboard layout.

3   In the command list area to the right of the keyboard layout map, drag the blue vertical scroll bar up and down to see the list of command sets.

The first nine sets contain all the commands in the Final Cut Pro menus. The topics that follow are organized by editing function.

4   At the top of the list, click the File Menu disclosure triangle to display the commands under that menu.

If a command currently has a keyboard shortcut, it is listed to the right of the command. There are a few functions that do not currently have keyboard shortcuts, such as Close Project and Import Folder. Let's create a shortcut for Import Folder.

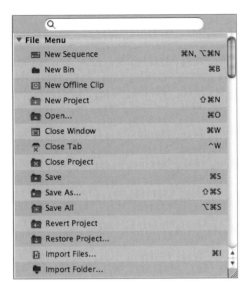

5   Click the shift-cmd modifier tab in the keyboard layout map.

Since Cmd-I is the shortcut for Import File, mapping the Import Folder function to the Shift-Cmd-I key will be easy to remember.

6   Drag the Import Folder name or icon from the command list onto the I key.

The new keyboard shortcut appears on the keyboard layout as well as to the right of the Import Folder command in the command list area.

7   On the Keyboard Layout window, click the Close button to close the window.

TIP   To reload the default U.S. layout, choose Tools > Keyboard Layout > Default Layout - U.S.

Adding Shortcut Buttons

Although the interface buttons you see in the Viewer and Canvas can't be changed, you can add shortcut buttons to a button bar in the Browser, Viewer, Canvas, and Timeline windows. The Timeline default layout has two buttons; the other windows have only the button tabs with no buttons in-between. If you edit extensively with your mouse, having buttons for specific functions you use frequently can significantly speed up the editing process. You can choose buttons from two places: the Keyboard Layout window or the Button List window. Both operate the same way.

1   To open the button list, choose Tools > Button List.

    This is the same list that appears on the Keyboard Layout window. In fact, you could use the Keyboard Layout window to perform these steps.

2   Click in the search entry area at the top of the commands list to bring up an alphabetized list of commands.

    NOTE ▶ To return to the main function and command menu listing, click the X to the right of the search entry field.

3   Type the word *audio* to search for all the audio commands in Final Cut Pro. Click the X to clear the entry field, or delete the individual characters, and type *transition*. Clear the field and type the word *import* to search for all the import commands.

A different list of commands is displayed every time a new word is entered in the search field. Each command has a unique visual icon depicting the function it represents.

TIP ▸ After entering a word in the search field, don't press Return. Final Cut Pro will read it as a keystroke and try to search for items that use that keystroke.

4   Click and drag the Import Files icon into the Browser between the button tabs and release the mouse.

The Import Files button is added to the button bar of the Browser.

5   Repeat step 4 with the Import Folder command.

The Browser now has an Import Files button and an Import Folder button.

6   Hold your mouse over one of these shortcut buttons to reveal the tooltip that identifies it.

7   One at a time, drag the Audio Mixer, Add Audio Transition, and Lock All Audio Tracks buttons to the Timeline button bar.

This adds a group of buttons that all involve audio. To distinguish them from the other non-audio buttons, you can color code them.

8   Ctrl-click the Audio Mixer button and choose Color > Blue from the shortcut menu. Make the other audio buttons blue as well.

TIP ▸ To separate the audio buttons from the default Timeline buttons, Ctrl-click the Audio Mixer button and choose Add Spacer from the shortcut menu.

9   To load a preset button bar, choose Tools > Button Bars > Audio Editing, and look at the new audio buttons in the Timeline button bar. Choose

Tools > Button Bars > Media Logging, and look at the new media buttons in the Browser button bar.

10 To remove the buttons from a window's button bar, such as the Browser, Ctrl-click in the Browser's button bar and choose Remove > All from the shortcut menu. To restore the default button bar layout, Ctrl-click in the Timeline button bar and choose Remove > All / Restore Default from the shortcut menu.

> **NOTE ▶** The button bar shortcut menu offers other options, such as saving customized button bars. To use your customized button bars on another computer station, you will need to save the layout as you did in the previous exercises.

Choosing an Easy Setup Preset

Customizing the Final Cut Pro interface is a personal choice, but choosing the audio/video settings is not. It's very important for FCP sequence settings to match the settings of the footage you will be editing. This will give you the best results throughout your editing process. Whether your project is NTSC or PAL, FCP has the flexibility to work with many different media formats in both standards and can also be connected to third-party hardware that expands those options even further.

FCP makes it easy to choose accurate audio/video settings by providing a list of default settings found in the Easy Setup window. These settings are organized as presets and include capture settings, sequence settings, device control settings, and output settings. By choosing an Easy Setup preset, you are simultaneously loading all these settings at one time. Keep in mind that Easy Setup presets change settings for all new sequences and are not attached to a specific project. A single project could contain sequences with different settings.

> **TIP ▶** Choose the correct Easy Setup preset *before* starting a new project. This will ensure that sequences automatically created in new projects will be set correctly.

1 Choose Final Cut Pro > Easy Setup, or press Ctrl-Q.

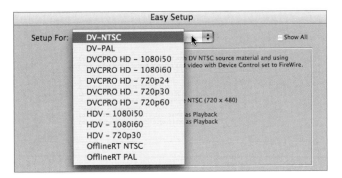

The Setup For pop-up menu displays the current or active preset. Beneath it is a summary of the settings that make up that preset.

2 Click the Setup For pop-up menu.

The presets in this list have already been created within FCP to facilitate an easier setup for you to get started. They represent many of the more standard presets, such as DV, HDV, Offline RT, and so on, in both PAL and NTSC.

3 To see an expanded version of preset options, move the mouse off the pop-up menu and select the Show All check box. Click the Setup For pop-up menu again.

You now see additional preset options, including Cinema Tools presets for film or HD projects, MPEG-IMX presets, as well as Anamorphic options for different formats.

NOTE ▶ If you have loaded additional presets from a third-party company, such as AJA or Blackmagic, in order to capture and edit other formats, those presets will also appear in the Setup For pop-up menu.

4   Deselect the Show All check box, and choose DV-NTSC from the Setup For pop-up menu. Click the Setup button to confirm this preset.

This is the preset for most of the media in this book. In a later lesson, you will work with PAL footage.

TIP ▶ If you need to create a new Easy Setup preset, choose File > Audio/Video Settings, and click the Create Easy Setup button. Enter a new preset name, and follow the steps to choose the appropriate settings. Refer to the Final Cut Pro 5 user's manual for more details on this process.

Selecting User Preferences

Once you've selected the correct settings for your project, you can take a closer look at User Preferences, a collection of options that determine how you want to work with Final Cut Pro. These options cover editing choices like preferred pre-roll duration, the level of undos, Timeline options such as number of tracks you want to appear when you create a new sequence, and so on. User Preferences settings apply to all open projects.

MORE INFO ▶ You can find a precise definition of each preference or setting in the Final Cut Pro 5 User Manual.

1   Choose Final Cut Pro > User Preferences, or press Option-Q.

The User Preferences window has six tabs that detail specific preferences. The General tab is where you choose assorted preference settings and those for capturing. Many of these options are covered in detail throughout the book. Two that have not been covered are

▶ Autosaving—Final Cut Pro will automatically save a backup of your project file as you work. You can choose how frequently a project will be saved, how many versions of the project will be saved, and the maximum number of projects saved. When the maximum number of versions is reached, Final Cut Pro moves the oldest version into the Trash before saving the current version.

▶   Auto Render—With auto rendering enabled, Final Cut Pro will automatically render the current sequence in the Timeline or all open sequences, when left idle for a specified amount of time.

2   Click the Editing tab.

As you have seen before, this is where you set preferences for certain editing functions, such as multi-frame trim size and previewing pre-roll and post-roll.

3   Click the Labels tab.

This is where you rename the color labels you apply to clips and bins. The colors themselves cannot be changed, only the label names.

4   Click the Timeline Options tab.

Here you choose settings for all *new* sequences. You can determine a default number of tracks so that each new sequence you create has that track configuration, or choose drop frame or non-drop frame timecode to ensure every new sequence displays that mode. Any changes made here will not affect any existing sequences or how they are displayed in the Timeline.

TIP ▶ To change Timeline settings for an existing sequence, choose Sequence > Settings and make adjustments in that window.

5   Click the Render Control tab.

This is where you enable or disable the most processor-intensive effects in Final Cut Pro.

6   Click the Audio Outputs tab.

Here you can create custom Audio Output configurations. You can use these different settings when laying off various audio tracks to tape. For example, if your hardware supports it, you can create an Audio Output configuration that outputs up to 24 distinct tracks at one time.

7   Click Cancel to leave the preferences unchanged.

NOTE ▶ To revert to the original Final Cut Pro preferences, quit the application, and find the Final Cut Pro 5 Preferences file in the Final Cut Pro User Data folder. Drag this file to the Trash, and relaunch FCP.

Viewing Clip Properties

As you're editing, there will be times when you may need to know some little detail about a clip you've captured. Maybe you want to know the size of the media file, where the clip is located on your hard drive, or what its pixel aspect ratio is. Some of this information appears in the Browser columns, where it's displayed for all clips. Another place to look is in the Item Properties window.

1   In the Browser, select the **98B-man** clip, and choose Edit > Item Properties > Format. (You can also press Cmd-9 to open the Item Properties window.)

The Item Properties window opens, displaying detailed information about every aspect of your clip. Notice under the Format tab that the frame size is 720 x 480, and the compressor is DV/DVCPRO – NTSC. These are some of the settings for DV-NTSC video. If you were using a capture card to work with high definition video, the frame size and compressor would be different.

Item Properties: 98B-man

Format \ Timing \ Logging \ Film	Clip	V1	A1	A2
Name	98B-man	98B-man	98B-man	98B-man
Type	Clip			
Creator	Final Cut Pro	Final Cut Pro	Final Cut Pro	Final Cut Pro
Source	G-RAID:FCP5 Book Files:Media:A	G-RAID:FCP5 Book Files	G-RAID:FCP5 Book Files	G-RAID:FCP5 Book Files
Offline				
Size	363.1 MB	363.1 MB	363.1 MB	363.1 MB
Last Modified	Today, 10:20 AM	Today, 10:20 AM	Today, 10:20 AM	Today, 10:20 AM
Tracks	1V, 2A			
Vid Rate	29.97 fps	29.97 fps		
Frame Size	720 x 480	720 x 480		
Compressor	DV/DVCPRO – NTSC	DV/DVCPRO – NTSC		
Data Rate	3.6 MB/sec	3.6 MB/sec	3.6 MB/sec	3.6 MB/sec
Pixel Aspect	NTSC – CCIR 601	NTSC – CCIR 601		
Anamorphic				
Field Dominance	Lower (Even)	Lower (Even)		
Alpha	None/Ignore	None/Ignore		
Reverse Alpha				
Composite	Normal	Normal		
Audio	1 Stereo		Left	Right
Aud Rate	48.0 KHz		48.0 KHz	48.0 KHz
Aud Format	16-bit Integer		16-bit Integer	16-bit Integer
Angle				

Cancel   OK

The Format tab displays clip settings, such as frame size, compressor, and data rate; the Timing tab displays timecode and length information. The Logging tab contains organizational information, such as what reel it came from and what scene, shot, and take it belongs to. The Film tab contains film information, if that was the originating format.

2   Click Cancel to close the Item Properties window without making any changes.

> **NOTE** ▸ You can also Ctrl-click a clip in the Timeline to access the Item Properties window for a sequence clip. Or select the clip, and use either of the methods listed in step 1.

Changing Sequence Settings

The Timeline options you selected in the User Preferences window will determine how new sequences are displayed in the Timeline. However, if you want to change any of these settings or preferences for a sequence that already exists, you have to open the Sequence Settings window.

1   Click in the Timeline to make it active, and choose Sequence > Settings, or press Cmd-0.

> **TIP** ▸ You can also Ctrl-click a sequence in the Browser and choose Settings from the shortcut menu.

This window has five tabs. The last three tabs also appear in the User Preferences window, where the settings apply to any newly created sequence. Here they apply to an existing, selected sequence.

Notice the settings in the General tab. These correspond to the Easy Setup parameters for frame size, aspect ratio, audio sample rate, and so on. These sequence settings should match your clip settings.

NOTE ▸ You cannot change the editing timebase (frames per second) of a sequence after clips have been edited into it.

2   Click the Video Processing tab.

You can change how Final Cut Pro processes the video in this particular sequence. If the material is DV, you will want the default settings of Render In 8-bit YUV and Process Maximum White As White.

3   Click the Timeline Options tab. Change the Track Size and Thumbnail Display.

Here you can change the starting timecode for a sequence, choose to see thumbnails on the video tracks, and make other display choices. These changes affect the selected or active sequence only. They *will not* affect any new sequences you create. Those settings are controlled in the Timeline Options tab of the User Preferences window.

NOTE ▶ If you edit a clip with one group of settings into a sequence with a different group of settings, an orange or red bar may appear over the clip in the Timeline ruler area. This means your sequence settings probably need to be changed to match the clip settings. You can use the Item Properties and Sequence Settings windows to compare the settings.

Lesson Review

1. How do you sort by a different column, other than the Name column?
2. How do you show a column that you can't currently see in the Browser?
3. Can the interface windows be dynamically resized? If so, how?
4. How do you search for a clip in the Browser using specific criteria?
5. What determines whether a clip is a master clip in Final Cut Pro?
6. Where are all customized layouts saved on your computer?
7. What does choosing an Easy Setup do? When should you select an Easy Setup preset?
8. Under what menu can you choose User Preferences?
9. How can you look at the detailed information about a single clip or item?
10. How do you make changes to an existing sequence?

Answers

1. Click a column head.
2. Ctrl-click a column head and show (or hide) from the shortcut menu.
3. Yes, dynamically resize them by dragging the boundary line between the windows.
4. Press Cmd-F to open the Find window and choose specific search criteria.
5. A clip is a master clip if it represents the first use of that clip in the project.
6. They are saved at Macintosh HD > Users > [user name] > Library > Preferences > Final Cut Pro User Data.

7. Choosing an Easy Setup preset ensures that your footage settings will match your new sequence settings. You should always choose the appropriate Easy Setup preset prior to creating a new project.

8. Choose User Preferences from the Final Cut Pro menu.

9. Select the clip, and press Cmd-9 to open the Item Properties window. You can also Ctrl-click the clip and choose Item Properties from the shortcut menu.

10. Make the sequence active in the Timeline, or select it in the Browser, and press Cmd-0 to open the Sequence Settings window. You can also choose Sequence Settings from the Sequence menu.

Keyboard Shortcuts

Cmd-F	Selects the Find window
Option-Q	Opens User Preferences
Shift-Q	Opens System Settings
Ctrl-Q	Opens Easy Setup
Cmd-9	Opens the Item Properties window
Cmd-0	Opens the Sequence Settings window

9

Lesson Files	None
Media	Your own
Time	This lesson takes approximately 60 minutes to complete.
Goals	Connect sources for capture
	Preview and mark source material
	Log clips
	Choose clip settings
	Choose capture presets
	Capture options
	Set capture preferences

Capturing Footage

As video technology continues to evolve, editors have the opportunity to work with a variety of video formats. Some of these formats, such as DV, HDV, and DVCPRO HD, can be captured via a single FireWire connector, whereas standard definition (SD) or other high definition (HD) formats, such as DigiBeta and Beta SP, require the use of a third-party capture card. Of course, film is another shooting alternative, but it needs to be transferred to video before capturing into Final Cut Pro.

Whatever video format option you choose, capturing footage is always the first step in preparing for the editing process. As in the preceding lesson, some capturing decisions must follow the particulars of your shooting format, whereas others can be personal preferences.

The Log And Capture window

Preparing the Project

To begin, you will launch Final Cut Pro and create a new project to use for capturing. You will also change the Easy Setup to your personal source tape format.

1   In the Dock, click the Final Cut Pro icon to launch Final Cut Pro.

   When you launch Final Cut Pro, any project that was active when you last quit the program will also open.

2   Choose Final Cut Pro > Easy Setup, and choose the appropriate option from the Setup For pop-up menu. This option should follow the specifications of your own source material.

3   Close all open projects.

   Remember that the Canvas and Timeline windows close when there are no open sequences to display.

4   Choose File > New Project to create a new project.

An Untitled Project tab appears in the Browser window along with a default sequence, *Sequence 1*. This sequence contains the settings of the Easy Setup you just selected.

5   To rename and save this project, choose File > Save Project As, and type *Lesson 9 Project* as the new name. Navigate to the Lessons folder on your hard drive, and click Save to save the project there.

Notice that the .fcp suffix for this project is automatically added for you in the Save As field, and just the name portion is highlighted. You simply have to type the new project name. If you don't want the .fcp extension to be part of the name, check the Hide Extension box in the lower-left corner of this window.

NOTE ▸   What you are saving is just the project file. It is not where the media will be stored. You will set that destination later in this lesson.

Connecting Sources for Capture

The first step in capturing your source material is to connect your capture device to the computer through a FireWire cable. Final Cut Pro can capture and control a variety of NTSC or PAL camcorders and decks using just a FireWire cable. You can also capture other video formats using a third-party capture card or analog-to-digital converter with FireWire output.

FireWire 400, also called IEEE-1394a, has two types of connectors. The smaller 4-pin connector usually attaches to a camera or deck. The larger 6-pin connector goes into your computer's FireWire port. Independent FireWire drives typically use a 6-pin-to-6-pin connector. FireWire 400 transfers data at 400 Mbps. The newer FireWire 800 is a higher-bandwidth version capable of transferring data at up to 800 Mbps. This cable uses 9-pin-to-9-pin connections, but you can also get 9-pin-to-4-pin and 9-pin-to-6-pin cables to work with other FireWire devices.

| 4-pin connector to
DV source | 6-pin connector to
computer | 9-pin connector
to G5 computer or
FireWire 800 device |

You can also connect your camera or deck to a separate video monitor or television set, or through a VCR, just as you would if you were screening a tape. However, this is not necessary because you can simply use the preview image area within the Final Cut Pro Capture function.

Previewing and Marking Your Source

Once the video source is connected, you can control the camera or tape deck by using controls in the Final Cut Pro interface. As you screen and preview the material, you can set an In and Out point to identify the area you want to capture. Marking source material for capture is very similar to marking clips for editing. You will learn other approaches to the capture process later in this lesson.

Opening and Sizing the Capture Window

All capturing is done in the Log And Capture window in Final Cut Pro. The Log And Capture window has two main areas: the preview area on the left, where you screen and mark your source tape, and the Logging area on the right, where you log information about your clips and make selections about where and how you will capture footage.

1   Choose File > Log And Capture, or press Cmd-8.

     NOTE ▶ If you are capturing HDV format, you will see a slightly different Log And Capture window.

Preview area   Logging area

NOTE ▶ If you see the following message appear, it means your playback source device is not properly connected to your computer's FireWire port. When you click OK, the Log And Capture window will open but you will only be able to simply log clips or use a non-controllable device. If you want to capture from a FireWire device, close the Log And Capture window, turn on the capture device, then reopen the Log And Capture window.

The preview area of the Log And Capture window defaults to the size of the Canvas window. To change the size of the Log And Capture window, you must first change the size of the Canvas window, or the Viewer and Canvas windows together. (You need to do this while the Log And Capture window is closed.)

2   Close the Log And Capture window by clicking its Close button in the upper left of the window.

3   To make the Log And Capture window larger, first choose Window >
    Arrange > Two Up to enlarge the size of the Viewer and Canvas together.

4   Choose File > Log And Capture to reopen the window again.

    A much larger Log And Capture window is displayed.

Playing the Source Tape

The preview area of the Log And Capture window is used to play your source
material and set In and Out points. If the capture device is connected through
FireWire or a third-party capture card with a device control cable, you will have
direct control of the device, meaning you can play and control it from within
the Final Cut Pro interface. If not, you will have to control the device manually.

1   To get started viewing the source material, put a source tape into your
    camera or deck.

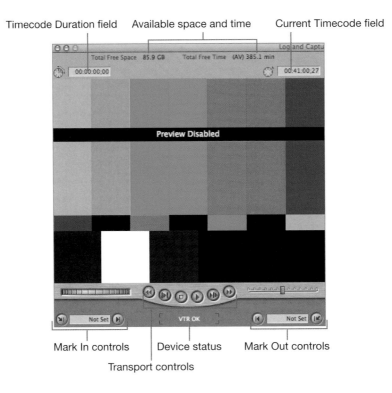

Timecode Duration field   Available space and time   Current Timecode field

Mark In controls   Device status   Mark Out controls

Transport controls

The preview area is similar in layout to the Viewer window. It has Timecode Duration and Current Timecode fields above the image area, a set of transport controls below the image area, plus shuttle and jog controls. The marking controls are in the lower left and lower right of the preview area. Between the marking controls is a device status area that indicates whether you have control over the capture device. In addition, the total amount of free hard drive space and time appears in the upper-middle area of the screen.

2 In the preview area, click the Play button to play the tape.

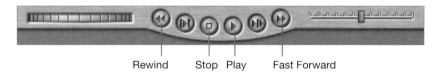

Rewind   Stop Play   Fast Forward

NOTE ▶ When you capture into Final Cut Pro through FireWire, you can choose to preview the audio through FCP, which you will do later in this lesson, or you can monitor it through headphones or speakers plugged into your device.

3 Click the Stop button to pause the tape.

4 Click the Stop button again to stop the tape.

When a tape in a camera or deck is stopped, the tape unwraps from the video heads. But the image in the preview area displays a freeze-frame of the most recent frame played.

TIP ▶ Pausing your tape is more efficient than stopping it completely. But leaving the tape in pause mode too long can damage the tape or cause video drop-outs.

5 Press the spacebar to play the tape, and the Play button lights up.

6 Press the spacebar again to pause the tape, and the Stop button lights up.

7 Click the Rewind or Fast Forward buttons to move quickly backward or forward.

8 Rewind your source tape to the beginning to prepare for the capture process.

Marking and Viewing Source Material

Marking a tape source is similar to marking a clip in the Viewer. In fact, you use the same marking controls or shortcut keys (I and O). The primary difference is that when you mark a clip in the Viewer, you make tight marks around the action you want to edit into the sequence. When you capture a clip, you mark a few seconds before the action and a few seconds after the action. This adds the additional pad, or handles, to the clip that you can use when adjusting edits in the Timeline.

In the preview mark area are Mark In and Mark Out buttons, Go To In Point and Go To Out Point buttons, and timecode fields for the In and Out points. The transport controls appear under the image as they do in the Viewer.

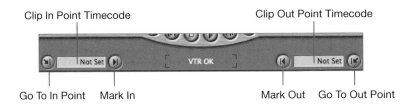

Clip In Point Timecode   Clip Out Point Timecode

| Not Set   VTR OK | Not Set |

Go To In Point   Mark In   Mark Out   Go To Out Point

1 Play the tape to the section you want to capture.

2 Press the spacebar, or click the Play (or Stop) button, to pause the tape at this point.

3 Click the Mark In button, or press the I key, to set an In point.

The timecode for your mark appears in the Clip In Point Timecode field. Unlike the Viewer marks, this mark will not appear in the image area, and there is no scrubber bar to scrub to the marks.

4 To adjust this mark and create a 3-second clip handle, click in the Clip In Point Timecode field, type *–3.* (minus three followed by a period), and press Return.

Typing –3. sets a new In point 3 seconds earlier than the previous mark, giving you a 3-second pad, or handle, before the desired action begins.

NOTE ▶ You may not need to create extra pad if your original mark allowed for pad prior to the action you want to use in editing.

5   Press the spacebar, or click the Play button, to move forward to where this portion of the action ends. Then press the spacebar to pause at this location.

6   Click the Mark Out button at this point, or press the O key, to set the Out point.

7   To create extra pad after the Out point, type +3. (plus three followed by a period) in the Clip Out Point Timecode field, and then press Return to add a 3-second handle to the Out point of this clip.

TIP ▶ When setting an Out point, you can also let the tape play past the end of the action a few seconds and set an Out point on the fly.

8   To see the marked portion, in the preview area, click the Play In To Out button.

9   Click the Go To In Point or Go To Out Point button to go to the In or Out point.

Go To In Point   Go To Out Point

Moving to the exact In or Out point can be a good double-check that you are capturing all the action you need in the clip.

10 Click the Play Around Current Frame button to see the area around the playhead position.

Logging Your Clips

Now that you have marked a source clip, you are ready to log information about that clip. If you look at the Logging tab of the Log And Capture window, you will recognize some of the topics you saw as Browser columns in the previous lesson, such as Name, Description, Scene, Angle, Log Note, and so on. Information you log at the capture stage appears in the Browser columns for reference later as you edit. Notice too there is an area where you can add markers during the logging process. But before you log a clip, you must determine the best approach to organizing the logged clips in the project.

Setting a Log Bin

When you capture a clip, Final Cut Pro needs to know where to place the new clip icons. The actual media files will be saved to your hard drive, but the clip icon linking you to that media will be saved to the current project in the Browser. If you want to move quickly, you can capture all your clips into the project tab area in the Browser and organize them later. If you want to organize as you capture, you can create a new bin for each category, such as reel/tape number or type of footage. In either case, Final Cut Pro needs to know where to place the clip icons. This destination is called the *log bin*. You can have only one log bin active at any given time, no matter how many projects you have open.

1   Position the Browser so you can see both the Capture and Browser windows at the same time while doing these steps.

In the Logging tab of the Log And Capture window, the project name, Lesson 9 Project, appears on the long, oval Log Bin button.

In the Browser window at the far left of the Name column heading, a slate icon appears, indicating that this project is the current logging bin.

At this point, you can capture all your clips into your project and organize the clips into bins after you've captured them. However, if you want to explore the other option of capturing to a new bin, continue with the following steps.

2   On the far right of the Log Bin button, click the New Bin button.

When you click this button, a new bin is created in the current project with the default name, Bin 1. The slate icon now appears next to this bin in the Browser to identify it as the target location for your new clips.

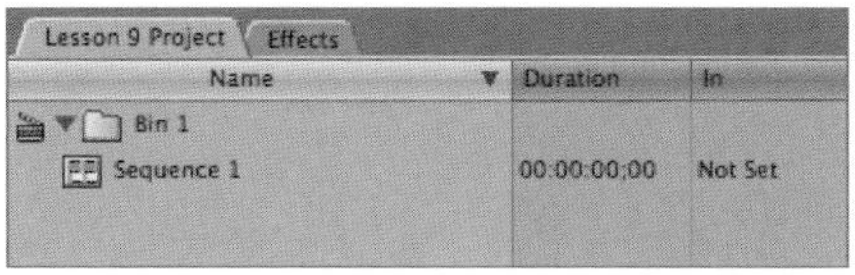

3   In the Logging tab, click the large Log Bin button with the new bin name on it.

The new bin opens as a separate window, which allows you to view just the new clips you are capturing without mixing them up with other clips already in your project.

4   Close this window by clicking its Close button.

5   In the Logging tab, click the Up button.

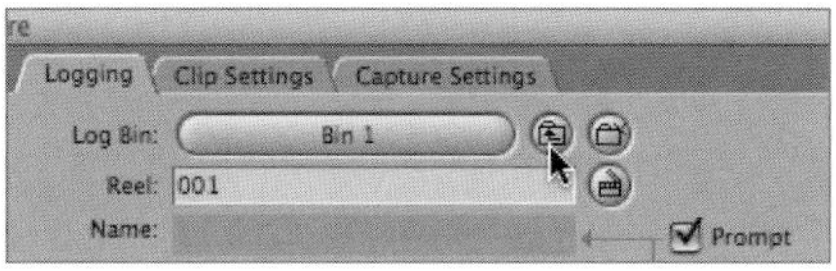

This takes the Log Bin destination up to a higher level, in this case back to the project level.

6   In the Browser, rename the new bin *Test Capture*.

The slate icon is now attached to the project, not to the Test Capture bin. However, you can assign the slate to the new bin.

7   To assign the Test Capture bin as the log bin, select it in the Browser, and choose File > Set Logging Bin.

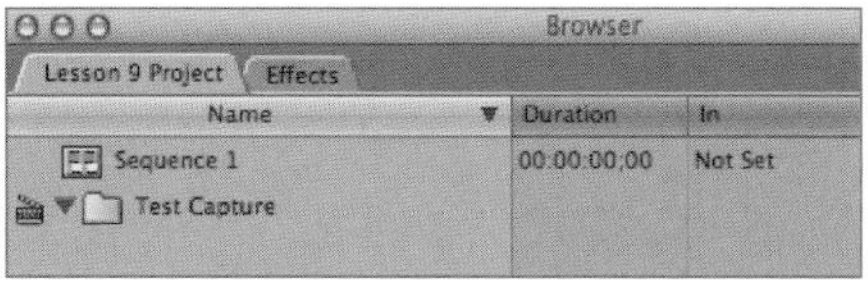

The slate icon now appears to the left of the Test Capture bin.

NOTE ▶ You can also Ctrl-click the bin in the Browser and choose Set Logging Bin from the shortcut menu.

Logging Clip Information

Certain logging information is required, such as reel number and clip name, or Final Cut Pro will not capture the clip. For reel numbers, you can use a simple numbering system or enter a reel name. The clip name is derived from any or all of the entry fields: Description, Scene, Shot/Take, and Angle. You can also add additional logging information any time after you have already captured the clip, as you learned in the preceding lesson. When you work with many clips on a complex project, you will appreciate the extra time you spent logging.

1   Enter an appropriate reel number or name for your source tape, or if you have just one tape, you can leave the default 001 reel number.

    TIP ▶ Ideally, you should use the same reel name or number that you used when labeling your tapes. That way you will always know from what source tape your clips were captured.

2 Try to click in the Name field.

The Name field is not for entering information, just displaying it. The name is actually compiled from any combination of the four descriptive fields below it that have an active checkmark.

3 Enter a description of the clip in the Description field, such as *dog runs to cam.* Use a name that will help you distinguish between that clip and another while you are editing.

4 Make sure the Description check box next to the slate button is checked, and press Tab or Return.

When checked, the information in the Description field automatically becomes part of the name.

5 If you're working with a script, enter the Scene information (such as 98), and press Tab or Return.

> **TIP** To use the scene and take numbers as the sole name, check those boxes, and deselect the Description and Angle check boxes.

6 Enter *1* as a Shot/Take number and *3* as the Angle.

7 Click on and off the check boxes next to each line to see how the name changes in the Name area.

Any one, or all four, of the descriptive entries can be included in the full clip name.

TIP ▶ Long clip names may be difficult to read when displayed on the clip in the Timeline. You might find it more useful to enter the information but not check the boxes to include it in the name. The information will still be attached to the clip, and you will have access to it in the Browser columns and through the Find function.

8   Next to the Angle entry, click the slate button.

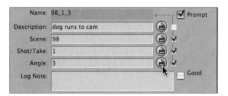

Every time you click one of the slates, the next consecutive number is added to the descriptive entry. This is true even if no number was originally entered. To change to another number, click the number to highlight it, and type the new number.

9   Click the Prompt check box on and off. Leave the box selected.

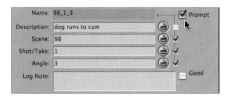

With the Prompt box selected, Final Cut Pro will display the information you've entered before logging the clip so you can check it, change it, or add to it before you complete the logging process.

10 Enter a log note about the clip, such as *pretty sunset,* and click the Good check box.

After you capture this clip, the log note will appear in the Log Note Browser column, and a checkmark will appear in the Good column

TIP ▶ A naming system can be a useful visual aid when working with different elements in the Browser. For example, for the lessons in this book, all clips are labeled with lowercase words and names, and sequences are in upper- and lowercase.

Adding Markers While Logging

In Lesson 7, you used markers to identify a specific location on a clip. You also used markers to create subclips of a longer clip. Depending on your project, you might want to add markers to a clip for these same purposes during the logging process. When you open the clip after capturing it, it will already have a marker identifying specific locations in the clip.

1 On the Logging tab, click the disclosure triangle next to Markers to expand the marker information pane.

2   With an In point selected on your source tape, play the tape from the In point, and click the Set Marker In button wherever you want to place a marker on the clip you are capturing. Then stop the tape.

NOTE ▶ Clicking the Set Marker Out button will give the marker a duration.

3   Enter a name for the marker in the Marker field.

4   Click Set Marker.

The timecode designating the marker location appears in the information fields. You are clear to add a new marker in this clip.

Choosing Clip Settings

In the Clip Settings tab, you make selections about *how* you want to capture a clip. Do you want to capture just the video, just the audio, or both? How do you want to capture the audio—as mono tracks or as a stereo pair? How many audio tracks do you want to capture—two or eight? Some of the options in the Clip Settings tab, such as the number of audio tracks you can capture, will depend on the type of deck or source you are using, and whether you are capturing via FireWire or through a capture card.

1 In the Log And Capture window, click the Clip Settings tab.

This pane is divided into Video and Audio sections. Each section has a check box to make that option active. If you are capturing through a FireWire device, the video controls will be dimmed. If you are working with a capture card, you can use these controls to adjust the incoming video levels of your clip.

2 To capture the logged clip's audio and video, make sure there are checkmarks in the Video and Audio boxes. To capture just one or the other, uncheck the appropriate option.

TIP Audio files do not take up as much room as video files. If you are trying to conserve hard-drive space and want to capture material from which you will only use the sound, such as an on-camera narration, capture just the audio to make the file size smaller. When you know you will use just the video portion of your source material, capture only video so you won't have empty audio tracks attached to the clip.

3   In the Audio area, click the Toggle Stereo/Mono button connecting the two audible speaker icons. Click it again to toggle between capturing two audio channels as a stereo pair and capturing them as separate mono channels.

When this option is deselected, as it is in this image, the audio tracks are *unpaired*, and the audio tracks are captured as separate channels. Capturing audio as mono tracks is helpful when you used a separate mic input during recording, as opposed to the stereo camera mic. Capturing the audio as mono channels gives you control over the individual tracks during editing.

Toggling to the Stereo option will create a connecting bracket around the two audio tracks, indicating they will be treated as a stereo pair. This will allow you to work with both audio tracks as one clip in the Timeline. The two audio tracks will also appear on just one audio tab in the Viewer. This can be helpful in editing because when you adjust one track, by changing the volume for example, the other track in the stereo pair is automatically adjusted the same way.

NOTE ▶ You can also pair or unpair the audio tracks in the Timeline during the editing process.

4   Deselect the Stereo option, and click the Channel 2 Audible control.

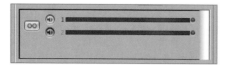

When the stereo option is deselected, you can choose whether you want to capture two mono channels or one individual channel of audio.

NOTE ▶ If you are using a capture card that supports multiple track capture, you can select the number of tracks you want to capture from the Input Channels pop-up menu. Whatever tracks you select appear in the audio track area. Here you can toggle stereo or mono off or on for any set of tracks.

5   To listen to the audio of your source as you are capturing, click the Preview box.

When the Preview box is checked, you can hear the audio of your source tape as you screen and mark your clips, and also as the clip is being captured.

6   If you have color bars at the head of your source tape, click the Video Scopes button to view them.

A Live Waveform Monitor And Vectorscope window appears where you can look at your incoming source levels. The Waveform Monitor on the left measures the brightness (luminance and black levels) of your incoming video; the Vectorscope on the right measures the color (saturation and hue).

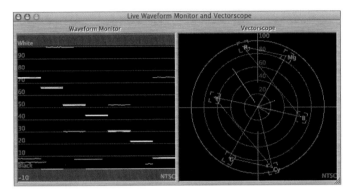

NOTE ▶ Keep in mind that although you can view the color bars at the head of a DV tape, you cannot change them at this point.

7   On the Live Waveform Monitor And Vectorscope window, click the Close button, or press Cmd-W, to close it.

Choosing Capture Settings

Before you begin capturing your clips, you have to choose how you will control the playback device, what Easy Preset option you will use to capture the footage, and where you will place it on your hard drive or FireWire drive.

NOTE ▶ HDV is a newer format that records video and sound as separate MPEG files. During capture, Final Cut Pro transcodes the MPEG files into a QuickTime movie with combined audio and video tracks. If you selected the HDV Easy Setup preset, you will see a slightly different capture window. The log and capture options that appear function the same as those in the default window.

1   In the Log And Capture window, click the Capture Settings tab.

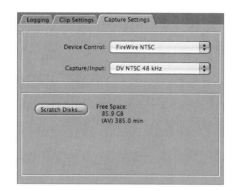

2   From the Device Control pop-up menu, choose FireWire NTSC, FireWire
    PAL, or another appropriate option.

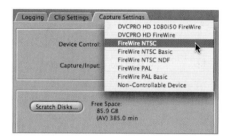

If you are capturing from a device that cannot be controlled through
FireWire, choose the appropriate preset, or choose Non-Controllable
Device. If you are using a third-party capture card, such as the AJA Io or
Kona card or Blackmagic DeckLink card, those options will appear here
as well.

3   Click the Capture/Input pop-up menu.

This is where you select the way your footage will be captured. The current option reflects the Easy Setup preset you selected earlier in this lesson.
You can capture a number of NTSC or PAL formats, including an assortment of options for DV, DVCPRO HD, and HDV.

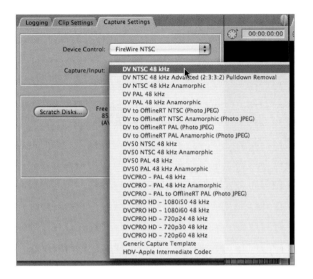

You can also capture at a lower quality resolution, such as DV To OfflineRT NTSC or PAL (Photo JPEG). The Offline RT option is good for large projects. You can edit your entire project using low-res files. Once the editing is complete, you can recapture just the footage you used in your sequence at a higher resolution. Read more about this process in the Final Cut Pro user's manual.

4   To select the destination for your captured media, click the Scratch Disks button.

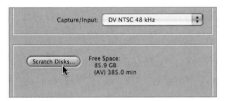

A window opens where you can set the path to the targeted scratch disk, or drive, to which you will be saving your media files. The current scratch disk is listed along with the amount of current available free space on that drive. You can choose a different scratch disk for audio and video, and for render files, which you will create in a later lesson. For now, capture them all to one destination.

NOTE ▶ You have the option of saving other types of files, such as Waveform, Thumbnail, and Autosave Vault, to other locations as well.

5   To change the currently selected scratch disk, click Set.

A file browser appears, where you can select a different scratch disk.

6   Navigate to where you want to save your captured files, and click Choose, then click OK in the Scratch Disks window.

7   Choose Final Cut Pro > System Settings, or press Shift-Q.

The first tab of this window shows the same Scratch Disk information that appears if you click the Scratch Disks button in the Capture Settings tab. You can set the scratch disk in either location. If the desired scratch disk is set in the System Settings window, and you are not changing it, you do not have to select it in the Capture Settings tab.

8   Choose Final Cut Pro > Audio/Video Settings, or press Cmd-Option-Q.

This is another place where you can select the device control and capture preset. If it is correctly selected here, the same setting will appear in the Device Control area of the Capture Settings tab.

Capturing Options

You can approach the capture process in different ways. In some situations, you may want to enter detailed information about a clip and then capture that clip before going on to the next one. In other situations, you may want to log information about all of your clips at one time, then capture them as a group. Other times, you may be working with footage that doesn't have timecode, and you won't be able to log any information. You can also choose to capture an entire tape and let Final Cut Pro automatically create the clips based on where the tape stopped and started.

> **NOTE ▶** If you're capturing a project that originated on film, you may need to use Apple's Cinema Tools to keep track of the relationship between the keycode of the original film frames and the timecode of the video you are capturing. Refer to the Cinema Tools user's guide for more information.

The lower portion of the Logging tab area has three capture buttons—Clip, Now, and Batch—and a Log Clip button. These buttons appear regardless of which tab is selected in the Log And Capture window. Each of the capture options converts footage from your tape source into computer media files. The Log Clip button builds a list to be captured later using Batch Capture. Although all the capture options create media clips, each goes about the process differently.

Capturing a Clip

If you have set In and Out points on your source footage, you have identified a specific clip. The Capture Clip option will capture just the marked portion of your source material, along with any additional log information and markers.

1   Mark a new clip from your source footage, or use the clip you marked in previous exercise steps.

2   Enter or amend the logging information.

3   In the Capture area of the Logging tab, click the Capture Clip button.

If the Prompt check box in the Name area was checked, the Log Clip dialog appears.

If you do not want to be prompted about your log information each time you click the Capture Clip button, deselect the Prompt check box in the Logging tab.

TIP ▸ If you do not want to be prompted about your log information each time you click the Capture Clip button, deselect the Prompt check box in the Logging tab.

4   If necessary, make changes to the clip log information, then click OK.

When capturing begins, a window appears that displays the material you are capturing. Don't worry if the image seems jagged at this point. The display during capturing does not reflect the quality of the captured image.

NOTE ▸ If you want to stop the capture process at any time, press the Esc (Escape) key.

Capturing Now

A second way to capture is to use the Capture Now option. You can still enter log information, but you cannot enter timecode In and Out points or markers. You can use this option to capture any format, or to capture material shot in the HDV format. You also use this capture option when you do not have FireWire control over a source device, such as a nondigital camera, that must be played through a digital converter box.

1   Enter the next clip name and reel number in the Logging fields.

> **TIP** ▶ Make sure you name the clip before you start the Capture Now process. If you don't, Final Cut Pro will give the clip a default name, and changing that default could make it difficult to link back to the media file.

2   Cue the source tape about 10 seconds before the action begins in the footage you would like to capture.

3   Play the tape from that point.

4   Click the Capture Now button.

> **TIP** ▶ This is a less exact method than the Capture Clip option, so make sure you give yourself adequate pad before and after the action you want to capture.

5   Press the Esc (Escape) key when you want to stop capturing.

> **NOTE** ▶ If you are capturing HDV footage, the sync between the audio and video may appear to be off. This is only how it appears during the capture process. It will capture in sync.

6   To automatically limit the amount of time you can capture in one stretch, click the Capture Settings tab and then the Scratch Disks button.

On the bottom of this tab is an option to limit the Capture Now process to a specified amount of time. When active, the default amount of time for Limit Capture Now is 30 minutes. To activate this option, click the check box and enter an amount of capture time. Click OK.

NOTE ▶ When using Capture Now, you can easily capture long pieces of material without realizing how large a file you are creating. Remember that about 5 minutes of DV or HDV media will consume about 1 GB of hard-drive space.

Another helpful option when using the Capture Clip *or* the Capture Now approach is to apply DV Start/Stop Detect to the captured clip. This function will place a marker at whatever point the original recording stopped and started—for example, when you paused and unpaused the Record button on your camera. This allows you to capture a long clip and then make subclips of it after capturing.

7   To apply DV Start/Stop Detect, follow these steps:

▶   Capture the clip, and open it in the Viewer.

▶   Choose Mark > DV Start/Stop Detect.
Markers will appear on the clip wherever the original tape was stopped and started during recording.

▶   In the Browser, select a marker, and choose Modify > Make Subclip. A new subclip is created from the location of this marker to the next marker.

TIP ▶ Select all the markers associated with a clip and drag them into a new bin to automatically make subclips with durations from one marker to the next.

Batch Capturing and Log Clip

Batch Capture and Log Clip are used together to streamline the process of marking and capturing footage. Rather than mark one clip and capture it, then mark another and capture it, you can play the source tape, mark and log clip after clip, and then capture all the logged clips at one time.

The first step is to log each individual clip, complete with reel names and descriptive notes. These clips are placed in the log bin just as any other clip would be, except they have a red diagonal line over them to indicate that they are offline media. This means the clip information is there, but not the media content, because the media has not yet been captured. When you have completed logging all the clips you want to capture, you can then capture them all at once using Batch Capture. Using all of your logged information, Batch Capture seeks out each clip on the specified reel and creates the respective QuickTime media file necessary for editing.

1   Mark a new section of footage, and enter the information in the Logging tab as you did before, but do not click a Capture button.

2   Click the Log Clip button, or press the keyboard shortcut, F2.

If the Prompt box was checked in the logging area, the Log Clip dialog will open, reminding you of your logging information. Click OK.

Name	Duration	In
Sequence 1	00:00:00;00	Not Set
Test Capture		
racing winners	00:00:07;23	Not Set

A new clip appears—with a red line through it—in the Browser.

3   Mark another portion of footage, and log the clip information in the Logging tab.

4   Click the Log Clip button again, or press F2.

Continuing this process will create a cumulative list of each clip you log. Each entry will appear with a red line through it in the Browser, indicating that the QuickTime file for that clip has not yet been captured.

5   To change the track selection of a logged clip before capturing it, select the clip in the Browser and choose Modify > Clip Settings. Make the changes, and click OK.

Using the Modify Clip Settings dialog is an easy way to change the settings of one or more clips before you capture. For example, if you logged a clip or group of clips as audio and video, but now realize you want to capture them as video-only clips, you can uncheck the Audio box to make the change. Or, you could toggle from mono channels to a stereo pair.

Modify Clip Settings
Modify Tracks of Type: Audio and Video
Number of selected offline files: 4
☑ Video
☐ Audio
Input Channels 2   ☐ Preview
Master Gain ⟨ ——————⟩ [1]

TIP ▶ You can also select a group of offline clips, choose Modify > Clip Settings, and make changes to the selected group at one time.

6   In the logging bin, select the logged clips you want to capture. You can select any or all of them.

NOTE ▶ If you placed all of your clips in a separate bin window, you can select them all by pressing Cmd-A, or by choosing Edit > Select All.

7   Click the Capture Batch button in the Log And Capture window.

A Batch Capture settings window opens. This is where you choose which logged clips you want to capture and how.

There are four options in the Batch Capture settings window:

▶   Capture—Click the pop-up menu to choose which clips you want to capture (All Items In Logging Bin, Offline Items In Logging Bin, or Selected Items In Logging Bin).

▶   Options: Use Logged Clip Settings—Click this box to capture the clips with all the settings that were present when you originally logged the clip.

▶   Options: Add Handles—Click this box to add additional handles to the current logged clip.

NOTE ▶ If you added additional handle material when you first marked the clip, you would not add extra handles here. If you prefer to mark your clip action tight and then log the clip, you can use this option to automatically add extra handles (maybe 2 or 3 seconds) of material on the head and tail of the clip.

▶   Capture Preset—If you want to capture the selected clips using a different preset than the one they were logged with, choose it from this menu.

At the bottom of the Batch Capture window are calculations based on the capture settings you select.

8   Make the appropriate selections, and click OK.

The Insert Reel dialog appears, indicating that you are ready to capture.

9   Click Continue.

The tape cues and captures each clip into the logging bin, based on the Capture option you selected. You will see the material you are capturing in a capture screen.

When all clips on that reel have been captured, the Insert Reel dialog opens again.

Insert Reel

001 - 00:00:00:00 - 0 clips - DONE

Successfully captured.

[Show Details...]   [Cancel] [Finished]

10 If all of the clips have been captured, click Finished.

> **NOTE ▸** If your list contains footage from another reel or tape, Final Cut
> Pro will prompt you to change reels and continue.

When Batch Capture is completed, each of the selected clips in the logging
bin will have footage connected to them, and the red lines will be gone.

Setting Capture Preferences

The General tab of the User Preferences window contains options that relate to
capturing. Certain user preferences will affect how you capture your video.
Some of these preferences help you troubleshoot or work around difficult
video. Others smooth the capturing process. Take a look at these options so
you will know what each of the capture preferences does.

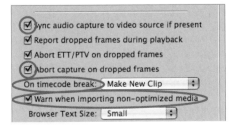

▸   Sync audio capture to video source if present—This option ensures sync
     for audio captured from a genlocked audio deck.

▶ Abort capture on dropped frames—If Final Cut Pro notices any frames of video being dropped or left out while capturing your source material, it will stop the capture process and report the dropped frames. You will lose all the media it had captured up to that point.

▶ On timecode break—If there is a break in the source-tape timecode, you have the option to make Final Cut Pro do one of three things: start a new clip at the timecode break, abort the capture process, or warn you that there was a timecode break after capturing is over.

▶ Warn when importing non-optimized media—Final Cut Pro will always optimize media files when capturing. On the rare occasion that it can't optimize a media file for multiple-stream, real-time playback, it will warn you if this option is checked. Unless you are editing with multiple uncompressed video streams that demand maximum media file performance, you can usually leave the files as they are and continue editing normally. If you are working with standard definition DV captured in Final Cut Pro, your files are already optimized.

TIP ▶ Try capturing using the default User Preference settings. If you have problems with dropped frames or timecode breaks, deselect one or more of the options and try again.

Lesson Review

1. Before you can capture footage, what is the first thing you must do?

2. Marking clips for capture is similar to marking clips while editing. True or false?

3. You can enter a variety of clip information in the Logging tab. Give an example of logging information that appears in the Browser columns.

4. When you choose your capture preset, what settings do you want it to match?

5. What are the three different capture modes you can use to capture footage?

6. What is a scratch disk?

7. How can you save time using the Batch Capture mode?

8. Where do you modify your logged clip settings?

9. You can choose only your computer hard drive as a scratch disk. True or false?

Answers

1. You must connect your source device via a FireWire cable or third-party capture card.

2. True.

3. Log note, good take, scene number, take number.

4. It must match your source footage.

5. Capture Clip, Capture Now, and Batch Capture.

6. The target destination for your captured media files.

7. With the Batch Capture mode, you can log individual clips and then capture them all together at the same time.

8. Modify logged clip settings in the Clip Settings window, which you access from the Modify menu.

9. False. You can set your computer hard drive or an external FireWire drive as your scratch disk, where the media files will be saved.

Keyboard Shortcuts

Spacebar	Plays and stops the tape
Shift-Q	Opens System Settings window
Option-Q	Opens User Preferences
Cmd-Option-Q	Opens Audio/Video Settings window
Cmd-8	Opens Log And Capture window
Ctrl-C	Batch Capture
Esc (Escape) key	Stops capture process
F2	Logs a clip in the Browser without capturing media

10

Lesson 10
Applying Transitions

Creating and refining a sequence is the core of the editing process. Once you've made decisions about edit selection and placement, you can start to focus on other aspects, such as adding transition effects to finesse the sequence. Transitions add variety to your video by changing how you get from one clip to the next. They can be used to fix an abrupt audio or video edit or to create a certain visual style when creating promos or show openings. In this lesson, you will explore different ways to apply a variety of transition effects to the video and audio clips in your sequence.

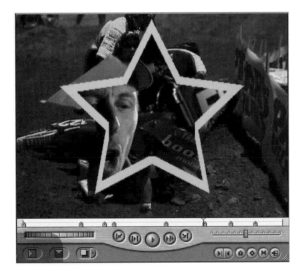

A Star Iris is one type of video transition that can be applied to an edit point between two clips.

Preparing the Project

To get started in Lesson 10, launch Final Cut Pro, and then open the project for this lesson.

1 Choose File > Open, or press Cmd-O, and select the **Lesson 10 Project** file from the Lessons folder on your hard drive.

2 Close any other open projects.

3 In the Timeline, play the open *Intro Cuts* sequence.

This is the *Intro* sequence you edited in Lesson 4. Each clip cuts from one to the next. For the finished *A Thousand Roads* movie, the editor added transitions between many of these shots.

4 Click the *Dissolves – Finished* sequence tab in the Timeline, and play this sequence.

This is the same sequence as the *Intro Cuts* sequence, but video dissolves have been applied to the edit points. Notice that the tracks have been customized so the V1 and A1 tracks you will use in these lessons are taller, and those tracks you won't use are smaller. You will add audio fades between some of the A1 clips later in this lesson.

5 To save a copy of the original *Intro Cuts* sequence to use throughout this lesson, duplicate it in the Browser, and rename it *Intro Cuts Backup*.

Understanding Transitions

A transition is an effect applied to the edit point between two clips in a sequence. Instead of cutting from one clip to the next and making an immediate change, a transition effect creates a gradual change over time from the outgoing clip to the incoming clip.

Several types of transitions can be applied in Final Cut Pro. One type of transition used frequently is a *cross dissolve*. A cross dissolve is a video transition that gradually mixes from the outgoing clip to the incoming clip at the edit point. As one clip fades out, the other clip fades in. This mixing process utilizes the *handles* of one or both clips that make up the transition. Handles are the additional source material that exists on the media file. In audio, this process is called a *cross fade*. The end of one audio clip fades out while the beginning of the next one fades in.

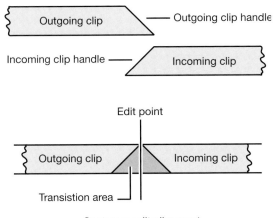

Center on edit alignment

Viewing Transition Options

In Final Cut Pro, you can choose a transition effect from one of two places: the Effects menu or the Effects tab in the Browser. Each contains the same set of transition effects organized in separate Video and Audio Transition bins.

1   In the Browser, select the Effects tab. If this tab is in icon view, Ctrl-click in the gray area and choose View As List from the shortcut menu.

The Effects tab has six bins. Three bins contain video effects, two contain audio effects, and one can be used to store your favorite effects. In this lesson, you will use just the Video Transitions and Audio Transitions bins.

2   Display the contents of the Audio Transitions bin.

▼ 🔒 Audio Transitions	Bin	
🔲 Cross Fade (0dB)	Audio Transition	00:00:01;00
🔲 Cross Fade (+3dB)	Audio Transition	00:00:01;00

This folder contains two audio cross fades: 0dB and +3dB. The +3dB cross fade is underlined, meaning it is the default transition.

3   Click the triangle next to the Audio Transitions bin to hide its contents. Then display the contents of the Video Transitions bin.

▼ 🔒 Video Transitions	Bin
▶ 🔒 3D Simulation	Bin
▶ 🔒 Dissolve	Bin
▶ 🔒 Iris	Bin
▶ 🔒 Map	Bin
▶ 🔒 Page Peel	Bin
▶ 🔒 QuickTime	Bin
▶ 🔒 Slide	Bin
▶ 🔒 Stretch	Bin
▶ 🔒 Wipe	Bin

There are nine bins of video transitions, each with its own set of transition styles and parameters.

4   Click the triangle next to the Dissolve bin to display its contents.

Name	Type	Length
▶ 📁 Favorites	Bin	
▼ 🔒 Video Transitions	Bin	
▶ 🔒 3D Simulation	Bin	
▼ 🔒 Dissolve	Bin	
🔲 Additive Dissolve	Video Transition	00:00:01;00
🔲 Cross Dissolve	Video Transition	00:00:01;00
🔲 Dip to Color Dissolve	Video Transition	00:00:01;00
🔲 Dither Dissolve	Video Transition	00:00:01;00
🔲 Fade In Fade Out Dissolve	Video Transition	00:00:01;00
🔲 Non–Additive Dissolve	Video Transition	00:00:01;00
🔲 Ripple Dissolve	Video Transition	00:00:01;00

Different dissolve transitions appear here, including the underlined Cross Dissolve, which is the default video transition. The 00:00:01;00 listed under the Length column indicates that the Cross Dissolve has a default duration of 1 second. All audio and video transitions have a default 1-second duration. Notice too that most of the Dissolve transitions are in boldface type, which means they can be played in real time (RT), or normal play speed, after you apply them.

5   Choose the Effects menu.

Five of the Effects bin titles appear here, including Favorites, Video Transitions and Filters, and Audio Transitions and Filters.

6   From the Effects menu, choose Video Transitions > Dissolve.

The same dissolve options appear here, although currently dimmed, that appear on the Effects tab in the Browser.

Applying Video Transitions

Video transitions can smooth the flow of a sequence or ramp it up if you're creating stylized effects for a television ad or promotional sequence. All video transitions are applied the same way, but more complex transitions have parameters you can adjust. You will learn to apply video transitions using the popular cross dissolve to the *Intro Cuts* sequence. Later in this lesson, you will apply these same steps to add other types of video transitions.

Applying a Cross Dissolve Transition

Some cross dissolves will simply mix from one image to another, but others of longer duration will create an interesting effect, almost as if the two images were superimposed on top of each other.

> **TIP** ▶ Throughout this lesson, zoom into the Timeline so you can identify clips and transitions more easily. Option-+ zooms into the playhead location, and Shift-Z returns the sequence to full view. When you zoom into the Timeline, you can use the Hand tool (H) to drag the sequence left or right.

1   In the *Intro Cuts* sequence in the Timeline, play the edit point between the **ruin steps** clip and the **canyon runner** clip. Then click the video edit point once to select it.

> **NOTE** ▶ You can also press the up or down arrows to move the playhead directly to an edit point as a way of identifying the transition target.

In this sequence, the V1 clips are not linked to the A1 audio clips, so only the video edit point is selected.

2   Choose Effects > Video Transitions > Dissolves > Cross Dissolve. Play the
new dissolve transition.

The **ruin steps** clip fades out as the **canyon runner** clip fades in. Since the
default length for all transitions is 1 second, this is a 1-second dissolve
centered over the edit point. Handles for each clip extend out 15 frames
to the other side of the edit point.

3   Move the playhead to the edit point, and press Option-+ (plus) a few
times until you can see the entire name of the transition.

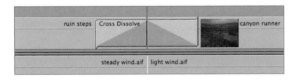

The transition name appears on the icon between the two clips. The dark
upward and downward shading represents the handle portion of each clip
fading in and out.

4   To apply a cross dissolve from the Effects tab, make sure you can see the
next edit point between the **canyon runner** and the **amanda rushing** clips.
From the Dissolve bin in the Effects tab, drag the Cross Dissolve icon to
this edit point, and release it. Play this transition.

NOTE ▸ This method of applying a transition does not require that you
select the edit point or position the playhead over it.

The cross dissolve is the default video transition. You can apply the default transition using a menu option or a keyboard shortcut. Each method requires that you select the edit point *or* park the playhead directly on the edit point to identify it.

5   Select the next edit point in the sequence between the **amanda rushing** and **johnny runs** clips. Press Cmd-T to add the default video transition.

> **TIP** ▶ There is a simple rule of thumb to remember when adding transitions. When using the Effects menu or keyboard shortcut, you *select and choose*, meaning you identify the transition target first before choosing the menu option. When using the Effects tab, you *drag and drop* the transition directly to the edit point in the Timeline.

6   Press Home to move the playhead to the head of the sequence, and choose Effects > Default – Cross Dissolve to add a fade up to the **sunrise** clip.

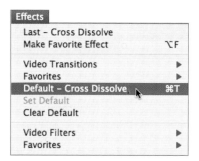

When a clip is at the beginning of the sequence, adding a transition will fade up from black into the clip. You can also use this approach to fade out a clip at the end of a sequence.

7   Press the down arrow twice to move the playhead to the next *video* edit point, and press Cmd-T to add the default cross dissolve. Add the default video transition to the next five video edit points, up to the **canyon runner** transition you applied earlier.

8   Play the last edit point in the sequence between the **ice fishers** and **healer cu** clips. Zoom into this area. Press S to select the Slip tool, and click and hold the **healer cu** clip. Do not drag it left or right.

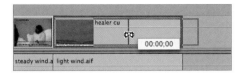

TIP ▶ A good trick for finding out how long your media handles are in a sequence clip is to click the clip with the Slip tool. You will see the handles extend on either side of the clip as part of the brown, hollow clip outline.

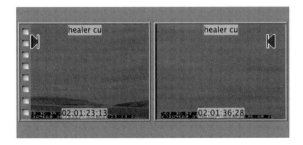

In the Canvas, you see the end-of-clip overlay in the left frame, indicating it's the first frame of the clip. This means there is no media at the head of the clip to mix with the outgoing clip before the edit point. In this situation, you can start the transition to begin at the edit point, instead of centering on the edit point. This extends the outgoing clip past the edit point the full length of the transition.

9   Press A to return to the default Selection tool. From the Effects tab, drag the Cross Dissolve icon to the right side of the edit point between the **ice fishers** and **healer cu** clips, but don't release the mouse.

When the Cross Dissolve icon is aligned on the right side of the edit point, you see the full length of the dissolve.

NOTE ▶ If you try to center the dissolve on this edit point, or apply one from the Effects menu, you will end up with a one-frame transition.

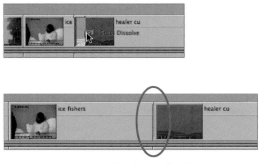

One frame dissolve

10 Release the transition on the right side of the edit point, and play the transition.

This is a Start On Edit type of transition, which is one of three transition alignments you can choose, along with End On Edit and Center On Edit. The transitions you've placed up to this point have all centered on the edit point. The End On Edit alignment is used when an outgoing clip has no extra media to extend past the edit point.

TIP ▶ You can apply the Ripple, Roll, Slip, and Slide tools to an edit point that has a transition. You can also edit a new clip to the Timeline and add a default transition at the same time. To do this, drag the source clip from the Viewer to the Canvas, and drop it in the Overwrite With Transition section in the Edit Overlay.

Changing and Copying Transitions

Once you have reviewed a transition, you might decide you want to change the duration or perhaps use the same transition on another edit point. You can change the duration of a transition several ways, including the drag-and-drop approach. With this method, you can drag the edge of the transition icon to change its duration or drag a transition to relocate it to another edit point. You can also copy and paste a transition.

1   Move the playhead to the cross dissolve between the **plowing fields** and **city street** clips. Press Option-+ (plus) to zoom into this area and then play this transition.

    Like all transitions, this cross dissolve has a default duration of 1 second. Extending the duration of this cross dissolve might create an interesting effect of the people walking in the field.

2   Move the pointer over either edge of the Cross Dissolve icon.

    The pointer changes to a resize arrow.

3   Drag the edge of this transition away from the edit point as far as possible, but don't release the mouse.

    A transition will only drag outward as far as there is clip material to support it. If you cannot drag any farther, either you have reached the limit of one or both of the clip's media, or you've reached the next edit point or transition in the Timeline. An information box indicates how much the transition has been lengthened and the new duration.

4   Release this cross dissolve at its longest possible duration, and play the transition.

Lengthening the duration of this cross dissolve gives the two clips a sense of being superimposed over each other.

> **TIP** ▶ When dragging a transition inward to reduce the duration, turning snapping off temporarily will give you greater control, as will zooming in to that area of the Timeline.

5 In the following edit point, between the **city street** and **ruin steps** clips, drag the edge of the cross dissolve icon out to 4:16. Play this transition.

With a longer dissolve duration, the city street walkers seem to be walking on the ruin steps.

> **NOTE** ▶ As you drag the transition icon, both sides of the hollow duration icon change by the same amount. If you begin with an even number, it will incrementally change by an even number as you drag, adding one frame to each side of the transition.

6 To change the duration of the next cross dissolve in the sequence, between the **ruin steps** and **canyon runner** clips, Ctrl-click one side of the Cross Dissolve icon, not on the actual edit point directly between the two clips.

A shortcut menu appears with options to adjust the transition. Here you can also choose a different transition alignment.

TIP ▶ Always click to the side of the actual edit point to select the transition icon. If you click in the middle, the edit point itself will be selected, and a different shortcut menu will appear.

7   Choose Duration from the shortcut menu.

A small Duration window appears with the length of the current transition in the Duration field. This duration is already highlighted, so you can begin typing a new duration without first clicking in the box.

8   In the Duration field, enter *20* for a new 20-frame duration. Press Return to enter the number, then press Return again, or click OK, to close the window. Play the new transition.

This 20-frame transition would work well applied to edit points later in the sequence. Once you've created a transition with a duration you like, you can copy and paste it to other edit points.

NOTE ▶ You can also enter the total number of frames. For example, if your tape source frame rate was 30 frames per second, you can enter 60 to represent 2 seconds. If you are editing in PAL, you would enter 50 frames for 2 seconds.

9   Click once on the Cross Dissolve icon between the **ruin steps** and **canyon runner** clips to select the transition. Press Cmd-C to copy it. You can also Ctrl-click the transition and choose Copy from the shortcut menu.

10   Press the down arrow three times to move the playhead to the empty edit point between the **johnny runs** and **truck on road** clips. With the playhead on the edit point, press Cmd-V to paste the 20-frame cross dissolve transition on this edit point. You can also Ctrl-click the edit point itself and choose Paste from the shortcut menu.

> **TIP** ▸ You can move a transition by dragging it from one edit point to another. You can also use the Option-drag approach to drag a copy of a transition from one edit point and drop the copy onto another edit point.

11   To delete the transition between the **johnny runs** and **truck on road** clips, select the transition icon, and press Delete.

You can always press Cmd-Z to undo the delete step and return the transition. Without a transition applied, the edit point is returned to a simple cut.

NOTE ▸ You can Cmd-click to select several transitions and delete them all at one time.

Project Practice

Continue to add cross dissolves in this sequence where none exist, or change the duration or alignment of existing transitions. When you're finished, press Cmd-S to save the changes to your project.

TIP ► Any transition can be the default transition. To change the default, Ctrl-click a different transition in the Effects tab and choose Set Default Transition from the shortcut menu. You can then use Cmd-T to apply it.

Applying Audio Transitions

In editing, the emphasis is often placed on the video portion of a sequence. However, if the audio clips in your sequence are jarring as they cut from one to the next, viewers will notice it immediately. Audio transitions are applied to the edit point between two adjacent clips, just as video transitions are. If an audio clip has two tracks that are a stereo pair, applying a cross fade to one track will automatically apply it to the adjoining stereo track. In this exercise, you will convert mono tracks to stereo tracks before adding audio transitions.

1 In the Browser, double-click the *Audio Cuts* sequence to open it in the Timeline and play the sequence.

   NOTE ► This sequence captures some behind-the-scenes moments of a director and his camera crew as they work out how to shoot a motocross race. You will work with the real motocross racing footage later in this lesson.

   The video clips in this sequence will remain unchanged as cuts. However, in order to smooth some of the abrupt audio cuts, you will add cross fades to some of the edit points.

2 Play the edit point between the second **gib arm & director** clip and the **two jump over** clip. Then position the playhead at the edit point.

Because you are cutting from one volume level and type of audio to another, this edit point sounds jarring and abrupt.

3   Choose Effects > Audio Transitions > Cross Fade (+3dB).

A 0 dB cross fade has a slight dip in the audio level at the midpoint of the transition. The +3 dB cross fade is designed to produce a fade without having this dip in the middle, which is why it is the default cross fade.

NOTE ▸ When working with your own sequences, experiment with both cross-fade options to make sure you're getting the best possible sound.

Since the A1 and A2 clips were captured as mono tracks, the Cross Fade transition icon appears over the edit point of just the A1 track. You can easily convert these mono tracks to stereo pairs and save many steps as you apply audio cross fades to these clips.

4   Press Cmd-Z to undo the previous step.

5   To convert all the audio tracks to stereo pairs at one time, select all the audio clips in the sequence, and choose Modify > Stereo Pair, or press Option-L. Deselect the clips.

Now the audio tracks of each clip have the stereo pair icon connecting them together.

6   Make sure the playhead is over the same edit point, and choose Effects > Audio Transitions > Cross Fade (+3dB). You can also choose Effects > Default – Cross Fade (+3d). Play this audio transition.

The cross fade has been applied to both audio tracks at the same time, and the abrupt cut has been smoothed considerably.

7   Press Option-+ to zoom in to that area of the sequence, and move the playhead away from the edit point.

All video and audio transition icons look alike except for the transition name that appears on it.

8   To apply a cross fade from the Effects tab, make sure you can see the next edit point between the **two jump over** and the **gib arm & director** clip that follows. From the Effects tab, drag the Cross Fade (+3dB) icon to the edit point and release it. Play this transition.

9   To use the shortcut to apply the default audio transition, move the playhead to the next edit point between the **gib arm & director** and **two bikers** clips. Press Option-Cmd-T.

> **NOTE ▶** You can change the duration of an audio transition or copy and paste it just as you did with video transitions.

Project Practice

To practice adding audio cross fades, click the *Intro Cuts* sequence tab in the Timeline. Toggle off the Audible controls for all but the A1 track to focus on just the sound effects. Add a cross fade wherever the sound transition is abrupt, and adjust the cross fade durations to match the length of the video dissolves above them.

> **TIP** ▶ You can also add buttons to add video or audio transitions to the Timeline button bar. Using buttons, like the menu and shortcut options, requires that you first target the edit point by positioning the playhead over it or by selecting it.

Using the Transition Editor

In addition to using shortcuts and menu options, you can also make changes to video transitions in the Transition Editor, which appears as a tab over the Viewer window. Most of the time, you will make changes to your cross dissolves using the methods covered earlier in this lesson. But if you apply more complex transitions to your edit points, as you will in the next exercise, the Transition Editor is the only place to make changes to those parameters.

1   In the current *Intro Cuts* sequence, Ctrl-click one side of the cross-dissolve icon between the **city street** and **ruin steps** clips, and choose Open 'Cross Dissolve' from the shortcut menu. You can also double-click one side of the icon.

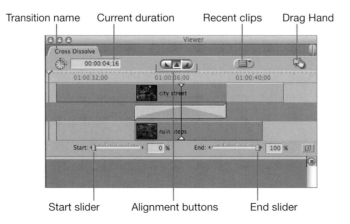

Transition name   Current duration   Recent clips   Drag Hand

Start slider   Alignment buttons   End slider

The Transition Editor opens in the Viewer with a graphic representation of the current transition. You have already adjusted or selected some of the options that appear here, such as duration and alignment, but the Transition Editor offers a few more options.

2   To use the current cross dissolve on another edit point, drag the Drag Hand icon in the upper-right corner of the window to the edit point between the **canyon runner** and **amanda rushing** clips.

Dragging the transition from the Transition Editor to this edit point replaces whatever transition was there previously with all the current transition parameters displayed in the Transition Editor.

3   In the Transition Editor, click the End On Edit alignment button (on the right) and then the Center On Edit alignment button (in the center).

The graphic representation of the dissolve in the Transition Editor changes, as does the transition on the edit point in the Timeline.

NOTE ▶ Clicking the Start On Edit alignment button opens a dialog indicating there isn't enough material to align the current transition in that way. Click Cancel.

4   In the Transition Editor, move the pointer over the transition icon.

The pointer turns into the Roll tool, allowing you to adjust or roll the edit point left or right to improve the timing of the edit without changing the transition. Notice the light blue area on the outer edge of each clip. This represents the clip's handles.

5   Drag the transition icon left about two seconds, where the camera is static in the right frame of the Canvas two-up display. Release the mouse, and play the transition.

In the Timeline, the edit point and transition appear earlier in the sequence.

6   Beneath the transition graphic in the Transition Editor, enter *50* in the Start field, and press Tab. In the End field, enter *50*, and press Tab again. Drag the playhead through the transition in the Timeline.

Most transitions create a mix between clips from 0% to 100%. With the Start and End each at 50%, the mix between the clips is not transitional, but fixed, creating a static blend of the two images at the edit point.

7   From the Effects tab in the Browser, drag the Dip To Color Dissolve onto the current edit point, between the **city street** and **ruin steps** clip. Play the transition.

In the Timeline, the new transition replaces the previous one but maintains the previous transition's duration. The outgoing clip dips to black as it transitions to the incoming clip.

In the Transition Editor, since this effect involves color, additional color parameters appear with sliders and entry fields you can change.

8   Click the black color tile on the Color parameter line. In the Colors window, if a color wheel appears, and it's black, drag the control on the vertical slider all the way up to see the brightest colors.

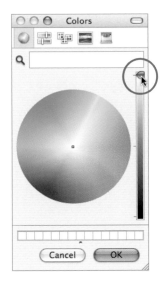

At the top of the Colors window are icons representing five color-picking layouts: Color Wheel, Color Sliders, Color Palettes, Image Palettes, and Crayons.

9 Click each icon to see how that option displays color choices. Then click the Crayons option. Click the lower-right crayon named Snow, and click OK.

The color tile changes to reflect your most recent selection.

10 Play the transition with the color change. To shorten this transition, click in the Transition Editor Duration field, enter *20*, and press Return. Play the transition again.

A shortened version of the Dip To Color Dissolve is often used between still images along with a camera-clicking sound effect. Anytime you create a transition effect you particularly like and may want to use again, you can save it as a favorite.

11 Before you save this transition, make sure you can see the Favorites bin in the Effects tab in the Browser. Click the disclosure triangle next to the Favorites bin to display its contents.

Unless you have added your own favorite effects to this bin, it will be empty.

12 Click the Viewer window, and choose Effects > Make Favorite, or press Option-F.

> **NOTE ▸** You can also drag the Drag Hand icon to the Favorites bin and release the mouse when the bin becomes highlighted.

In the Favorites folder, a new Dip To Color Dissolve with all of your changes appears. Notice in the Length column that the duration is 20 frames, not the default 1:00.

13 Click in the name field for this transition, and rename it *dip to white*.

> **TIP ▸** Although all transitions have a default 1-second duration, you can change the default duration for any transition by clicking in the Length column in the Effects tab and entering a new duration .

Changing Transition Parameters

Cross dissolves can have a smoothing effect on a sequence, but other transitions can jazz it up. The more complex a transition is, the more parameters you can adjust in the Transition Editor. Most of these transition effects can be played in real time; some may have to be *rendered*, which you will learn to do in the next exercise.

TIP To make sure you see as many real-time effects as possible, click the RT pop-up in the Timeline and choose Unlimited RT from the shortcut menu. Click the RT pop-up again, and make sure Dynamic is checked in both places it appears. You will learn more about these options in the next exercise.

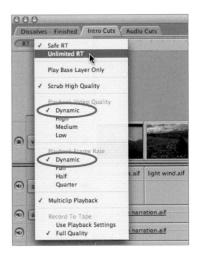

1 Close all the sequences that are open in the Timeline. In the Browser, open both the *Racing – Cuts* and the *Racing – Transitions* sequences. Click between the two tabs, and play the *Racing – Transitions* version.

NOTE ▶ Depending on your computer, you may see some of the transitions *stutter* a bit as they play in the sequence. You can render these in the next exercise.

This sequence uses an assortment of transitions to create a fast-paced, promo-style piece that may be used to advertise a documentary series on motocross racing. There is a marker in the ruler area above each transition labeling its type, with the bin location in parentheses.

TIP If you want to preserve the *Racing – Cuts* sequence to experiment with other transitions on your own, make a backup copy of it before you begin these steps.

2   Click the *Racing – Cuts* sequence tab, make sure the playhead is at the head of the sequence.

3   Choose Effects > Video Transitions > Wipe > Checkerboard Wipe. Play this transition.

Each new square reveals another portion of the incoming image. You can preview other wipe transitions on this edit point by choosing a different transition from the Effects > Video Transitions options, or by dragging it from the Effects bin to the edit point. A new transition will replace whatever transition was there before it.

4   Move the playhead to the marker labeled *star (iris)*. Choose Effects > Video Transitions > Iris > Star Iris. Play the transition. Then move the playhead back to the center of the edit point.

This iris transition has a number of parameters that can be modified in the Transition Editor.

> **TIP** ▶ Parking the playhead on the transition allows you to see the adjustments in the Canvas as you make them. Make sure you do this in the following steps before you make changes.

5   Double-click the Star Iris transition in the Timeline to open it in the Transition Editor.

Under the transition graphic display, there are additional parameters that can be controlled or adjusted using a slider or numerical-entry box. Some parameters in other effects use pop-up menus. Most parameters are self-explanatory after you've changed the parameter values and looked at the effect in the Canvas.

NOTE ▸ Clicking the tiny triangle at the end of each slider will change the numerical value of that parameter by single increments.

6   Experiment with the different settings for this transition as you view the results in the Canvas window. When you are through making changes, click the red X reset button to return to the default settings for this effect.

You can add borders to many transitions, including the iris and wipe effects, and choose a color from the color tile as you did in a previous exercise. But you can also pick a color from an image for the border color.

7   In the Border field, enter 6 to create a thin border. To select a border color from the images involved in this transition, drag the playhead earlier in the transition to see the effect *and* the yellow-gold flag. Click the Select Color eyedropper in the Color parameters, and click once in a bright yellow area of the flag.

TIP To search or preview different border colors before selecting one, select the eyedropper, and click and drag around the Canvas image area without releasing the mouse. The border and color tile will reflect whatever color the eyedropper picks up. When you see the color you want, release the mouse.

The color tile in the Color parameters has changed to the color you picked. Once you've selected a color, you can adjust it and save it to use for other borders in other effects.

8   To make adjustments to this color, click the triangle next to the Select Color eyedropper. Drag the S (Saturation) and B (Brightness) sliders to

create a rich gold color. Don't drag the H (Hue) slider, or you will change the original color you picked from the flag.

9   To save this color to use on other transitions, click the color tile. Drag the yellow color from the top horizontal color bar (with the magnifying glass on the left) down to any color tile at the bottom of the window and release it. Click OK.

Many television shows use a favorite color repeatedly for borders, text, backgrounds, and so on, as part of the show style. This is how you save a favorite color.

NOTE ▶ This is the OS X Colors window, so the saved color swatch will be available for use on other projects or applications on the same computer.

10 Adjust the playhead so you can see the motorbike behind the man speaking. To reposition the center of the star iris, click the Center button in the Center parameter line. Move the pointer into the Canvas image area and,

with the crosshair icon that appears, click somewhere over the numbers on the bike. Play the transition.

Now the origin or position of the star is centered over the bike. Try it again centered over the man's face.

11 In the Timeline, move the playhead to the marker labeled *cross zoom (3D simulation)*. From the 3D Simulation bin in the Effects tab, drag the Cross Zoom transition to this edit point, and play the transition.

In the Timeline ruler area, a colored line appears above the effect. This is discussed in the next exercise.

Previewing and Rendering Effects

You can view many effects, even multiple streams or layers of effects, in real time in Final Cut Pro. How FCP plays back these effects depends on your computer hardware and video format, as well as some options you can choose. You sometimes have to give up either image quality or a consistent frame rate to see all the effects play together. Or you may have to preview or *render* the transition. Rendering is a process that takes just the transition between two clips and makes a separate clip out of it. That clip is stored in the Render Files folder on the designated scratch disk and played back in the sequence as a separate but invisible clip—meaning that it does not appear in the Browser or the Timeline.

There are settings that guide Final Cut Pro on how to play effects in each sequence, and an area in the Timeline that displays a color for each effect, indicating whether or not it needs to be rendered.

1   In the current sequence, in the upper left of the Timeline under the sequence tabs, click the RT pop-up, but don't release the mouse.

You have been working in Unlimited RT. This setting tells Final Cut Pro to do what it has to do to play as many effects as possible in real time, even if it has to drop out some of the effect parameters or not play every frame. The other option is Safe RT. This option tells Final Cut Pro to play an effect only if it can do so without dropping frames.

2   Look at the ruler area in the Timeline for any yellow or orange bars. Choose Safe RT from the RT pop-up menu, and release the mouse. Now look at the Cross Zoom transition you applied in the previous exercise.

3   Click the RT pop-up again and look at the quality settings under Playback Video Quality and Playback Frame Rate.

The lower the quality and frame rate, the more effects Final Cut Pro will be able to play in real time. Choosing Dynamic will ensure that at any given moment you will have the best quality possible at the best frame rate possible while also maximizing the number of effects that will play in real time.

The more complex the effects, the lower the quality will be, so your computer will still be able to play it in real time. When there are fewer demands on your computer, Final Cut Pro will use a higher video quality and frame rate.

4   In the current sequence, zoom in to the Timeline where the cross zoom is located. You can use the markers as a reference.

The colored line above the transition is a render bar. The render bar actually contains two thin regions. The upper region represents video, the lower region audio. A render bar can appear in the ruler area above a transition, or above the body of a clip when a *filter* type effect has been applied.

NOTE ▶ You will see render lines above the bodies of some clips in this sequence because their colors were adjusted using a filter effect. You will learn to do this in a later lesson.

Different colored lines can appear in the render bar, indicating the status or capability of Final Cut Pro to play this effect in real time given the current RT settings. The render status of an effect will depend on the speed of the computer you are using. The status of an effect may be one of the following:

▶   Red   Needs to be rendered to play in real time.

▶   Orange   Exceeds computer's real-time playback capabilities but can still play if Unlimited RT is selected, although it may drop frames.

▶   Yellow   Transition can play in real time but may approximate certain attributes.

▶   Green   Will play in real-time but not at full quality.

> ▶ Dark green Capable of real-time playback and output with no rendering required.

> ▶ Steel gray   Material has been rendered.

> ▶ Dark gray   No rendering is required.

5 Move the playhead to before the cross zoom transition and play it.

The outgoing clip plays at normal play speed until it gets to the transition, when *Unrendered* appears in the Canvas image area for the duration of the transition. With the Safe RT option, Final Cut Pro doesn't even try to play this effect in real time. Yet there is a way to preview this effect.

6 Drag the playhead back before the transition once again. This time, press Option-P. You can also press Option-\ (backslash) or choose Mark > Play > Every Frame.

The clip plays at normal play speed until the playhead reaches the transition. At that point, the play speed slows down to process the transition, then picks up again when it has passed the transition area. When Final Cut Pro can't play all the effects, even set to the Unlimited RT option, previewing is a good way to get a sense of the effect without rendering it.

TIP ▶ If you use Option-P a lot, you might consider adding that function, Play Every Frame, to the Timeline or Canvas button bars.

7   This time drag the playhead manually through the transition area to see unrendered transition frames. Use the left and right arrow keys to move through it frame by frame.

This is somewhat like scrubbing an effect. But to see this effect play in real time at Safe RT, you must render it.

8   In the Timeline, click the Cross Zoom transition once.

9   To render it, choose Sequence > Render Selection, but don't release the mouse.

Sequence		
Render Selection ▶	Both	⌘R
Render All ▶	Video	
Render Only ▶	✓ — Needs Render	
Settings... ⌘0	— Rendered Proxy	
	Proxy	
Lift ⌫	— Preview	
Ripple Delete ⇧⌫	— Full	
Close Gap ⌃G	— Unlimited	
Solo Selected Item(s) ⌃S	Audio	⌃⌥R
Nest Item(s)... ⌥C	✓ — For Playback	
Add Edit ⌃V	— Item Level	
Extend Edit e		
Add Video Transition ⌘T		
Add Audio Transition ⌥⌘T		
Transition Alignment ▶		
Trim Edit ⌘7		
Insert Tracks...		
Delete Tracks...		

In the Render Selection submenu, the different render status colors appear. If the render color in the Timeline effect is not checked in this menu, your effect will not be rendered.

10   Make sure the red render bar is checked, or whatever color appears in your Timeline, and choose Sequence > Render Selection > Video, or press Cmd-R.

Writing Video...

39%   (Cancel)

A window appears with a render progress bar. When rendering is complete, a blue render status line appears above the transition, indicating it has been rendered.

NOTE ▶ If a transition has already been rendered, changing its duration or any other aspect will require it to be rendered again.

11 In the Timeline, click the RT pop-up and choose Unlimited RT.

This is the best option to choose when trying out different effects.

NOTE ▶ To view or change the scratch disk designation where render files are saved, press Shift-Q to open the System Preferences window.

Project Practice

To continue applying transitions and changing their parameters, use the markers in the ruler area of this sequence as a reference for what transition to apply at each location. You can also apply the yellow color you saved in the Colors window to the last transition in the sequence. Or you can be creative and add any transition you choose to any edit point. Don't forget to save your favorites!

Lesson Review

1. From what two places can you choose a transition effect?

2. In which option do you need to target the edit point by selecting it or positioning the playhead over it?

3. What are three ways to change the duration of a transition in the Timeline?

4. What are the three ways a transition can be aligned to an edit point?

5. How can Cmd-C and Cmd-V be used on transitions?

6. How do you open the Transition Editor?

7. How are wipes and iris transitions different from dissolves?

8. What RT setting should you choose when you want to preview as many effects in your sequence as possible?

9. In what three ways can you save a favorite transition?

10. How do you set a new default transition?

Answers

1. Choose transition effects from the Effects tab in the Browser and the Effects menu.

2. Before applying a transition from the Effects menu, you must target the edit point.

3. Drag the edge of the transition icon; Ctrl-click the transition icon, choose Duration from the shortcut menu, and enter an amount in the Duration window; and open the Transition Editor, and change it in the Duration field.

4. Use Center On Edit, Start On Edit, and End On Edit.

5. Selecting a transition and pressing Cmd-C copies the transition. Moving the playhead to the target edit point and pressing Cmd-V pastes the copied transition.

6. Either Ctrl-click one side of the transition icon and choose Open *type of transition* from the shortcut menu, or double-click one side of the icon in a sequence clip.

7. These types of transitions have additional parameters, such as border width and color, that can be adjusted in the Transition Editor.

8. Choose Unlimited RT and Dynamic.

9. From the Transition Editor, drag the Drag Hand icon to the Effects tab and release it in the Favorites bin; choose Effects > Make Favorite; or press Option-F.

10. Ctrl-click the transition in the Effects tab and choose Set Default Transition from the shortcut menu.

Keyboard Shortcuts

Cmd-T	Applies default video transition
Cmd-C	Copies a selected transition
Cmd-V	Pastes a copied transition
Option-Cmd-T	Applies default audio transition
H	Selects the Hand tool
Option-P	Previews a transition (Play Every Frame command)
Cmd-R	Renders a selected transition
Option-R	Renders all transitions in the Timeline
Shift-Q	Opens System Settings window
Option-F	Saves a favorite transition

11

Lesson Files	Lesson 11 Project
Media	A Thousand Roads > Canoe Club folder
	Motocross > Racing Footage and Team Story folders
Time	This lesson takes approximately 90 minutes to complete.
Goals	Organize and preview audio tracks
	Adjust audio levels in the Timeline
	Use waveforms for audio editing
	Add edits to create audio fades
	Create audio fades using keyframes
	Use the Audio Mixing tool
	Record a voice-over
	Import CD tracks

Mixing Audio Tracks

Organizing and mixing tracks creates a unified, cohesive-looking and sounding sequence. Although mixing audio tracks together is often the last step in the editing process, there are many times when you need to make important audio adjustments *as* you're editing. You can work with up to 99 tracks of audio in one sequence, giving you the opportunity to preview numerous music options or other audio tracks before making your final clip selection. There are also additional Timeline controls to help manage or change audio clips, as well as two separate tools for mixing audio and recording your own voice-over.

Audio controls and waveform displays in the Timeline

Preparing the Project

To get started in Lesson 11, you will launch Final Cut Pro and open the project for this lesson.

1   Launch Final Cut Pro and choose File > Open, or press Cmd-O. Select the **Lesson 11 Project** file from the Lessons folder on your hard drive.

2   In the Timeline, click between the *Canoe Club – Mono* and *Canoe Club – Finished* sequence tabs. Play the *Canoe Club – Finished* sequence.

The volume levels in the *Canoe Club – Finished* sequence have been adjusted and mixed together. In the *Canoe Club – Mono* sequence, the audio clips are at their original sound levels, and the narration clips are mono. In this lesson, you will convert the mono clips into stereo pairs and adjust the volume of the music and sound effects tracks to create a good mix with the narration.

3   Click the *Team Story* sequence tab, and play the sequence.

This sequence combines reflections from the Yamaha of Troy Motocross Racing Team. To add to the dramatic effect, the speed was changed on the first three clips. You will learn to change clip speed in the next lesson. In this lesson, you will add music and sound effects to this sequence, learn to isolate and preview tracks, and then mix the audio tracks together.

NOTE ▶ In the Timeline, most of the clips contain the team members' initials. They are: PA - Phil Alderton, DS - Danny Smith, BS - Brock Sellard, and MB - Mike Brown.

4   Close the *Canoe Club – Finished* sequence, and click the *Canoe Club – Mono* sequence tab so it is active for the next exercise. In the Sequences bin in the Browser, change the name of the *Canoe Club – Mono* sequence to *Canoe Club Mix*.

When you change the name of an open sequence, the new name appears on the sequence tab in the Timeline.

Organizing and Previewing Audio Tracks

The most important aspect of organizing audio tracks is to place similar types of clips on the same or neighboring tracks. For example, you might place all your dialogue on A1 and A2, and use A3 and A4 for sound effects. If you use two music sources, you can position them on neighboring tracks for easy access.

In this exercise, you will prepare two sequences for an audio mix by converting mono clips to stereo to enrich the primary track, add multiple tracks at one time, and preview tracks in different ways.

1   To add a new audio track between the A3 and A4 tracks, Ctrl-click the Timeline A3 track control area and choose Add Track. Don't click directly on the A3 destination control or you will get a different shortcut menu.

A new A4 track is added beneath the A3 track, and the bottom two tracks have been moved down in position, becoming A5 and A6.

2   To select all the clips on the A3 track, press T to select the Select Tracks Forward tool, the third tool in the Tool palette.

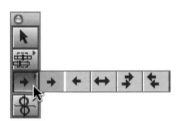

There are five track selection tools in the Tool palette. Each tool selects clips forward or backward from where you click on one or all tracks.

3 Click the first narration clip in the A3 track, **VO_01**.

4 To turn the mono tracks to stereo, press Cmd-C to copy these clips. To target where the pasted clips will be placed in the sequence, snap the playhead to the first frame of the **VO_01** narration clip, and Option-click the A4 Auto Select control. Press Cmd-V to paste the clips.

The copied clips are aligned beneath the original clips.

5 Press A to return to the default Selection tool and select the two **VO_01** clips. Choose Modify > Stereo Pair, or press Option-L. Repeat this for the remaining two sets of narration clips.

TIP If a clip was shot using two different microphones, and you want to strip away the weaker track, reverse this process. Make the tracks mono, and delete the bad track. Then copy and paste the good track, and group the two as a stereo pair.

6 Click the *Team Story* sequence tab. To add several audio tracks to this sequence at one time, choose Sequence > Insert Tracks.

The Insert Tracks window appears. Here you can choose to insert a specific number of new video or audio tracks.

TIP > You can access the Delete Tracks window by choosing Sequence > Delete Tracks. Here you can delete all unused video or audio tracks at the same time.

7 In the Insert Audio Tracks field, enter *4,* and make sure the After Last Track button is selected. Click OK.

In the Timeline, four new audio tracks are added after what was previously the last track.

8 From the Team Story Clips bin in the Browser, drag the **dramatic trumpet.aif** music clip to the A3 and A4 tracks in the Timeline, and release it at the head of the sequence as an Overwrite edit. Repeat the process for the **bike sfx.aif** clip on the A5 and A6 tracks.

With different types of audio now in the sequence, you may want to preview just the music with the video, without hearing the other tracks. There is a way to solo this track while muting the others, without toggling the Audible controls.

NOTE ▶ If you toggle off the Audible or Visible control for a track, you can lose your audio or video render files.

9   In the lower left of the Timeline, click the Audio Controls control, which is represented by a speaker icon.

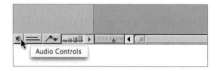

This expands the audio controls area of your Timeline window to reveal the Mute and Solo buttons. The Mute buttons are the speaker icons on the left, and the Solo buttons are the headphone icons on the right.

10 To hear how the music alone plays against the video, click the A3 and A4 Solo buttons, and play the sequence. Then click the A1 and A2 solo buttons to add the sync sound to the mix.

Clicking a Solo button isolates that track while simultaneously muting all the other tracks. When you click an additional Solo button, it adds that track to the preview. Although you can click the Solo and Mute buttons on one track, Solo overrides Mute.

TIP ▶ Unlike with the Audible controls, you can toggle the Solo and Mute buttons off or on even while the sequence is playing.

11 Toggle off the Solo buttons for the music tracks. Look at the audio meters as you play just the A1 and A2 tracks.

For this shoot, two microphones were used to record the sound. One was a lavalier mic attached to the person speaking, and the other was a boom mic that also picked up room sound. The audio levels for these clips fall around –12 dB on the audio meters, which is a good level for your primary audio tracks.

Using the Solo buttons, you can distinguish what audio source is on what track and adjust them accordingly.

12 Solo just the A1 and then the A2 track as you play these clips until you can determine which track is which.

NOTE ► If your sequence has more tracks than can be seen at one time, you can create a separate *static track* area in the Timeline to isolate the first few tracks, then scroll through the additional tracks below them. To create a static track area, drag the lower static tab down to include the number of tracks you want in constant view. To remove the static track area, drag this same tab upward.

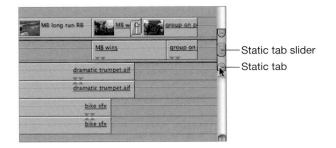

Adjusting and Editing Audio in the Timeline

After you've prepared your tracks and added additional sound sources, you can set the audio level for each clip according to its purpose in the sequence. You begin by setting the level for the highest priority tracks—those tracks that must be heard above all others. Often, those are the sync or dialogue tracks. But when narration is present, in addition to dialogue, as in the *Amanda* sequences, the dialogue may become secondary at times.

In digital audio, no part of the *overall* audio signal of the *combined* tracks can go above 0 dB, or the sound will be clipped off and distorted. This differs from analog audio, which uses a different dB scale and often averages sounds at around 0 dB. In order not to exceed the 0 dB level for all tracks, you set the primary audio tracks, such as dialogue and narration, well below that, perhaps between –12 dB and –6 dB. You can set the music volume to -15 or -18. As you add additional sound tracks to the mix, you have some room to raise the volume without peaking. If, however, adding the additional audio tracks causes the volume to peak, you have to adjust your mix accordingly.

There are two displays that can be toggled on in the Timeline that will help you adjust and edit your audio: clip overlays and audio waveforms.

Using Clip Overlays to Set Audio Levels

You have already adjusted volume levels for clips in the Viewer by entering a dB amount or dragging the pink volume level overlay line up or down. You can also adjust volume on clips directly in the Timeline. To do this, you toggle on a clip overlay that displays a pink volume level line like the one in the Viewer.

1   Click the *Canoe Club Mix* sequence tab. Click the Audio Controls control for this sequence, then solo the A3 and A4 narration tracks. As you play these clips, watch the dB levels in the audio meters.

    Although the narration clips are fairly consistent, they fall beneath –12 dB on the audio meters. Since the narration is the primary audio in this sequence, you will need to raise the volume of these clips.

2   To turn on clip overlays for this sequence, click the Clip Overlays control. You can also press Option-W.

A pink volume level line appears in each audio clip representing the volume of that clip. Black overlay lines appear on the video clips. These represent the percentage of video opacity. The audio overlay lines appear on the one-third line of the clip, allowing room to raise the volume above the original level. The video opacity lines, when in their default position, are at the top of the video clips at 100%, or full, opacity.

Opacity line

Volume level line

NOTE ▸ The Audio Controls and Clip Overlay controls can be toggled off or on in each individual sequence open in the Timeline. When you save the project, the sequence will reopen in that state.

3 In the **VO_01** clip, move the pointer over the volume level line on the A1 or A2 track, and drag the line up and down.

As you drag, both lines move up or down because these tracks are grouped as a stereo pair. An information box displays the dB amount you are changing the volume relative to its original 0 dB level.

NOTE ▸ Remember, the 0 dB level for each clip represents the original audio level as it was captured. It does not mean it will appear at 0 dB on the audio meters.

4 Drag the volume level line 4 dB above 0, and play the clip again. Try it 8 dB above its original level.

TIP ▸ As you drag, the volume level overlay will change in different increments depending on the height of the track. To see each increment and have greater control, hold down the Command key as you drag.

Determining a starting point is the first step in setting levels. When you preview the sequence audio with this clip, you may need to come back and readjust these narration clips.

5 Play and adjust the volume of the **VO_02** and **VO_03** narration clips to be consistent with the first one.

6 Now click the Solo controls for the A5 and A6 music tracks to add them to the mix. Play the areas where the music and narration clips overlap in the sequence.

TIP ▶ As you finish listening to one narration clip, and without stopping the playhead, just click in the ruler area above the next narration clip, and the playhead will continue playing from that point.

At full volume, the music overpowers the narration. Let's adjust the music volume to create an optimum mix level that supports the narration.

7 Drag the volume level line on one of the stereo music tracks down –12 dB, and play the area again. Adjust the level so the music is clearly heard but not distracting to the narration.

NOTE ▶ Later in this lesson, you will learn how to raise and lower the sound level within the music clip, allowing you to bring it up to a fuller level when the narrator isn't speaking.

8   To turn off all the Solo buttons and listen to all tracks, Option-click the A1 Solo button, then Option-click it again.

Option-clicking a deselected Solo button first selects all the Solo buttons. Option-clicking again deselects them all.

9   Play the sequence where the first narration clip, **VO_01**, overlaps with the first **rowing sound** clip. Lower the first **rowing sound** volume to a mix level you like.

10 To apply the volume level of the first **rowing sound** clip to the others, select the first clip, and press Cmd-C to copy it. Select the remaining **rowing sound** clips.

11 Ctrl-click one of the selected clips and choose Paste Attributes from the shortcut menu. In the Paste Attributes window under Audio Attributes, click the Levels check box, and click OK.

The volume lines on all the **rowing sound** clips move down to the same level as the first sound effect clip in this sequence.

NOTE ▶ If the sound level of a sequence clip peaks at 0 dB, the sound may have been recorded too high during the original shoot, and the audio may be distorted. Changing the level as outlined in this lesson may help but may not completely correct the problem.

Project Practice

To practice adjusting sound levels, click the *Team Story* sequence tab and adjust the team members tracks first, then blend the music and then the motorbike sound effects into the mix. Remember, you will animate the volume level later in this lesson. Here you want to find the right mix or balance between the tracks. You may notice that the **bike sfx.aif** clip has sound on only one track. You will work with this clip more in the next exercise.

> **TIP** ▶ You can also choose Modify > Levels to open the Gain Adjust window. Here you can adjust the relative level of the selected clips up or down by a specific amount. You can also set an absolute volume level in this window.

Using Waveforms for Audio Editing

In addition to the volume level overlay line, you can also see the waveform displayed for the audio tracks in the Timeline. Seeing the actual representation of the audio can be very helpful as you adjust volume and edit audio tracks. As you edit, you may want to display the volume level overlay lines and audio waveforms together in the Timeline. To help you focus on the waveform display in this exercise, you will turn off the clip overlays.

1   If you balanced the volume levels of the *Team Story* sequence in the previous Project Practice, continue with that sequence. If not, open the *Team Story Mixed* sequence in the Sequences bin in the Browser.

    This is the same sequence but with mixed audio levels.

2   Choose Show Audio Waveforms from the Timeline Layout pop-up menu. You can also press Option-Cmd-W.

> **TIP** ▶ Sometimes it's easier to remember similar shortcuts together. Option-W toggles clip overlays, and Option-Cmd-W toggles the waveform display.

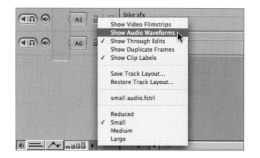

3 Move your pointer into the Timeline track area over the A1 and A2 boundary line. When the cursor changes to the resize arrow, press Option and drag down.

As you enlarge the audio tracks, the waveforms appear larger as well, allowing you to take a closer look at the shape of your audio signals.

4 Look at the A1 and A2 tracks to see which is the boom track and which is the more robust lavalier, or lav, microphone track.

5 Look at the **bike sfx.aif** clip on A5 and A6.

If you played this clip in the previous Project Practice, you may have seen there was no audio registering in one of the audio meters. Viewing the waveform display provides a visual clue to the audio content of your clips without playing them.

6 To delete the empty track from the stereo **bike sfx.aif** clip, select the clip, and press Option-L to ungroup the stereo pair. Select the lower track, and press Delete.

Now only the good **bike sfx.aif** track appears in the Timeline.

7 Move the playhead to the end of the fourth team member clip, and play to the end of the sequence. Look at the waveform display for the **MB wins** clip.

From the waveform display, it looks as though there could be additional crowd clapping sounds earlier in this clip. Extending that sound under the image of the **MB long run** clip before it would add the sound of the audience before you see them, making the sequence more interesting.

8 In the Timeline button bar, click the Linked Selection button to toggle it off. Drag the In point of the **MB wins** clip to the left, and snap it to the Out point of the **MB championship** clip. Play from this location.

Even though the extended portion of this clip is not synched to the video above it, it coincidentally syncs perfectly with the man clapping.

Another use for the waveform display is when you edit audio tracks in the Timeline.

9 Open the *Waveform Editing* sequence from the Browser. Play the two unedited clips, and then play the group of edited audio clips that follows in the sequence.

The edited version of these two clips was used in the *Racing – Transitions* sequence in the previous lesson. When you remove the ums and ahhs from the team manager's comments, you end up with a tightly edited and much more effective sound bite.

TIP ▶ If the audio waveform does not appear, make the track taller or zoom into the clip to see the waveform display.

10 Zoom into the head of the first clip, **JM stakes rise**.

When zoomed in, it's easy to see where the pauses occur in this clip by the shape of the waveform display. You can mark the pauses and delete them to shorten these two clips and improve the sound bite.

11 Play from the beginning of the clip, and set an In point just after the team manager says, "When the stakes rise," but before he pauses. Set an Out point just after the next "hum," but before he says, "You'll see…"

TIP ▶ When viewing the waveform display on stereo audio clips, such as in this sequence, you can enlarge one track but make the other small, since whatever you do to one track of a stereo pair, you do to the other simultaneously.

12 Press Shift-Delete to delete the pause and pull up the remaining portion of the clip. Play the new edit point to see how it sounds.

NOTE ▶ You can also click the Razor Blade tool on either side of a pause, which creates a separate clip of just the pause, then delete that clip.

Project Practice

To continue editing using the waveform display, go through the **JM stakes rise** and **JM what you see** clips, and delete the pauses or ums and ahhs. To complete the audio editing process and make the individual clips sound more polished, use the Ripple tool (or bracket keys) to trim frames at the edit points, and add short audio cross fades where the edit points are abrupt. Use the edited version in the sequence, and the script below, as a reference to help you.

"When the stakes rise, you will see some situations that are interesting, to say the least."

"You're going to witness a tremendous amount of desire, and passion, and emotion. All of the components that make a competitive athlete who and what they are."

TIP Working with the audio waveform display in the Timeline uses additional RAM, just like working with video thumbnail images does. When you are not focusing on audio, turn off the waveform display.

Changing Audio Levels Over Time

In the previous exercises, you've set sound levels on individual clips in the *Canoe Club Mix* and *Team Story* sequences. There are music and sound effects tracks that continue throughout the sequence. At times, you may want to fade them down, allowing the primary sound to dominate, only to fade up seconds later. There are two ways to change, or *animate,* the sound levels. One method involves adding an edit point and a cross fade where you want to change an audio level. The other method involves setting a *keyframe* directly on the volume level line. A keyframe identifies a frame in a clip where you want to change a clip property, such as audio level or, in a video clip, the opacity.

1   In the Timeline, click the *Canoe Club Mix* sequence tab, and make sure clip overlays are toggled on for this sequence. Make sure all tracks can be heard—that no solo buttons are on—and that snapping is active.

You set a mix level for the **battlesong** clip on A5 and A6 in a previous exercise. To raise the music volume in the areas when the narrator isn't speaking, you can divide the music track into separate clips.

2 Move the playhead to snap to the In point of the **VO_01** narration clip. Choose one of the following three methods to add an edit point and divide the clip at this location:

▶ Press B to select the Razor Blade tool, and click the A5 track at the playhead location. Press A to return to the default Selection tool.

▶ Toggle off the Auto Select controls for all video and audio tracks except the A5 and A6 tracks. Choose Sequence > Add Edit.

▶ With the Auto Select controls off for all but the A5 and A6 tracks, press Ctrl-V.

TIP ▶ You can use the keyboard shortcut (Ctrl-V) to add edits as a clip is playing. Blue markers will appear in the ruler area when you press Ctrl-V and when you stop, edit points will appear at the marker locations.

A new edit point is added to the music clip, creating two separate clips.

3 To change the volume of the first **battlesong** clip, drag the volume level line up to 0 dB. Play through the edit point to hear the change in volume.

Cutting from one audio level to another makes this an abrupt transition.

4 To smooth the transition, select the edit point and press Option-Cmd-T to add the default audio cross fade between these two clips.

You used a cross fade in the previous lesson to smooth a transition between two sound clips. Here, since the two clips play a continuous music track, the cross fade transitions from one audio level to the next.

5 Add edit points on the **battlesong** clip using the beginning and end of each narration clip as a guide. On the clips where narration is not present, raise the volume level line to 0 dB. Apply the default cross fade at each edit point, and play the sequence.

6 Click the *Team Story* (or *Team Story Mixed*) sequence tab. To prepare this sequence, turn on clip overlays and turn off the audio waveforms. Make sure no track is soloed, and mute the A5 track.

To raise and lower the music volume a different way, you will set a keyframe where you want to change the audio level.

7 As a visual guide, move the playhead to the In point of the **PA team owner** clip. Press P to select the Pen tool, and move the pointer into the **dramatic trumpet.aif** clip and over the pink volume level line before the playhead.

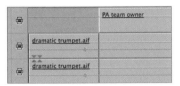

The tool looks like a pen only when the pointer is over the clip's over-lay line.

TIP You can also use the default Selection tool and hold down Option to temporarily select the Pen tool.

8   Click the Pen tool before the playhead position. Make sure you click *on* the clip overlay line.

A pink diamond, or keyframe, appears on the line at the playhead posi-tion. This is where you want to *begin* fading the audio.

TIP To delete a keyframe, press PP to select the Pen Delete tool and click a keyframe, or Ctrl-click a keyframe and choose Clear from the shortcut menu. You can also use the Option key with either the default Selection tool or the Pen tool to delete an existing keyframe.

9   Move the Pen tool to the right of the playhead and again click the volume level line.

This is the point where you want the fading to stop and level off.

10 To raise the volume of the first portion of the music, press A to return to the default Selection tool. Move the pointer over the volume line. When you see the resize arrow, drag the volume line up to 0 dB and release it. Play the audio fade.

11 Play the last **group on podium** clip in the sequence, then zoom into it to make it larger. To create a simple fade-out on this clip, add two keyframes anywhere on the second half of the audio clip by Option-clicking the volume level overlay.

Once a keyframe has been placed on an overlay line, it can be raised or lowered to change the volume at that location, or repositioned left or right to change where the volume change starts or stops.

TIP Setting a keyframe inside the edge of the clip gives you greater control as you position it.

12 Move the pointer over the second keyframe. When the pointer changes to a crosshair icon, drag the keyframe down and to the right corner of the clip, but stay inside the clip's edge. Play the clip.

NOTE ▶ The crosshair is not a selectable tool. It is a part of the Pen function and allows you to move a keyframe.

As you drag a keyframe up and down or left and right, an information box appears displaying the distance and direction you've moved the keyframe from its original position, or the dB level change.

NOTE ▶ You can also set keyframes in the Viewer's audio tab, either before or after editing the clip to the Timeline.

Project Practice

In the *Team Story* sequence, continue adding keyframes to the music track around the team members In and Out points, as you did in the previous steps. Raise the music volume when no one is speaking. When you've finished mixing the music, apply either method of changing volume to the **bike sfx.aif** clip to fade in and out with the bikers racing video clips. You can look at the *Team Story Final* sequence in the Browser to see the finished version.

TIP ▶ To create a video fade-up, set two keyframes at the head of the first video clip, and drag the first keyframe down into the lower left corner of the clip.

Mixing Tracks Using the Audio Mixer

Now that you understand how to set keyframes and mix audio manually in the Timeline, you're ready to mix tracks in real time using the Audio Mixer tool. There are two ways to access the Audio Mixer. One is to select the Audio Mixing window layout, which incorporates the Audio Mixer into the interface. The other is to choose Tools > Audio Mixer. This opens the Audio Mixer as a separate window that you can place wherever you like.

1   From the Sequences bin in the Browser, open the *Racing Promo* sequence. Turn on clip overlays for this sequence.

2 Choose Tools > Audio Mixer, or press Option-6. Drag the Audio Mixer tool to the left over the Browser window area.

When you open the Audio Mixer, it appears within the Tool Bench window as a tab. There are six audio tracks represented in the Audio Mixer—the same number of tracks you have in your sequence. If the active sequence had 20 audio tracks, 20 tracks would appear in the Audio Mixer.

TIP If you are working with several tracks and can't see them all at one time, you can hide a track by clicking its number in the Tracks selection pane.

3   In the Audio Mixer, make sure the Record Audio Keyframes button in the upper-right button bar is deselected so that no keyframes will be created while you practice.

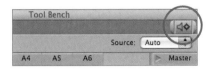

4   In the Timeline, play the *Racing Promo* sequence from the beginning, but watch the faders in the Audio Mixer.

The track faders move in response to the keyframes and sound levels currently set in the clips. These faders can also be used to set a different audio level, just as you would raise or lower the volume level line.

NOTE ▶ The Solo and Mute buttons here work the same as they do in the Timeline Audio Controls panel.

5   In the Timeline, move the playhead over the first **JM stakes rise** clip and look at the position of the clip's volume level line. In the Audio Mixer, drag the A1 fader down to about –25 dB and release the fader. Look again at the clip's volume level line in the Timeline.

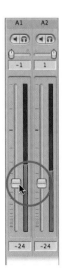

Changing the volume of a clip in the Audio Mixer changes the volume level line on the clip in the Timeline. In the Audio Mixer, the dB level in the box below the fader changes to reflect how much higher or lower you have changed the sound from its original 0 dB level. You can also enter a value here and press Return, which will move the fader to that level.

NOTE ▶ When changing volume on a stereo pair, dragging one fader adjusts the volume on both tracks in tandem.

Once the individual mix levels are set for each track, you can adjust the overall output level for your sequence by using the Master fader on the far right of the Audio Mixer window. You can also mute all tracks at once using the Master Mute button.

6   If the Master fader is not open, click its disclosure triangle to reveal it.

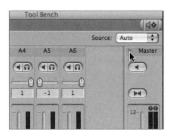

7   Play the sequence from the beginning and, as it plays, look at the Master fader meters. Drag the fader up to raise the overall volume level or down to lower it, making sure the combination of all tracks never exceeds 0 dB.

The levels in the Master fader reflect the output levels of the active sequence. When you change the level in a sequence using the Master fader, that output level will remain until you change it again.

NOTE ▶ Any changes made to the Master fader will affect the level of the mix as it's played back or output to tape. For this lesson, you will focus on balancing or mixing the individual tracks, and not outputting them to tape.

8   Before you remix the music track using the Audio Mixer, remove the keyframes by Ctrl-clicking the **promo music** clip and choosing Remove Attributes from the shortcut menu. In the Remove Attributes window, make sure Levels is checked under the Audio Attributes column, and click OK.

9   In the Audio Mixer button bar, click the Record Audio Keyframes button to toggle it on.

With this option on, any adjustments you make by dragging a track fader while the sequence is playing will automatically add keyframes to the clip in the Timeline.

TIP ▶ In the Editing tab of the User Preferences, you can choose a different level of automatic keyframing, either more or less sensitive to your fader movements. Start with the current default, which is the middle level.

Since mixing with the Audio Mixer happens in real time, take a moment to think about the process. First you will begin to play the sequence, then click and hold the A3 (or A4) fader button and watch the playhead move in the sequence. As the playhead approaches the first section of dialogue, drag the A1 fader down and under while the man is speaking, then back up to its original level at the end of the first dialogue section. Continue holding the fader button and repeat the process for the second dialogue section. Only when the sequence has finished do you release the mouse.

10 Follow these steps to create a live mix:

▶ Move the playhead to the head of the sequence, and press the spacebar to begin playing. Immediately click and hold the A3 fader. Do not release the mouse until the sequence has finished playing.

▶ As the playhead approaches the first dialogue section, drag the A3 fader down so you can clearly hear the dialogue but still hear the music in the background.

▶ At the end of the first dialogue section, drag the A3 fader back up to its original level.

▶ Keep watching the playhead, and as it approaches the second dialogue section, drag the A3 fader down and under again, then up full.

▶ When the sequence is finished playing, release the mouse.

In the Timeline, keyframes appear that identify peaks in the music clip where you raised and lowered the faders. To adjust your mix, you can raise or lower these keyframes, reposition them, or manually add new ones as you did in a previous exercise.

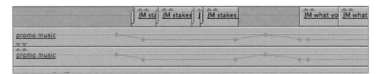

NOTE ▶ The Audio Mixer can be a powerful tool, but it requires some practice before you can achieve the desired results. Sometimes, manually controlling the individual keyframes, with the Pen tool for example, may give you the best result.

Recording a Narration Track

Depending on your project, you may need to record a voice-over to your sequence, perhaps to try out a narration or simply to provide a track you can use for timing purposes as you cut video for a documentary or news story. To record a voice-over in Final Cut Pro, you can use a digital camera or other audio recording device, such as a USB microphone, PCI card, or internal mic on a laptop computer. Recording an audio track this way creates a new clip directly in the Timeline. To create the voice-over clip, you will use the Voice Over tool.

1 If you are using an external microphone or camera mic, connect the device to your computer.

2 In the Timeline, click the *Canoe Club Mix* sequence tab. Mute the A3 and A4 tracks so you won't hear the existing narration.

You will record yourself saying what the narrator says in the clip.

TIP ▶ Recording a rough narration allows you to begin editing, even if the final narration script has not been recorded or captured. A rough voice-over track is often referred to as a *scratch track*.

3 Move the playhead to the beginning of the **VO_01** clip, where you will start recording the voice-over. Press I to create an In point. In the Canvas Duration field, enter *1400*, and press Return.

This sets an Out point a little farther than the original narration clip, and gives you some extra pad as you record.

NOTE ▶ If there are no In and Out points, the voice-over clip begins recording at the playhead location and continues until the end of the sequence.

4 Choose Tool > Voice Over to open the Voice Over tool window.

If Final Cut Pro does not detect a recording device, a warning window appears. If Final Cut Pro detects a microphone source, the Voice Over tool appears as a tab in the Tool Bench window. Notice the Audio Mixer tab is still open in this window as well.

The Voice Over tool is divided into four areas: Status, Audio File, Input, and Headphones.

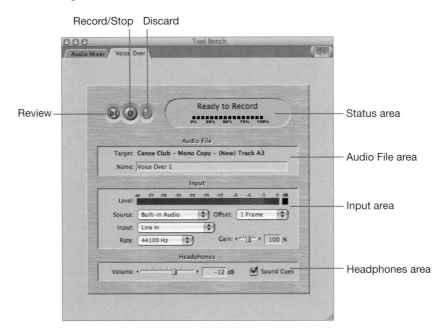

5   In the Audio File area, look at the Target information and track destination. Then, in the Timeline, drag the a2 source control to the A6 destination control. Look again at the Target information.

TIP   If you don't see an a2 source control in the Timeline track control area, open a clip with audio into the Viewer, and source controls will appear.

With the a2 source control patched to the A6 destination track, the target for the new voice-over is A7. This track will be created automatically after you record the voice-over.

NOTE ▶ The Voice Over function records only one channel of audio, or mono audio. It does not record in stereo.

6   In the Audio File area, type *Canoe Club Intro* as the name for this voice-over track.

7   In the Input area, choose the correct source from the Source pop-up menu. If it's DV, choose 48000 Hz from the Rate pop-up menu and 3 Frames from the Offset pop-up menu.

NOTE ▶ Final Cut Pro will display a default Input configuration based on the audio recording device it detects. A recording offset amount is included as one of the default settings. If your device does not support 48000 Hz, you won't see that as an option.

8   Start talking to set the Headphones level as well as the Gain level in the Input area.

TIP ▶ If you use headphones for this process, you can hear the other audio in the sequence as you record the narration without recording the other audio tracks.

9   Select the Sound Cues check box.

This will cause beeps to sound during the five-second countdown before recording, and once again as a signal prior to the Out point.

If you're not using headphones and you have Sound Cues selected, the beeps will be picked up and recorded as part of your clip. Deselect the Sound Cues option, and instead watch the Starting countdown in the Record area to see when recording begins and ends.

When you are sure you are ready to record, look for the Ready to Record signal in the Status area. Here's what will happen. You will click the Record button. The playhead will immediately jump backward five seconds for the pre-roll, while the Ready to Record window will turn yellow and count down from five. It will then turn red and begin recording. When you are finished reading the narration line, click the black Stop button.

10 Click the Record button, and record the following line:

"Over at the western edge of the hemisphere, skimming across a deep water inlet of the Puget Sound, I see my northwest relatives, the Salish Canoe Club."

The recording ends at the Out point, and the new voice-over clip appears in the Timeline.

11 Play the clip back by clicking the Review button or playing the sequence in the Timeline.

Each time you record a new version, or *take*, a new clip is placed in another track in the Timeline and is labeled with the next highest take number.

TIP ▸ If you want to stop a recording in process, or if you don't have an Out point, click the Stop button. You can also click the Discard button to discard an unwanted track. This step cannot be undone.

Importing CD Tracks

For these lessons, you've been using music tracks already contained in the project. As you edit your own material, you will most likely use music tracks from other sources, especially CDs. Standard CD audio is recorded at the 44.1 kilohertz (kHz) *sampling rate*, whereas high-quality video audio, including DV, XDCAM, HD, and so on, is recorded at 48.0 kHz. Although Final Cut Pro will play a CD track in the Timeline without rendering it, convert the CD tracks to 48.0 kHz so the CD tracks will match the audio tracks from your video source. In the image below, the audio clip on the right displays a green bar in the upper portion of each track indicating it doesn't match the sequence settings of 48.0 kHz.

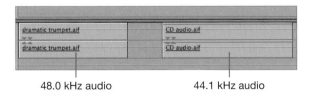

48.0 kHz audio   44.1 kHz audio

NOTE ▸ In digital audio, a sampling rate represents the number of times a sample from an audio source has been taken over a period of time to create a good representation of that sound. The more samples taken, the more accurately the audio is represented in digital form. Audio sample rates are measured in hertz and written as hertz or kilohertz, such as 48.0 kHz or 48000 Hz.

1   In the Browser, press Cmd-B to create a new bin. Name the bin *CD 48*.

2   With this bin selected, choose File > Batch Export.

An Export Queue window opens with the empty bin selected. This window is a portal for exporting or converting a group of clips at one time. Although you will cover other exporting options in later lessons, for now you will use this window to convert your own CD tracks to 48.0 kHz.

3   Arrange your interface so you can see the Export Queue window and the Desktop. Insert your own CD into the computer. Open a Finder window, and drag several audio tracks from the CD into the Final Cut Pro Export Queue window and release them onto the CD 48 bin.

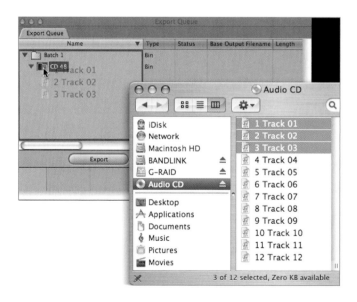

4   With the CD 48 bin selected, click the Settings button.

A Batch window appears with different options.

5   Click the Set Destination button, and select a location where you want to save the new music tracks. Click Choose.

6   Click the Format pop-up, and from the menu choose AIFF as the file type.

7   Click the Options button. When the Sound Settings window appears, change the Rate to 48.0 by either entering it in the Rate field or clicking the lower arrow to the right of the field and choosing 48.000 from the pop-up menu.

8   Leave the other settings at their defaults and click OK. In the Export Queue window, click the Export button.

An Export Queue progress bar appears, indicating the CD tracks with the current settings are being exported to the destination you selected. When this process is complete, you can import those tracks into your project and edit them into your sequences.

Project Practice

As time allows, you can come back to this project file and apply the techniques you learned to two different sequences in the Practice Project bin, which is located in the Sequences bin. If you are working with Final Cut Pro Studio and have Soundtrack Pro, you can add additional sound effects to these sequences and mix those levels.

Save your project changes frequently.

Lesson Review

1. What control do you click in the Timeline to display the Mute and Solo buttons?

2. What result do you get when you click the Solo button on a track?

3. In what two ways can you add tracks to the Timeline?

4. How do you make the volume level line appear on clips in the Timeline?

5. When would you turn on audio waveforms in the Timeline?

6. What are two of the three ways you can add an edit point to an existing clip at the playhead location?

7. What tool do you use to set a keyframe on the volume level line?

8. How can the Pen tool be accessed without selecting it from the Tool palette?

9. How do you reposition a keyframe or change its volume level?

10. On what menu do you find the Audio Mixer?

11. To mix tracks in real time and automatically create keyframes on a clip, what must you do in the Audio Mixer?

12. What tool do you use to record your own voice-over, and where do you access it?

13. When you want to use CD audio tracks in your sequence, what can you do to convert them to 48 kHz?

Answers

1. The Audio Controls control in the lower left of the Timeline.

2. That track becomes the only audible track as you play the sequence.

3. Ctrl-click in the Timeline audio or video track controls area and choose Add Track from the shortcut menu; or choose Sequence > Insert Tracks.

4. Click the Clip Overlay control in the lower left of the Timeline, next to the Track Height control.

5. When you want a visual representation of a clip's audio signals and to edit audio clips.

6. Click the clip with the Razor Blade tool, choose Sequence > Add Edit, or press Ctrl-V.

7. The Pen tool, or you can Option-click it with the default Selection tool.

8. Hold down Option and move the pointer over the volume level line on a Timeline clip. The Pen tool appears on the overlay line.

9. Drag left and right to change its position and up and down to change its volume level.

10. The Tools menu.

11. Click the Record Audio Keyframes button in the Audio Mixer button bar to toggle it on.

12. The Voice Over tool, found on the Tools menu.

13. Drag the tracks into the Export Queue window, and change the settings to 48 kHz. Export with these settings.

Keyboard Shortcuts

Option-W	Toggles clip overlays on and off in the Timeline
Option-Cmd-W	Toggles waveforms on and off in the Timeline
P	Selects the Pen tool
PP	Selects the Pen Delete tool
Option-6	Opens the Audio Mixer

12

Lesson 12
Changing Motion Properties

Changing the motion properties of a clip opens a world of possibilities in your editing. You can change the speed of a clip to slow down, speed up, freeze, or do all three. You can resize, reposition, and crop images, then stack them on top of each other to create a composite image of all the clips in the stack. You can also rotate and distort clips, and animate all motion properties so the changes happen over time. In addition, you can even fit a clip of one length into a sequence space of a different length using an edit called Fit To Fill.

Two images cropped and repositioned to fit together on screen

Preparing the Project

1 Launch Final Cut Pro, and open the **Lesson 12 Project** file from the Lessons folder on your hard drive.

2 Close any other open projects.

3 Click between the *Speed – Starting* and *Speed – Finished* sequences. Play the latter to see what you will create in this lesson.

These sequences are similar to the *Team Story* sequence you mixed in Lesson 11, with a few minor adjustments to the video clips. You will make speed changes to the B-roll footage on the V2 track.

NOTE ▶ Some of the clips in these two sequences would benefit from a color adjustment. You will learn to correct color in the next lesson.

4 To create a backup of the *Speed – Starting* sequence, duplicate it in the Browser and rename it *Speed – Starting Backup*.

TIP ▶ Choose Unlimited RT and Dynamic in the RT pop-up to see the highest number of speed changes in real time.

Changing Clip Speed

There are different ways to change the speed of a clip. You can enter a percentage amount, such as 50% to play the clip half as fast, or a total duration for the clip, which will slow it down or speed it up accordingly. You can also use a type of edit—called Fit To Fill—that will automatically fit a clip into an existing space in the sequence. Each of these methods will change the clip from one constant speed to another.

You can find all the source clips for this exercise in the Team Story Clips bin in the Browser.

1 Click the *Speed – Starting* sequence tab in the Timeline. To prepare the sequence for the first edit, do the following:

▶ Disconnect the a1 and a2 source controls, if they appear, and patch the v1 source control to the V2 destination track.

▶ Set an In point after the team owner says, "Factory Yamaha's official" and an Out point just before he says, "And it's our job."

▶ Zoom into the sequence at this location.

The first B-roll, or cutaway, will be edited to this location on the V2 track.

2 Open the **team truck** clip into the Viewer. To change this clip's speed, choose Modify > Speed, or press Cmd-J.

A Speed window opens with options for setting duration, clip speed, reverse direction, and frame blending.

NOTE ▶ When playing a clip at a slower speed, you sometimes see a strobe effect. Selecting the Frame Blending option helps minimize this effect.

3 Enter 50 in the Speed percent field, and click OK. Play the clip.

The entire clip now plays at 50% of its original speed. You can mark any portion of this clip to use in an edit, and that portion will play at 50%.

4 Set an In point where the camera begins to pan the truck, and edit this clip as an Overwrite edit. Play the clip in the sequence.

5 Open the **TB with tool** clip and play it. Press Cmd-J to open the Speed window. To have the mechanic reverse his motion and put the tool back into its slot, click the Reverse check box. Enter 30% for the Speed and click OK.

6 Set an In point at 14:18:14:13 and an Out point at 14:18:13:28. Edit this clip to the Timeline next to the team truck clip, and play the clip.

NOTE ▶ When you reverse a clip in the Viewer, the timecode number in the Location Timecode field appears in italics, and the numbers move in reverse as well.

When you zoom into this clip, you see the speed percentage and reverse direction, indicated by a minus sign next to the clip name.

TIP ▶ Changing clip speed in the Viewer will alter the master clip. To return a master clip back to its original speed or direction, open it in the Viewer and choose Modify > Speed, enter *100* in the Speed percent field, and deselect Reverse. This will not affect the speed of the sequence clip.

7 In the Timeline, set an In point in the first frame of the gap on V2 after the **TB with tool** clip, and set an Out point after the team owner says, "125 National Championship," for the next slow motion clip.

The duration of these marks is about 1:22.

8   Open the **BS drinking water** clip, and play it. Set an In point where he starts to lift the water bottle up to his mouth, and set an Out point where the bottle becomes horizontal, about a 22-frame duration.

To fit the 22-frame portion of this source clip into the Timeline marks area, the clip will have to be slowed down. You can set a specific duration for the marked portion of this clip in the Speed window. But you can also let Final Cut Pro handle it for you by using the Fit To Fill edit. The Fit To Fill edit takes the source content between its In and Out points and changes the speed so it fits (or fills) the duration between the sequence's In and Out points.

9   Drag the **BS drinking water** clip from the Viewer into the Canvas and release it on the green Fit To Fill option of the Edit Overlay, or press Shift-F11. Play the clip in the Timeline.

The clip is slowed down to fill the space between the Timeline edit points. If you zoom into the sequence clip, you can see it has a speed of about 48%, depending on where you set your edit points.

TIP To change the third edit button in the Canvas window from the default blue Replace button to any of the other Edit Overlay edit options, such as Fit To Fill, click and hold the arrow and choose a different edit type.

10 Open the **MB high jump** clip, and play it. Set an In point where the biker first comes up over the hill, and set an Out point after the second jump in the clip, just before the red bike enters the frame, about a 6:25 duration.

11 In the Timeline, move the playhead into the first gap, and press X to mark the gap's duration, which is 5:00 in length. Edit the **MB high jump** clip as a Fit To Fill edit, and play the sequence to this point.

In this case, to fit the 6:25 source clip into the 5:00 sequence slot, the clip had to play faster.

TIP ▶ To use Fit To Fill to cover several clips in a sequence, set an In and an Out point around the clips or area you want to fill, then mark and edit your source clip as a Fit To Fill edit.

12 You can change the speed of a sequence clip the same way you change a source clip. Move the playhead over the next clip on the V2 track, the **DS good ride** clip, and press X to mark this clip's current duration. Select the clip, and press Cmd-J, or Ctrl-click the clip and choose Speed from the shortcut menu. Enter *70* as the clip speed, and click OK. Play the clip.

In the Timeline, this clip is lengthened while all the clips that follow are pushed down to accommodate the speed change. If you made the clip faster than 100%, it would appear shorter, and the following clips would be pulled up.

TIP ▶ After you apply a speed change to a sequence clip, you can slip the clip because the entire clip content is at the same speed.

13 Press RR for the Ripple tool, and ripple the end of this clip to snap to the Out point. Remove the edit points by pressing Option-X, and press A to return to the default Selection tool. Press Cmd-S to save your changes.

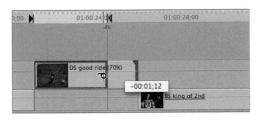

The remaining clips in the sequence are pulled up to their original positions.

Creating a Freeze-Frame

Another way to modify the speed of a clip is to stop the motion altogether to freeze a specific frame in a clip. In video, a freeze-frame is actually created by repeating one frame over and over for a specific length of time. This process is handled automatically by Final Cut Pro. Freeze-frames can be created in the Timeline or in the Viewer. But unlike changing a clip's speed in the Viewer, creating a freeze-frame will not alter the master clip.

In this exercise, you will create a freeze-frame in the Viewer of each of the racers, and create a *run and freeze* effect on two clips in the sequence.

1 In the Browser, Ctrl-click the Team Story Clips bin and choose New Bin from the shortcut menu. Name this bin *Freeze Frames*, and click its disclosure triangle to see its contents.

2 Open the **DS good ride** clip, and move the playhead to the marker labeled *freeze*. To create a freeze-frame at this location, choose Modify > Make Freeze Frame, or press Shift-N.

A separate clip is created in the Viewer with a total length of 2 minutes and a marked default duration of 10 seconds. Notice the freeze-frame name contains the timecode number where the freeze was created.

TIP ▶ If you anticipate creating a lot of freeze-frame images and want them to be a specific length, you can change the default of the Still/Freeze Duration in the Editing tab of the User Preferences window.

3   To save this freeze-frame, drag the image from the Viewer into the Freeze Frames bin you created in the Browser.

The freeze-frame appears as a graphic icon, also used to represent other graphic files such as TIFFs or JPEGs.

NOTE ▶ If you were to open the Freeze Frame bin and change it to an icon view, you would see the frame as a thumbnail image.

4   Repeat the process in steps 2 and 3 for the **BS over hill**, **MB high jump**, and **MB long run** clips to complete the set of four images.

You will use these freeze-frames to create motion effects later in this lesson.

5   To create a run and freeze effect in the Timeline, drag the playhead and snap to the marker in the **BS over hill** clip. Choose Modify > Make Freeze Frame, or press Shift-N.

A 2-minute freeze-frame appears in the Viewer with a 10-second marked duration, just as it did in the previous steps. To create a run and freeze effect, this freeze-frame must be edited back into the sequence exactly where it was created.

6   In the Timeline, set an In point at the *freeze* marker location, and an Out point on the last frame of the **BS over hill** clip. Click the Overwrite edit button. Play the clip, then zoom into to this area.

Freeze-frame clips in the sequence appear as a slightly different shade of blue to distinguish them from normal clips. The name of the freeze-frame is the sequence name and location, since it was created from that frame in the sequence.

7   To add a freeze-frame to the last clip in the sequence, **group on podium**, move the playhead to the marker in that clip, and repeat the process outlined in steps 5 and 6.

NOTE ▶ Later in this lesson you will use another method of creating freeze-frames and apply variable speed changes to the last bike jumping clip in this sequence.

8   Close the two open sequences, and press Cmd-S to save changes.

Changing Motion Parameters

In addition to changing clip speed, you can also resize, reposition, crop, rotate, distort, and create a variable speed effect in a single clip. Every clip comes with these built-in motion parameters, all of which can be changed. You access and change motion properties in the Motion tab in the Viewer.

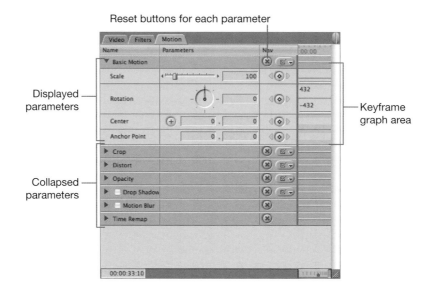

The Basic Motion category includes the most primary motion attributes, such as Scale and Center, which you use to resize and reposition an image. The other motion parameters, such as Crop, Distort, Opacity, and so on, are not displayed until you click one of the disclosure triangles next to their names. The Motion tab also has a keyframe graph area, which you will use later in this lesson to animate parameters.

Sizing, Positioning, and Cropping an Image

You can adjust a clip's size, position, and other parameters by entering numbers and dragging sliders in the Motion tab. In addition, there is an Image+Wireframe mode that helps you create motion effects directly on the image in the Canvas.

1   From the Sequences bin, open the *Motion – Finished* and *Motion – Starting* sequences. Play the *Motion – Starting* sequence.

This sequence contains the same clips you worked with in the previous exercise, as well as some of the speed and freeze-frame effects, but the clips are laid out differently on the tracks. The team member clips have been placed on the V2 track over their slow-motion racing shots.

2   Click the *Motion – Finished* sequence, and play it.

By changing motion parameters such as size, crop, and position, you can see multiple images on the screen at the same time. Also, some of the video clips in the sequence have opacity keyframes to fade the video in or out, and some have been color-corrected.

3   Click the *Motion – Starting* tab, and toggle off the Clip Overlays. Move the playhead into the second clip, **DS intro**, and double-click the clip to open it in the Viewer. Click the Motion tab.

> **TIP**▸ Always position the playhead over the clip you opened in the Timeline so you can see both the Motion tab in the Viewer and the image in the Canvas as you make changes.

4   Drag the Scale slider to the right as far as possible and then left, looking at the image in the Canvas as you drag. Then enter *65* in the Scale percentage field.

With this clip sized less than 100%, you can see the clip beneath it on the V1 track. Notice there is a turquoise border around this clip because it is selected in the Timeline.

5   To reposition this clip to the left, click the Center crosshair button in the Motion tab, and move the cursor into the Canvas. Click the midpoint of the left turquoise border, but don't release the mouse. Drag right or left to make sure you can fully see the man's face and then release the mouse.

6   To crop the right portion of this image, click the disclosure triangle next to Crop to reveal the Crop controls. Drag the Right slider to the right to about *32*.

7   In the Timeline, double-click the **DS good ride** clip to open it in the Viewer. If necessary, click the Motion tab. Enter *65* for the Scale percentage to match the previous clip.

To reposition this clip a different way, you will drag the clip's image in the Canvas.

8   In the Canvas, click the View pop-up and choose Image+Wireframe.

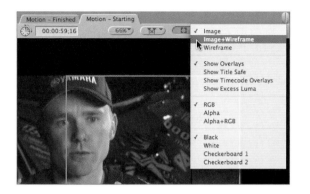

NOTE ▶ You can also choose View > Image+Wireframe, or press W with the Timeline or Canvas window active.

A large white X appears corner to corner over the image area, and a number appears at the center point, indicating the clip's track number. With this mode selected, you can position the clip manually by dragging it around in the Canvas image area.

9 Move the pointer into the Canvas over the **DS good ride** clip. When you see the Move pointer, drag the image, but don't release the mouse. Now hold down the Shift key and drag the image up and down and left and right.

The Shift key constrains your movements and helps you stay aligned with the clip to the left.

NOTE ▶ When you move your pointer over an image in the Canvas, there are several icons you might see, depending on the exact location of the pointer over the image's wireframe.

Move pointer in image area

10 While holding down Shift, drag the clip to the right until you see some black space or separation between the two clips, and release the mouse. Play the clips in the Timeline.

11 To ensure the outer edges of these two images will appear within a viewable area on home television monitors, click the Canvas View pop-up and choose Show Title Safe. Make any necessary adjustments, then toggle off this overlay.

The Title Safe overlay has two turquoise guidelines. The inner guideline is used to position text; the outer one indicates an "action safe" area. Any action you want the viewers to see should appear within the outer guideline.

Rotating and Distorting an Image

Rotating an image involves two motion parameters: Rotate and Anchor Point. The *anchor point* is simply the point around which an image is rotated. The default anchor point is the center point of the image. Distorting an image changes its aspect ratio. There are two approaches to changing the Distort parameters. One way is to reposition individual corners in the image, and the other is to change its overall aspect ratio, making the image tall and thin or short and squat.

> **TIP** ▶ Whenever you open a clip from the Timeline in the following steps, click the Motion tab to access those parameters.

1   In the Timeline, drag the playhead through the last stack of clips until you see all three racers in the Canvas image area.

In the *Motion – Finished* sequence, the lower two clips were angled or rotated to create a more interesting combined or composite image.

> **NOTE** ▶ Normally, the V3 clip would prevent you from seeing the V2 or the V1 clip. Since these clips have already been sized down, you can see all three of them in the Canvas at the same time.

2   In the Timeline, double-click the V2 clip, **DS good ride**, to open it in the Viewer. In the Rotation parameter, drag the rotation angle control clockwise and counterclockwise. Now, move the pointer into the Canvas

and over the turquoise bounding box edge on the right. This is referred to as a *rotation handle.*

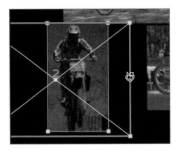

A Rotate pointer appears when you move the cursor across any rotation handle of the clip.

3   Drag the image as though you were turning the steering wheel of a car. Finish your movements with an angle toward 11 o'clock, or −22 degrees in the Rotation field.

4   To change the rotation of the **BS over hill** clip, just select the clip in the Timeline and move the pointer over one of the turquoise rotation handles in the Canvas. When the cursor changes to the Rotation tool, drag clockwise, toward 1 o'clock.

When Image+Wireframe mode is active, and a clip is selected in the Timeline, you can make changes directly in the Canvas without accessing the Motion tab.

5   To see the composite of all three images in the Canvas without the high-
     lighted edges, deselect the clip in the Timeline.

     NOTE ▶ The turquoise bounding box around a selected clip appears only
     when the playhead is stopped. When you play these clips, it will not appear.

6   Move the playhead to the middle of the **BS king of 2nd** clip, and select this
     clip. Move the pointer into the Canvas and over any one of the four corner
     points. These are referred to as *corner handles*. When the cursor changes to
     a crosshair icon, drag inward toward the center of the clip until it's a little
     over half its original size, around 60%.

     Dragging any corner handle inward makes the clip smaller, and dragging
     outward resizes it larger.

     TIP ▶ When you move the pointer into the corner of the image area,
     you may see other pointers appear that you could use here. To make it eas-
     ier to grab the corner handle with the crosshair, drag the image away from
     the corner, then complete the resizing.

7   In the Tool palette, click the Crop tool (the eighth tool), or press C. Move
     the pointer into the Canvas and over the right edge of the **BS king of 2nd**
     clip. When you see the Crop tool appear, drag left to crop out the motor-
     bike in the background.

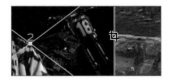

     Cropping is measured in percentage. To see the percentage cropped, you
     can double-click this clip in the Timeline, click the Motion tab in the
     Viewer, and click the disclosure triangle next to the Crop parameter.

8   Press D to select the Distort tool. Move the Distort tool over the upper-right corner handle of the **BS king of 2nd** clip. When the pointer changes to the Distort tool, drag the corner down, then up; left then right.

NOTE ▶ You can also click and hold the Crop tool in the Tool palette. The alternative tool that appears is the Distort tool.

Distorting one corner of an image changes its perspective. You can also change or distort all four corners at once.

9   Press Cmd-Z to undo the previous change. Hold down Shift and drag down the upper-right corner until the left top and bottom corners reach the upper and lower limits of the Canvas image area. Then release the mouse.

Holding down Shift here works similarly to the way it did when you positioned a clip. It constrains the movements so the distort effect is applied evenly to each side of the clip.

10   Drag the image left until its left edge is just out of the image area.

11 Apply the process in the preceding steps to the **BS over hill** clip so it mirrors the **BS king of 2nd** clip. Use the *Motion – Finished* sequence as a visual guide as you scale, crop, distort, and position this clip.

> **TIP** Don't forget to press A to return to the default Selection tool when you want to resize the clip.

Sharing Motion Attributes

If you are working with a group of images, and you want them to share a common motion attribute such as size, crop, or position, you can adjust the parameters in one clip and copy and paste those attributes to another, just as you did with audio levels.

> **TIP** Before you perform these steps, review the **MB high jump** clips at the beginning of the *Motion – Finished* sequence, and return to the *Motion – Starting* sequence.

1 In the Timeline, drag the playhead toward the head of the sequence and over the middle of the **MB high jump** clips. Select the clip on the V1 track.

In the Canvas, notice the number 1 over the center point of the wireframe X, indicating the selected clip is on V1.

2 Move your pointer over this wireframe in the Canvas, and when the pointer changes to the Move pointer, drag the **MB high jump** clip around in the image area, then release it.

In the previous rotation exercise, the clips at the end of the sequence were already resized so you could see all three together. Here, the clips are full frame, and the uppermost clip takes priority over the clips on the lower tracks. As you drag the wireframe, you are in fact moving the V1 clip, although you see only the wireframe representation of the image move.

To see the changes you make to the V1 clip, you must turn off visibility to the upper two clips. You can do this without turning off visibility to the entire V2 and V3 tracks.

3   In the Timeline, Ctrl-click the **MB high jump** on the V3 track, and choose Clip Enable from the shortcut menu. Repeat this process for the **MB high jump** clip on V2.

Clip Enable turns off visibility for one or more clips without turning it off for the entire track. This is helpful because turning off Visibility for an entire track may cause you to lose render files for other unassociated clips.

TIP   To accomplish the same thing using a different approach, select the V1 clip and choose Sequence > Solo Selected Item, or press Ctrl-S. This approach disables all other clips that overlap the selected clip.

4   Double-click the V1 **MB high jump** clip, and in the Motion tab, click the red Reset button in the Basic Motion section to return these parameters to their default settings.

5   Perform the following motion parameter changes to this clip, either in the Motion tab or directly on the clip in the Canvas. It may take a little tweaking to get the desired result.

▶   Move the playhead to the marker in the V1 **MB high jump** clip.

▶   Crop the left and right sides so you see only the racer in the middle of the frame.

▶   Crop some of the top and bottom of the image, but don't crop the racer.

▶   Scale the image down to allow for two additional racers the same size within the frame.

▶   Position the clip toward the left, with a comfortable black margin, staying within the action safe area.

▶   In the Timeline, drag the playhead through the clip to ensure the motocross bike is seen throughout the majority of the clip.

6   Select the V2 and V3 clips. Ctrl-click either one, and choose Clip Enable.

You can toggle Clip Enable for one clip or a group of clips at the same time.

7   To paste the motion attributes from the V1 **MB high jump** clip to the V2 and V3 clips, select the V1 clip, and press Cmd-C to copy it. Select the V2 and V3 **MB high jump** clips, and Ctrl-click either one. Choose Paste Attributes from the shortcut menu.

In the Paste Attributes window, you can select the specific motion parameters you want to paste.

8   Click the Basic Motion and Crop check boxes, and click OK.

In the Canvas, it appears as though there is only one image. All three images, since they share the V1 clip's attributes, are aligned on top of the V1 clip.

9   In the Timeline, select the V2 **MB high jump** clip. In the Canvas, Shift-drag the V2 clip to the right, and release it in the center of the Canvas image area.

10   In the Timeline, click the V3 **MB high jump** clip, and in the Canvas, drag it to the right of the center clip. Make any additional adjustments, and play these clips.

TIP   To fine-tune the position and alignment between these images or the other images in this sequence, click the View pop-up in the Canvas, and choose one of the Checkerboard options from the pop-up menu. When the playhead is stopped, the background changes from its default black to a checkerboard pattern. When the sequence plays, you see the default black behind the images.

Project Practice

To continue practicing with motion parameters, review the **MB championship** clip in the *Motion – Finished* sequence. This clip was cropped, resized, and repositioned to the upper part of the frame. The lower image was cropped, resized, and positioned, and the aspect ratio of the clip was changed to appear shorter. Make these changes to this clip in the *Motion – Starting* sequence. Save your changes.

Animating Motion Parameters

In addition to changing motion parameters, you can also set keyframes to animate those parameters over time. Just as audio keyframes set locations where the audio levels change, motion keyframes provide locations for motion parameters to begin, end, or change. When you set motion keyframes to move a clip's position around the image area, you create a *motion path*. You can set keyframes in the Viewer or Timeline, or use a keyboard shortcut. For these exercises, you will set keyframes in the Viewer.

Viewing Motion Keyframes

Before you begin setting motion keyframes, you will reposition the Viewer window and enlarge it to display the keyframe graph area where you will set and adjust the keyframes.

> **NOTE ▶** You may want to create a backup of the *Motion – Starting* sequence before you begin adding keyframes.

1   In the Timeline, drag the playhead to the marker in the ruler area labeled *all in*. Double-click the **DS good ride** clip on the V2 track to open it in the Viewer, and click the Motion tab.

The *all in* marker in the Timeline identifies the location where all three images are in view. You will set keyframes to rotate and resize the lower two clips that appear on the V2 and V3 tracks.

2   Drag the Viewer window to the left edge of the computer screen, over the Browser window, and extend the right edge of the Viewer to snap to the Canvas. Click the Opacity disclosure triangle so you can see its parameter details along with those of the Basic Motion parameters.

> **TIP ▶** You can save this window layout to use the next time you want to animate keyframes.

Keyframe button

Keyframe navigation buttons | Keyframes   Keyframe graph

Zoom control   Zoom slider

Each parameter has a keyframe button to set keyframes, and a keyframe graph where individual keyframes appear. The playhead moves in tandem with the Timeline playhead, and a zoom control and zoom slider help to focus on a specific area. The brighter portion of the graph represents the length of the sequence clip. You can zoom into that area so it is prominent in the keyframe graph.

3   In the Timeline, with snapping on, drag the playhead over the **DS good ride** clip and notice the places *within* the clip where the playhead wants to snap. Look at the Opacity keyframe line in the Viewer, and drag again over the clip in the Timeline.

Two opacity keyframes have already been set for the current clip, and the playhead is snapping to those locations. The playhead snaps to keyframes whether or not they are visible. Although you can set opacity keyframes in the Timeline, opacity is included with the Motion parameters and can be set or adjusted in that tab.

4   In the Motion tab, drag the playhead between the two opacity keyframes. Click the left and then the right keyframe navigation buttons next to the Keyframe button. Jump back and forth between these two keyframes and look at the Opacity parameter area.

TIP ▶ You can also press Shift-K to move forward to the next keyframe, and press Option-K to move backward to a previous keyframe. These shortcuts also work in the Timeline, and will move to any keyframe on any track, as long as Auto Select is on for that track and no other clips are selected.

The Opacity slider and percentage amount change from 0, or fully transparent, to 100, or fully visible. When the playhead is directly over a keyframe, the diamond on the Keyframe button is solid green. The arrows next to the Keyframe button are *keyframe navigation buttons,* which become solid when there is a keyframe in that direction you can move to.

5   To enlarge the keyframe graph for one parameter, move the pointer over the bottom portion of that parameter boundary. When the pointer turns into the resize arrow, drag down. Drag back up to return it to its original height.

6   In the Motion tab, hide the Opacity parameter, and look at the two blue diamonds in the keyframe graph area.

Although the Opacity parameter is collapsed, the two blue keyframes indicate the exact location of the two Opacity keyframes.

7   Display the Opacity parameter so you can use those keyframes as a reference in the following exercise.

Setting Motion Keyframes

To animate a motion effect, you need at least two keyframes. One identifies where a parameter begins to change, and the other where the parameter change ends, or changes again. In Final Cut Pro, this process is automated. With the first keyframe set, changing the parameter at a different location will automatically add a new keyframe.

In this exercise, you will rotate a freeze-frame image over time. The first keyframe will set the starting Rotation angle, and the second keyframe will set the ending angle. It doesn't matter which keyframe you set first. You often set the second, or end, keyframe first. For example, the racer freeze-frames are already in their ending position. Why not take advantage of that by setting those keyframes first? Once the rotation keyframes are set, you will animate the Scale parameter to change size as the image rotates.

> **NOTE ▶** For this exercise, always keep the highlighted or brighter portion of the keyframe graph, which represents the clip length, in full view.

1   In the Viewer, use any method to move the playhead to the second Opacity keyframe, the ending position of the **DS good ride** clip. Click the Rotation Keyframe button.

A green keyframe is added to the rotation graph at this location. This sets the ending angle for this clip.

2   Now move the playhead back to the previous Opacity keyframe. You will use this position as the starting Rotation keyframe. Drag the Rotation angle control wheel counter-clockwise around the circle until you see –360 in the field, or enter that number directly in the field.

Without clicking the Keyframe button, a new keyframe is automatically added on the Rotation line because you changed the parameter after setting an initial keyframe. As you dragged the wheel, the position of the keyframe on the line was adjusted up or down.

3   Play the clip to see the rotation effect. Then reposition the playhead to the first keyframe again, enter *−90* in the Rotation field, and play that version of the effect.

TIP ▶ If you don't reposition the playhead back to the starting position, a keyframe will be added wherever the playhead is located. Remember, keyframes mark an action at a specific location, and the placement of the playhead determines that location.

4   To change the scale of the **DS good ride** clip as it rotates, move the playhead to the second keyframe, the ending position. To set a keyframe so the scaling will stop at this current size, click the Scale Keyframe button.

5   Move the playhead back to the starting keyframe, and enter *10,* in the Scale field. Play the effect.

TIP ▶ If you want to delete a keyframe, move the playhead to it in the keyframe graph and click the Keyframe button. The diamond on the Keyframe button is no longer solid green, it becomes hollow. You can also Ctrl-click the keyframe and choose Clear from the shortcut menu.

6   To add motion keyframes to another freeze-frame image, double-click the
BS over hill clip on the V3 track. In the Viewer, you can reveal the Opacity
parameter details to see those keyframes, or just use the blue keyframes as
a reference.

This time, you will use a keyboard shortcut to add keyframes.

7   Move the playhead to the second keyframe, the ending location, and press
Ctrl-K to add keyframes for all motion parameters at once.

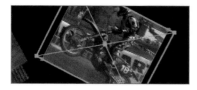

In the Canvas, the wireframe X turns green, indicating a keyframe is present on this frame.

NOTE ▶ You can also click the Keyframe button in the Canvas to add
keyframes to all motion parameters at one time. If you Ctrl-click the
Keyframe button, you can choose the specific parameter for which you
want to set a keyframe.

8   Move the playhead to the first keyframe. To change this image in the Canvas,
move the pointer over the right rotation handle of the selected clip.
When you see the Rotation pointer appear, drag clockwise about 90 degrees,
or a quarter turn.

9   With the playhead still on the first keyframe, drag a corner handle of the
clip wireframe inward until you get close to 10% in the Scale field. Play
the effect.

> **TIP** To save a specific set of keyframes as a favorite, select the clip in the Timeline and choose Effects > Make Favorite Motion, or press Ctrl-F. The motion will be saved in the Effects Favorites bin in the Browser.

Creating a Motion Path

In the preceding exercise, the clips you animated used the Scale and Rotation parameters but did not change the position of the clips. When you animate the position of an image over time, you create a *motion path* along which the image travels. Motion paths can be as simple as a straight line so that the image moves across the screen from one point, or keyframe, to another. Or it can include several keyframes that dictate very specific twists and turns. Creating complex motion paths is an art. These steps will expose you to some of the basic principles.

In this exercise, you will add keyframes to the uppermost freeze-frame image to change its position over time.

1   Double-click the **MB long run** clip on the V4 track. In the Motion tab, move the playhead to the second, or ending, Opacity keyframe as a reference.

> **TIP** To double-check if the playhead is really on the keyframe, display the Opacity parameters and look for the solid green diamond on the Keyframe button.

2   To set an ending Center (position) keyframe at this location, click the Center Keyframe button.

The Center parameter controls the position of the image on the screen. The center point default is 0 pixels horizontal and 0 pixels vertical. The first field represents horizontal movement. If you move a clip past center to the right, you will see a positive number. If you move a clip to the left past center, you will see a negative amount. The second field represents vertical movement—up shows as a negative number and down shows positive.

3 Move the playhead to the first Opacity keyframe, where you will change the starting position of this clip and its size.

At this frame, the opacity for this clip is zero, so you don't see the clip image in the Canvas. There is, however, a small white rectangle in the upper portion of the Canvas representing the cropped portion of the clip. Since this is the only portion of the clip you will see in the final effect, you can focus on positioning the white rectangle.

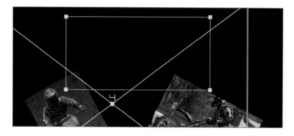

4 To see the space around the image area and create more room to reposition this clip, click the Zoom pop-up and choose 25%.

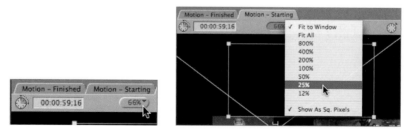

Zoom pop-up   Zoom pop-up menu

NOTE ▸ The percentage amount on the Zoom pop-up button will be different depending on the size of your computer screen.

You can use this pop-up to zoom in to or out from an image. When you zoom out, you see a wider view, so you can reposition clips outside the image area.

5   If a black background does not appear behind this clip, click the View pop-up and choose Black.

6   In the Canvas, Shift-drag the clip straight down until the *cropped* image is completely beneath the black image area. Play the clip.

A line with tic marks stretches from the first keyframe to the second. This is the motion path of this clip, which represents the clip's movement over time.

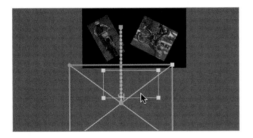

NOTE ▶ If you don't see the clip wireframe in the Canvas, select the clip in the Timeline. If you don't see the clip's parameters or keyframes in the Motion tab, double-click the clip you are changing to reopen it in the Viewer.

7   To return the Canvas view back to its default setting, click the Zoom pop-up, and choose Fit To Window. To turn off the wireframe display, click the View pop-up menu and choose Image. Press Cmd-S to save your changes.

NOTE ▶ In the Zoom pop-up menu, the default Fit To Window setting will always fit the entire clip image in the Canvas window regardless of how you change the window size. Like zooming in or out of the Timeline, changing the percentage in the Zoom pop-up menu does not change the actual scale of the image.

Project Practice

To continue working with motion keyframes, add Opacity keyframes on the first three clips in the current sequence to fade up each clip at a different time. Add Center keyframes to the **DS intro** and **DS good ride** clips so they move from offscreen into their current position. Do the same for the other two racing clip sets.

Creating a Variable Speed Change

Earlier in this lesson, you changed the speed of several clips to different yet constant speeds. You also edited a freeze-frame to a clip in motion to create a run and freeze effect. In this exercise, you will use keyframes to create a variety of these speed changes, all within the same clip. As with other motion parameters, you will add these keyframes in the Viewer Motion tab.

1   Drag the Viewer window to the right to access the Browser window, and, in the Browser double-click the *Speed – Starting* sequence to reopen it in the Timeline. Reposition the Viewer over the Browser.

2   Play the **MB long run** clip. Double-click this clip to open it in the Viewer, and click the Motion tab.

3   In the Motion tab, collapse the Basic Motion parameters section, and display the Time Remap parameters. If necessary, scroll down to see the full keyframe graph display, and zoom in so the highlighted area fills the graph.

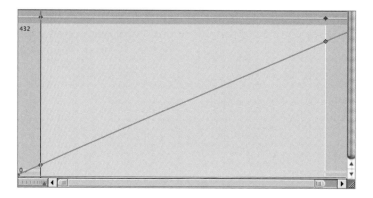

A 45-degree angle diagonal line, going from the lower left to the upper right, represents a constant 100% speed.

4   To create a freeze-frame in the middle of this clip, move the playhead to where the bike is at its highest point in the jump.

When using the keyframe graph to control speed, you set keyframes on the diagonal line. The location of the playhead on the line represents the frame you see in the Canvas.

5   To set a keyframe to *begin* the freeze, hold down Option and move the pointer over the diagonal line at the playhead location. When you see the Pen tool appear, click the green line.

Since there is ongoing motion in this clip, it will take two keyframes to create the freeze. The first keyframe is where the freeze begins, and the second keyframe is where the freeze ends and the motion begins again.

6   To create a 3-second freeze, press Shift-right arrow three times to move the playhead forward 3 seconds.

In the Canvas, you see the current frame at the playhead location. This will change in the next step.

7   Option-click the diagonal line at the playhead position, and drag the keyframe down until it's *exactly* even with the first freeze-frame keyframe. Play the clip.

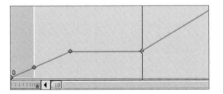

In order to stop time and accommodate the 3-second freeze-frame in the middle of this clip, the frames that follow play faster than normal speed.

Let's change the effect so rather than a freeze-frame you see the entire jump in slow motion.

8   In the keyframe graph, move the playhead to the first freeze-frame keyframe, and drag the keyframe down until you see the bike leave the ground in the Canvas.

Dragging a keyframe up or down changes the actual frame you will see *at that location*.

9   Now move the playhead to the second freeze-frame keyframe, and drag that keyframe up until you see the bike land on the ground. Play the clip.

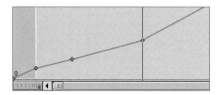

In the keyframe graph, the angle of the line determines the speed. A sharper angle creates a faster speed, and a lower angle creates a slower speed. The angle between these two keyframes is not that different from the normal 45-degree play-speed angle.

10   Move the playhead forward about 4 seconds in the keyframe graph. Drag the second freeze-frame keyframe horizontally to this location. Don't drag it vertically or you will be choosing a different frame of media. Play the clip.

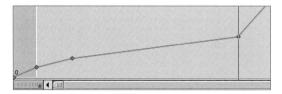

Now the angle of the line between these two keyframes is lower, and that portion of the clip plays more slowly, while the remainder of the clip accommodates the speed change.

11 If you want this clip to play in reverse after the slow-motion jump, drag the last keyframe on the upper right of the clip area down to the bottom of the graph. Play the clip.

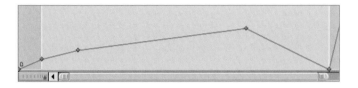

The clip plays backward when the line moves down.

TIP ▶ To create a smoother speed change at a specific keyframe, Ctrl-click the keyframe, and choose Smooth from the shortcut menu.

By applying keyframes to the keyframe graph, you can create numerous speed combinations. Here are some helpful aids to guide you:

▶ Upward line   Indicates forward speed

▶ Downward line   Indicates reverse speed

▶ Line angle   Indicates speed of the clip

▶ Flat line   Indicates freeze-frame

▶ Sharp corner   Indicates immediate speed change

▶ Curved line   Indicates smooth speed change

NOTE ▶ You can also add a Drop Shadow, which is another Motion parameter, to an image or text. You will work with this parameter in a later lesson when you work with text.

Lesson Review

1. From what menu do you select the Speed option?

2. How can you tell if the speed of a sequence clip has been changed?

3. What type of edit can change clip speed automatically as you edit it into the Timeline?

4. When you create a freeze-frame, does a new freeze-frame clip appear in the Browser automatically?

5. Where do you access motion parameters?

6. Can you change motion parameters directly in the Canvas? If so, how?

7. Can motion attributes be copied and pasted? If so, how?

8. Where are motion keyframes set and adjusted?

9. What is a motion path?

10. Under what motion parameter can you set speed keyframes?

Answers

1. From the Modify menu.

2. A speed percentage will appear next to the sequence clip name.

3. A Fit To Fill edit.

4. No, but you can drag the freeze-frame image from the Viewer to the Browser if you like.

5. In the Motion tab.

6. Yes, by choosing Image+Wireframe in the Canvas View menu.

7. Yes, by copying the clip and accessing the Paste Attributes window.

8. In the Motion tab keyframe graph.

9. The path a clip moves along between two or more keyframes.

10. Under the Time Remap parameter.

Keyboard Shortcuts

Cmd-J	Opens Speed window
Shift-N	Creates freeze-frame from playhead position
W	Toggles among Image, Image+Wireframe, and Wireframe modes
Shift-K	Moves forward to next keyframe
Option-K	Moves backward to previous keyframe
Ctrl-K	Sets a keyframe for Basic Motion parameters, Crop, and Distort

13

Lesson Files Lesson 13 Project

Media Motocross > Racing Footage and Team Story folders; Graphics folder

Time This lesson takes approximately 75 minutes to complete.

Goals Apply audio and video filters

View and modify filters

Apply filters for image correction

Apply filters to multiple clips

Use tools for viewing and adjusting filters

Nest a group of clips

Apply a matte to a clip or sequence

Apply a key filter

Animate filters using keyframes

Applying Filters

In Final Cut Pro, effects that can be applied to a clip are divided into two groups: transitions and filters. Transitions, of course, are applied to the edit point between two clips; filters are applied to the content or body of a clip. Although there are numerous reasons why you might apply a filter to a clip, there are three primary uses for filters.

First, on a lighter note, filters can give your sequence a special look or style, jazz it up, or create some fun and exciting visuals. Some call this *eye candy*. On a more serious note, filters can correct something that's wrong with an image, such as its color or contrast, or it can blur a product label you didn't get permission to use in your show. And finally, you can use certain filters to key or mask portions of images to create a simple letterbox effect or a complex visual composite combining several images.

You can apply filters to audio clips as well, either to improve the sound or to create an audio effect.

Preparing the Project

1   To launch Final Cut Pro, double-click the **Lesson 13 Project** file from the Lessons folder on your hard drive.

2   Close any other open projects.

3   In the Timeline, click the *With Filters* sequence tab, and play the sequence.

TIP ▶ In order to see as many filter effects play in real time as possible, click the RT pop-up menu in the Timeline and make sure Unlimited RT and Dynamic are selected. You can also select a clip and render it to see it play in real time.

Each clip has had a filter applied to it that changes it in some way.

4   Play the *Without Filters* sequence.

You don't see the effects that added some fun and style to the images, but there are still corrective filters applied to some of these clips that improved their image color.

5   To remove the filters in these clips, select all the video clips in the sequence, and Ctrl-click any one of them. In the shortcut menu, choose Remove Attributes. Make sure Filters is checked, and click OK. Play this sequence.

All the filters are removed from the selected clips, and now you see what the clips actually looked like after capturing them. In this lesson, you will first learn the mechanics of applying filters to add style to the sequence. And then you will apply filters to correct the color of the bluish images.

6   Before you begin making changes, create a backup of the *Without Filters* sequence in the Browser.

Applying Video Filters

You apply a video filter in one of two ways, similar to the way you applied transitions. You can drag it from the Video Filters bin in the Effects tab directly to a clip in the Timeline. Or you can select the clip in the Timeline, and choose a filter from the Effects menu. But unlike transitions, which are applied to an edit point, filters are applied to the body of the clip. Filters can be applied to a clip in the Viewer or in the Timeline.

In this exercise, to acquaint you with some of the filters used to create style, you will apply a different filter to each clip in the *Without Filters* sequence. Each of these filters can be modified, which you will do in the next exercise.

1   Move the playhead to the first clip, **CU pan starting line**. Select this clip.

As with transitions, parking the playhead on the clip allows you to see in the Canvas how that clip is changed as you apply a filter.

2   Choose Effects > Video Filters, and drag your pointer through some of the categories in the submenu.

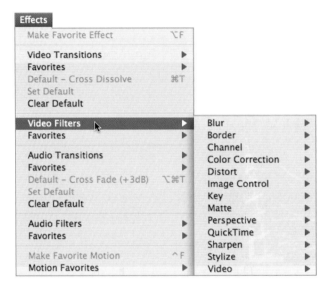

As with transitions, each filter category has a submenu of options. Based on the names of the filters, you can anticipate that some might add an interesting visual effect to a clip, whereas others might be used to correct images.

3   To apply a filter to the selected clip in the Timeline, choose Effects > Video Filters > Stylize > Find Edges. Play the clip.

The Find Edges filter creates an effect of extreme contrast that outlines the edges of the image in the clip.

Look at the Timeline ruler area. If an orange render bar appears above this clip, the clip will play in real time but may drop frames along the way. If the render bar is red, the clip must be rendered to view it in real time. You can also press Option-P to preview the effect but not in real time.

NOTE ▶ When you apply a filter in the Timeline, you are not changing the master clip in the Browser or the media file on your hard drive; you are changing only the sequence clip.

4   To add a filter to the next clip, click the Effects tab in the Browser, display the contents of the Video Filters bin, and then the Distort bin.

▼ 🔒 Distort	Bin
🎞 **Bumpmap**	Video Filter
🎞 **Cylinder**	Video Filter
🎞 **Displace**	Video Filter
🎞 **Fisheye**	Video Filter
🎞 **Pond Ripple**	Video Filter
🎞 **Ripple**	Video Filter
🎞 **Wave**	Video Filter
🎞 **Whirlpool**	Video Filter

NOTE ▶ All filter icons look the same regardless of how a specific filter affects a clip.

5   Drag the Pond Ripple filter to the second clip in the sequence, **race begins**, but *don't release the mouse.*

When you use the drag-and-drop approach to applying a filter, you see a brown selection outline around the entire clip.

6   Release the filter, and play the clip.

7   Move the playhead to the third clip, **BS over hill**, and select it. Choose Effects > Video Filters > Stylize > Solarize, and play the clip.

This is another filter that changes the look or style of a clip.

8   Select the fourth clip, **lots of bikers over hill**, and choose Effects > Video Filters > Perspective > Mirror. Play the clip.

This effect splits the action with one side mirroring the other.

9   For the last three clips, apply the following filters by using either the Effects tab drag-and-drop approach, or by choosing an option from the Effects menu:

▶   **DS good ride**   Border > Bevel

▶   **MB high jump**   Stylize > Replicate

▶   **biker down**   Stylize > Diffuse

Viewing and Modifying Filter Parameters

Every filter has a set of parameters you can modify to fine-tune the effect you want. These parameters appear in the Filters tab in the Viewer. Here you can modify parameters, delete the filter, toggle it off or on to compare before and after, save it as a favorite, or copy the same filter to another clip in the Timeline. You can also change the priority of filters, which can change the look of the effect. But before you can make any of these changes, you open the clip from the Timeline into the Viewer.

1   In the Timeline, move the playhead to the **DS good ride** clip, and double-click to open it in the Viewer.

2   Click the Filters tab.

Filter name   Reset button

You modify the parameters as you would motion effects, using sliders, rotation angle controls, and numerical fields. Some filters use color pickers for color selection.

3   In the Filters tab, click the Video Filters disclosure triangle to hide and then display the video filters applied to this clip. Click the Bevel disclosure triangle to hide and display its parameters.

4   Click the enable check box next to Bevel to toggle the filter off and on.

Toggling a filter off or on does not delete it from the clip. It simply allows you to view the clip with or without it.

5   Make your own changes to the Bevel parameters on this clip.

TIP   If you want to return a filter to its default settings, click its red Reset button.

6   Move the playhead to the **race begins** clip, and double-click it to open it in the Viewer. Change the Radius to 45, Ripple to 2, and Amplitude to 12.

7   To add an additional filter to this clip, choose Effects > Video Filters > Blur > Gaussian Blur.

Since this clip is already open in the Viewer, the filter appears as soon as you choose it.

You can apply several different filters to one clip to create a special effect. How they affect the image depends on the parameter settings and the order in which they are applied.

NOTE ▸ The first filter is always the first applied, and the last filter will be applied to the clip as well as to the filters that are listed before it.

8   In the Gaussian Blur parameter, change the Radius to 10, and look at the image in the Canvas. Click the enable check box for each filter to see how it is affecting the image, then enable both filters.

When you apply the Gaussian Blur *after* the Pond Ripple filter, the entire image, along with the ripples, is blurred. Changing the order of these filters will give you a different result.

9   To change the order of the filters, click the Gaussian Blur filter name and drag it up above Pond Ripple. When a dark bar appears above Pond Ripple, release the mouse.

When the Gaussian Blur filter is positioned *on top of* the Pond Ripple filter, the blur is applied only to the image, not to the Pond Ripple effect, and the ripples are no longer blurry.

10 Drag the Pond Ripple filter above the Gaussian Blur filter, to its original location, and the ripples become blurry again.

11 To delete the Gaussian Blur filter from this clip, click its name in the Filters tab, and press Delete. Press Cmd-S to save your changes.

TIP ▶ To remove all filters for a clip, click Video Filters, and press Delete. You can always press Cmd-Z to undo the most recently applied or deleted filter or filter adjustment.

Project Practice

To practice applying, modifying, and deleting filters, and to explore further the filter categories that change style, open several clips in this sequence, and disable their current filters. Apply other filters to the clips, and modify changes to that filter's parameters. For example, you can flop a clip to make it play in the opposite direction. Choose from the following Video Filter categories: Blur, Border, Distort, Perspective, and Stylize.

NOTE ▶ The QuickView tool in the Tools menu is an aid to previewing effects that may need rendering, or that don't play every frame. When open, it will play a marked portion of the Timeline and render the effect to your computer's RAM without creating a separate render file. After an initial slow play of the clip while rendering, QuickView then plays an area in real time.

Applying Corrective Filters

There are several video filters that can help correct a clip's color or improve its look in some way. Some of these filters can change the color balance of an image, adjust the luminance and black levels, add more color, or take color away. In these exercises, to understand how to use the color correcting filters, you will work with the motocross racing clips and correct the bluish tint.

Understanding Color Basics

Before you make color adjustments to a clip, you need to understand a few basic color principles. First of all, video is an additive color system, meaning that all colors added together will create white. So your reference to white is very important. If your white balance is off, as it is in some of the racing clips, the overall balance of colors in the image will be off as well.

Another aspect of color correction is the *hue* of the image. Hue is the color itself, sometimes represented by a name (red) but most often represented by a number on a 360-degree color wheel. Each color comes up at a different location around the wheel. For instance, the three primary colors in video are red, green, and blue, and they fall at 0 degrees, 120 degrees, and 240 degrees.

Some color wheels display more than just the hue. They reflect the *saturation* of a color. Saturation is the amount of hue present in an image. For all colors, 0 percent saturation shows the color as white. If red is fully saturated at 100 percent, decrease the saturation to 50 percent and you get rose. Decrease it to

25 percent and you get pink. Each of these colors is part of the red family in that they share the same hue but not the same amount of saturation.

The brightness, or *value*, of an image is the amount of lightness or darkness present. A 100 percent value is the highest or brightest level, whereas 0 percent gives you black, regardless of the hue or saturation numbers.

Using the Color Corrector 3-Way Filter

In Final Cut Pro, there are different filters you can apply to correct or adjust the color in an image, each offering a different approach for the same result. For example, you could choose the Image Control > Proc Amp filter, whose parameters are similar to controls on a professional VTR. Also from the Image Control category, you could choose Brightness and Contrast, or Levels, to adjust those specific aspects of your clip.

However, there is a general all-purpose filter you can use to color correct an image, and it is a real time effect. This is the Color Corrector 3-way filter. In this exercise, you will work with this filter to correct the bluish tint on the racing footage.

1   In the current sequence, move the playhead to the marker in the last clip, **biker down**, and double-click to open the clip into the Viewer. Click the Filters tab, and disable the Diffuse filter so you can see the original clip.

> **TIP** ▶ When working with multiple filters, it's helpful to hide or collapse the parameters of one filter as you focus on the parameters of another.

If the colors in a clip don't appear quite right, it may be because the color balance of the image is off. That can happen if the step of white balancing a camera was skipped prior to shooting the original material, or if the lighting for the shoot was hard to control, as it was in the racing footage.

2   Choose Effects > Video Filters > Color Correction > Color Corrector 3-way.

The Color Corrector 3-way filter appears in the Filters tab, but the parameter details are not in view. Instead you see a button named Visual and a separate tab called Color Corrector 3-way. There is a very good reason for this.

3   Click the disclosure triangle next to the Color Corrector 3-way enable check box, and drag the vertical scroll bar down to see all the parameters. Then click the disclosure triangle again to hide those parameters.

These parameters control the color of an image, but there is a much easier approach—a more *visual* approach.

4   Click the Visual button next to the Color Corrector 3-way name, or click the Color Corrector 3-way tab.

Although this filter is very complex and has lots of parameters, it also has a streamlined visual interface. Working within the visual interface lets you focus on the look of the image without getting distracted by the numbers you saw in the standard numeric interface.

In the visual display, the Color Corrector 3-way filter has three wheels: Blacks, Mids, and Whites. Each wheel controls the color balance in those ranges, and the sliders beneath the wheels control the different level of brightness in the image pixels. The Saturation slider beneath the wheels increases or decreases the amount of color in the image.

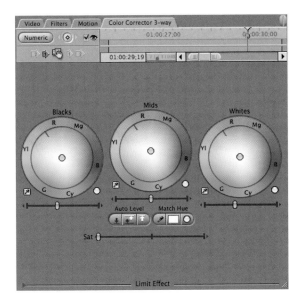

NOTE ▶ The Limit Effect area under the color wheels is used to change or control a specific color in an image.

One way to improve the color of the **biker down** clip is to *reset* (or redefine) what true white is in the clip's image.

5 Under the Whites color wheel, click the small Select Auto-balance Color eyedropper.

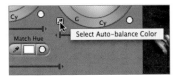

With this tool, you can select a new white reference from the image in the Canvas.

6 In the Canvas, click the white shirt-sleeve of the man on the right behind the flag.

Clicking a white area of the Canvas image rebalances all the colors and resets the colors in the image as though the white you clicked was true white. Look at the Whites balance control color wheel. The indicator in the center of the wheel has moved away from blue toward yellow.

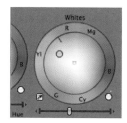

7 Click the enable check box so you can see the image with and without the Color Corrector 3-way filter enabled. Leave the filter enabled.

Just changing the white balance for this image has improved it considerably. Other racing clips in this sequence also appear bluish. You can apply this Color Corrector 3-way filter, with its current settings, to another blue clip.

8 Move the playhead to the **MB high jump** clip. From the Color Corrector 3-way filter tab, drag the Drag Filter icon to the **MB high jump** clip and release it.

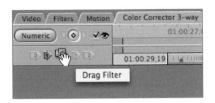

The settings that improved the **biker down** clip also work for the **MB high jump** clip. There are two more bluish clips in this sequence. You can apply this filter to both of these clips at the same time.

9   Move the playhead to the **DS good ride** clip. Select this clip, and Cmd-click the **race begins** clip to add it to the selection. To apply the current Color Corrector 3-way settings from the **biker down** clip, drag the Drag Filter icon to either selected clip and release it.

In the Canvas, you see the **DS good ride** clip is much improved. If you drag the playhead to the **race begins** clip, it too will have a new white balance. Since the **biker down** color filter changes were so effective on these clips, you might want to save this filter as a favorite to use on other bluish clips.

TIP ▸ Another way to copy the filters from one clip to another is to copy a clip and use the Paste Attributes option to paste all of the clip's filters to another clip.

10   In the Browser, select the Effects tab. From the **biker down** Color Corrector 3-way tab, drag the Drag Filter icon into the Effects tab and release it in the Favorites bin. Rename it *Blue Correction*.

TIP ▶ You can also choose Effects > Make Favorite Effect to save an effect. However, if there is more than one filter applied to the clip, all the filters will be saved together in a bin in the Favorites bin. You can drag this bin to any clip or group of clips if you want to apply the entire set of filters.

Viewing and Modifying Color Correction Changes

Sometimes, resetting the white balance for a clip solves the problem, and sometimes it just gets you in the ballpark. If you're only in the ballpark, you will need to tweak or adjust settings in the Color Corrector 3-way filter. To help you do that, there are two tools you can use to view the color changes and other filters you apply to a clip. One is the Frame Viewer, which displays a clip in a before-and-after, split-screen configuration. The other tool is the Video Scopes tool, which displays certain properties of an image, such as amount of brightness and color, or *luminance* and *chroma*.

1   In the Timeline, move the playhead to the marker in the **biker down** clip. Double-click this clip to open it in the Viewer.

2   Choose Tools > Frame Viewer, or press Option-7. When the tool opens in the Tool Bench window, reposition it over the Browser.

NOTE ▶ The Tool Bench window is placed over the Viewer or at the last position it was used in the interface.

In the Frame Viewer, you can choose what you want to see on each side of the frame and easily compare one clip to another or compare one clip with and without filters.

3   In the lower left of the window, click the Frame Viewer pop-up, and choose Current Frame, if it's not already selected. Click the pop-up on the right side, and choose Current w/o Filters.

In this view, you see the color-corrected image on the left and the original, uncorrected image on the right. You can change the size of each frame by dragging the boundary indicator.

NOTE ▶ You can also click the V-Split (Vertical), Swap, or H-Split (Horizontal) buttons to divide the frame differently or swap the images.

4   To use video scopes to help color correct a clip, choose Tools > Video Scopes.

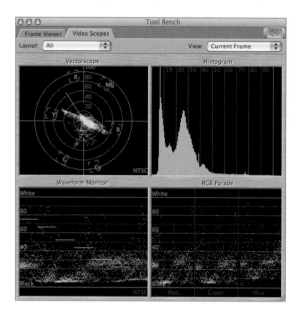

Now there are two tabs in the Tool Bench: Frame Viewer and Video Scopes. You can pull away either of these tabs to create its own separate window. You can also change the size of the window itself.

NOTE ▶ You don't use Video Scopes to make any adjustments, only to view your image in different ways. Another way to work with Video Scopes is to change your window layout to the preset Color Correction option.

5   To view just the luminance levels of your image in the Video Scopes tab, click the Layout pop-up on the left and choose waveform. Make sure the View pop-up on the right is set to Current Frame.

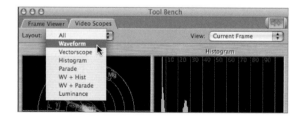

Each option in the Layout pop-up menu displays the pixels of your image differently, according to luminance, chroma, and so on. The waveform displays the luminance of the image over a 0 to 100 percent graph, with 0 being Black and 100 being White. Broadcast luminance levels should not exceed 100 percent.

6   In the Viewer, experiment with the Blacks level by dragging the Blacks slider left and right, then reposition it back to center. Click the left adjustment arrow, maybe eight times, until you see the lower group of pixels in the waveform creep down toward the 0% Black line.

TIP ▶ If you're working with a scrolling mouse, you can position your pointer over one of these sliders and scroll to change the levels.

The luminance of a clip is often divided into three areas, representing the darker pixels, the midrange pixels, and the brighter pixels in the image. The sliders beneath the color wheels in the Color Corrector 3-way tab are used to adjust these groups of luminance levels, and the waveform is used to monitor these levels.

7   To raise the level of the middle-range pixels, click the right adjustment arrow on the Mids slider. If the uppermost pixels in the waveform are not at 100%, you can click the right adjustment arrow on the Whites slider to make the brighter pixels a little brighter.

TIP ▶ Adjusting the Mids slider is a good way to bring out more detail of an image that is too dark or underexposed, or to remove the washed-out effect of an overexposed image.

In addition to changing the luminance properties of a clip, you can adjust the color balance even further by working with the three color balance control wheels.

8   To remove some of the blue cast in the darker dirt areas, drag anywhere within the Blacks color balance control to move the balance control indicator toward yellow. If the darker areas appear a little green, move the indicator upward away from green on the color balance control.

> **TIP** When making adjustments in the balance control wheel, hold down the Command key as you drag to move the indicator faster. To reset a color balance control to its default setting, click the Reset button on the lower right of the wheel.

In addition to changing the luminance and hue of a clip, you can adjust the Saturation slider beneath the wheels to increase or decrease the *amount* of color in the image.

9   Drag the Saturation slider to the right to add more color, or chroma, to this image.

10   In the Viewer, click the enable check box on the Color Corrector 3-way tab to see the image with and without the adjustments, or look at the split-frame image in the Frame Viewer tab.

Project Practice

Open the *Motion with Filters* sequence from the Browser. Follow the process in the previous exercise and reset the white balance for one of the first bluish racing clips, and then apply that correction to the other bluish clips in that sequence. Then make any additional level adjustments to the Blacks, Mids, Whites, and the Saturation of each clip. You can also experiment with filters in the Image Control category, or apply the Color Corrector filter from the Color Correction category to make these same adjustments a different way.

Applying Audio Filters

Applying filters to the audio portion of a clip is very similar to the way you apply video filters: you drag the filter from the Audio Filters bin in the Effects tab or select the clip and choose an option from the Effects menu. You can use an audio filter to help improve overall audio quality or to create a special effect such as an echo. You can also add a corrective filter to remove a specific sound.

1   Close the Tool Bench window, and open the *Motion with Filters* sequence from the Browser, if it's not already open from the previous Project Practice. Listen to the **MB wins** clip of the announcer speaking over the PA system.

An audio filter added to this clip could make the announcer sound like he's in a large stadium.

2   Double-click the **MB wins** clip to open it in the Viewer.

3   Click the Filters tab, and choose Effects > Audio Filters > Final Cut Pro > Reverberation.

> **TIP** ▶ Applying an audio filter to this clip may produce a red audio render line in the Timeline ruler area. If this occurs, open the User Preferences and, in the General tab, change the Real-time Audio Mixing to 12 tracks. If the red line is still present, render the clip.

The Reverberation filter is displayed under the Stereo 1 Filters heading in the Filters tab. The filter has four parameters. You will use the default settings.

4   Play the **MB wins** audio clip in the Timeline.

The default Reverberation filter makes the announcer sound like he's larger than life.

5   In the Browser, click the Effects tab, and click the Audio Filters triangle to display its contents. Display the contents of the Final Cut Pro folder.

The audio filter icon is a speaker with a filter overlay covering it.

6   To make the narrator sound like he's speaking to a crowd, drag the Echo filter to the **MB wins** audio clip.

When you drag the Echo filter onto the audio tracks of this clip, the audio tracks become outlined, just as they do when you drag a video filter to a clip.

7   Before playing the clip, deselect the enable check box next to the Reverberation filter so you will hear how only the Echo filter sounds. Play the clip in the Timeline. Then play the clip with both filters active.

These audio filters add an effect to create an entirely different sound, however, other audio filters, such as 3 Band Equalizer, just change the equalization (EQ) of a clip.

8   Close all open sequences in the Timeline, and press Cmd-S to save your changes.

Compositing Clips

In the previous lesson, you cropped and resized images in order to see more than one clip in the Canvas at the same time. By applying certain filters, such as keys or mattes, you can combine two or more clips together to create one *composite* image. Sometimes you composite clips out of necessity to cover up something you don't want to see in an image. Other times you use them to create a visual effect by combining the foreground from one clip with a background image from another.

Matting Portions of an Image

Mattes are filters that mask out a portion of an image. They can be used to create a simple letterbox or wide-screen effect for your entire sequence, or to mask a portion of an image you don't want to see, perhaps because of an unwanted object in the background. In fact, some mattes are referred to as *garbage mattes* for this reason. When you add a matte to create a wide-screen effect, you can save several steps by combining the video clips into a *nest*, and then applying the matte to the nested sequence.

1 From the Browser, open the *Intro with Matte* sequence, and play it.

To matte or mask the number information in the images and to see a letterbox or widescreen version of this sequence, you could add a matte filter to each clip. But then, if you wanted to make a change to the matte parameters, you would have to change the parameters for each clip. An easier way is to create a nest of the video clips.

2 Select all the video clips in this sequence. Choose Sequence > Nest Items, or press Option-C. In the Nest Items window, enter the name *Intro NEST*, and click OK.

In the Timeline, one single clip appears where the individual clips used to be. This is a nest of the clips you selected. In the Browser, there is a new *Intro NEST* sequence.

TIP If you want to get back to the individual clips, just double-click the sequence in the Browser, or the nest in the Timeline, and a sequence opens with just the individual clips you nested together.

3 To apply a matte to the nest of clips, select the nest in the Timeline, and choose Effects > Video Filters > Mattes > Widescreen. Drag the playhead through the sequence.

The upper and lower portions of the video clips have been equally masked, and you no longer see the numbers on the images.

4   To adjust the Matte filter settings, you *can't* double-click the nest in the Timeline, as you would a clip, or the nested sequence would open with the individual clips. Press Option and double-click the nest in the Timeline. In the Viewer, drag the playhead through the scrubber bar.

The entire nest of all the individual clips, including transitions, appears in the Viewer.

> **TIP** ▶ There are other ways to open a nest from the Timeline into the Viewer. You can Ctrl-click the nest and choose Open in Viewer, select the nest and press Return, or drag the nest from the Timeline to the Viewer.

5   Click the Filters tab. In the Matte parameters, click the Type pop-up and choose 2:35:1, and watch the sequence.

Because the clips are nested, you have to make only one selection in one filter to change the matte option.

> **NOTE** ▶ Each matte option is an aspect ratio that represents the image's width by its height. 35mm film is generally 1.85:1. The *A Thousand Roads* film is screening at the Smithsonian National Museum of the American Indian in an aspect ratio of 2.35:1.

6   To apply a different kind of Matte filter, open the *Garbage Matte* sequence from the Browser, and drag the playhead through this clip.

This is the freeze-frame you used in the previous lesson. Let's say the producer wants you to remove the man in the lower-left corner. Cropping the image from the bottom or side won't work here because it will crop the entire bottom or left edge of the image.

7   Double-click the **MB long run FREEZE** clip to open it in the Viewer. Click the Filters tab, and choose Effects > Video Filters > Matte > Four-Point Garbage Matte.

▼ ✔ Four-Point ...		⊗ ☑▾
View Mode	Preview ⬍	
Corners		
Point 1	⊕ -360 , -240	◁◉▷
Point 2	⊕ 360 , -240	◁◉▷
Point 3	⊕ 360 , 240	◁◉▷
Point 4	⊕ -360 , 240	◁◉▷
Edges		
Smooth	⬚———————▸ 0	◁◉▷
Choke	◂——⬚————▸ 0	◁◉▷
Feather	⬚———————▸ 0	◁◉▷
Options		
Invert	☐	
Hide Labels	☐	

In the parameters area of this filter are four points. In the Canvas window, the default points are set in each of the corners and are numbered clockwise from the upper-left corner. You will set new points to create a box around the man's body.

8   To set the first point of the matte, click the crosshair in the Point 1 parameter line. Move the pointer into the Canvas, and click to the left of the man's body, above his head.

TIP If you click and drag the point before releasing the mouse, the point will continuously update. If you release the mouse, you have to click the Point 1 crosshair again in the Filters tab and repeat the step.

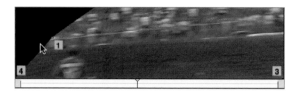

9 Continue setting Points 2, 3, and 4 clockwise around the man to isolate him. Also, drag Points 3 and 4 down beneath the image to include the area up to the clip's edge.

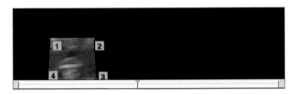

With the points isolating just the man, which is the portion of the image you don't want, you can now invert the image to reverse the matte.

10 In the Four-Point Garbage Matte filter, click the Invert check box, and drag the Feather slider to the right to 30. You may have to readjust the points to completely eliminate the man from the picture.

Feather		30	
	Options		
Invert	✔		
Hide Labels	☐		

Now you need to fill the hole. You do this by placing a clip beneath the current one so material from that clip will show through. You can use a duplicate of this clip as the background image and adjust it as necessary.

11 With the **MB long run FREEZE** clip selected in the Timeline, press Option and drag the copy down to the V1 track, release the Option key, then release the clip.

12 Press W to toggle on Image+Wireframe mode. In the Canvas, with the V1 clip selected, drag the wireframe left until you see a good match to fill the hole. You can also rotate the V1 image slightly to match the angle of the racing track. Toggle off the wireframe mode.

NOTE ▶ If the matte points are visible in the image area, double-click the V2 clip. In the 4-Point Garbage Matte parameters, click the View Mode and choose Final.

TIP ▶ Garbage mattes work well for many situations, such as masking an image to appear inside an object like a picture frame or television screen.

Applying a Key Filter

Another way to composite two clips is to make a clip's background transparent. This isolates just the foreground of the clip, perhaps a person, object, or graphic, so you can combine it with a different background. This is called a *key* effect and is created by applying a Key filter. There are two primary types of keys. One is used to key out the luminance of an image area, based on its darkness or brightness. The other is used to key out a particular color, or *chrominance*, of the image. Final Cut Pro offers several types of key filters. In this exercise, you will explore one that will key out a color in a graphic image.

1	In the Browser, open the *Key Filter* sequence.

	This sequence has all the filters that have been applied to this point.

2   To import a new file, press Cmd-I. In the Choose A File window, navigate
    to FCP5 Book Files > Media > Graphics > **Logo FLAT.jpg**, and click Choose.

    This single-layer JPEG file is displayed in the Browser as a graphic icon,
    like freeze-frames.

3   In the Browser, double-click the **Logo FLAT.jpg** file to open it in the Viewer.

    In the Viewer, the graphic has a marked 10-second duration, which is the
    default setting for still images in the User Preferences. You will edit this
    clip over the first clip in the sequence. Placing one clip on top of another
    is called *superimposing*. To make the graphic duration match the duration
    of the V1 clip, you will use the Superimpose edit.

4   In the Timeline, move the playhead anywhere within the **CU pan starting
    line** clip. Make sure the **v1** source control is patched to the V1 destination
    control. In the Viewer, drag the graphic image into the Canvas and release
    it on the Superimpose edit option.

The **Logo FLAT.jpg** clip is automatically placed on the track *above* the V1 track and is given the **CU pan starting line** clip's exact duration. To see the V1 clip, you will have to key out the graphic's blue background.

5 Double-click the **Logo FLAT.jpg** clip, and click the Filters tab. Choose Effects > Video Filters > Key > Color Key.

> **NOTE ▶** When you want to remove a color from a video image, which is a more complex key, apply the Chroma Key filter.

6 In the Color parameters, click the Select Color eyedropper button, and then click the blue background in the Canvas. Drag the Edge Feather slider all the way to the left. Drag the Tolerance slider right until you no longer see the blue edge around the graphic.

With the blue background keyed out, you now see the **CU pan of starting line** clip appear beneath the graphic.

7 In the Filters tab, click the View pop-up and choose Matte.

With Matte selected, only the alpha channel of the image appears in the Canvas, and you see how clean the graphic key really is.

All video clips are made up of three channels of information: red, blue, and green—or RGB. Images are formed by the combination of these three colors. When you add certain filters onto clips, such as keys and mattes, a fourth channel is created: the *alpha channel*. Alpha channels are displayed in black and white. The white area is opaque and protects or maintains that portion of the foreground image. The black area is transparent and allows the background image to show through.

TIP ▶ To create the cleanest keys in your images or graphics, always take a quick look at the matte of the keyed image. Make sure the white opaque area is as solid as possible so that portions of the RGB background image won't show through.

8 Adjust the Color Key parameters until the key is as tight around the graphic as possible, and you don't see any black artifacts in the white matte area.

9 To take an even closer look at the details of this image, click the Canvas Zoom pop-up and choose 200%. Press H to select the Hand tool, move the pointer into the Canvas image area, and drag the image to see other areas of the matte in this zoomed-in view.

When you see an area that has black specs, adjust the parameters in the Key filter until the black no longer appears.

10 To return the image to its normal size, click the Canvas Zoom pop-up and choose Fit To Window. In the Viewer Filters tab, click the View pop-up again and choose Final.

> **TIP** ▶ Another way to combine clips together is to apply a composite mode to a selected clip. Composite modes in Final Cut Pro are similar to those found in Adobe Photoshop and After Effects. You can choose composite modes from the Modify menu.

Adding Keyframes to Animate Filters

If you want to change a filter's parameter over time, you can add keyframes as you did with motion parameters, and you do it in exactly the same way. In this exercise, you will apply the Curl filter to a clip and animate it to cause the corner of the image to rise.

1 In the *Key Filter* sequence, move the playhead to the *curl* marker. Double-click the **biker down** clip, and, if necessary, click the Filters tab. Choose Effects > Video Filters > Perspective > Curl.

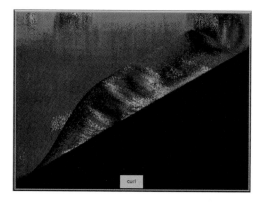

In the Canvas, the image's lower-right corner is curled upward. This is the default Curl setting.

2 In the Viewer, with the playhead at the *curl* marker, drag the Amount slider to 0.

Without a curl amount, no curl appears in the image. This will be your starting position, or where you place your first keyframe.

TIP ▸ When adding keyframes in the Viewer, expand the window, as you did when setting motion keyframes, to see more of the keyframe graph.

3   Click the Keyframe button for the Amount parameter.

Radius		30	
Amount		0	
Peel			

4   Press Shift-right arrow two times to move the playhead forward 2 seconds. Drag the Amount slider to 32, or enter that amount. Play the clip.

Since you have a starting keyframe, changing the amount at a different location automatically adds a new keyframe. Now the corner curl is animated over time.

NOTE ▸ You may want to disable the Diffuse and Color Corrector 3-way filters in this clip as you make changes to the Curl filter.

In this effect, the front of the image shows through to the back as the corner peels, which is a little distracting. But you can place a different image on the back of this clip.

5   From the Browser, drag the **Logo FLAT.jpg** image into the Filters tab of the Viewer, and drop it onto the Back graphic box, or well. Play the **biker down** clip.

Amount		0	
Peel			
Back		Logo FLAT.jpg	

Now as the corner curls, you see the original blue background of the **Logo FLAT.jpg** image appear in the lower-right corner. If you continued the curl through the entire image, you would see the full graphic.

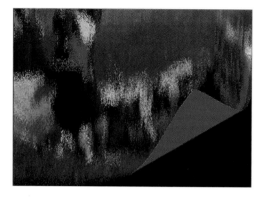

In a later lesson, you will add a graphic in the lower-right corner.

TIP Whenever you see a graphic well in a parameter, you can drop a different clip into the box to add an image to that parameter.

Project Practice

To continue practice setting filter keyframes, open the **Logo FLAT.jpg** image from the Timeline, and choose Effects > Video Filters > Perspective > Basic 3D. In this filter, you can change how the image is positioned on the X, Y, or Z axis, as well as change the scale or size of the image. Move the playhead 2 seconds from the head of the sequence, and set keyframes for each parameter in the default full-screen state of this filter. Then move the playhead to the beginning of the sequence and experiment with different starting possibilities as you preview the effect. Save your changes.

Lesson Review

1. What two ways can you apply a video or audio filter?

2. What is the procedure to view and modify filters for sequence clips?

3. How do you delete one or all filters in the Filters tab?

4. What two filters do you use to change luminance and chroma settings on a clip via its visual interface?

5. What two tools can be helpful when adjusting image color?

6. How do you apply a filter from one clip to another clip? To several clips?

7. How can you work with a group of clips as a single clip?

8. What two filter categories can you use to composite clips?

9. How do you add filter keyframes in the Viewer?

Answers

1. You can drag and drop a filter from the Effects tab to the clip in the Timeline, or you can identify the clip by selecting it or moving the playhead over it and choosing an option from the Effects menu.

2. Open the clip in the Viewer, and click the Filters tab. To change the priority of a filter, drag the filter name above or below another filter. To disable the filter, click the enable check box.

3. Click the filter name, and press Delete. To delete all video filters, click Video Filters, and press Delete.

4. Use the Color Corrector 3-way filter and the Color Corrector filter.

5. The Frame Viewer and Video Scopes tools are used to view color changes.

6. You can drag the Drag Filter icon from the Filters tab to another clip in the Timeline. To copy a filter to several clips at once, select those clips before dragging the filter. You can also use the Paste Attributes option.

7. Nest them together.

8. Use mattes and keys to composite clips.

9. Position the playhead where you want to start or end a filter change, and click a parameter keyframe button. Reposition the playhead, and change that parameter.

Keyboard Shortcuts

Option-7	Opens Frame Viewer tool
Option-9	Opens Video Scopes tool
Option-P	Previews an effect
Option-click	Sets a keyframe in the Viewer keyframe graph

14

Multicam Editing

Many shows use multiple cameras at the same time to shoot a production, event, or performance. Depending on the type of event, you might see anywhere from 3 or 4 cameras up to 20 or more. Reality television shows can use an even larger number of cameras to follow individual characters over a period of time. Daytime programming, such as soap operas and prime-time sitcoms, have four or five cameras rolling at once. Even dramatic television shows shoot some scenes rolling A and B cameras at the same time.

In Final Cut Pro, you edit multiple camera source material by using the *multi-clip* function. This function enables you to group multiple clips together according to angle and then cut between them, as though you were cutting the show live or in real time. But you don't have to shoot multiple cameras to use this feature. With FCP's multiclip approach to grouping clips, you can sync and play any set of clips together at one time. The material does not have to share the same timecode, or even be shot at the same time or location.

Preparing the Project

In this lesson, you will edit multicam footage using a different video standard than DV-NTSC, which you have been using throughout this book. The multicam footage is a music video originally shot using the HDV format, then converted to DV-PAL using the QuickTime Conversion within Final Cut Pro. (You will learn to convert media files in a later lesson.) To preserve the original aspect ratio of the HDV footage, which is 16:9, the DV-PAL Anamorphic setting was used in the conversion process.

NOTE ▶ The HDV footage was shot at 29.97 frames per second with the pixel dimensions of 1440 x 1080, which has an aspect ratio of 16:9 and was converted to DV-PAL Anamorphic, which is a 25-frames-per-second format with the pixel dimensions of 720 x 576. The DV PAL Anamorphic format has an aspect ratio of 4:3, but since it is anamorphic, it will automatically stretch to 16:9.

1   Launch Final Cut Pro and open the **Lesson 14 Project** file from the Lessons folder on your hard drive.

2   Close any other open projects.

Currently there are no sequences in this project, so the Canvas and Timeline will not appear. The underscore in front of the word *Sequences* tells Final Cut Pro to place this bin at the bottom of the other project elements when sorting alphabetically.

3   In the Browser, display the contents of the Audio Pops bin. Drag the scroll bar to the right until you see the Frame Size, Vid Rate, and Compressor column headings.

NOTE ▶ The two clips bins in this project are named after the method you will use to synchronize those clips during this lesson.

These clips all share the same properties of the DV-PAL format. If you scroll the columns farther to the right, you will find an Anamorphic column heading, and each clip will have a check in that column. To edit these

clips, you need to create a sequence that matches all of these clip properties. You do this by choosing the appropriate Easy Setup preset.

4   Choose Final Cut Pro > Easy Setup. Click the Show All check box in the
    upper-right corner of the Easy Setup window. Then click the Setup For
    pop-up menu and choose DV-PAL Anamorphic. Click Setup.

5   In the Browser, Ctrl-click the Sequences bin and choose New Sequence
    from the shortcut menu. Name this sequence *In Points*. Scroll back to the
    Vid Rate, Frame Size, and Compressor columns.

    The new sequence contains the same PAL settings as the clips in this proj-
    ect. You will use this sequence to practice synching clips by In points.

6   Double-click the *In Points* sequence to open it in the Timeline.

    Notice that the Canvas size appears wider than it did in the other
    sequences you have edited. The Canvas size follows the sequence
    settings—in this case, the 16:9 aspect ratio.

Organizing a Multiclip Editing Workflow

Although this lesson focuses on *editing* using the multiclip function, there are
some important things to consider while shooting, capturing, and organizing a
multiple camera (multicam) project that can make the editing process smoother.

The following suggestions may be useful when planning a multicam shoot that you will edit in Final Cut Pro, or when preparing footage to use as part of a multiclip.

Shooting Multiple Cameras

▶   Syncing the multiple camera sources is an important part of the multiclip process. There are different ways you can sync multiple cameras. On a professional multicam shoot, a master timecode generator is used to feed the same timecode to each camera or recorder. With this approach, the timecode number on each source identifies the same point in a scene or event. If this isn't an option, you can also record a visual or sound cue, such as a clapboard, an audio pop, or a camera flash, on all sources before the action begins or after it ends.

▶   When shooting with multiple cameras, you often assign each camera a number or letter that identifies the camera angle. Cameras are often numbered or labeled from left to right as you look at the stage or action. As part of the multiclip functionality in Final Cut Pro, clips are organized according to angle number or letter. Take time before and during the shoot to assign angle numbers and properly label the source tapes accordingly.

NOTE ▶ You can group up to 128 sources or angles into one multiclip.

Logging and Capturing Multicam Footage

▶   When capturing multicam footage, you capture each source independently. You can mark and capture footage as separate clips, or use the Capture Now function to capture an entire tape.

▶   In the Log tab of the Log And Capture window, there is an Angle field where you can enter or assign an angle number or a letter (A through E) for a source. Angle numbers are important when creating multiclips, because Final Cut Pro uses them to determine how a clip is sorted in the multiclip group. If no angle information is present for a clip, Final Cut

Pro uses the name of the clip to sort angles in the multiclip. Also, be sure
to enter the correct reel number.

Customizing Your Interface for Multiclip Editing

▶   There is a preset button bar you can use for working with multiclips, as
well as a preset keyboard layout for editing multicam material. You will
work with these options later in this lesson. If you have personalized your
button bars in the interface, take a moment to save that layout so you can
return to it after this lesson.

Synchronizing Camera Angles by In Points

Before you group clips into a multiclip, you need to synchronize them by
determining a common starting point. If all the recording devices were being
fed the same timecode information during the shoot, Final Cut Pro could
automatically synchronize the multiple camera sources according to their
timecode. However, if recording the same timecode on all media was not an
option, or if you are creating a multiclip from material that was not shot con-
currently, you can set an In or Out point to establish a sync reference. In this
exercise, you will sync sources by setting In points at an audio cue.

1   From the Audio Pops bin in the Browser, open the **CD Track – In Points** clip and listen to the introduction of the song. Then move the playhead to the beginning of the clip, and select the Stereo tab.

This is the mixed track of "Box Office Stud," performed by the All Hours band and written by bandleader Gilly Leads. The music video was shot at The Viper Room in Los Angeles with just two cameras as the band played to the mixed CD track. With repeated takes, additional camera angles were added. An image of the CD cover was added to this music track as a visual reference to this clip.

NOTE ▸ The All Hours band members are Gilly Leads on vocals and guitar, Dean Moore on bass, Nick Burns on drums, and Amit LeRon on lead guitar.

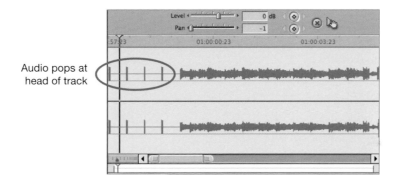

Audio pops at head of track

Audio pops were recorded at the beginning of the CD track to cue the band. Since every take recorded these audio pops, you can use them as a reference to sync the clips together before creating a multiclip.

2   Set an In point the frame *before* the last audio pop before the music plays.

You will set the same In point on the other video clips to sync to this location.

NOTE ▸ In this short intro, you will learn to sync sources by setting an In point on each clip's audio pop. You will edit a longer portion of the music video later in this lesson.

3 In the Browser, drag the scroll bar to the left, if the Frame Rate column is still in view, until you see the Media Start column.

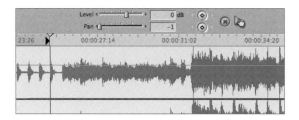

The clips in the Audio Pops bin do not share the same timecode information to synchronize these clips, which is why you are setting In points at the last audio pop in each clip.

4 From the Audio Pops bin, open the **wide right** clip and play it in the Viewer. Click the Stereo (a1a2) tab.

Even though this audio track will not be used in the final edited version, it serves as a good reference for syncing this video with the master CD track, and the video clips with each other.

5 Move the playhead to the frame before the last audio pop, and set an In point at this location as you did with the master CD track.

NOTE ▶ Whether you set an In point the frame before or on the frame where the pop begins is unimportant. The key is to set the In point consistently in all clips.

6   Open the `Gilly_cu guitar` clip and, using the waveform as a guide, set an In point on the frame before the last audio pop on this clip. Set an In point at the same location in the remaining video clips in the Audio Pops bin.

Each clip may have a different number of audio pops, but each has one before the music begins.

7   In the Browser, scroll the columns to the right until you see the Angle column.

If an angle is entered during the capture process, it would appear in this column. Currently these clips have not been assigned an angle.

NOTE ▶ It is not required that a clip have an angle number before you include it in a multiclip, but it can be a helpful step, especially in organizing a large project.

8   Click in the Angle column for the `Gilly_cu guitar` clip, and enter *1*. Enter *2* for the `Dean_bass` clip, *3* for the `Amit_lead` clip, and *4* for the `Nick_drums` clip. Click the Angle column head to sort by angle number.

You will not assign angles to the remaining clips.

Name	ot/Take	Angle ▼	Reel	Mast
▼ ☐ Audio Pops				
☐ CD Track – In Points				
☐ wide right			001	
☐ Gilly_cu guitar		1	002	
☐ Dean_bass		2	002	
☐ Amit_lead guitar		3	002	
☐ Nick_drums		4	001	

Lesson 14 Project · Effects

These angle numbers determine how the clips will be sorted and displayed in the multiclip configuration.

NOTE ▶ You can also change the angle number in the Item Properties window. To do this, select the clip, and choose Edit > Item Properties > Format.

Creating and Viewing Multiclips

With an In point set and some of the angles entered for the Audio Pops clips, you can now create a multiclip. By creating a multiclip, you group together a set of clips for the purposes of seeing them play at the same time. This gives you the opportunity when screening sources in the Viewer to choose from an assortment of clips playing in real time, rather than just one.

1   Select the four clips in the Audio Pops bin that have angle numbers. To create a multiclip from these four clips, choose Modify > Make Multiclip. You can also Ctrl-click one of the selected clips and choose Make Multiclip from the shortcut menu.

    NOTE ▶ A multiclip can contain any type of clip in the Browser, such as a graphic file or still image. You can also choose a bin and make a multiclip of all the clips in that bin.

A Make Multiclip window appears, displaying the clips in order of their angle numbers. The solid blue bars represent the clip content. The gray portion of the bar indicates areas where there is no clip content.

2   Click the Synchronize Using pop-up to view the options. You can synchronize these clips by In points, Out points, or Timecode. Choose In Points from the pop-up menu. This is the default option.

Clip In points

	Angle Name		Media Alignment
☑	[1] – Gilly_cu guitar		
☑	[2] – Dean_bass		
☑	[3] – Amit_lead guitar		
☑	[4] – Nick_drums		

The clips are aligned according to the In points you set on the audio pops.

NOTE ▸ To deselect one of the clips from the multiclip selection, click the angle check box next to that clip.

3   Click OK.

In the Browser, a multiclip icon appears in the Audio Pops bin. This icon always represents a group of clips. Notice the name is italicized and begins with the angle 1 clip, **Gilly_cu guitar**.

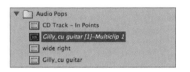

NOTE ▸ The number following the word *Multiclip* indicates the number of multiclips that have been created in this project as you've been working, not necessarily the number of multiclips currently *in* the project.

4   Click the name portion of the multiclip. When it becomes highlighted, enter *Audio Pops*, then press Return.

Since the angle and clip name are added automatically, only the name of the multiclip is changed.

5 Double-click the multiclip to open it in the Viewer, and press the spacebar to play it. If the Viewer image changes to a single clip, click the RT pop-up in the Timeline and choose Multiclip Playback.

> **NOTE ▶** Depending on your computer processor, you may not see all the clips play together for the duration of the multiclip. In the Timeline, you can adjust the RT Playback Video Quality and Playback Frame Rate settings to improve the performance.

In the Viewer, a 4-up view displays all four clips simultaneously. The clips are positioned left to right, top to bottom, in the order of the angle numbers you entered in the Browser. You can use all of the play functions and shortcuts in a multiclip you've used to play single clips.

6 To create a larger Viewer image area, choose Window > Arrange > Two up.

7 In the Viewer, drag the playhead to any location where you see all four clips in the image area. Without playing the clips, click from image to image.

The selected or *active* angle is highlighted with a blue-green outline. In the Browser, the angle name and number on the multiclip changes to reflect the active angle, while the name of the multiclip itself, Audio Pops, remains constant. The multiclip will reposition itself within the Audio Pops bin according to the current sort order.

	Name
▼ 🗀 Audio Pops	
	Amit_lead guitar [3]–Audio Pops
	CD Track – In Points
	wide right

You can use keyboard shortcuts on the number pad of an extended keyboard to change angles if you load the multicam Keyboard preset layout.

8   To use the keyboard shortcuts on an extended keyboard, choose Tools > Keyboard Layout > Multi-camera Editing. Switch between the multiclip angles using numbers 1 through 4 on the number pad. If you're working on a laptop, toggle on Number Lock and use the number keys that appear in the J-K-L area of the keyboard.

NOTE ▶ Without using the Multi-camera Editing keyboard layout, you can change angles on an extended keyboard number pad by using the Shift key.

9   In the Viewer, click the View pop-up and choose Show Multiclip Overlays.

The multiclip overlay displays each clip's angle number, clip name, and timecode number. It works like other overlays in that you see these only when you scrub through the multiclip, not when you play it.

NOTE ▶ When you are using the Multi-camera Editing keyboard layout, some editing functions—such as trimming, rolling, moving, or slipping by numbers—are not available.

Modifying Multiclips in the Viewer

Once you have created a multiclip and have opened it in the Viewer, you can modify certain aspects of it. You can change the arrangement of the clips in the 4-up view, delete an angle from the multiclip selection, or add a different angle to the grouping. You can also resynchronize a clip to start earlier or later in the group. In this exercise, you'll begin by rearranging the current layout of the clips in the Viewer.

1   To reposition the **Nick_drums** clip in the multiclip, Cmd-click that angle and drag it to the left. Release it over the **Amit_lead guitar** clip.

As soon as you begin to drag a clip to a new angle position, the clip in the original angle position moves to allow for the new clip arrangement.

TIP ▶ If at any time you no longer see the multiclip angles in the Viewer, just double-click the multiclip in the Browser to reopen it.

2   Cmd-click the **Nick_drums** clip, drag it to the upper-right corner, and release it. Look at the angle number of this clip.

Changing the position of a clip in the Viewer 4-up display changes the angle number of that clip within the multiclip. It does not, however, change the clip's angle number in the Angle column of the Browser. The original angle 2 clip, **Dean_bass**, has been moved down to the next line as angle 3.

3   To add a fifth clip to the multiclip group, drag the **wide right** clip into the upper-left corner of the Viewer, but don't release the mouse.

An overlay appears over the image, giving you the option to insert the new clip as the new angle 1 or overwrite the current angle, removing it from the multiclip group.

4   To add this clip to the multiclip group at this location, release it onto the Insert New Angle option.

The other clips are moved to the right and then down. At this point you will not see the fifth angle. In a moment, you will change a setting to see all the angles.

5   From the Audio Pops bin, drag the **CD Track – In points** clip to the Viewer and insert it in the lower-right corner.

This is the final mixed track of the song, "Box Office Stud." It will provide a better soundtrack for the music video than the music on the video clips.

NOTE ▶ When you drag a new clip onto an active angle, only the Insert New Angle option appears. You cannot overwrite the active angle.

6   Move your pointer to the lower-right corner of the Viewer, and click the down arrow to scroll to the offscreen angles, **Dean_bass** and **Amit_lead guitar**. In the upper-right corner, click the up arrow to return to the first four angles.

7   In the Viewer, click the View pop-up menu and choose Multiclip 9-Up
    from the pop-up menu.

When you change to the Multiclip 9-up view, you can see all the angles
contained in this multiclip. You can view up to 16 angles in real time.

8   To select a clip a different way, click the Viewer Playhead Sync pop-up.
    Make sure Video + Audio is checked toward the top of the pop-up menu,
    then drag your pointer down the menu and choose either the video or
    audio of the **CD Track – In Points** clip.

Playhead Sync pop-up

This clip becomes highlighted in the Viewer. When Video + Audio is the
active mode, you are selecting the video *and* audio of the clip you select.
But when you change the mode to Video, you can switch between just the
video sources and allow the audio from the CD mixed track source to
continue playing.

9   Click the Playhead Sync pop-up and choose Video as the switching mode.
    Now click the **Gilly_cu guitar** clip.

The blue-green highlight separates when not in Video + Audio mode. The green highlight stays over the active audio source, and the blue highlight switches to the **Gilly_cu guitar** clip, indicating it is the active video angle.

NOTE ▶ You can also change the switching mode by choosing View > Multiclip Active Tracks and selecting the appropriate option. The switching mode remains until you change it to a different option.

10 Now play the multiclip and watch the angles against the mixed CD track.

11 To delete the **Amit_lead guitar** clip from the multiclip and return to just four video angles, Cmd-click and drag it anywhere outside of the Viewer, then release the mouse.

NOTE ▶ You cannot delete an active angle.

A smoke puff will appear, indicating that you have removed the clip from the multiclip grouping.

12 Reposition the CD Track angle to be the last angle, or lower-right angle, in the group. Then click the View pop-up and choose Multiclip 4-Up to return to that display.

The audio source will be out of view, but since you are only switching between video angles, it won't matter.

> **TIP** ▶ If you need to adjust the sync of a clip after it's been included in a multiclip, hold down the Shift and Control keys and drag the clip in the Viewer left or right, then release the mouse.

Editing with Multiclips

Once you have created and adjusted your multiclip as necessary, you can move on to the editing process. Editing multiclips is a little different than editing single clips. With multiclip editing, you edit the multiclip to the Timeline and *then* make editing choices about when you want to cut to a different angle. You can even edit between angles on the fly, in real time, directly in the Timeline. This is similar to productions such as music performances or football games, during which a director or technical director chooses between camera inputs on a video switcher. The output of the video switcher is often broadcast live.

Editing a Multiclip to the Timeline

Except for one important difference, getting a multiclip into the Timeline is the same as it is when you edit a single clip. You position the playhead in the Timeline, patch the source controls, and mark your multiclip in the Viewer, if you want to edit only a portion of it. You can even click the Overwrite or Insert edit buttons in the Canvas to make the edit. The only difference is that when you choose the drag-and-drop approach to making the edit, either dragging the image to the Canvas Edit Overlay or directly to the Timeline, you must use the Option key.

1 In the Viewer, set an In point just after the audio pop at the head of the multiclip. Move the playhead toward the end of the multiclip, and set an Out point where all the images are still in view.

2   Make sure the **CD track – In Points** clip is the active audio source and has a green highlight around it. Click the **wide right** clip as the active video angle.

3   In the Timeline, make sure the playhead is at the beginning of the sequence, and that the video and audio source controls are patched to the V1, A1, and A2 destination tracks.

4   To edit the multiclip into the Timeline, click the red Overwrite edit button in the Canvas. You can also use the drag-and-drop approach, but you must hold down the Option key as you drag.

In the Timeline, a stereo audio track appears along with one video track. Multiclips are contained within one track in the Timeline. The audio is the **CD Track – In Points** audio that was selected prior to making the edit. The video is the active video angle you selected prior to making the edit.

NOTE ▶ Think of the multiclip in the sequence as a layer cake. The top layer is visible, but you can switch to a different layer beneath it at any time.

5   Play the sequence.

When you play the sequence, you see only the active angle, or the top layer, play in the Canvas. To see the other angles play in the Viewer at the same time, you have to change the playhead sync.

NOTE ▶ Although you can double-click the multiclip in the sequence to open it in the Viewer, you still need to perform the following step to see all the angles play simultaneously.

6 In the Canvas, click the Playhead Sync pop-up and choose Open. You can also choose View > Playhead Sync Open, or press Ctrl-Shift-O. Play the multiclip again.

With this option, Final Cut Pro literally *opens* the multiclip into the Viewer and keeps it open as you continue editing so you can see all the angles—as many as 16—play at once. Notice in the Viewer scrubber bar that the two rows of dots, or sprocket holes, appear as they do when you open a single clip from the Timeline.

> **TIP** ▶ To ensure that you see all angles play in the Viewer during multiclip editing, make sure you have Multiclip Playback checked in the Timeline RT pop-up and the Playhead Sync set to Open.

7 Without playing the multiclip, click the different angles in the Viewer to see each one appear in the Canvas.

In the Timeline V1 track, the thumbnail image changes whenever you switch to a different angle, as does the angle name on the clip. However, since the switching mode is set to Video in the Playhead Sync pop-up menu, the audio track doesn't change.

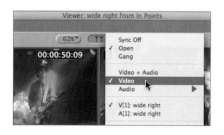

NOTE ▶ In the Timeline, make sure the multiclip is deselected. Anytime the multiclip is selected in the Timeline, many of the multiclip functions are disabled.

8   You can also switch angles by using a shortcut menu. Move the playhead
    to the head of the sequence and Ctrl-click the multiclip on the V1 track.
    From the shortcut menu, choose Active Angle, and then choose Gilly_cu
    guitar from the submenu.

    This menu lists the clip names along with their angle numbers.

9   To switch angles on an extended keyboard, click the numbers between 1
    and 4 to switch between the different video angles.

    As in many Final Cut Pro functions, there is yet another way to switch
    between the camera angles. There is a preset button bar layout you can
    load to use in multicam editing.

    TIP If you haven't already saved your customized button bar layout,
    take a moment to do that so you can load it back into the interface when
    you complete this lesson.

10 To load the preset multiclip button bars, choose Tools > Button Bars >
    Multiclip.

    New buttons have been added automatically to the button bars in each
    window. These buttons are placed in the most logical window to help you

with that function. For example, a Make Multiclip button appears in the Browser, and a Show Multiclip Overlays button appears in the Viewer.

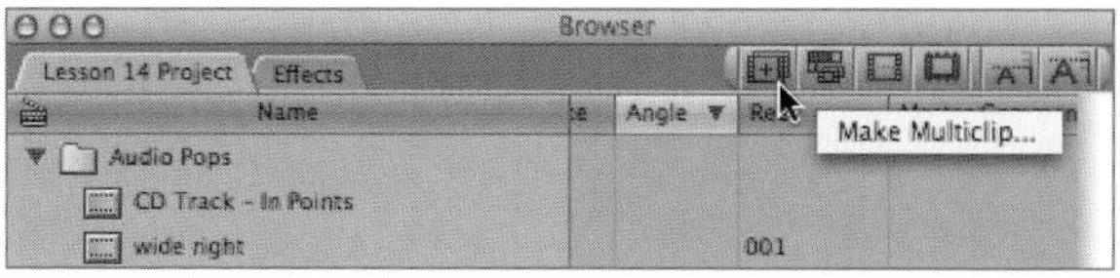

11 Move your pointer over some of the new multiclip buttons to familiarize yourself with these options.

12 In the Timeline button bar, there are three sets of multiclip buttons; each set has a different color. Click the far-left gray button, and then click the button to the right of it. Now move your pointer over each of the first eight buttons.

These eight gray buttons are really just two sets of four buttons, with each set divided by a spacer. The first four buttons switch to video angles 1 through 4; the second four switch to audio sources 1 through 4.

Cutting Between Angles in a Multiclip

In the previous exercises, you clicked a camera angle in the Viewer to switch to it and make it the active angle. In this exercise, you will *cut* between angles to create edit points in the multiclip. In order to understand and observe everything that is happening when you cut to a different multiclip angle, in this exercise you will move the playhead to a specific area where you want to make an edit and then cut to an angle. In the *next* exercise, you will cut from angle to angle in real time.

1 To coordinate the steps in this exercise with the angle layout in your own Viewer, move the playhead in the Timeline to the head of the sequence and position the clips as they appear in the following image.

2   To start the sequence with the close-up guitar shot, use any method you like to *switch* to the `Gilly_cu guitar` angle. As the active angle, this image will appear in the Canvas when you select it, as well as in the Timeline thumbnail image on the V1 track.

3   Play the sequence, and look for where the band comes in, around 1:00:06:06. Stop playing and reposition the playhead a few seconds before this point.

4   Play from this location and this time click the angle 1 image in the upper-left corner. Then press the spacebar to stop playing.

NOTE ▶ You can cut to angles using similar methods as when you switched to angles.

5 Play the new edit. Then move the playhead about 4 seconds past this edit point, where you will cut to the next angle.

NOTE ▶ Throughout these steps, general times will be used as a simple reference for creating new edit points. You can choose more specific cut points if you like.

6 To cut to the **Dean_bass** angle 3 clip at this location, move your pointer over the Cut Video To Angle 3 button (the third cyan-colored button in the Timeline button bar). Click this button, then play the new edit.

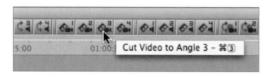

The eight cyan buttons cut to video angles 1 through 4 or audio angles 1 through 4.

NOTE ▶ The icon for this function is a razor blade over a video camera. Applying this button at the playhead location creates a new edit point in the multiclip, just as the Razor Blade tool does to single clips.

7 Move the playhead forward another 4 seconds from the edit point you just created to the next cut point. This time, if you have an extended keyboard, press Cmd-4, using the number pad, to cut to the angle 4 clip, **Nick_drums**. If you don't, just click this clip in the Viewer.

8 Move the playhead 4 seconds forward from the previous edit point, and press Cmd-1 on the number pad to cut to the angle 1 clip, **wide right**, or click this clip in the Viewer.

9   Move the playhead over the second clip in the multiclip. Change this angle to a different angle using any of the *switching* methods.

Once an edit has been made in the multiclip, you can change the active angle at that location by moving the playhead to the clip and switching to a different angle.

NOTE ▶ When you edit a multiclip into a sequence that has additional audio and video tracks of other sources, keep in mind that cutting and switching multiclip angles follows the Auto Select controls.

Project Practice

Before you move on to cutting angles in real time, practice switching or cutting angles in the current sequence. Or delete the multiclip from this sequence and repeat the process to edit the multiclip again. To refine the precise location of each edit point, you can use the Roll tool, and the individual angles will all stay in sync.

TIP ▶ To remove an edit you just created, press Cmd-Z.

Cutting Multiclip Angles Live

Finally, you can put on your director's hat and let the footage roll as you cut to different angles in real time. This is often called *cutting on the fly*. To do this, you have to be somewhat of a multitasker. You watch the individual images in the Viewer and position your fingers over the number pad of your keyboard. When you see an angle in the Viewer you want to cut to, you Cmd-click that angle number. Remember, you can always go back to any edit in the multiclip and switch to a different angle. You can also adjust edit points with the Roll tool.

1   In the Browser, create a new sequence in the Sequences bin, and name it *Cutting Live*. Open this sequence in the Timeline.

2   In the Browser, double-click the Audio Pops multiclip to reopen it in the Viewer. If necessary, reset the In and Out points where all the angles are in view. Click the `Gilly_cu guitar` clip to begin with that angle.

When you reopen the multiclip from the Browser, the Viewer scrubber bar does not contain the sprocket holes as it does when you are viewing the multiclip from the Timeline.

3 Edit this multiclip to the head of the sequence. Remember to hold down Option if you use the drag-and-drop approach.

4 Double-check that the Viewer Playhead Sync is set to Open.

At this point, you are ready to play the sequence and begin cutting live. But before you start, take a moment to think through your plan of action. (Even directors rehearse themselves by taking a closer look at their camera angles before the event begins.) What camera angle do you want to cut to after the guitar close up? Do you want to cut to the wide shot in the middle of the guitar introduction? It may be helpful to play the music track a few times as you watch the angles in the Viewer, and begin to formulate ideas.

When you do cut to a new angle in the following step, you will see blue markers appear in the Timeline ruler area at your cut points. When you stop playing the sequence, these markers become edit points in the multiclip.

TIP Before you begin cutting, you can rehearse by playing through the sequence and switching angles. Switching also places blue markers in the Timeline ruler area, but does not cut the multiclip.

5 When you're ready, play the sequence and get ready to press Command and the angle number you want to cut to next, or click that image in the Viewer.

When you stop playing the sequence, edit points appear at the blue marker locations.

TIP ▶ To undo the live cuts and return to the single-angle multiclip, press Cmd-Z.

Project Practice

If you'd like to keep working with this portion of the music video, create a different version by adding a new angle to the multiclip from the Audio Pops bin. Cut the music video live using the process just outlined. You will work with a new section of the music video in the following exercise.

Synchronizing Camera Angles by Timecode

Another way to sync clips is to use timecode as a reference. When clips share the same timecode, you don't have to set an In point to sync them together. A timecode number in one clip should identify the same action in an event as that same timecode number in a different clip. The method of switching and cutting angles in the multiclip is the same, no matter how the clips are synchronized. For this exercise, you will use a different set of clips and a different section of the music video.

1   In the Browser, Ctrl-click the Sequences bin and choose New Sequence from the shortcut menu. Name this sequence *Timecode,* and open it in the Timeline.

    Each new sequence you create contains the same PAL settings you chose from the Easy Setup window earlier in this lesson.

2   Hide the contents of the Audio Pops bin, and display the contents of the Timecode bin.

3 Double-click the `Gilly_cu` clip, and play from the beginning of the clip. When Gilly steps up to the mic to start singing, stop the clip and look at the timecode number in the Current Timecode field in the Viewer.

4 Open a few other clips from the Timecode bin and compare the timecode numbers at the location where Gilly starts to sing.

   The same timecode number in all of these clips identifies the same event or clip location. For this group of clips, you can synchronize by timecode, even though they don't all start or stop on the same frame.

5 To make a multiclip of all the clips in the Timecode bin, Ctrl-click the bin and choose Make Multiclip from the shortcut menu.

6 In the Make Multiclip window, click the Synchronize Using pop-up and choose Timecode as the sync option.

	Make Multiclip	
Synchronize using: Timecode		
Angle Name	Media Alignment	Sync Time
☑ [1] – Gilly_Dean		01:01:25:18
☑ [2] – Amit_lead guitar		01:01:25:00
☑ [3] – CD Track – Timecode		01:01:23:20
☑ [4] – Dean_bass		01:01:21:24
☑ [5] – Gilly_cu		01:01:25:17
☑ [6] – Gilly_med		01:01:24:17
☑ [7] – Nick_drums		01:01:25:16
☑ [8] – Wide_left		01:01:21:21
☑ [9] – Wide_right		01:01:23:24
	Cancel	OK

The blue bars of each angle reposition to align the clips by timecode. Notice how the blue bars seem to cover the same relative area. They were taken from the same portion of the song but are not exactly the same length.

7   Click OK. In the Timecode bin, rename the new multiclip *Timecode,* and double-click to open it in the Viewer.

8   In the Viewer button bar, click the Show Multiclip Overlays button to toggle off the overlays in this multiclip.

9   In the Viewer, click the View pop-up and choose Multiclip 9-Up from the pop-up menu to see all the multiclip angles. Play this portion of the music video.

10 To edit this multiclip, use the same process you used with the Audio Pops multiclip. Start by changing the sync to Video+Audio and selecting the **CD Track - Timecode** clip. Then change the sync to Video and select the first video angle. Set an In point and an Out point where the angles are all in view, and edit the multiclip to the Timeline.

11 To see the clips play in the Viewer as you play the sequence, click the Playhead Sync pop-up, and choose Open from the menu, or press Shift-Ctrl-O. This will allow you to see the angles as you play and cut in real-time.

At this point, you can edit these clips as you did in previous exercises: either by moving the playhead to an exact edit location and cutting to a new angle, or by cutting live.

NOTE ▶ If you are using a laptop or slower computer, this nine-clip multiclip may play slowly.

Project Practice

Create a few new sequences, and open them in the Timeline. Edit this same multiclip into each sequence, but then cut each sequence differently. In one sequence, you might decide to feature Gilly Leads, the lead singer. In another, you might feature Nick, the drummer, or other members of the band.

Changing Clip Timecode

Syncing by timecode is a convenient process. It saves the step of having to set In points as a sync reference for each clip. If you want to use this approach but your source material does not share the same timecode, you can change the timecode within Final Cut Pro of your original QuickTime media file. Keep in mind that whenever you change the timecode in the QuickTime media file, you change it for *all* uses in *all* projects.

Another option is to create a secondary Aux timecode, which will not change the primary timecode but can still be used as a reference point. You can also use an Aux timecode to sync clips in the Make Multiclip window. The steps that follow are general ones you can apply to your *own* footage, not to the clips in this project.

1   To change the timecode number (or reel number) in a media file or to add an Aux timecode number, open the clip in the Viewer and choose Modify > Timecode.

2   In the Modify Timecode window, click the Frame To Set pop-up and choose either Current or First.

If you want a specific timecode number, such as 1:00:00:00, to begin at a specific point in the action, such as the first note of the song, you must position the playhead at that location and choose Current.

3   Enter the new timecode number, make any other selections such as frame rate and timecode type (drop frame or non-drop frame), and click OK.

Switching Angles with Effects

You can apply filter, speed, and motion effects to angles you've cut in the multi-clip in the Timeline. You do this the same way you would with a single clip. But if you decide to switch an angle with an effect to another angle at the same location, the new angle will not have the effect. There is a way you can switch to a different angle and also apply the previous angle's effects to the new angle:

1   With a multiclip in the Timeline, move the playhead over any clip and choose Effects > Video Filters > Image Control > Desaturate. Play this clip.

The Desaturate filter has removed the saturation from this clip, but only on this specific angle, not on the other angles located at this position in the multiclip.

2   Move the playhead over the desaturated clip, and switch to a different camera angle.

The different angle has color. Only the angle that was previously active in the sequence at this location has the Desaturate filter.

NOTE ▶ Remember that a multiclip is like a layered cake stacked with individual single clips. If a filter is applied to an angle, it is like icing on the top layer of the cake. Applying a filter (the icing) on the top layer does not automatically apply it to any of the angles (or layers) below.

3   Press Cmd-Z to return to the previous desaturated angle.

4   This time, switch to a different angle by clicking one of the first four purple Switch Video With Effects buttons in the Timeline button bar. Make sure you are switching to a different camera angle than the one with the Desaturate filter.

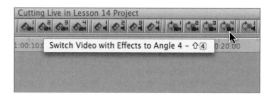

Any filters, speed, or motion effects that were applied to the previous angle are now applied to the current angle. In this case, the new angle is also desaturated.

Collapsing a Multiclip

Once you've completed editing your multiclip, refined your edit points, and settled on your camera angles, you may need to output your sequence and pass it along to someone else, such as a colorist or audio mixer. Instead of passing along the sequence with a multiclip in it, you can *collapse* the multiclip so that only the active angles are accessible. In this way, no one can make any unwanted changes to your sequence. You can *uncollapse* a sequence at any time, returning it to the original multiclip state.

> **NOTE ▶** Once you've finished your edit, collapsing a multiclip will make playback less taxing on the processor and free up speed for other editing functions or effects.

1 In the Timeline, press Cmd-A to select all the clips.

2 Ctrl-click any portion of the multiclip and choose Collapse from the shortcut menu. You can also choose Modify > Collapse Multiclips.

When you collapse a multiclip, only the actual clip name—not the angle number or multiclip name—appears on the clips.

3 Try to switch to a different angle for any one of the clips.

The other clip angles are not available to you in this mode.

4 To uncollapse or bring the multiclip state back, select all the clips, and choose Modify > Uncollapse Multiclips, or Ctrl-click a selected clip and choose Uncollapse Multiclip from the shortcut menu.

The angle numbers and multiclip name appear once again on the clips in the Timeline. You can collapse or uncollapse one or several clips in the multiclip at one time.

5 Switch to a different camera angle for any clip in the sequence.

With the multiclip state restored, you once again have access to the different angles at the playhead location.

NOTE ▶ If you are going to do a lot of multicam editing, there are a few other topics you may want to read about in the Final Cut Pro user's manual, such as optimizing system performance and using the Make Multiclip Sequence option.

TIP ▶ To revert back to your normal editing setup and continue working with the remaining lessons, change the Easy Setup preset back to DV-NTSC. Then, from the Tools menu, reload the default layouts for the keyboard and button bar, or reload your customized layouts.

Lesson Review

1. What is the frame rate of PAL video?

2. What does it mean when a production is shot multicam?

3. Where can you enter angle information once a clip has already been captured?

4. When creating a multiclip, what are the three ways you can sync clips or angles?

5. How do you create a multiclip?

6. What modifier key do you use to modify the arrangement of multiclip angles in the Viewer?

7. What modifier key do you use to drag and drop a multiclip from the Viewer to the Canvas Edit Overlay or directly to the Timeline?

8. What's the difference between switching angles and cutting angles?

9. When you apply an effect to an angle in a multiclip, can you keep that effect when you change angles? If so, how?

10. Can a multiclip in a sequence be collapsed for output as single clips? If so, how?

Answers

1. 25 frames per second, or fps.

2. Multiple cameras shoot the same action at the same time but from different angles.

3. In the Angle column in the Browser, or in a clip's Item Properties window.

4. In points, Out points, or timecode.

5. In the Browser, select the clips you want to include in the multiclip and choose Modify > Make Multiclip, or Ctrl-click a selected clip or bin and choose Make Multiclip from the shortcut menu.

6. The Command key.

7. The Option key.

8. Switching changes the angle you see at the playhead location; cutting makes a new edit point at that location.

9. You can apply the same effect to a different angle at the same location if you use the Switch Video (or Audio) Angle With Effects buttons in the Timeline button bar.

10. Yes, you collapse a multiclip by choosing Modify > Collapse Multiclip.

Keyboard Shortcuts

Shift-Ctrl-O	With the Multi-camera Editing keyboard layout loaded, it changes the Playhead Sync to Open

15

Lesson Files   Lesson 15 Project

Media   Motocross > Racing and Team Story folders;
Graphics folder

Time   This lesson takes approximately 90 minutes to complete.

Goals   Create text edits

Control text options

Superimpose a title

Create a lower third

Create animated text edits

Work with multilayered graphic files

Add motion effects to text

Work with Boris text

Adding Titles and Graphics

No matter how simple or complex a sequence is, adding text, titles, and graphics makes it seem complete. In Final Cut Pro, titles—along with other items such as color mattes and color bars—are generated within the application. You can add titles to your project for a number of purposes and in a number of ways. For example, you can create stand-alone title clips for simple slates or a production title card before your sequence even begins. Or you can add text on top of existing sequence clips to identify a person, place, or thing. There are specialty text effects you can use, such as placing an image inside of text letters. And most projects require either an opening or a closing title and a credit roll of some type.

Preparing the Project

1   Launch Final Cut Pro, and open the **Lesson 15 Project** file.

2   Close any other open projects.

3   If you haven't removed the multiclip buttons from the preceding lesson, Ctrl-click in the button bar of each window and choose Remove > All.

4   In the Timeline, click each sequence tab. Play the *Adding Text - Finished* sequence to see what you will create in this lesson.

> **TIP**   If the effects in this sequence don't play in real time, press Option-R to render them. Make sure the render bar color or type is selected in the Sequence menu before rendering.

There are a variety of clips in this sequence that display text—some share style attributes such as color or font size and type, others don't. You generally limit these options when working with text and graphics in order to create a uniform look. However, the purpose of this lesson is to introduce you to the different text options.

NOTE ▶   If you did not change the Easy Setup at the end of the preceding lesson, choose Final Cut Pro > Easy Setup, and change it to DV-NTSC so all new sequences will match the media in this lesson.

Working with Text Generators

The clips you have used so far have been captured from source material or imported from other files. But Final Cut Pro can create certain clips—called *generators*, or generated items—internally. These include color bars and tone, which are used as color references; slugs to fill a space with black; color mattes to create background color; and other items. Some generated items stand alone, such as color bars at the head of a sequence. Other items can be used in conjunction with other video clips. When selected, most generated items appear in the Viewer with a length of 2 minutes and a marked 10-second default duration. Color bars and slugs are not marked. All generated items are video-only except for color bars and tone.

Text is one of the generated items that Final Cut Pro can create. Within that category are different types of text options, each with their own set of parameters. Although you may choose a graphic artist or use Apple's Motion or the bundled LiveType applications to create special titles for your project, the generated text options within Final Cut Pro offer many ways to create and control your titles.

> **NOTE ▶** LiveType is a 32-bit title-animating program that comes bundled with Final Cut Pro. You can find an introductory PDF for LiveType on the DVD that accompanies this book.

Applying a Text Generator

Generated items can be selected from two different locations: the Effects tab in the Browser, and a pop-up menu in the Viewer. The most basic of the text generators is simply called Text. You can use this text option to create a number of title clips, including slates, basic titles, and a production title card that identifies the title of the sequence, film, or project. In this exercise, you will add a title card following the logo to introduce the sequence.

1   In the Timeline, click the *Adding Text - Starting* sequence tab, and position the playhead at the start of the gap following **Logo FLAT.jpg**.

2   In the lower-right corner of the Viewer, click the Generator pop-up and choose Text > Text from the pop-up menu.

NOTE ▶ As with transitions, bolded text options will play in real time.

In the Viewer, the words *SAMPLE TEXT* appear over the image area. This is a default text line. The In and Out points create a 10-second default duration, which you can change in the User Preferences.

NOTE ▶ The background behind the text defaults to the last background you chose in the View menu.

3   For the purposes of this exercise, choose View > Background > Checkerboard 1. Click the Canvas window, and repeat this process.

All title clips contain an alpha channel. This allows you to use the text as a stand-alone item or superimposed over another clip. The checkerboard background behind the text indicates the portion of the text image that is being dropped or keyed out.

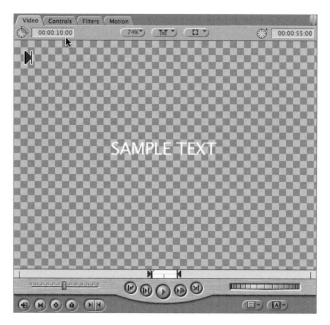

TIP You can also choose a background from the View pop-up menu in the Viewer or the Canvas.

4 Change the duration of this text clip to 3 seconds.

5 Edit the text onto the V2 track in the Timeline at the playhead location.

TIP To better organize your sequence, place all of your text on one track. If you ever need to create a copy of your project without titles, you can just toggle off the Visible control for the Text track. For this exercise, you will place your text edits on the V2 track.

6 Move the playhead to the center of the **Text** clip in the Timeline to see it in the Canvas.

Controlling Text Options

Once you edit a generated Text item into the sequence, you make changes to it the same way you would if you were adding a filter to a sequence clip—you open it back up into the Viewer. As with other generated items, Text provides a Controls tab in the Viewer where you can modify its attributes.

1 To make changes to the **Text** clip, double-click it to open it in the Viewer.

2   In the Viewer, click the Controls tab.

Note the attributes you can modify, such as Font, Size, Style, and Alignment. Scroll down to look at the other attributes, then scroll up to the Text parameter.

3   Click in the Text field, and when Sample Text is highlighted, type *Presents*.

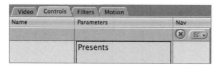

4   Press the Tab key to apply this information, and look in the Canvas to see what you've typed.

5   Make the following text selections by choosing from the pop-up menus, adjusting the sliders, or typing the information:

   ▶   Font: Impact

   ▶   Size: 70

   ▶   Alignment: Center

6   To change the color of the text, click the Font color picker.

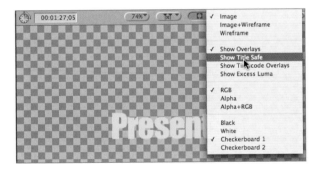

7   Select a bright yellow color, and click OK.

NOTE ▸ You can reset parameters to their default status by clicking the red X reset button in the upper-right corner of the Controls tab.

8   Adjust the Tracking, Leading, and Aspect sliders to see how they affect the text in the Canvas. If you don't like a change, return to your previous settings by pressing Cmd-Z.

9   To double-check that the text is positioned within the proper guidelines, click the Canvas View pop-up menu and choose Show Title Safe. Toggle off Show Title Safe when you finish viewing the text.

TIP ▸ To make sure your titles will be visible on a television set, always position them within the inner title safe boundary.

Adding a Title over a Background

In this exercise, you will utilize the alpha channel of a text item by placing a title over a background clip.

1   Set an In point at the start of the **team truck** clip, and set an Out point at the end of the **BS drinking water** clip.

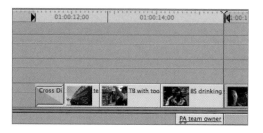

2   In the Viewer, click the Video tab. From the Generator pop-up menu, choose Text > Text.

3   Make sure the v1 source is patched to the V2 track. Edit this **Text** clip as an Overwrite edit, and move the playhead over the new text clip.

4   With the playhead parked over any one of the three clips, you see *SAMPLE TEXT* appear in the Canvas.

4   In the Timeline, double-click the new text clip to open it in the Viewer.

5   Click the Controls tab, and in the Text box, type *Yamaha of Troy.*

6   In the Controls tab, make the following changes to this text:

▶   Font: Impact

▶   Size: 63

▶ Style: Bold

▶ Alignment: Center

▶ To make the color of this text the same as that of the first text clip, click the Select Color tool (eyedropper), and move the Timeline playhead over the first text edit, Presents. In the Canvas, click the yellow text with the Select Color tool.

▶ Tracking: 6

Adding a Lower Third

Lower thirds are lines of text used to identify a person, place, or thing in a clip. Final Cut Pro's Lower 3rd text clip is preformatted and automatically creates two lines of text information within the title safe boundary in the lower left of the image area. You can choose to use only one line of text in a lower third, but you cannot use more than two. The name *Lower 3rd* is derived from the placement of the text in the lower third of the image area.

In this exercise, you will use the Superimpose edit function to edit the Lower 3rd text clips.

1   In the Timeline, patch the v1 source control to the V1 track, and move the playhead into the **DS intro** clip.

2   Click the Video tab in the Viewer, then click the Generator pop-up menu and choose Text > Lower 3rd.

In the Viewer, a new text clip appears with two default lines of sample text. (The background of the screen shot shown here has been changed to black for easier viewing.)

3   To superimpose this text clip over the **DS Intro** clip, drag the text clip into the Canvas and drop it on the Superimpose section of the Edit Overlay.

The **Lower 3rd** text clip is placed on the V2 track above the V1 clip, and is automatically given the same duration as the V1 clip.

NOTE ▶ The Superimpose edit function determines the new clip duration by looking at the clip on the assigned destination track under the playhead location at the time of the edit.

4   In the Timeline, double-click the **Lower 3rd** clip to open it in the Viewer.

5   Click the Controls tab.

There are Sample Text 1 and Sample Text 2 entry areas, along with a separate set of attribute controls for each line of text.

6   In the Text 1 field, enter *Danny Smith*, and make it Arial Black, Italic, and 36 point. In the Text 2 field, enter *Number 59*, and make it Arial and 30 point. Play this clip.

When you create a text clip you like, you can make a copy of it and use it elsewhere in your sequence. You will apply a lower third to the other two racers but will copy and paste the original to keep all the control parameters the same.

7   In the Timeline, select the **Lower 3rd** clip. To use a copy of this text clip over the next racer, Option-drag it over the **BS king of 2nd** clip. First release Option and then the mouse to make an Overwrite edit.

8   Double-click this **Lower 3rd** clip to open it in the Viewer. In the first text field, replace Danny Smith's name with *Brock Sellard*; in the second field, enter *Number 18*.

9   Scroll down to see the Background attributes. Click the Background pop-up menu and choose Solid.

This places a solid bar behind the text. This bar can be used for style purposes or to help make text more readable.

10 Use the Background's Select Color tool to sample the blue of Brock's bike, below the handlebars to the right. Change the background Opacity to 50.

NOTE ▶ You cannot apply the solid bar to the Danny Smith lower third without cutting into the image of his face. You will enhance his lower third in others ways later in this lesson.

Project Practice

Add a lower third clip over the **MB championship** clip, either by starting from scratch and superimposing it, or by dragging a copy from the Brock Sellard **Lower 3rd** clip. Match the Brock Sellard font sizes and styles, but use Mike Brown's name and his number (3).

To finesse the text clips you've created, adjust the duration of each **Lower 3rd** clip to match that of its background clip, and add opacity keyframes to the **Lower 3rd** clips to fade them in and out. You can use the *Adding Text – Finished* sequence as a reference.

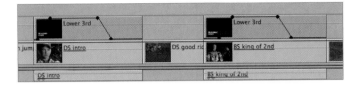

Using the Outline Text Generator

The Outline Text generator allows you to create an outline around the letters of your text, add a background image to your text, or even fill the text, outline, or background with different images from other clips. This exercise will guide you through some of Outline Text's possibilities, but there are numerous ways to adjust this type of text clip.

1   Park the playhead over the **PA team owner** clip. Because of the position of the man in the frame, a lower third is inappropriate here.

2   In the Viewer, click the Video tab, and from the Generator pop-up menu choose Text > Outline Text.

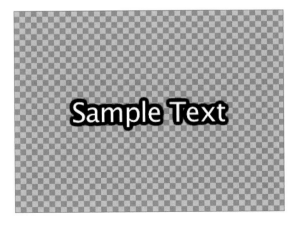

The default *Sample Text* appears in the Outline Text style.

3 Drag the image from the Viewer to the Canvas and drop it on the Superimpose section of the Canvas Edit Overlay.

4 In the Timeline, double-click the **Outline Text** clip to open it in the Viewer. Click the Controls tab.

5 In the Text field, enter *Phil Alderton*, and press Return. On the second line, enter *Team Owner*, and press Tab to see it in the Canvas. Choose Arial Black for the Font, choose Bold for the Style, and enter *35* for the Size.

	Text Settings		
Text	**Phil Alderton** **Team Owner**		
Font	Arial Black		
Style	Bold		
Alignment	Center		
Size	35		

6 Set Tracking to 3, Leading to −20, Line Width to 20, and Line Softness to 3.

7 Use the Select Color tool to choose a blue from the bike as the outline color of the text.

Text Graphic			
Line Color			

Although the text looks good, it isn't positioned properly. You can reposition text easily by toggling on the Image+Wireframe mode in the Canvas and dragging the text into place.

8 Click in the Canvas to make it active, and press W to toggle on Image+Wireframe. In the Canvas, drag the **Outline Text** clip up and to the right. Toggle on the Title Safe overlay to make sure the text sits within the title safe boundary. When you've finished positioning the text, toggle off Title Safe, and return the Canvas to just the Image mode.

Project Practice

Outline Text has additional options. You can insert an image or graphic either within the text itself, within the outline surrounding the text, or in both places at once. To create this effect in the current sequence, move the playhead to the end of the sequence, and edit a 5-second **Outline Text** clip at this location. Open the clip, change the text to *The End,* and choose Impact as the font. Adjust the size and aspect of this clip so the letters fill the frame, staying within the title safe area.

> **NOTE ▶** You can open the **Outline Text** clip at the end of the *Adding Text – Finished* sequence as a reference for parameter settings.

To fill the text letters with an image, scroll down to the Text Graphic parameter. From the Freeze Frame bin in the Browser, drag the **Photo Finish** clip into the Viewer and release it in the Text Graphic image well.

The image fills the text letters. You can also choose an image to fill the outline around the text, and another to appear in the background behind the text.

TIP ► To clear an image from one of the graphic image wells, Ctrl-click the image and choose Clear from the shortcut menu.

Creating a Credit Roll

You can create credits as single clips with one name on the screen at a time. Or you can use the Final Cut Pro animated Scrolling text option to roll the credits over the screen, which is the standard approach for television shows and films.

1   Position the playhead on the first frame of the *The End* **Outline Text** clip at the end of the sequence. Press Shift-F5 to lock all audio tracks.

    You will insert a credit roll at this location, but you don't want to change or split any of the audio clips.

2   In the Viewer, click the Video tab, then click the Generator pop-up menu and choose Text > Scrolling Text. Change the clip duration to 5 seconds.

NOTE ▶ The Scrolling Text option in the Generator Items pop-up menu is not bold, so it may not play in real-time on your computer.

3   Edit the **Scrolling Text** clip into the Timeline as an Insert edit at the playhead position.

4   Double-click the **Scrolling Text** clip to open it in the Viewer, and click the Controls tab. In the Timeline, move the playhead into the **Scrolling Text** clip to see it in the Canvas.

The Scrolling Text has a built-in animation that moves the text up from the bottom of the screen and rolls it off the top of the screen, like typical movie credits. If the playhead is parked at the end or beginning of the clip, you won't see the text.

5   In the text entry area, enter the following information, including the asterisks between the credit and person's name, and press Return after each line. Press Tab after the last line to see the text update in the Canvas:

Produced by*Name

Directed by*Name

Edited by*Name

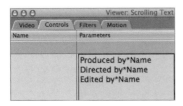

Final Cut Pro creates two symmetrical columns separated by a gap where the asterisks were entered in the text. When no asterisk is entered, all the text is centered together.

NOTE ▶ It may seem intuitive to place a space before and after the asterisks, but it is not necessary and will not create the desired effect.

6   Drag the scroll bar down to the lower Controls parameters. Make the Size 34 and set Spacing to –2. Adjust the Gap Width to 10% to increase the distance between the two columns.

7   To fade your credits in and out as they appear on and off the screen, enter a Fade Size of 25%.

TIP ▶ Drag the playhead to the beginning or end of the clip to see where the credits fade in or out.

8   Change the Leading to 190%.

9   Play the **Scrolling Text** clip. If your computer has trouble playing it, preview it by pressing Option-P.

The length of this clip determines the amount of time it takes for all of the text to scroll through the frame. If you shorten the clip, the scrolling text moves faster. If you lengthen the clip, the scrolling text moves slower.

NOTE ▶ There are two other animated text generators you can experiment with on your own: Crawl and Typewriter text. Crawl reveals text horizontally across the screen from the left or right. You may have seen weather warnings broadcast this way. The Typewriter text reveals one letter at a time until the full text is revealed, as though a typewriter is typing the text.

Adding Color Mattes

There is more to the list of video generators than just text. There are color mattes, render items, such as Gradient and Noise, and shapes. A color matte can add a simple color background to use behind text. Like all generated items, color mattes can be sized, cropped, or even animated. In this exercise, you will edit and crop four color mattes and place them around the **Scrolling Text** clip to frame the credit roll.

1   Click the Generator pop-up menu and choose Matte > Color.

2   Connect the v1 source control to the V1 destination track, and move the playhead over the **Scrolling Text** clip. Edit the color matte as a Superimpose edit.

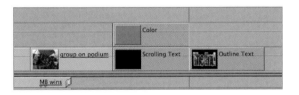

3   In the Canvas, click the View pop-up menu and choose Show Title Safe. Press W to toggle to the Image+Wireframe mode in preparation for the next step.

> **NOTE ▶** You may want to review the *Adding Text – Finished* sequence to see how these color mattes will look in the final version.

4   In the Timeline, select the **Color** clip. Press C to select the Crop tool, and move the pointer into the Canvas over the turquoise bounding line on the bottom of the image.

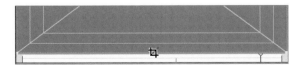

5   When you see the Crop tool appear, drag up until the lower portion of the matte is in line with the upper title safe line. Drag down from the top of the matte to the outer bounding line, which identifies the action safe area. You should see a thin horizontal bar at the top of the image area.

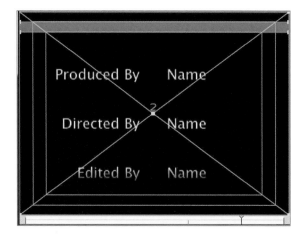

Because you have cropped the color matte, the text beneath it is revealed.

6   Press A to return to the default Selection tool. To duplicate this already cropped **Color** clip, Option-drag it up to the V3 track. Remember to release Option before releasing the mouse to make an Overwrite edit. Repeat this two more times for a total of four **Color** clips. Play these clips.

   TIP ▶ With a little concentration, you can still use the Shift key in this step to ensure you are positioning the copied clip directly above the original. The trick is this: don't release the Shift key before releasing the mouse.

In the Canvas, you still see only a single gray bar because the four **Color** clips are currently stacked on top of each other.

7 In the Timeline, select the V3 clip. In the Canvas, drag the bar down until it sits between the action safe and title safe boundary lines in the lower portion of the image area. Hold down Shift to prevent any horizontal adjustments.

8 In the Timeline, select the V4 clip. To rotate this clip 90 degrees, move the pointer over one of the rotation handles and drag clockwise in a circular motion until the matte is vertical. You can also use Shift to help snap to the 90-degree position.

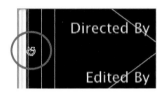

9 Repeat this process for the V5 **Color** clip, but position it to the left, completing the square.

With the cropped mattes in position, you can now change each bar's color. As a color reference, you will use the colors found in the **Logo FLAT.jpg** file at the head of the sequence.

10 Move the playhead to the start of the sequence so the **Logo FLAT.jpg** clip appears in the Canvas. Double-click the V2 **Color** clip to open it in the Viewer, and in the Controls tab click the Select Color tool.

11 In the Canvas, click in the blue background of the graphic to choose this color for the V2 **Color** clip.

12 Follow the same process to add colors to the other three **Color** clips. Use a different color for each bar. Choose your colors from the graphic at the head of the sequence.

> **NOTE ▶** It's not necessary to match the color bars as they appear in the *Adding Text – Finished* sequence; but it is necessary to take the colors from the graphic image.

Working with Graphics

Final Cut Pro can import different types of graphic files, such as TIFF, JPEG, and so on. In an earlier lesson, you imported a single-layer graphic file of the 5th Dragon logo. In this exercise, you will import a multilayered graphic file that was created in Adobe Photoshop. With this type of multilayered file, you can edit each layer separately within Final Cut Pro and even access the originating program from within FCP.

Preparing Graphic Files for Editing

Before editing graphic files into your sequence, keep in mind that video's pixel aspect ratio is different than graphic files'. This is because computers and graphic programs display square pixels, whereas digital video uses nonsquare pixels. If you create a graphic of a circle and import it into Final Cut Pro, the output of that file will not look perfectly round. To be absolutely accurate, you need to take certain steps when preparing your graphic files to accommodate this pixel difference. These steps apply both to single-layer and multilayer graphics.

> **NOTE ▶** When you're working with graphics in video, the dpi settings are irrelevant. A 300 dpi image will look the same as a 72 dpi image. The pixel dimensions of an image—such as 1440 x 1080 or 720 x 480—determine the resolution of the video image.

1   In your graphics application, begin with a file image size that is 720 x 540 pixels for DV-NTSC or 768 x 576 for DV-PAL. These represent the square-pixel dimensions you should use in any still-image graphic program.

2   When you have completed the graphic, save a copy of it, and change the image size to 720 x 480 for NTSC or 720 x 576 for PAL.

3   Without making changes to the 720 x 480 (720 x 576 for PAL) file, import it into Final Cut Pro.

    The image will look as it did in the original version of your graphic file.

> **MORE INFO ▶** The Final Cut Pro user's manual contains a chart of additional graphic format conversions.

Editing Multilayered Graphics

When you import a graphic file that has layers, Final Cut Pro detects this and creates a new sequence in which it can display those layers. In this exercise, you will import a multilayered Photoshop file of the 5th Dragon logo, insert it beneath the curl in the **group on podium** clip, and change the graphic to make it fit in the space.

1   To import a graphic directly into the Graphics bin, Ctrl-click the Graphics bin and choose Import > Files from the shortcut menu. In the Choose A File window, navigate to the FCP5 Book Files > Media > Graphics folder, and select the image named **Logo LAYERS.psd**. Click Choose.

A new sequence icon appears in the Graphics bin with the name of the graphic file.

Graphics	
Logo FLAT.jpg	00:00:05;00
Logo LAYERS.psd	00:00:10;00
Sequences	

2   Double-click the *Logo LAYERS.psd* sequence to open it in the Timeline.

V5			Dragon-text		Dragon-text
V4			Layer 1		Layer 1
V3			th–text		th–text
V2			5–text		5–text
v1 V1			background		background

Each Photoshop image layer is placed on a separate track so you can access or change individual layers. Since there is only video in a graphic file, the audio/video dividing line is automatically repositioned in the sequence to display just the video tracks. The default duration of all layers is 10 seconds, as it is with other still images.

You edit a multilayered graphic into a sequence as though it were a source clip.

3   Click the *Adding Text – Starting* sequence tab. Make sure the v1 source control is patched to the V1 destination track. To superimpose the graphic over the **group on podium** clip, position the playhead over the **group on podium** clip, drag the *Logo LAYERS.psd* sequence from the Browser into the Canvas window, and drop it on the Superimpose section of the Edit Overlay.

In the Timeline, the layers are nested together in a single clip.

4   To see the graphic beneath the corner curl, hold down Shift and drag the **group on podium** clip up to the V3 track, above the graphic. To bring the two clips back down to the V1 and V2 tracks, select both clips, and press Option-down arrow.

   NOTE ▶ You can use Option-up arrow or Option-down arrow to move one or more clips vertically in the Timeline, as long as no other clips block the move.

5   Play these clips.

   Because the graphic is full-screen, you don't see it in the lower-right corner.

6   Select the **Logo LAYERS.psd** clip. Toggle on the Image+Wireframe mode, and the Title Safe overlay. Resize and position this clip until you see most of the graphic appear in the lower-right corner within the title safe area.

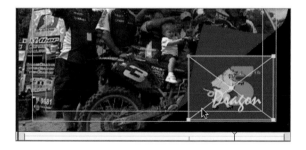

With the graphic positioned in the corner, you may see some additional adjustments that would improve this effect. For example, turning off the graphic's blue background might make the overall effect more interesting. You would make this change on the individual graphic layer.

7   In the Timeline, double-click the **Logo LAYERS.psd** clip.

This opens the Photoshop file with the individual layers. Here you can toggle off visibility for a track, add additional tracks, or resize individual tracks.

8   In the *Logo LAYERS.psd* sequence, toggle off visibility for the V1 track. Click the *Adding Text – Starting* sequence tab to see the difference.

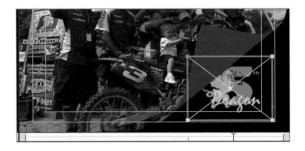

9   Toggle off the Image+Wireframe mode and the Title Safe overlay.

> **NOTE** ▶ For more control of the final effect, you can restore the default size and position of the nested graphic and change the size and position of the individual layers in the graphic sequence. You can also add layers to that sequence, such as a white color matte for the background.

Using an External Editor

An external editor is a separate program that you can use to modify your files as you edit. Final Cut Pro includes a link to external editors for three types of files: still image files, video files, and audio files. The beauty of linking to other programs in this way is that you can modify a file in its originating program, and Final Cut Pro will automatically update your clip with the changes you made in the other program. There is no need to re-import the clip.

1   Choose Final Cut Pro > System Settings, and click the External Editors tab.

2   To set an external editing application for any of the listed file types, click the Set button, and navigate to the location of that application on your hard drive. Click OK.

3   In the Timeline, Ctrl-click the **Logo FLAT.jpg** file at the head of the sequence.

To make changes to this clip in your own external graphic editor, you can choose Open In Editor from the shortcut menu to launch that application and edit this file. Any saved changes will appear in the sequence.

4   In the Timeline, Ctrl-click the **Logo LAYERS.psd** clip toward the end of the sequence. In the shortcut menu, choose Send To.

You can also send a file to other Apple applications to make changes.

Adding Motion Effects to Text

You have already used some basic motion effects to crop and reposition the color matte clips in this sequence. Another frequently used motion effect you can add to text is a drop shadow. In Final Cut Pro, this function is located in the Motion tab of the Viewer. You can also add motion keyframes to a text clip or graphic clip to create a motion path, just as you did in Lesson 12.

> **TIP**   Always resize text in the Controls tab using the Size slider, not on the Motion tab using the Scale slider. Using Scale will make the text look pixilated.

Adding a Drop Shadow

Most of the text that appears on television programs has some type of drop shadow applied to it. Drop shadows are often used to make the text stand out from the background image, but you can also use them to create a style. As one of the Motion attributes in Final Cut Pro, drop shadow can also be applied to any video clip. In this exercise, you will add a drop shadow to the **Text** clip above **DS intro**.

1   In the *Adding Text – Starting* sequence, move the playhead over the **DS intro** clip, and double-click the **Lower 3rd** clip above it to open it in the Viewer. Click the Motion tab.

2   To add a drop shadow, click the Drop Shadow check box to make it active.

The default drop shadow appears around the text in the Canvas.

3   Click the Drop Shadow disclosure triangle to display the parameters, enter the following information, and press Tab. Then play the clip.

▶   Offset: 2

▶   Angle: 135

▶   Color: Use the Select Color tool to sample the red on Danny's shoulder.

▶   Softness: 10

▶   Opacity: 72

NOTE ▶ Depending on your computer, you may not see this effect play in real time. You can press Option-P to preview it, or render the clip.

As with any parameter, you can copy and paste the drop shadow to other clips.

4   Ctrl-click the **Lower 3rd** clip above **DS intro** and choose Copy from the shortcut menu. Then Ctrl-click the **Outline Text** clip above **PA team owner** and choose Paste Attributes from the shortcut menu.

Under the Video Attributes column in this window, Drop Shadow is listed among the other Motion attributes.

5   In the Paste Attributes window, click Drop Shadow, and click OK.

The attributes from the clip above **DS intro** are now applied to this clip. Remember the blue outline in this text was created in the **Outline Text** itself.

Animating Text and Motion Effects

As with filters and motion effects, you can also animate certain text parameters, such as scale, tracking, or even color. You can animate the tracking of the text and stretch the letters horizontally over time. Or you can animate the color to change at a specific time. You can also animate motion effects when they're applied to a text clip. For example, when a drop shadow is applied, you can animate the offset over time so it appears as though the sun or light source is changing behind the text.

However, some of the more basic uses of motion effects as applied to text are simply to change the position of the text in the image area, or to move the text onscreen or off. Of course, you can make it zoom in and swoop past the viewer as well. In this exercise, you will move the first two text clips onscreen.

1 Move the playhead to the beginning of the first **Text** clip in the Timeline, and select the clip.

2 To see outside the image area, click the Canvas Zoom pop-up menu and choose 25%. Press W to change to the Image+Wireframe mode.

3 Hold down the Shift key as you drag the **Text** clip offscreen to the left until you no longer see the *s* in *Presents*.

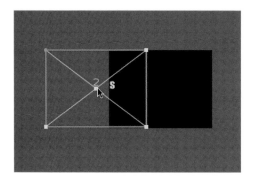

4 Press Ctrl-K to set a keyframe for this starting position.

5 In the Timeline, press Shift-right arrow to move the playhead 1 second to the right.

6 Hold down Shift as you drag the **Text** clip into the center of the screen.

A keyframe is automatically created for this new position.

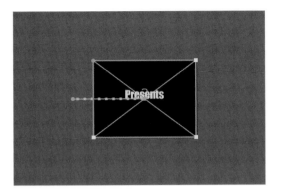

TIP If the text clip you are adjusting becomes deselected in the Timeline, just click to select it again, and the wireframe for that clip will appear in the Canvas.

7   To bridge the gap between the Presents text and the Yamaha of Troy **Text** clip, drag the Yamaha of Troy **Text** clip In point to the left and snap it to the Presents **Text** clip Out point.

8   Repeat the process of setting keyframes to animate the Yamaha of Troy text to come onscreen the same way Presents does.

TIP You can also copy the Presents **Text** clip and paste the Basic Motion attributes to the Yamaha of Troy **Text** clip, which will paste the same keyframes you used in the first clip to the second clip. With the Scale Attributes Time check box enabled, you will stretch or contract the keyframes if the clip lengths differ; with it disabled, the motion timing remains the same as the original clip.

9   When you've completed setting the keyframes, click the Canvas View pop-up, and choose Fit To Window. Play the clips.

Project Practice

Depending on the type of text and its purpose in a sequence, it might cut in and out or fade in and out to create a smoother transition. Smooth the text edits in this sequence by either adding transitions to the text clips or by setting opacity keyframes. You can refer to the *Adding Text – Finished* sequence as a reference and turn on the clip overlays to see the opacity keyframes.

You can also add motion keyframes to the color matte bars to animate them moving into place before the credits roll and then moving offscreen toward the end of the edit.

> **NOTE ▶** If you add a transition to fade out a text clip, you will first have to change the length of the text clip if you don't want it to appear over the entire background clip.

Working with Boris Text Options

There is another category of text generators—called Boris—in the Generator pop-up menu. (In Final Cut Pro 4 and HD, this option was referred to as Title 3D.) Boris contains an advanced set of text generators that provide great flexibility and high-quality output. The Boris submenu lists four text generators. Unlike the previous text options covered in this lesson, these access a separate window, offering a wider variety of parameters, including 3D control of individual characters (Title 3D). The Boris text options allow you to make a number of style choices and then save them as part of a style palette you can then apply to other clips in other projects.

The Boris Text Scrambler option allows you to create an animation in which your text letters scramble and then slowly resolve to the correct text. In this exercise, to sample a Boris effect, you will edit the Text Scrambler text effect over the **MB long run** clip toward the end of the sequence.

1   Move the Playhead to the middle of the **MB long run** clip, and target the V1 track.

2   In the Viewer, click the Video tab, and then click the Generated Items pop-up menu and choose Boris > Text Scrambler. Edit this clip to the Timeline as a Superimpose edit. Double-click to open this clip in the Viewer.

3   Under the Controls tab, click in the Text Scrambler box.

In the Boris text options, you don't enter text information in the Controls tab; instead, you use a separate window.

A large window opens with several text options. The options are organized via small tabs running vertically down the left side of the window. The different tabs are Text Style, Text Wrap, Text Fill, Edge Style, and Shadow Type. Next to some of the tabs are tiny check boxes for toggling the options on and off.

4   With the first tab selected, type *Champion* in the large gray text area, and drag over the letters to select the text.

TIP ▶ To see the true colors of the text, not the highlighted version, as you make changes, click in a numerical entry box after highlighting the text.

5   Choose Impact from the pop-up menu. Click in the font size box, and enter *72*.

6   Click the Style Palette button.

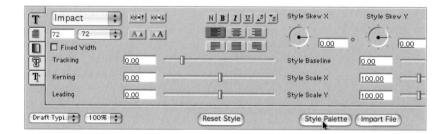

A new window opens with a number of style options.

7   From the upper pop-up menu in the Style Palette, choose *bevel gradient fill. B2D*, and double-click the second sample when it appears in the pane to the right.

8 Click Apply.

The window closes, and *Champion* appears as text in the Canvas.

9 In the Canvas, select Image+Wireframe and Show Title Safe. Reposition the Champion text to the top center of the image within the title safe boundary.

10 Place the playhead at the end of the **MB long ride** clip, and press Shift-left
arrow three times to park the playhead 3 seconds before the end of the
clip. Double-click to make sure that the Champion text is in the Viewer. In
the Controls tab in the Viewer, click a Keyframe button for Scramble
Characters and for Opacity.

11 Position the playhead at the head of the clip. Slide the Scramble Characters
slider all the way to the right. Set Opacity at 0, and play the clip.

Project Practice

To continue practicing creating text edits, open the *Racing Promo* sequence
from the Browser. Add a lower third to the first **JM stakes rise** video so it cuts
in and out with the clip. Add a slate, opening title, and end credits, using the
methods detailed in this lesson, or you can experiment with other options. Try
adding a text crawl over several clips to announce the most recent earthquake
results. You can also open previous lesson project files and add text to those
sequences.

> **TIP** ▶ If you want to work with the text settings you've created in one
> sequence in a different project, make sure both projects are open, then
> copy a sequence from one open project, and paste it into another open
> project.

Lesson Review

1. From what two places can you choose a generated item such as text?

2. What tab in the Viewer do you select to make changes to text clips?

3. When you superimpose an edit over a V1 clip, to what track should the
    source control be patched for the superimposed clip to be placed on V2?

4. What type of generated text identifies a person, place, or thing?

5. To animate a text clip, what two visual clues are helpful to have on in the
    Canvas?

6. When you import a multilayered Adobe Photoshop file, what icon will you
    see for this file in the Browser?

7. Where can you find the Drop Shadow attribute?

8. In what set of text generator options does a separate window appear for making text changes?

Answers

1. Choose from the Browser Effects tab or from the Generated Items pop-up menu in the Video tab in the Viewer.

2. The Controls tab.

3. The V1 track.

4. A lower third.

5. Image+Wireframe mode and Title Safe overlay.

6. A sequence icon.

7. In the Motion tab in the Viewer.

8. The Boris text options.

Keyboard Shortcuts

Ctrl-K	Sets a keyframe at the playhead location for motion parameters

16

Lesson 16
Finishing and Outputting

Once a sequence is complete, with titles and effects all in, it's time to finish and output it. The finishing stage is when you look at your sequence with a different eye. It's less about making editorial decisions than about ensuring that your program looks and sounds its best before you present it to others. Once this has been accomplished, you are ready to output the sequence. Outputting can include creating a tape of the sequence for screening. It can also include exporting the sequence using various file formats for a variety of delivery possibilities, including the Web or DVD. Along the way, you will want to consider archiving the project and managing the project media.

Image with out-of-range video levels

Preparing the Project

Since this lesson is about fixing and outputting completed sequences, you will work with sequences you've already completed from other lessons.

1 Launch Final Cut Pro and open the **Lesson 16 Project** file.

2 Close any other open projects.

3 Play the *Racing Promo* sequence in the Timeline.

   This sequence is not quite ready to output because some of the audio and video clips do not meet appropriate broadcast specifications. In this lesson, you will learn how to fix these problems before outputting the sequence.

   In the Browser, there are only three sequences but no clip icons. These sequences were not edited in this project—they were copied from earlier projects and pasted into this project to use for outputting. If you want to access individual clips that were used in creating these sequences, you can create a new set of master clips.

4 In the Browser, select the *Racing Promo* sequence. Choose Tools > Create Master Clips.

   In the Browser, a new bin appears with a set of master clips that support just those clips you used in the selected sequence. These clips link back to the media files that were originally used to edit the sequence.

5 Display the clips in the Master Clips For Racing Promo bin and double-click the **biker down** clip to open it in the Viewer.

   Each clip is unmarked and is the full duration of the media file.

   NOTE ▶ You can create master clips this way for any sequence in any project.

Reconnecting Media

Whether your project elements were captured or imported into your project, the clips always link back to a specific place on the hard drive where those media files are stored. If you move the media or rename the media file, the link between the clip in the project and the media file on the hard drive is broken. The clip icon in the Browser goes offline, and a red slash appears over the clip icon. The clip no longer knows where to find the actual media file. This occurred when you logged clips in an earlier lesson in preparation for using Batch Capture. The logged clips had no real media to link to and, therefore, were offline.

Breaking the connection with your media can happen for various reasons. You may want to move a project from your computer to someone else's computer, or from your G5 tower to your laptop so you can edit on the go. Or maybe you decided to rename all the media files on your hard drive in the middle of a project. Any of these situations will cause a break in the original clip's link to the media locations and cause the clip to go offline. To continue working with the clip, you must reconnect the project clip to the media file's new location.

1   In the Timeline, move the playhead over the last clip in the sequence, **BS big jump**.

    This clip is currently connected to the **BS big jump** media file in the FCP5 Book Files folder on your hard drive. If you move the media file from its current location, this clip will become *offline,* or disconnected from its media file.

2   To find this media file on the hard drive, select the **BS big jump** clip in the Browser, and choose View > Reveal in Finder.

    Above the Final Cut Pro interface, a Finder window appears with the **BS big jump** clip in view.

3 In the Finder window, drag the **BS big jump** clip from its current column or folder into the Motocross folder so it appears along with the other motocross folders.

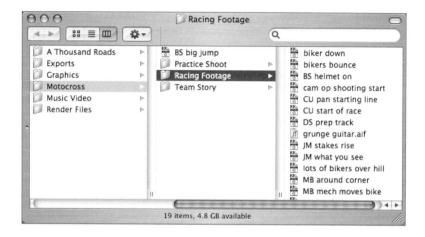

4 Click the Browser to make Final Cut Pro active again.

> **TIP** ▶ You can also press Cmd-Tab to toggle to any open application.

In Final Cut Pro, there are several indications that something has changed:

▶ An Offline Files window appears, indicating that some files went offline. You have the option of reconnecting the files or continuing with them offline. If you check Media Files in the Forget Files section and then click Continue, Final Cut Pro will assume that you don't want to connect the file, and it won't remind you in the future.

▶   Look at the clip in the Browser, but don't select it. The **BS big jump**
clip has a red slash over it.

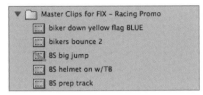

▶   In the Timeline, the clip appears white with a red and black thumbnail image. With the Playhead parked over the **BS big jump** clip in the
Timeline, Media Offline appears in the image area of the Canvas along
with the clip name.

5   To reestablish a link between the clip icon in the Browser and the original
clip media in its new location, click the Reconnect button in the Offline
Files window.

A Reconnect Files window appears. Under the Files To Connect portion of
the window, the offline file is listed along with the path where it was last
located before you moved it. If you know where the files are located, you
can check Search Single Location and then choose the appropriate location. This will speed up Final Cut Pro's search, since it won't have to search
all the available hard drives and directories. Leave it unchecked for now.

You have two options for finding your missing media files: Locate or
Search. Click the Locate button to look manually for the missing files.

(Choose this option when the name of the media file has changed.)
Clicking the Search button initiates an automatic search for the file.

6   Click Search.

A Reconnect file browser appears, and the **BS big jump** file should be
selected.

7   If Final Cut Pro does not find this clip at its new location on the Desktop,
navigate to the clip and select it. Click Choose.

> **TIP** If the file you want to connect to is dimmed and can't be selected,
> you can click the Show pop-up menu in the lower left of the Reconnect
> window and choose All Files. This will enable you to click any file. Also,
> you can deselect Matched Name Only if the filename has changed and
> you'd like to relink to the clip with the new name.

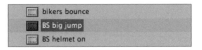

Once found, the **BS big jump** clip is listed in the Files Located section along with the file path to its new location.

NOTE ▶ If something has changed about your clip, such as reel number, timecode, or number of tracks, a warning will appear. If you are aware of the conflict and know this to be the right clip, go ahead and connect to it. When a mismatch does occur, the number of conflicts appears in the lower left of the window and the clip name is italicized.

8   Click Connect.

In the Browser, the red offline slash on the clip icon is removed because it knows where to find the media file when you play the clip in the project. In the Timeline, the clip's thumbnail is restored because the sequence clip is an affiliate of the master clip, and the Canvas window again displays a frame of the video clip.

NOTE ▶ If you change the name of the clip in the Browser, it will still be able to link back to the media file. If you rename the media file on the hard drive, you will have to reconnect the project clip.

9   Repeat the process from the previous steps to place the **BS big jump** clip back into the Media > Racing Footage folder. Then reconnect to that new location.

10   Hide the contents of the Master Clips bin.

TIP ▶ To reconnect a clip that is offline, you can also Ctrl-click the clip in the Browser or Timeline and choose Reconnect Media from the shortcut menu.

Finishing Audio and Video

During the editing process, you often deal with audio and video from different sources that were recorded at different levels and under different conditions. Perhaps you were given a narration recorded in a studio and ambient sound recorded in the field. Or you worked with some footage that was shot indoors at night and some that was shot outdoors in the bright sunlight. After you've made your creative decisions and finished editing your sequence, you can turn your attention to refining the video and audio so all the clips will work together as a whole.

The video and audio levels should not be too high or too low. As you know, audio levels that are too high can become distorted. And high video levels may result in video that is not broadcast safe, meaning it exceeds the limits of the FCC standards.

Detecting Audio Peaks

When adjusting the audio level of your sequence, the one absolute rule is never to allow the audio to peak over 0 dB. Final Cut Pro can help you pinpoint exactly where the audio is peaking in your sequence by placing a marker in the Timeline at each peak.

1   In the Timeline, play the *Racing Promo* sequence, and watch the audio meters to see if there are any peaks in the sequence. You can also open the Audio Mixer and look at the audio levels on the Master fader.

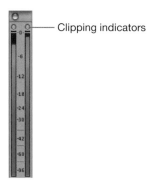
Clipping indicators

When the audio peaks in the Timeline, the red clipping indicator lights up on one or both audio meters, depending on which track peaked. The indicators stay red until you stop playing the sequence. Although these indicators tell you there *was* an audio peak, they don't pinpoint exactly where in the sequence it occurred.

2   In the Timeline, deselect all clips by clicking in the empty gray area of the Timeline or pressing Shift-Cmd-A. Choose Mark > Audio Peaks > Mark.

A progress bar appears while Final Cut Pro examines the sequence.

> **Detecting Audio Peaks**
>
> Detecting Audio Peaks
>
> 51%   (Cancel)

When the detection is complete, markers are placed in the Timeline ruler area wherever the audio peaks occur in the sequence. If the peak is sustained for more than an instant, a long marker—or marker with a duration—appears over the clip to indicate the length of the peaking audio.

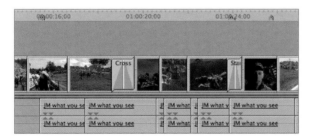

NOTE ▶ When the playhead is over an audio peak marker, Audio Peak appears as an overlay in the Canvas to identify it.

3   Move the playhead over the first audio peak marker, and zoom in to get a better view.

Audio meters reflect the levels of the combined audio tracks in the sequence. You will have to judge which individual tracks are causing the peaking. Since the music and sound effects are very low at this location, it's most likely that the A1 and A2 voice-over clips are the problem.

4 Move the playhead over the next group of audio peak markers.

Here again, the VO clip is causing the sound to peak.

5 Select the **JM what you see** clip under the first two audio peak markers. Cmd-click the **JM what you see** clip under the next two markers to add it to this selection.

NOTE ▶ You can toggle on clip overlays if you want to view the volume level lines on the clips in the Timeline.

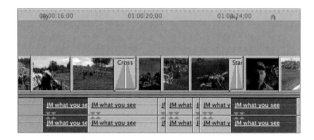

6 Choose Modify > Levels.

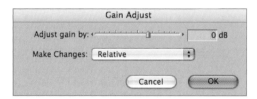

A Gain Adjust window opens. You can use this window to adjust current levels for a single clip or a group of clips. Gain adjustments that you make in this window can be relative or absolute. Making a *relative* adjustment changes the current level of the selected clips by the amount you enter and maintains any keyframes those clips may contain. Making an *absolute* adjustment removes any keyframes and resets the audio to a specific level.

NOTE ▶ If you select a video clip and choose Modify > Levels, an Opacity Adjust window will appear, allowing you to adjust the opacity level of the clip.

7   In the Gain Adjust window, in the Adjust Gain By field, enter –3 dB, and leave the Make Changes option set to Relative. Click OK. Watch the audio meters as you play through these two clips.

These clips no longer cause the audio to peak.

8   If there are any other peak markers in the sequence, select the clip and adjust its levels using the Gain Adjust window.

> **TIP** ▶ A good time to use the Absolute option in the Gain Adjust window is when you have changed the audio level of one or more clips and want to return them to their original 0 dB level, or to another specific level. You would enter *0*, or other number, in the Adjust Gain By field and choose Absolute from the Make Changes pop-up. This option removes all keyframes.

9   To clear the audio peak markers from the Timeline, choose Mark > Audio Peaks > Clear, or press Ctrl-~ (tilde key).

> **TIP** ▶ If you've changed the peak levels and want to reassess whether there are still audio peaks, choose Mark > Audio Peaks > Mark again. Remember to deselect all clips before choosing this option.

Adjusting Video Levels for Broadcast

One of the most common problems with video levels is that sometimes the whites of an image, or the luminance levels, are too bright. This can be a serious consideration, because the FCC mandates that no video should be broadcast with a luminance level over 100 IRE, which is considered to be broadcast safe. (IRE is a unit of measurement in video that was named for the organization that created it—the Institute of Radio Engineers.) If video does go over 100 IRE, the video level is clipped during broadcast, similar to the way audio is clipped when it peaks over 0 dB. Some networks or facilities may reject the tape and choose not to air it at all.

To prepare the video portion of your sequence for output, you will need to monitor the luminance levels of your clips, then lower those that are too bright. Final Cut Pro has a tool called Range Check that will check both the luma and chroma of a clip to determine whether they are within an acceptable broadcast range. When you find clips that are not within broadcast specifications, you can apply the Broadcast Safe filter to correct them. Use the Video Scopes tool as a reference when viewing video levels.

1   In the Timeline, move the playhead to the beginning of the **biker down** clip, the sixth video clip from the end of the sequence.

2   Open the Video Scopes tool by choosing Tools > Video Scopes. When the Tool Bench window appears with the Video Scopes tab, position the window over the Browser.

3   In the Video Scopes tab, click the Layout pop-up menu and choose Waveform.

The Waveform Monitor enables you to see the luminance values of the current frame. Broadcast standards specify a maximum luminance level for any video. This is represented in the Waveform Monitor as 100%.

4   Move the pointer up and down over the Waveform Monitor.

A yellow horizontal line follows the movement of the pointer, and a number in the upper-right corner displays the luma percentage of the current pointer location in the scope.

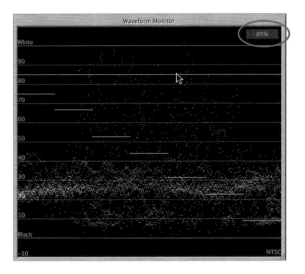

5   To check the luma level of the current clip, make the Timeline active and choose View > Range Check > Excess Luma, or press Ctrl-Z.

When you toggle on Range Check, each clip in the sequence will appear with one of three symbols indicating whether the luminance level of that clip is or is not within *legal* range for broadcast use. For the current clip, a green circle and a checkmark appear in the Canvas, indicating that the luminance levels for that frame are broadcast safe and below 90 percent.

6 Move the playhead to the beginning of the second clip in the sequence, the **BS helmet on** clip.

An *in-range* icon appears with a checkmark and an upward arrow, indicating that some luma levels are between 90 and 100 percent. The affected areas are indicated by green zebra stripes. Although it's reaching the upper limit, this is still acceptable video.

7 Press the down arrow to move the playhead to the next video clip, the **DS prep track** clip.

A yellow warning icon appears, indicating that some luminance levels are above 100 percent. The red zebra stripes show the areas of the image that are above 100 percent. The waveform shows how much the luminance values exceed 100 percent.

8 Select the **DS prep track** clip, and choose Effects > Video Filters > Color Correction > Broadcast Safe. Double-click the clip to open it in the Viewer, and click the Filters tab to see the filter parameters.

With the Broadcast Safe filter added to this clip, the red zebra stripes in the Canvas turn to green, and the Waveform Monitor shows that the luminance levels have been clipped at 100 percent.

NOTE ▶ If you suspect that some of your color levels are too intense, you can choose View > Range Check > Excess Chroma and view the Vectorscope to identify any problem areas.

Project Practice

To continue fine-tuning the video, step through this sequence and practice applying the Broadcast Safe filter to the clips that need it. For more practice, open the Team Story sequence from the Browser and check it for audio peaks and video levels. This video was shot outdoors in bright daylight, so you may find that several clips are out of the broadcast-safe range.

When you've finished practicing, close the Tool Bench window and choose View > Range Check > Off.

Exporting Finished Sequences

One of the most common output options you'll choose for your completed sequences is to export a media file that can be digitally distributed. You can choose to export a high-quality file to import into special-effects applications, burn on a DVD, or archive on a FireWire drive. You can also experiment with lower-quality file formats for delivery on the Internet through email or on a cell phone. Often you will want to export multiple versions of your project for delivery in a number of different ways.

Final Cut Pro utilizes QuickTime as its standard media format. You can export using several different QuickTime-compatible file formats. The specific type of compression or decompression you choose during exporting is called a *codec*, short for compression/decompression. You can choose to export using the current codec for Final Cut Pro clips and sequence material, or you can use a different QuickTime codec for other types of video, audio, or graphics files.

Understanding File Formats

Before getting into the specific steps of exporting, let's review some of the common compression types you might use when exporting from a Final Cut Pro project.

Video Formats

▶ DV-NTSC and DV-PAL codecs are used to capture video and audio from FireWire devices, such as camcorders, decks, and analog-to-DV converter boxes. The data rate is 3.6 megabytes per second (MB/sec).

▶ DVCPRO 50 is similar to the DV codec, but it has higher quality and a larger data rate—7 MB/sec.

▶ MPEG-2 is a compression standard used most commonly on commercial DVDs.

▶ HDV is an MPEG-2–based high-definition video format that records on a DV cassette tape.

▶ MPEG-4 (.mp4) is used for Internet posting, streaming, and wireless devices. It has high quality and low data rates, which allow its file size to stay relatively small.

▶ H.264 is based on MPEG-4 and provides the highest quality at the lowest data rate (or smallest file size). It encodes with about twice the efficiency of the MPEG-2 format, allowing better quality at the same data rate. It is very versatile and can be used for Web video as well as for high-definition DVD projects.

▶ AVI (.avi) is the standard video and audio file format for Windows-compatible computers.

Audio Formats

▶ AIFF (.aif) is a high-quality format that is native to Final Cut Pro and many OS X audio applications. It is also used for audio output for DVD use.

▶ AAC (.m4p) is the Apple format for downloading music from the iTunes Music Store. It is similar to MP3 but is a higher quality with a reduced file size. It is often used in MPEG-4 multimedia files, and it can support sur-round sound.

▶ Wave (.wav) is the standard audio file format for Windows-compatible computers.

Still Image Formats

▶ JPEG (.jpg) has variable compression levels, which makes it an excellent format for Web sites.

▶ Photoshop (.psd) can contain multiple layers and be imported into Final Cut Pro as a single layer or with multiple layers intact.

▶ PICT (.pct) is a widely used, high-quality graphic file format that can contain an embedded alpha channel. This is the format of choice for single-layer graphics in Final Cut Pro.

▶ TIFF (.tiff or .tif) is designed for use in desktop publishing. This format can also be used to convert a Final Cut Pro clip to an image sequence, converting each frame to a separate file.

▶ Other file formats supported are BMP (.bmp), PNG (.png), and TGA (.tga).

Exporting a QuickTime Movie

The most basic way to export from Final Cut Pro is to use the QuickTime Movie option. This option is set up to output a clip, sequence, or marked portion of a sequence using current or preset sequence settings. By using the current settings, you create a QuickTime file at the same settings and quality as your clips and sequences; no extra media compression is necessary. This allows Final Cut Pro to export your clips quickly with virtually no quality loss. Use this option when you want a full-quality version of your sequence to archive or to import into other applications or, for example, when you want to burn a DVD in iDVD.

1 In the *Racing Promo* sequence, set an In point at the beginning of the sequence and an Out point right before the second group of interview narration clips start at 1:00:15;11.

   This marks approximately 15 seconds of the sequence, starting from the beginning.

2   Choose File > Export > QuickTime Movie.

A Save window opens with the name of this sequence automatically entered in the Save As field.

3   Add *DV* to the end of the filename, navigate to the Media folder, and select the Exports folder as the destination for the new media file.

> **TIP** ▶ Adding *DV* or another descriptive name to your files when exporting will help you remember what settings were used for that file. This will give you a way of comparing how the quality of your clips changes when you use different compression settings.

4   Make sure Current Settings is selected in the Setting pop-up menu. The Include pop-up menu should be set to Audio and Video, and the Markers pop-up menu should be set to None.

> **NOTE** ▶ The Markers pop-up is where you can select markers that may have been created for a DVD or Soundtrack Pro audio project.

5   Leave the Recompress All Frames box unchecked.

When enabled, this option will recompress all frames in the selected export item. This can introduce additional compression artifacts to the file and increase the export time. If Final Cut Pro ever has trouble processing certain frames in your clips, exporting with this option enabled may be a good troubleshooting technique.

6 Make sure the Make Movie Self-Contained box is checked.

There are two types of QuickTime movies: One is self-contained, and the other is not. A self-contained QuickTime movie can play on your computer or anyone else's because it contains all of the media elements (not just the clip links) from your hard drive that are in the clip or sequence. However, you can also export a QuickTime movie without making it self-contained. This enables you to create and play the movie on your computer but not on anyone else's unless it, too, has all of the media files on its hard drive. A self-contained movie is a larger file size because the media files are contained within the movie.

7 Click Save.

A window appears with a progress bar as the clip is being exported. Sometimes, especially with audio files, the exporting is so quick that no window appears.

8 To view this clip in a QuickTime Player, press Cmd-H to hide Final Cut Pro. In the Finder, navigate to the FCP5 Book Files > Media > Exports folder, and double-click the **Racing Promo DV** clip.

Because you created this clip with Final Cut Pro settings, it opens within the application.

9 Close the **Racing Promo DV** clip window by clicking the Close button in the upper-left corner.

> **NOTE ▶** Once you've exported a sequence, you can import it into a project, and then view and edit it as you would any other clip.

Exporting Using QuickTime Conversion

Using the QuickTime Movie export function works for many situations when you want to use preset sequence settings. But there are times when you need to convert what you're exporting to a specific file type—perhaps to an audio file such as AIFF, or to a file you can play on the Web.

In Final Cut Pro, you have numerous file type options for exporting your finished sequence. Keep in mind there is always more than one way to configure your export settings. Preparing media for digital distribution is an exercise in compromise between quality and performance—the higher the data rate, the higher the quality, but the poorer the performance. Through practice and trial and error, you can decide for yourself the correct balance based on your distribution medium and your intended audience.

In this exercise, you will export a movie for the Web using the QuickTime H.264 compressor.

1 In the Timeline, mark the first 10 seconds of the *Racing Promo* sequence.

You will export this portion of the sequence using a different format than the current sequence settings.

2 Choose File > Export > Using QuickTime Conversion.

A Save window opens with the name of this sequence automatically entered in the Save As field, along with the QuickTime suffix, .mov.

3   In the Save As field, add *H264-web* to the filename. If it's not already the destination, navigate to the Media > Exports folder as the destination for this file.

4   With QuickTime Movie as the default format, click the Options button next to the Format pop-up menu.

The Movie Settings window opens, displaying the current settings for Video, Sound, and Internet Streaming.

NOTE ▶ Each option in the Format pop-up has its own variety of settings. For example, if you choose Still Image, you can choose a format, such as BMP, TIFF, or Photoshop, to export a single frame from a clip or sequence.

5   In the Video section, click the Settings button.

The Standard Video Compression Settings window opens, displaying the current compression settings.

6   Make sure H.264 is chosen for Compression Type, restrict the Data Rate to 400 kilobits per second, and leave the other settings at their defaults. Click OK.

7   In the Movie Settings window, click the Size button. When the Export Size Settings window appears, click Use Custom Size. Enter a custom size of 320 pixels for width and 240 pixels for height.

NOTE ▶ These pixel dimensions are one of the standards for smaller-sized movie files.

8   Click OK to close the Export Size Settings window, and then click OK again to close the Movie Settings window.

NOTE ▶ When preparing video for the Web, you should also experiment with different Format settings for your audio by clicking the Settings button under the Sound section. Audio doesn't take up as much space as video, but it can still impact the performance of a Web movie.

9   With all settings selected in the Save window, click Save.

Because QuickTime conversion is processor-intensive, it may take several moments for Final Cut Pro to finish exporting your video.

10 When the export is complete, press Cmd-H to hide Final Cut Pro. Navigate to the Media > Exports folder, and double-click the **Racing Promo H264-web** file.

This movie opens in QuickTime Player, where you can view it. You can also import this movie file into Final Cut Pro and compare it to the QuickTime movie you exported earlier in this lesson.

11 In the dock, click the Final Cut Pro icon to return to the application.

TIP ▶ You can use these steps and settings to post a movie for download on the Web.

Exploring QuickTime Movie Export Options

During editing, you may want to export a low-resolution sample of your sequence to send to your producer for approval, or you may need to send your sequence to another system that accepts only certain formats. In these situations, it is important to find out what format is required, and then use the following steps to export your sequence in that format.

1   In the Timeline, press Option-X to remove the In and Out points in the *Racing Promo* sequence. In the Browser, select this sequence.

When you want to export a sequence in its entirety, you can simply select it in the Browser. However, if there are In or Out points in the sequence, only that portion of the sequence will be exported.

2 Choose File > Export > Using QuickTime Conversion.

3 Leave the default name as is, Racing Promo.mov. Navigate to the Exports folder, leave the default format on QuickTime Movie, and click the Options button.

4 In the Movie Settings window, click the Video Settings button. When the Standard Video Compression Settings window appears, click the Compression Type pop-up menu.

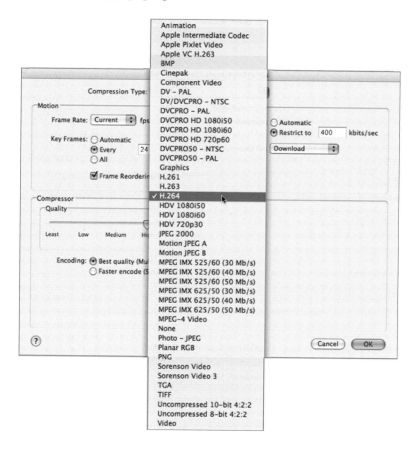

A long list appears of the available codecs on your computer. Different codecs are good for different types of situations. Ask the person for whom you are creating the QuickTime movie which codec to use, or experiment with different codecs to find the one that's best for you.

NOTE ▶ Once you choose a codec, you will also need to adjust the settings for that codec. Again, experiment to find the optimal settings for your situation.

5   Click Cancel to close the various windows.

Outputting to Tape

When outputting your sequence to tape, Final Cut Pro can work with a wide variety of tape formats. It can output through FireWire to DV, DVCPRO, HDV, and DVCPRO HD. It can output to other tape formats, from VHS to DigiBeta, as long as you have the hardware to support it. You will usually record a master copy of your sequence to the same tape format you started with or the format that's required for delivery, but you may also want to make a viewing copy on a different format, such as VHS.

As part of the output to tape, you will generally record additional material consisting of color bars and tone, program slate, countdown, and black before the sequence begins. This is collectively called *leader material* and is added in different ways, depending on the output method you choose.

NOTE ▶ Before you begin outputting, make sure your recording device is hooked up to your computer and turned on.

As in exporting, you can output the entire sequence or a partial sequence using In and Out points in the Timeline.

There are three ways to output your sequence to tape:

▶   Manual record

▶   Print To Video

▶   Edit To Tape

The first two methods, manual record and Print To Video, are available through any FireWire recording device. The third method, Edit To Tape, is available only with devices that Final Cut Pro can control remotely.

Recording Manually

The easiest way to output to tape is to simply play the sequence and press Record on the connected camera or deck. This is referred to as a manual recording process. You use this option when you want to make a quick dub to tape.

Though this output method is the simplest, it is also the least precise. It is very much a "what you see is what you get" proposition. To record manually, you must have any preprogram, or leader, elements (such as bars and tone, slate, black, countdown, and so on) edited before the head of your sequence in the Timeline. And you must also mix down your audio and render any unrendered video.

1   From the Browser, open the *Team Story* sequence, if it's not already open in the Timeline.

2   In the Viewer, click the Generator pop-up menu and choose Bars And Tone (NTSC).

The video in the *Team Story* sequence is DV-NTSC. When working with other video formats, you would choose the appropriate option.

3   Insert the 10 seconds of bars and tone at the head of the sequence.

4   To create a slate, click the Generator pop-up menu and choose Text > Text. Click the Controls tab, and enter *Team Story,* today's date, and your name as editor. Insert 5 seconds of this slate after the bars and tone you just edited.

5   To add black before the **Logo FLAT.jpg** graphic, click the Generator pop-up menu and choose Slug. Edit 5 seconds after the slate. Edit the same 5 seconds after the last clip at the end of the sequence.

NOTE ▶ You don't have to edit leader material before the sequence to record it manually. But it's good to have at least 5 seconds of black at the head and tail of a sequence.

6   If there are any render bars in the Timeline ruler area that are red, yellow, or orange, choose Sequence > Render All, and make sure the same render level colors that appear in the Timeline ruler area are checked here. Press Option-R to render everything in the Timeline.

7   Park the playhead at the head of the Timeline.

The output of the Timeline begins wherever the playhead is parked. You will record a freeze-frame of the playhead location *until* you play the sequence. When the playhead reaches the last frame of the sequence, it will again freeze on that frame. This is why it's good to have a slug of black before your sequence begins and after it ends.

8   In the Timeline, click the RT pop-up menu, and choose these settings: Safe RT mode, High under Video Quality, and Full under Frame Rate. You will have to click the RT pop-up menu, to select each option.

9   Cue up your recording device, and begin recording.

10   After at least 5 seconds, play the sequence.

> **NOTE ▶** If you want the sequence to repeat, select the Loop Playback option in the View menu. The amount of black you want to play between the looped sequences is determined by the slug edit at the end of each sequence.

11   When the taping is complete, allow additional seconds of black to be recorded, then stop the recording device.

Printing to Video

The Print To Video option enables you to select the preprogram leader elements from a list before outputting to tape. During the output process, Final Cut Pro will automatically generate these items as though they were edits in your sequence. This is a good method to use when you want to take advantage of the automatic leader options but don't have a device that can be controlled by timecode. Also, this method automatically renders anything that needs rendering and plays your sequence back at high quality even if the Timeline playback settings are set to low quality or dynamic.

> **NOTE ▶** To output HDV material to tape, you would use the Print To Video option.

NOTE ▶ The Audible controls in the Timeline turn tracks on and off from the computer processor. Tracks turned off using this method will not be included on output. Solo and Mute effect audio only during playback, and will not exclude tracks during output.

1   Make sure the Timeline is active and there are no In or Out points in the sequence.

2   Select all of the leader clips you edited in the previous exercise and press Shift-Delete to delete them along with the gap. Choose File > Print To Video, or press Ctrl-M.

There are four parts to this window: the Leader, Media, Trailer, and Duration Calculator areas. In each area, you can check a box to include that option in the output or choose an option from the pop-up menus. You can also enter a specific amount of time for items.

3   In the Leader area, click the Color Bars box, and change the duration to 10 seconds.

NOTE ▶ Generally, you record anywhere from 10 to 60 seconds of color bars, depending on its use.

4   Click in all the boxes in the Leader section. Since this is a sample output, shorten the Black durations to 2 and Slate to 5.

5   In the Slate pop-up menu, choose Text. In the text box that will appear to the right, type *Team Story*, today's date, and your name.

TIP You can also create your own slate with graphics and a company logo. To use a personal slate, choose File from the Slate pop-up menu, and click the folder button to the right to navigate to the file.

6   In the upper-right corner of the Print To Video window, click the Preview button to test the audio level going into your recording device. If the level is not high enough, adjust it using the dB slider. Then click Stop.

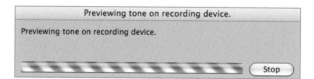

7   In the Media area, choose Entire Media from the Print pop-up menu to output the entire Timeline contents, and select Loop.

TIP If your sequence is short, such as a promo, commercial, or music video, use the Loop option to loop it several times. This saves having to rewind the tape to see it again.

8   In the Trailer area, click Black, and change the duration to 10 seconds.

9   Check the Duration Calculator to see how long the total output will be, and make sure the tape you have selected is long enough.

10 Click OK.

A progress bar appears as the output is configured and prepared.

11 When Final Cut Pro is ready to play back the sequence and other elements, a message will appear telling you to begin recording. Click OK.

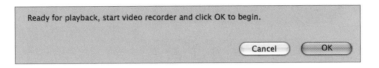

Ready for playback, start video recorder and click OK to begin.

Cancel OK

12 Begin recording from your recording device, and after about 5 seconds, click OK to start the playback and output of your sequence and elements.

Editing to Tape

The third way you can output your sequence to tape is the Edit To Tape method. It is similar to Print To Video in that the same set of leader and other options appear for you to select and include with your output. The primary difference is that the Edit To Tape window also has transport buttons for controlling the deck and setting an In point where you will begin recording your sequence.

In a professional environment, having this kind of frame-accurate control can be especially helpful. For example, you may want to begin recording your program exactly at 1:00:00:00. If so, you can backtime the amount of time you need for your preprogram elements, maybe 1 or 1.5 minutes, and begin recording those elements at that specific time—say, 58:30:00 or 59:00:00. Then your sequence will hit at precisely 1:00:00:00.

1 With the Timeline active, choose File > Edit To Tape.

If you do not have a controllable device connected, a warning window will appear.

⚠ Unable to initialize Edit to Tape. Please check your current Device Control Preset in Audio/Video Settings.

OK

If the device is properly connected, the Edit to Tape window opens.

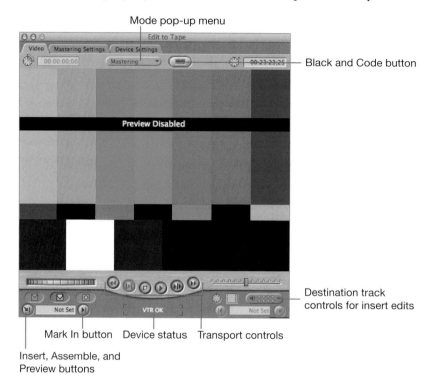

Mode pop-up menu

Black and Code button

Preview Disabled

Destination track controls for insert edits

Mark In button   Device status   Transport controls

Insert, Assemble, and Preview buttons

2   Click the Play button, play the tape, and click the Mark In button (or press I) to mark where you want to begin recording.

3   Click the Mastering Settings tab, and choose your settings just as you did in the Print To Video exercise.

4   Click the Video tab. From the Browser, drag the *Team Story* sequence to the preview area of the Edit To Tape window and into the Assemble section, then release the mouse.

5   When the Ready For Playback dialog box appears, click OK to start the
    recording process.

    The tape is cued up automatically, and the first elements of the output are
    recorded, starting at the In point you set.

6   Close the Edit To Tape window.

    NOTE ▶ When using DV material, you cannot use the Edit to Tape
    option to insert just video or audio.

Making a Timecode Window Burn

Often during the editing and output process, someone will request a screening
tape of the current version of the sequence with a visual timecode superimposed on top of the image. This visual timecode display is sometimes called a
timecode burn-in or window burn. A window burn of your sequence is helpful
when others need to screen your sequence and provide feedback referencing
precise locations, or when you're working with a deck that cannot read timecode from the tape.

In Final Cut Pro, the visual timecode, or window burn, is created by applying
the Timecode Reader filter. Since the objective is to have a visual timecode for

every clip in the entire sequence, you will first nest the sequence, then apply the filter.

1   In the Browser, duplicate the *Racing Promo* sequence. Name the duplicate *Racing Promo Burn-in*. Open this sequence in the Timeline.

2   In the Timeline, choose Edit > Select All, or press Cmd-A, to select all the clips in this sequence.

3   Choose Sequence > Nest Items.

> **TIP** When you want to apply the same filter to a large group of clips or to the entire sequence, it's often easier to make a nest of those clips and apply the filter to the nest.

4   Add the word *NEST* to the end of the name, and click OK.

All the clips in the Timeline are nested into a single track of video and two tracks of audio.

5   Move the playhead forward in the sequence so you see a full image in the Canvas. Choose Effects > Video Filters > Video > Timecode Reader.

This applies a Timecode Reader filter to the entire sequence.

6   Click a few different places in the Timeline ruler area and make sure the visual timecode display in the Canvas matches the timecode number in the Current Timecode field.

7   To change the appearance of the visual timecode, Option-double-click the nested sequence in the Timeline to load it into the Viewer, and click the Filters tab. You can also select the nest in the Timeline and press Return.

8   Adjust the size, color, opacity, and position of the visual timecode so it is easily seen over the video in the sequence, yet not too distracting.

9   Output the *Racing Promo Burn-in* sequence to tape using any one of the output methods described earlier in this lesson.

Managing Project Media

Managing media is the process of organizing, converting, and removing the media files that live on your hard drives. You may go through an entire project without having to address the issue of managing project media on your computer. On the other hand, during the editing process you may find that you need to move your project to a different computer, copy the media files for someone else to work on, delete files you aren't currently using to make room for new media, or recapture the media at a different resolution.

In Final Cut Pro, there is a Media Manager tool that enables you to perform these functions when needed, during or after the editing process. Media management can be a complex process, depending on the project's needs. The following exercises will serve as an introduction to this tool.

Copying a Project

If you have to copy your project from one computer to another, you can use the Media Manager Copy function to search for and gather all of the media files associated with that project. No matter where they are located, or whether they are graphic files, audio files, or media files, the Media Manager will find them and copy them to the specified destination.

1   To make a copy of your entire project, click in the Browser and press Cmd-A to select all items.

> **NOTE ▶** For this exercise, you can select the items in the Browser for the Lesson 16 Project and move through the exercise steps. At the end of the exercise, you can choose not to copy the material.

2   Choose File > Media Manager.

The Media Manager window opens and displays five sections. The Summary section describes what will happen based on the current settings; the green bars provide a visual indication of the media involved with the settings; and the Media options indicate how the media is processed. The Project and Media Destination sections enable you to create a new project for the media changes and choose a destination for the media files.

3   Click the Media pop-up menu.

There are five media processing options—Copy, Move, Recompress, Use Existing, and Create Offline—which tell the Media Manager how to process your media files.

4   Leave the Media pop-up menu on the default, Copy.

> **NOTE ▶** An important difference between the Copy and Move options is that when you move a project, the original project files will be deleted after you complete the move.

5   If you want to copy the render files as well, check the Include Render Files option. Deselect the Delete Unused Media From Duplicated Items option, and keep the Base Media File Names On option on the default, Existing File Names.

> **TIP▶** If you don't want to copy the portions of the media files you aren't using in the project, click the Delete Unused Media From Duplicated Sequences option. You can then give each clip a specific duration of handles if you choose.

6   Check the Duplicate Selected Items And Place Into A New Project option.

7   In the Media Destination area, click the Browse button, and navigate to the external drive where you want the copied media files to be placed. Create a folder for the new files.

8   When the Save window appears, enter a name for the new project and destination. For this exercise, click Cancel.

Recompressing Project Media

If you're an editor who wants to take your work home or work off-site, you may choose to recompress the media files you've been using in the editing bay and create lower-resolution media files you can put on your laptop to edit on the go.

1   In the Browser, select the Intro sequence and choose File > Media Manager.

2   In the Media Manager window, click the Media pop-up, and choose Recompress from the menu. Deselect Delete Unused Media From Duplicated Items.

3   Click the Recompress Media Using pop-up and choose OfflineRT NTSC
(Photo JPEG).

With a lower-resolution format selected, the Modified bar in the Summary
section of the Media Manager window shows a reduced amount of total
media.

4   In the Media Destination section, navigate to the Exports folder, then
click OK.

5   In the Save window that appears, name the project *Intro-Offline*. Before
you click Save, note that doing so will add media to your hard drive. If you
do not want to do this, click Cancel.

After the media has been processed, a new project tab will appear in the
Browser with the new recompressed media files. The clips will appear at a
lower offline resolution and not as clear as the original clips.

NOTE ▸ Each option in the Media Manager tool has an effect on how the
media will be copied or processed. To understand more about the details
of this tool, refer to the Final Cut Pro user's manual.

Backing Up Projects

After you have fine-tuned and output your sequence, it is time to back up your
project. It is important to have a backup strategy, not only for when you are
finished with a project, but all along the way. If the Autosave Vault is active,
Final Cut Pro will automatically save a backup of your project at set time

intervals as you work. In addition to this automatic backup system, here are a few other strategies to keep in mind:

▶ Store your project files on a separate drive from your Autosave Vault. That way, if either drive goes down, you will always have your project on the other drive.

▶ Save a few different versions of your project throughout the life of the project. This reduces the chance of file corruption by ensuring that you don't work on the same physical file for an extended period of time.

▶ Back up your project every few days to removable media, such as CDs, Zip disks, an iPod, or other FireWire devices. You can even back up your project to a server. The idea is to protect the project and yourself in case your computer or drive goes down.

Lesson Review

1. What does it mean when a clip has a red slash through the clip icon?
2. What is the most efficient way of finding the audio peaks in a sequence?
3. How are audio peaks indicated in the Timeline?
4. What can you do to determine whether an image falls within the broadcast safe category?
5. How can you correct an out-of-range clip so its range is in tolerance?
6. What is a self-contained QuickTime movie?
7. When might you use the QuickTime Conversion option to export a sequence?
8. What are the three ways you can output a sequence to tape?
9. What tool do you access to make changes to your project's media files?

Answers

1. The clip is offline and disconnected from its media file.
2. Using the Audio Peaks function, located in the Mark menu.
3. By markers in the ruler area where the audio peaks occurred.

4. Choose View > Range Check > Luma, and move through the sequence to see where the out-of-range clips are.

5. Apply the Broadcast Safe filter to the clip.

6. A movie that has the same settings as the sequence or clip and that can be played on any computer without having the original media files present.

7. When you want to export a sequence at settings other than the current ones (for example, for the Web, or DVD).

8. Manually, or by using the Print To Video or Edit To Tape options.

9. The Media Manager tool.

Keyboard Shortcuts

Cmd-Option-L	Opens Audio Gain Adjust or Video Opacity Adjust
Ctrl-Z	Toggles excess luma range check on and off

Appendix **A**

Introduction to LiveType

LiveType, a stand-alone application that ships with Final Cut Pro, lets you create high-quality animated titles and graphics, even if you have minimal motion graphics experience. Rather than spending hours building complex animations, LiveType lets you simplify the process, providing pre-keyframed effects that can be customized quickly and easily. To find out how to build titles and graphics in LiveType, refer to Appendix A on the DVD that accompanies this book. See Lessons > **x_Apndx A-LiveType**.

Appendix **B**

Final Cut Studio Workflows

Apple's family of professional audio and video applications are designed to work together seamlessly, even in the most demanding postproduction workflows. The Final Cut Studio product line—a comprehensive and integrated postproduction package—includes Final Cut Pro 5, Soundtrack Pro, Motion 2, DVD Studio Pro 4, Compressor 2, LiveType 2, and Cinema Tools 3. These tools, in conjunction with Shake 4 and Logic Pro 7, provide professional editors with the most comprehensive toolkit in the industry.

Appendix B, on the DVD accompanying this book, details the roles of each application in the Final Cut Pro production process. You will also find a sample Final Cut Studio workflow, and information on "round-tripping," the ability to embed and open application project files while working in another application. See Lessons > **x_Apndx B-Final Cut Studio Workflows**.

Glossary

16-bit   A standard bit depth for digital audio recording and playback.

16 x 9   The standard display aspect ratio of a high-definition television set.

32-bit   A four-channel image with each channel 8 bits deep. Typically, a CGI image with red, green, blue, and alpha channels.

4 x 3   The standard display aspect ratio of a standard video home television set.

8-bit   For video, a bit depth at which color is sampled. 8-bit color is common with DV and other standard-definition digital formats. Some high-definition acquisition formats can also record in 8-bit, but usually record in 10-bit.

Action safe   The area inside a border that is five percent smaller than the overall size of the video frame. Most of the time, anything in your video image that's outside of this border will not be displayed on a video screen.

A

Add Edit   Working like the Razor Blade tool, adds an edit point to all clips in the Timeline at the current position of the playhead.

A/D converter box   Equipment that changes an analog signal into a digital signal.

AIFF (Audio Interchange File Format)   Apple's native uncompressed audio file format created for the Macintosh computer, commonly used for the storage and transmission of digitally sampled sound.

Alpha channel   An image channel in addition to the R, G, and B color channels that is used to store transparency information for compositing. In Final Cut Pro, black represents 100 percent transparent, and white represents 100 percent opaque.

Ambience   A type of sound that includes background room noise, traffic noise, and atmospheric sound effects.

Analog   A signal that consists of a continuously varying voltage level, measured on a Waveform Monitor, which represents video and audio information. Analog signals must be converted to digital signals (digitized or captured) for use in Final Cut Pro. VHS and Beta SP are both analog tape formats.

Anamorphic   An image shot in a widescreen format and then squeezed into 4 x 3 frame size. When played back in Final Cut Pro, the image is played wide screen.

Anchor point   In the Motion tab, the point that is used to center changes to a clip when using motion effects. A clip's anchor point does not have to be at its center.

Animation   The process of changing any number of variables such as color, audio levels, or other effects over time using keyframes.

Aspect ratio   The ratio of the width of an image to its height on any viewing screen. Standard TV has an aspect ratio of 4:3; HDTV's is 16:9.

Attributes   All of the unique settings that have been applied to either audio or video clips.

Audio meters   A graphic display of the audio level (loudness) of a clip or sequence. Used to set incoming and outgoing audio levels and to check for audio distortion and signal strength.

Audio mixing   The process of adjusting the volume levels of all audio clips in an edited sequence, including the production audio, music, sound effects, voice-overs, and additional background ambience, to turn all of these sounds into a harmonious whole.

Audio sample rate   The rate or frequency at which a sound is sampled to digitize it. 48 kHz is the standard sampling rate for digital audio; CD audio is sampled at 44.1 kHz.

Audio waveform   A graphical representation of the amplitude (loudness) of a sound over a period of time.

Autosave Vault   A function to automatically save backup copies of all your FCP open projects at regular intervals. It must be turned on, and you can specify the intervals.

AVI   A PC-compatible standard for digital video no longer officially supported by Microsoft but still frequently used. AVI supports fewer codecs than QuickTime.

Axis   An imaginary straight line (horizontal, vertical, 3D diagonal) along which an object can move or rotate in space.

B

Backtiming   Using In and Out points in the Viewer and only an Out point in the Timeline, the two Out points will align, and the rest of the clip will appear before or to the left of this point.

Batch capture   Capturing multiple clips and or sequences with a single command.

Batch export   The ability to export multiple clips and or sequences with a single command by being able to stack them up in a queue. It is particularly useful when exporting will take a lot of time.

Bars and tone   A series of vertical bars of specific colors and an audio tone that are used to calibrate the audio and video signals coming from a videotape or camera to ensure consistent appearance and sound on different TV monitors.

Bezier handle   The "control handles" attached to a Bezier curve on a motion path that allow you to change the shape of the curve.

Bin   A file folder in the Browser window used to keep media clips grouped and organized. Derived from film editing where strips of film were hung over a cloth bin for sorting during the editing process.

Black level   The measurement of the black portion of the video signal. In analog television, this should not go below 7.5 IRE units. In digital television, black may be 0 units.

B-roll   A term used to describe alternate footage that intercuts with the primary soundtrack used in a program to help tell the story, or to cover flaws. B-roll is usually referred to as *cutaway* shots.

Blue screen   A solid blue background placed behind a subject and photographed so that later the subject can be extracted and composited onto another image.

Broadcast safe   The range of color that can be broadcast free of distortion, according to the NTSC standards, with maximum allowable video at 100 IRE units and digital black at 0 IRE, or analog black at 7.5 IRE units. FCP has a Broadcast Safe color-correction filter that provides a fast method of dealing with clips that have luminance and chrominance levels exceeding the broadcast limits for video.

Browser   An interface window that is a central storage area where you organize and access all of the source material used in your project.

C

Cache   A special high-speed memory area that the computer uses to store information that it can retrieve much faster than from main memory.

Canvas   The window in which you can view your edited sequence.

Capture   The process of digitizing media in the computer.

Center point   Defines a clip's location in the X/Y coordinate space in the Motion tab of the Canvas.

Chroma   The color information contained in a video signal consisting of hue (the color itself) and saturation (intensity).

Clip   Media files that may consist of video, audio, graphics, or any similar content that can be imported into Final Cut Pro.

Clipping   Distortion occurring during the playback or recording of digital audio due to an overly loud level.

Close-up   Framing a subject so that it fills the frame. Usually used for dramatic storytelling.

Codec   Short for compression/decompression. A program used to compress and decompress data such as audio and video files.

Color balance   Refers to the overall mix of red, green, and blue for the highlights (brightest), midtones, and shadow (darkest) areas in a clip. The color balance of these three areas can be adjusted using the Color Corrector 3-way filter.

Color correction   A process in which the color of clips used in an edited program is evened out so that all shots in a given scene match.

Color depth   The possible range of colors that can be used in a movie or image. In computer graphics, there are usually four choices: grayscale, 8-bit, 16-bit, and 24-bit. Higher color depths provide a wider range of colors but also require more disk space for a given image size. Broadcast video is generally 24-bit, with 8 bits of color information per channel.

Color matte   A clip containing solid color created as a generated item in the effects.

Composite Mode   One of the options in the Modify menu that offers many different methods of combining two or more images.

Compositing   The process of combining two or more video or electronic images into a single frame. This term can also describe the process of creating various video effects.

Compression   The process by which video, graphics, and audio files are reduced in size. The reduction in the size of a video file through the removal of redundant image data is referred to as a *lossy* compression scheme. A *lossless* compression scheme uses a mathematical process and reduces the file size by consolidating the redundant information without discarding it. See also *codec.*

Compression marker   A marker placed in a Final Cut movie that will flag DVD Studio Pro to stop so an I-frame can be changed.

Contrast   The difference between the lightest and darkest values in an image. High-contrast images have a large range of values from the darkest shadow to the lightest highlight. Low-contrast images have a more narrow range of values, resulting in a "flatter" look.

Crop tool   A tool used to slice a specified amount from the total frame size of a clip. You can crop the top, left, right, and bottom of a clip independently.

Cross fade   A transition between two audio clips where one sound is faded out while the other is faded in. Used to make the transition between two audio cuts less noticeable.

Cut   The simplest type of edit where one clip ends and the next begins without any transition.

Cutaway   A shot that is related to the current subject and occurs in the same time frame; for instance, an interviewer's reaction to what is being said in an interview or a shot to cover a technically bad moment.

D

Data rate   The speed at which data can be transferred, often described in megabytes per second (MB/sec). The higher a video file's data rate, the higher quality it will be, but it will require more system resources (processor speed, hard disk space, and performance). Some codecs allow you to specify a maximum data rate for a movie during capture.

Decibel (dB)   A unit of measure for the loudness of audio.

Decompression   The process of creating a viewable image for playback from a compressed video, graphics, or audio file. Compare with *compression*.

De-interlace filter   Used to convert video frames composed of two interlaced fields into a single unified frame; for example, to create a still image of an object moving at high speed.

Desaturate   To remove color from a clip. 100 percent desaturation results in a grayscale image.

Device control   A cable that allows Final Cut Pro to control a video deck or camera. Three protocols are used most frequently to control video devices: serial device control via the RS-422 and RS-232 protocols, and FireWire for DV camcorders and decks.

Digital   Data that is stored or transmitted as a sequence of ones and zeros.

Digital video   Video that has been captured, manipulated, and stored using a digital format, which can be easily imported into your computer. Digital video can come in many different formats such as Digital-8, DVC Pro, DVCAM, or DV.

Digitize   To convert an analog video signal into a digital video format. A method of capturing video. See also *capture.*

Dissolve   A transition between two video clips where the first one fades down at the same time the second one fades up.

Distort   An option in the Tool palette that allows you to change the shape of an image by moving any of its four corners independently of the others.

Dock   A strip on the Desktop where you can store the program alias icons that you use most frequently.

Drop frame timecode   A type of timecode that skips ahead in time by two frame numbers each minute, except for minutes ending in "0" (10, 20, 30, and so on). Although timecode numbers are skipped, actual video frames are not skipped. Drop frame timecode is a reference to real time.

Drop shadow   An effect that creates an artificial shadow behind an image or text.

Dub   Making a copy of an analog tape to the same type of format.

Duration   The length of a clip or a sequence from its In to its Out point, or the length of time that it takes that piece of video to play.

DV   A standard for a specific digital video format created by a consortium of camcorder vendors, which uses Motion JPEG video at a 720 x 480 resolution at 29.97 frames per second (NTSC) or 720 x 546 resolution at 25 fps (PAL), stored at a bit rate of 25 MB per second at a compression of 4:1:1.

DVD   A disc that is the size of a CD, but uses higher-density storage methods to significantly increase its capacity. Usually used for video distribution, DVD-ROM discs can also be used to store computer data.

DVD marker   A location indicator that can be seen in DVD Studio Pro used to mark a chapter.

Dynamic range   The difference, in decibels, between the loudest and softest parts of a recording.

E

Easy Setup   Preset audio/video settings, including capture, sequence, device control, and output settings.

Edit point   (1) Defines what part of a clip you want to use in an edited sequence. Edit points include In points, which specify the beginning of a section of a clip or sequence, and Out points, which specify the end of a section of a clip or sequence. (2) The point in the Timeline of an edited sequence where the Out point of one clip meets the In point of the next clip.

Edit to Tape   The command that lets you perform frame-accurate Insert and Assemble edits to tape.

EDL   A text file that uses the source timecode of clips to sequentially list all of the edits that make up a sequence. EDLs are used to move a project from one editing application to another, or to coordinate the assembly of a program in a tape-based online editing facility.

Effects   A general term used to describe all of Final Cut Pro's capabilities that go beyond cuts-only editing. See *filters, generators,* and *transitions.*

Export   A menu option that allows you to move files or media out of Final Cut Pro to a variety of destinations via a variety of codecs; lets you translate the current file format into a number of different formats.

Extend edit   An edit in which the edit point is moved to the position of the playhead in the Timeline.

F

Fade   An effect in which the picture gradually transitions to black.

Faders   In the Audio Mixer, vertical sliders used to adjust the audio levels of clips at the position of the playhead.

Favorite   A customized effect that is used frequently. You can create favorites from most of the effects in Final Cut Pro.

Field   Half of an *interlaced video* frame consisting of the odd or the even scan lines.

Field Dominance   The choice of whether field one or field two will be displayed on the monitor first. The default should be Lower (even) for DV and Targa captures.

Filters   Effects you can apply to video and audio clips or group of clips that change some aspect of the clip content.

Finishing   The process of fine tuning the sequence audio and video levels and preparing the sequence for output to tape or other destination, such as the Web or DVD. Finishing may also involve recapturing offline resolution clips at an uncompressed resolution.

FireWire Apple's trademark name for the IEEE 1394 standard used to connect external hard drives and cameras to computers. It provides a fast interface to move large video and audio files to the computer's hard drive.

Fit to Fill edit An edit in which a clip is inserted into a sequence such that its duration matches a predetermined amount of specified track space.

Frame A single still image from either video or film. For video, each frame is made up of two interlaced fields (see *interlaced video*).

Frame blending A process of inserting blended frames in place of frames that have been duplicated in clips with slow motion, to make them play back more smoothly.

Framing Composing a shot for the best presentation of the subject, taking into consideration the size of the subject in the frame and how it is centered.

Frequency The number of times a sound or signal vibrates each second, measured in cycles per second, or hertz.

Gain In video, the level of white in a video picture; in audio, the loudness of an audio signal.

G

Gamma A curve that describes how the middle tones of an image appear. Gamma is a nonlinear function often confused with "brightness" or "contrast." Changing the value of the gamma affects middle tones while leaving the whites and blacks of the image unaltered. Gamma adjustment is often used to compensate for differences between Macintosh and Windows video cards and displays.

Gap Locations in a sequence where there is no media on any track. When output to video, gaps in an edited sequence appear as black sections.

Generators Clips that are synthesized by Final Cut Pro. Generators can be used as different kinds of backgrounds, titles, and elements for visual design.

Gradient A generated image that changes smoothly from one color to another across the image. The change can occur in several ways: horizontally, vertically, radially, and so on.

Green screen   A solid green background placed behind a subject and photographed so that later the subject can be extracted and composited into another image.

H

Handles   Extra frames of unused video or audio that are on either side of the In and Out points in an edit.

Head   The beginning of a clip.

Histogram   A window that displays the relative strength of all luminance values in a video frame, from black to super-white. It is useful for comparing two clips in order to match their brightness values more closely.

Hue   A specific color or pigment, such as red.

I

Icon   An onscreen symbol that represents a program or file.

Import File   The menu option that allows you to bring one or more media files into an FCP project.

Import Folder   The menu option that allows you to import a folder of media files into an FCP project.

Incoming clip   The clip that is on the right-hand side, or B-side, of a transition or cut point.

In point   The edit point entered either in the Viewer, Canvas, or Timeline that determines where an edit will begin.

Insert edit   To insert a clip into an existing sequence into the Timeline, which automatically moves the other clips (or remaining frames of a clip) to the right to make room for it. An Insert edit does not replace existing material.

Interlaced video   A video scanning method that first scans the odd picture lines (field 1) and then scans the even picture lines (field 2), which merges them together into one single frame of video. Used in standard-definition video.

IRE   A unit of measurement for luminance in an analog signal established by the Institute of Radio Engineers (IRE).

Jog   To move forward or backward through your video one frame at a time.   **J**

JPEG (Joint Photographic Experts Group)   A popular image file format that lets you create highly compressed graphics files. The amount of compression used can vary. Less compression results in a higher-quality image.

Jump cut   A cut in which an abrupt change occurs between two shots.

Keyframe   A point at which a filter, motion effect, or audio level changes   **K**
value. There must be at least two keyframes representing two different values to see a change.

Keying   The process of dropping out a specific area of an image, such as its background, in order to composite it with another image. You can key out information in a clip based on brightness and darkness, or color.

Labels   Terms that appear in the Label column of the Browser such as "Best   **L**
Take" and "Interview." Labels can also be assigned to clips and media to help distinguish and sort them. Each label has an associated color that is also applied to clips.

Letterbox   When widescreen video is displayed to fit within a standard 4 x 3 monitor, putting black at the top and bottom of the picture.

Lift edit   An edit function that leaves a gap when material is lifted from the Timeline.

Link   (1) To connect an audio clip and video clip together in the Timeline so that when one item is selected, moved, or trimmed, all other items linked to it are affected. (2) The connection between a clip and its associated source media file on disk. If you move source media files, change their names, or put them in the Trash, the links break and associated clips in your Final Cut Pro project become *offline clips.*

Linked selection   An option in the Timeline that, when enabled, maintains connections between linked clips. When linked selection is turned off, linked items behave as if they are not connected.

Lock Track control   The lock icon in the Timeline tracks control area, which locks and unlocks tracks. See *locked track.*

Locked track   A track whose contents cannot be moved or changed. Cross-hatched lines distinguish a locked track on the Timeline. You can lock or unlock tracks at any time by clicking the Lock Track control on the Timeline.

Log and Capture   The process of playing clips from a device and logging and capturing the clips you want to use in editing.

Log bin   A specific bin where all the logged or captured clips go when using the Log and Capture window.

logging   The process of entering detailed information including the In and Out points from your source material, log notes, and so on, in preparation to be captured.

Looping   A playback mode of repeatedly playing the same portion of a clip or sequence from an In point to an Out point.

Lower third   Lines of text used to identify a person, place, or thing in a clip.

Luma   Short for luminance. A value describing the brightness part of the video signal without color (chroma).

Luma Key   A filter used to key out a luminance value, creating a matte based on the brightest or darkest area of an image. See *keying* and *matte*.

M

Mark In   The process of indicating with a mark in the Timeline the first frame of a clip to be used.

Mark Out   The process of indicating with a mark in the Timeline the last frame of a clip to be used.

Markers   Location indicators that can be placed on a clip or in a sequence to help you find a specific place while you edit. Can be used to sync action between two clips, identify beats of music, mark a reference word from a narrator, and so on.

Marquee   When dragging the pointer over items in the Browser or Timeline, the dashed lines that create a rectangular area used to select items in that area.

Mark in Sync   Placing a marker that labels the audio from another source as being in sync with a selected video clip. This disables the normal out-of-sync warnings.

Mask   An image or clip used to define areas of transparency in another clip. Similar to an *alpha channel.*

Master clip   The status given to a clip when it is the first time that clip is used in a project. It is the clip from which other affiliate clips, such as sequence clips and subclips, are created.

Master shot   A single, long shot of some dramatic action from which shorter cuts such as close-ups and medium shots are taken in order to fill out the story.

Mastering mode   A mode in the Edit to Tape window that lets you output additional elements such as color bars and tone, a slate, and a countdown when you output your program to tape.

Match Frame   A command that looks at the clip in the Timeline at the playhead, and puts that clip's master into the Viewer. The position of the playhead in the Viewer matches that of the playhead in the Canvas, so both the Canvas and the Viewer will display the same frame, and the In and Out points of the clip in your sequence will be matched to those of the copy in the Viewer. In addition, all the original source material for this clip will also be displayed.

Matte   An effect, such as a widescreen matte or a garbage matte, that hides or reveals a part of a clip.

Media file   A generic term for captured or acquired elements such as QuickTime movies, sounds, and pictures.

Media Manager   A tool that helps you manage your projects, media files, and available disk space quickly and easily in Final Cut Pro without using the Finder.

Midtones   The middle brightness range of an image. Not the very brightest part, nor the very darkest part.

Mono audio   A single track of audio.

Motion Blur   An effect that blurs any clip with keyframed motion applied to it, similar to blurred motion recorded by a camera.

Motion path   A path that appears in the Canvas when Image+Wireframe mode is selected and a clip has Center *keyframes* applied to it.

MPEG (Moving Picture Experts Group)   A group of compression standards for video and audio, which includes MPEG-1, MPEG-2, MPEG-3 (referred to as *MP3*), and MPEG-4.

Multicam editing   This feature lets you simultaneously play back and view shots from multiple sources and cut between them in real time.

Multiclip   A clip that allows you to group together multiple sources as separate angles and cut between them, up to 128 angles, of which 16 can be played back at a time.

N

Natural sound   The ambient sound that is used from the source videotape.

Nest   To place a sequence that is edited within another sequence.

Non-drop frame timecode   A type of timecode, in which frames are numbered sequentially. Non-drop frame timecode is off by 3 seconds and 18 frames per hour in comparison to actual elapsed time.

Noninterlaced video   The standard representation of images on a computer, also referred to as progressive scan. The monitor displays the image by drawing each line, continuously one after the other, from top to bottom.

Nonlinear editing (NLE)   A video editing process that uses computer hard disks to randomly access the media. It allows the editor to reorganize clips very quickly or make changes to sections without having to re-create the entire program.

Nonsquare pixel   A pixel whose height is different than its width. An NTSC pixel is taller than it is wide, and a PAL pixel is wider than it is tall.

NTSC (National Television Systems Committee)   Standard of color TV broadcasting used mainly in North America, Mexico, and Japan, consisting of 525 lines per frame, 29.97 frames per second, and 720 x 486 pixels per frame (720 x 480 for DV).

O

Offline clip   Clips that appear in the Browser with a red slash through them. Clips may be offline because they haven't been captured yet, or because the media file has been moved to another location. To view these clips properly in your project, you must recapture them or reconnect them to their corresponding source files at their new locations on disk.

Offline editing   The process of editing a program at a lower resolution to save on equipment costs or to conserve hard disk space. When the edit is finished, the material can be recaptured at a higher quality, or an *EDL* can be generated for re-creating the edit on another system.

OMF (Open Media Framework)   OMF is an edit data interchange format.

On the fly   The process of setting an In or Out point as the clip is playing in the Viewer or on the Timeline.

Opacity   The degree to which an image is transparent, allowing images behind to show through.

Outgoing clip   The clip that is on the left-hand side of the cut point or the A-side of the transition.

Out of sync   When the audio of a track has been shifted horizontally in the Timeline from the video track causing it to no longer match the video track.

Out point   The edit point entered in the Viewer, Canvas, or Timeline where an edit will end.

Overlays   Icons or text that are displayed over the video in the Viewer and Canvas windows while the playhead is parked on a frame to provide information about that frame.

Overwrite edit   An edit where the clip being edited into a sequence replaces an existing clip. The duration of the sequence remains unchanged.

P

PAL (Phase Alternating Line)   The European color TV broadcasting standard consisting of 625 lines per frame, running at 25 frames per second, and 720 x 546 pixels per frame.

Pan   To move a camera left or right without changing its position.

Parade Scope   A modified Waveform Monitor that breaks out the red, green, and blue components of the image, showing them as three separate waveforms. Useful for comparing the relative levels of reds, greens, and blues between two clips, especially in a graphics situation.

Paste Attributes   The ability to copy attributes from one clip and transfer (paste) them to another clip of the same type.

Patch panel   The section of the Timeline containing the Audio, Source, Destination, Track Enabling, Locking, and Edit Select controls.

Peak   Short, loud bursts of sound that last a fraction of a second and can be viewed on a digital audiometer that displays the absolute volume of an audio signal as it plays.

Phase   An attribute of color perception, also known as *hue.*

PICT   The native still-image file format for Macintosh developed by Apple Computer. PICT files can contain both vector images and bitmap images, as well as text and an alpha channel.

Pixel   Short for "picture element," one dot in a video or still image.

Pixel aspect ratio   The width-to-height ratio for the pixels that compose an image. Pixels on computer screens and in high-definition video signals are square (1:1 ratio). Pixels in standard-definition video signals are nonsquare.

Playhead   A navigational element on the scrubber bar that shows you on what frame you are in the Timeline, Canvas, or Viewer. You drag the playhead to navigate through a sequence.

Post-production   The phase of film, video, and audio editing that begins after all the footage is shot.

Post-roll   The amount of time that a tape machine continues to roll after the Out point of an edit, typically between 2 and 5 seconds.

Poster frame   The representative still frame of a clip that is the Thumbnail image.

Pre-roll   A specified amount of time, usually 5 seconds, given to tape machines so they can synchronize themselves to the editing computer before previewing or performing an edit.

Preview   To play an edit to see how it will look without actually performing the edit itself.

Print to Video   A command in Final Cut Pro that lets you *render* your sequence and output it to videotape.

Proc amp (processing amplifier)   A specific piece of equipment that allows you to adjust video levels on output.

Project   In Final Cut Pro, the top-level file that holds all the media associated with a program, including sequences and clips of various kinds.

QuickTime   Apple's cross-platform multimedia technology. Widely used for editing, compositing, CD-ROM, Web video, and more.

Q

QuickTime streaming   Apple's streaming media addition to the QuickTime architecture. Used for viewing QuickTime content in real time on the Web.

QuickView tool   Provides an alternate way of viewing your composition outside of the Canvas as you work. It takes advantage of Final Cut Pro's ability to cache frames of your sequence as you play it. This is useful for fast previews of complex composites and effects. It's also a good way to see how your final composite looks if you are zoomed into the Canvas while making adjustments.

RAID (Redundant Array of Independent Disks) drive   A method of providing nonlinear editors with many gigabytes of high-performance data storage by formatting a group of hard disks to act as a single drive volume.

R

Range check   Options that enable zebra striping to immediately warn you of areas of a clip's image that may stray outside of the broadcast legal range.

Razor Blade   An option on the Tool Palette that allows you to slice the clip into two separate edits to be manipulated individually and is also used as a quick way to trim frames off of a clip.

Real-time effects   Effects that can be applied to clips in an edited sequence and played back in real time, without requiring rendering first. Real-time effects can be played back using any qualified computer.

Record monitor   A monitor that plays the previewed and finished versions of a project when it is printed to tape. A record monitor corresponds to the Canvas in Final Cut Pro.

Redo   To reverse an undo, which restores the last change made to a project.

Render   To process video and audio with any applied effects, such as transitions or filters. Effects that aren't real time must be rendered in order to play them back properly. Once rendered, your sequence can be played in real time.

Render file   The file produced by rendering a clip to disk. FCP places it in a separate hidden folder so it does not show up in the Browser, but is retrieved with the Timeline.

Render status bars   Two slim horizontal bars, in the Timeline ruler area, that indicate which parts of the sequence have been rendered at the current render quality. The top bar is for video, and the bottom for audio. Different colored bars indicate the real-time playback status of a given section of the Timeline.

Replace edit   Allows you to replace an existing shot in a sequence with a different shot of the same length.

RGB   An abbreviation for red, green, and blue, which are the three primary colors that make up a color image.

Ripple edit   An edit in which the start and end times of a range of clips on a track is adjusted when the duration of one of the clips is altered.

Roll edit   An edit that affects two clips that share an *edit point.* The Out point of the outgoing clip and the In point of the incoming clip both change, but the overall duration of the sequence stays the same.

Rotation   To rotate a clip around its anchor point without changing its shape.

RT Extreme   Real-time effects processing that scales with your system.

Ruler area   The measurement bar along the top of the Timeline, which represents the total duration of an edited sequence. Also displays the timecode corresponding to the location of clips in the Timeline. You can move the playhead on the ruler in order to navigate through clips in a sequence.

Sampling   The process during which analog audio is converted into digital information. The sampling rate of an audio stream specifies how many samples are captured. Higher sample rates yield higher-quality audio. Examples: 44.1 K, 48 K.

Saturation   The purity of color. As saturation is decreased, the color moves towards pastel then towards a white.

Scale   In the Motion tab of the Viewer, an adjustable value that changes the overall size of a clip. The proportion of the image may or may not be maintained.

Scratch disk   The hard drive that is designated as the destination to hold your captured media, rendered clips, and cache files.

Scrub   To move through a clip or sequence with the aid of the playhead. Scrubbing is used to find a particular point or frame or to hear the audio.

Scrubber bar   A bar below the Viewer and the Canvas that allows you to manually drag the playhead in either direction to playback.

SECAM (Séquentiel Couleur à Mémoire)   The French television standard for playback. Similar to PAL, the playback rate is 25 fps and the frame size is 720 x 546.

Selection tool   The default arrow-shaped pointer, which allows you to select items in the interface. For example, you use it to select a clip or edit point. You can choose the Selection tool by pressing the A key.

Sequence   An edited assembly of video, audio, or graphics clips. In Final Cut Pro, sequences can be up to four hours long and contain as many clips as you need to tell your story. A sequence can contain your entire edited program or be limited to a single scene.

Sequence clip   A clip that has been edited into a sequence.

Shuttle control   The slider control located at the bottom of the Viewer and the Canvas. This control is useful for continuous playback at different speeds, in fast and slow motion. It also shifts the pitch of audio as it plays at varying speeds.

Slate   A small clapboard that is placed in front of all cameras at the beginning of a scene, which identifies the scene with basic production information such as the take, date, and scene. A slate or clapper provides an audio/visual cue for synchronization of dual system recordings.

Slide edit   An edit in which an entire clip is moved, along with the edit points on its left and right. The duration of the clip being moved stays the same, but the clips to the left and to the right of it change in length to accommodate the new positioning of the clip. The overall duration of the sequence and of these three clips remains the same.

Slip edit   An edit in which the location of both In and Out points of a clip are changed at the same time, without changing the location or duration of the marked media. This is referred to as *slipping* because you slip a pair of In and Out points inside the available footage.

Slug   A solid black video frame that can be used to represent a video clip that has not yet been placed in the Timeline.

SMPTE (Society of Motion Picture and Television Engineers)   The organization responsible for establishing various broadcast video standards like the SMPTE standard timecode for video playback.

Snapping   A setting in the Timeline that affects the movement of the playhead. When snapping is enabled, the playhead "snaps," or moves directly, to markers or edit points when it is moved close to them.

Solo   An audio monitoring feature in which one audio track from a group may be isolated for listening without having to remove it from the group.

SOT   Acronym for *sound on tape*.

Sound byte (SOT, sound on tape)   A short excerpt taken from an interview clip.

Split edit   An edit in which the video track or the audio track of a synchronized clip ends up being longer than the other; for example, the sound is longer than the video at the head of the clip, so it is heard before the video appears. Also referred to as an *L-cut*.

Spread   An audio control that allows you to adjust the amount of separation of stereo channels.

Square pixel   A pixel that has the same height as width. Computer monitors have square pixels, but NTSC and PAL video do not.

Static region   An area in a sequence in the Timeline that you lock so that it is visible even when you scroll to see other tracks. The static area can contain audio tracks, video tracks, or both.

Stereo audio   Sound that is separated into two channels, one carrying the sounds for the right ear and one for the left ear. Stereo pairs are linked and are always edited together. Audio level changes are automatically made to both channels at the same time. A pair of audio items may have their stereo pairing enabled or disabled at any time.

Storyboard   A series of pictures that summarizes the content, action, and flow of a proposed project. When using the Browser in icon view, clips can be arranged visually, like a storyboard. When dragged as a group into the Timeline, the clips will be edited together in the order in which they appear in the Timeline, from left to right, and from the top line down to the bottom.

Straight cut   An edit in which both the video and audio tracks are cut together to the Timeline.

Streaming   The delivery of media over an intranet or over the Internet.

Subclip   A clip created to represent a section of a *master clip*. Subclips are saved as separate items within a bin in the Browser, but do not generate any additional media on the hard disk.

Superimpose edit   An edit in which an incoming clip is placed on top of a clip that's already in the Timeline at the position of the playhead. If no In or Out points are set in the Timeline and Canvas, the previously edited clip's In and Out points are used to define the duration of the incoming clip. Superimposed edits are used to overlay titles and text onto video, as well as to create other compositing effects.

Super-black   Black that is darker than the levels allowed by the CCIR 601 engineering standard for video. The CCIR 601 standard for black is 7.5 IRE in the United States, and 0 IRE for PAL and for NTSC in Japan.

Super-white   A value or degree of white that is brighter than the accepted normal value of 100 IRE allowed by the CCIR 601.

Sweetening   The process of creating a high-quality sound mix by polishing sound levels, rerecording bad sections of dialogue, and recording and adding narration, music, and sound effects.

Sync   The relationship between the image of a sound being made in a video clip (for example, a person talking) and the corresponding sound in an audio clip. Maintaining audio sync is critical when editing dialogue.

T

Tab   In Final Cut Pro, tabs delineate projects in the Browser, sequences in the Canvas and Timeline, and functions within the Viewer. You click a tab to open a project or go to a specified function window, such as Video, Audio, Filters, or Motion. Tabs can also be dragged out of the main window to create a separate window.

Tail   The end frames of a clip.

Target track   The yellow light that indicates which track is active.

Three-point editing   The process of creating an edit by setting just 3 edit points that determine source content, duration, and placement in the sequence. With 3 edit points selected, Final Cut Pro calculates the fourth one.

Thumbnails   The first frame of a clip, shown as a tiny picture for reference. In Final Cut Pro, the thumbnail is, by default, the first frame of a clip. You can change the frame used as that clip's thumbnail by using the Scrub Video tool.

TIFF (Tagged Image File Format)   A widely used bitmapped graphics file format that handles monochrome, grayscale, and 8- and 24-bit color. There are two types of TIFF images, one with an alpha channel and one without.

Tilt   To pivot the camera up and down, which causes the image to move up or down in the frame.

Timecode   A unique numbering system of electronic signals laid onto each frame of videotape that is used to identify specific frames of video. Each frame of video is labeled with hours, minutes, frames, and seconds (01:00:00:00). Timecode can be drop frame, non-drop frame, or time of day (TOD) timecode, or EBU (European Broadcast Union) for PAL projects.

Timecode gap   An area of tape with no timecode at all. Timecode gaps usually signify the end of all recorded material on a tape, but timecode gaps may occur due to the starting and stopping of the camera and tape deck during recording.

Timeline   A window in Final Cut Pro that displays a chronological view of an open *sequence.* Each sequence has its own tab in the Timeline. You can use the Timeline to edit and arrange a sequence. The order of the tracks in the Timeline determines the layering order when you combine multiple tracks of video. Changes you make to a sequence in the Timeline are seen when you play back that sequence in the Canvas.

Time remapping   The process of moving a frame in a clip to another time relative to the Timeline. All frames in that clip from the beginning of the clip to that keyframe are either sped up or slowed down to accommodate the new duration that's been specified.

Title safe   Part of the video image that is guaranteed to be visible on all televisions. The title safe area is the inner 80 percent of the screen. To prevent text in your video from being hidden by the edge of a TV set, you should restrict any titles or text to the title safe area.

Tool Bench   A window that contains interface elements that supplement information displayed in the Viewer and Canvas. The Tool Bench can contain up to three tabs—QuickView, Video Scopes, and Voice Over.

Tool palette   A window in Final Cut Pro that contains tools for editing, zooming, cropping, and distorting items in the Timeline. All tools in the Tool palette can also be selected using keyboard shortcuts.

Tracks   Layers in the Timeline that contain the audio or video clips in a sequence. Also refers to the separate audio and video tracks on tape. Final Cut Pro allows up to 99 video and 99 audio tracks to be used in a single sequence.

Track Lock   An icon that indicates a track has been locked to prevent accidental change.

Track Visibility   A control in the track controls area of the Timeline that you click to turn track visibility on or off. Invisible tracks don't play in the Canvas or on an external monitor, nor will they be rendered or output to tape. When a track is invisible, it appears darkened in the Timeline, but its contents remain in your sequence and you can still edit them.

Transition   A visual effect that is applied between two edits, such as a dissolve, wipe, or iris.

Transition Editor   A specialized editor that appears in the Viewer when you double-click a transition in the Timeline and is used to make detailed changes to a transition's timing and effects parameters.

Trim Edit window   A window in Final Cut Pro that displays both sides of an edit: the Out point of the outgoing clip on the left and the In point of the incoming clip on the right. You can use this window to adjust the edit point between two clips very precisely, frame by frame.

Trimming   To precisely add or subtract frames from the In or Out point of a clip. Trimming is used to fine-tune an edited sequence by carefully adjusting many edits in small ways.

Two-up display   A display in the Canvas that appears when using some type of trim or adjustment mode, such as Roll, Ripple, Slip, or Slide. Two individual frames appear to display either the frames being adjusted or the border frames.

U

Undo   A feature that allows you to cancel the last change made.

User Preferences   The area where you set up how you want to work with your media inside Final Cut Pro.

V

Variable speed   Dynamic alteration of the speed of a clip, alternating among a range of speeds, in forward or reverse motion.

Vectorscope   A window in Final Cut Pro that graphically displays the color components of a video signal, precisely showing the range of colors in a video signal and measuring their intensity and hue.

Video level   The measurement of the level (amplitude) of a video signal. It is measured using the Waveform Monitor in FCP.

Video scopes   Tools you can use to evaluate the color and brightness values of video clips in the Viewer, Canvas, or Timeline. Video scopes display an analysis of the video frame located at the current playhead position.

Video Scopes tab   A tab in the Tool Bench that contains the four Final Cut Pro Video scopes: Waveform Monitor, Vectorscope, Parade Scope, and Histogram.

Viewer   A window in Final Cut Pro that acts as a source monitor. You can use the Viewer to watch individual source clips and mark In and Out points in preparation for editing them into your sequence. You can also customize transitions, modify filters, and view and edit various effects. Clips from the current sequence in the Timeline can be opened in the Viewer to refine edits, effects, and audio volume.

Voice Over tool   Allows you to record audio in Final Cut Pro while simultaneously playing back a specified section of a sequence from the Timeline. Audio can be recorded using any Sound Manager-compatible device, such as a USB audio capture device, PCI audio card, or the built-in microphone on a DV camcorder.

VTR / VCR   Videotape recorder/Videocassette recorder. A tape machine used for recording pictures and sound on videotape.

VU meter (Volume Unit meter)   An analog meter for monitoring audio levels.

Waveform Monitor   A window in Final Cut Pro that displays the relative levels of brightness and saturation in the clip currently being examined. Spikes or drops in the displayed waveforms make it easy to see where the brightest or darkest areas are in your picture.

W

White balance   The reference to white that is made during recording. This reference can be changed within FCP to reset the white balance, correcting or improving it.

White level An analog video signal's amplitude for the lightest white in a picture, represented by *IRE* units.

Wide-screen An aspect ratio such as 16:9 or 2.35:1 that allows for a wider image, suitable for widescreen television or film projection.

Wide-screen matte filter Adds a mask, blacking out the top and bottom of a 4 x 3 image, which creates a wide-screen image, such as 16:9.

Wipe A type of transition that uses a moving edge to progressively erase the current clip to reveal the next clip.

Wireframe A visual substitute for a clip that simply represents the outline of the clip's video frame. Clips in the Viewer and Canvas can be viewed in Wireframe mode.

Window burn Visual timecode and keycode information superimposed onto video frames. It usually appears on a strip at the bottom or top of the frame, providing code information to the editor without obscuring any of the picture.

X

X axis Refers to the x coordinate in Cartesian geometry. The x coordinate describes horizontal placement in motion effects.

Y

Y axis Refers to the y coordinate in Cartesian geometry. The y coordinate describes vertical placement in motion effects.

YcrCb The color space in which digital video formats store data. Three components are stored for each pixel—one for luminance (Y) and two for color information, Cr for the red portion of the color difference signal and Cb for the blue color difference signal.

YUV The three-channel PAL video signal with one luminance (Y) and two chrominance color difference signals (UV). It is often misapplied to refer to NTSC video, which is YIQ.

Z axis   Refers to the z coordinate in Cartesian geometry. The z coordinate describes perpendicular placement in motion effects.

Zebra stripes   Animated diagonal "marching lines" that are superimposed over illegal areas or areas that are very near the broadcast legal limits in an image. Zebra stripes are enabled when you use Final Cut Pro's range-checking options.

Zoom   To change the view of your image or Timeline.

Zoom control   Used to zoom in or out while keeping the material in the waveform display area centered. Clicking to the right of the control zooms out to show more of the duration of your clip; clicking to the left zooms in to show more detail.

Zoom slider   The slider control that appears at the bottom of the Timeline. The Zoom slider allows you to navigate throughout the total duration of the currently displayed sequence; you can use the thumb tabs on the left and right of the slider to zoom in to and out of a sequence for a more detailed view.

Index

Hear Your Vision?

THE INDEPENDENT CHOICE

megatrax®

Film & TV

PRODUCTION MUSIC   ORIGINAL SCORING

Love? Terror? Or both? Bring your audience into the scene with the perfect sound. Offering the highest quality production music & original scoring, Megatrax can put the right track to any film, TV, advertising or multimedia project.

With three new high quality libraries: **Amusicom, Intervox and Arts Classical, Megatrax** now offers over 450 CDs to choose from!   Call us or go to **megatrax.com** to search, preview & download more than 12,000 tracks online.

t: 818.255.7177   888.MEGA.555   f: 818.255.7178
e: **filmtv@megatrax.com**   **www.megatrax.com**

All Hours

InFlagranteDelicto

Featuring:
"Box Office Stud"
"Make Up" &
"Make It Right"

www.allhoursmusic.com

H hybrid

Welcome TO A NATIVE PLACE

www.AmericanIndian.si.edu • 202.633.1000

Above Right: *Raven Steals the Moon*, by Ed Archie NoiseCat (Salish, b. 1959), 2003. Santa Fe, New Mexico. Cast glass. Photo by Ernest Amoroso.

Above Left: *Raven Steals the Sun*, by Preston Singletary (Tlingit, b. 1963), 2003. Seattle, Washington. Blown and sand-blasted glass. Photo by Ernest Amoroso.

Right: The east-facing main entrance to the National Museum of the American Indian in Washington, D.C. Photo © 2004 Judy Davis/Hoachlander Davis Photography.

Left: Objects from the *Window on Collections*, which showcases thousands of works from the NMAI collection.

Smithsonian
National Museum of the American Indian

The Apple Pro Training Series

The official curriculum of the Apple Pro Training and Certification Program, the Apple Pro Training books are a comprehensive, self-paced courses written by acknowledged experts in the field.

- Focused lessons take you step-by-step through the process of creating real-world digital video or audio projects.
- All media and project files are included on the companion DVD.
- Ample illustrations help you master techniques fast.
- Lesson goals and time estimates help you plan your time.
- Chapter review questions summarize what you've learned.

**Apple Pro Training Series:
Final Cut Pro 5**
0-321-33481-7

In this best-selling guide, Diana Weynand starts with basic video editing techniques and takes you all the way through Final Cut Pro's powerful advanced features. Using world-class documentary footage, you'll learn mark and edit clips, color correct sequences, create transitions, ply filters and effects, add titles, work with audio, and more.

**Apple Pro Training Series: Advanced
Editing Techniques in Final Cut Pro 5**
0-321-33549-X

Director and editor Michael Wohl shares must-know professional techniques for cutting dialogue scenes, action scenes, fight and chase scenes, documentaries, comedy, music videos, multi-camera projects, and more. Also covers Soundtrack Pro, audio finishing, managing clips and media, and working with film.

**Apple Pro Training
Series: Color
Correction and
Effects in
Final Cut Pro 5**
0-321-33548-1

This Apple-authorized guide delivers hard-to-d training in real-world color correction d effects techniques, including motion ects, keying and compositing, titling, ene-to-scene color matching, and rrecting for broadcast specifications.

**Apple Pro Training
Series: Optimizing
Your Final Cut Pro
System**
0-321-26871-7

Written and field-tested by industry pros Sean Cullen, Matthew Geller, Charles Roberts, and Adam Wilt, this is the ultimate guide for installing, configuring, optimizing, and trouble-shooting Final Cut Pro in real-world post-production environments.

**Apple Pro Training
Series: Final Cut Pro
for Avid Editors**
0-321-24577-6

Master trainer Diana Weynand takes you through a comprehensive "trans-lation course" designed for professional video and film editors who already know their way around Avid nonlinear systems.

he Apple Training Series:

ple Training Series: iLife '05
321-33020-X
ple Training Series: GarageBand 2
321-33019-6
**ple Training Series: Mac OS X
pport Essentials**
321-33547-3

**Apple Training Series: Desktop and
Portable Systems, Second Edition**
0-321-33546-5
**Apple Training Series: Mac OS X
Server Essentials**
0-321-35758-2

**Apple Training Series: Security
Best Practices for Mac OS X v 10.4**
0-321-36988-2
**Apple Training Series: Mac OS X
Server Administration Reference**
0-321-36984-X

To order books or find out about the Apple Pro Training Series, visit: **www.peachpit.com/appleprotraining**

To order books or find out about the Apple Pro Training Series, visit: **www.peachpit.com/appleprotraining**

Apple Pro Training Series: Soundtrack Pro
0-321-35757-4

Create original soundtracks with Apple's exciting new sound design software. Author Mary Plummer guides you through the secrets of editing, repairing, mixing, and and arranging multi-track audio files.

Apple Pro Training Series: Shake 4
0-321-25609-3

The leading compositing choice for cutting-edge visual effects in feature films, Shake is pure magic. This Apple-certified guide uses stunning real-world sequences to reveal the wizardry of keying, matting, painting, rotoscoping, and more.

Apple Pro Training Series: Shake 4 Quick Reference Guide
0-321-38246-3

This compact reference guide includes cheat sheets, quick-glance tables, and a concise explanation of the Shake interface, work-space, views, and tools.

Apple Pro Training Series: Getting Started with Motion
0-321-30533-7

This Apple-certified guide is designed to make Motion's sophisticated visual effects accessible to newcomers. Author Mary Plummer starts with the fundamentals and takes you through more than a dozen real-world projects. Fully compatible with Motion 2.

Apple Pro Training Series: Motion
0-321-27826-7

In this guide to Apple's revolutionary motion graphics software, commercial artist Damian Allen shows you how to harness Motion's behavior-based animations, particles, filters, and effects to create professional TV promos and other projects. Fully compatible with Motion 2.

Encyclopedia of Visual Effects
0-321-30334-2

The ultimate recipe book for visual effects artists working in Shake, Motion, and Adobe After Effects, this is a compendium of the coolest and most useful effects from A to Z ("Adding Clouds" to "Zapping Wires"). Written by Hollywood and independent pros, it covers everything from rotoscoping and painting to advanced greenscreen techniques.

Apple Pro Training Series: Logic Pro 7 and Logic Express 7
0-321-25614-X

Audio producer Martin Sitter shows you how to create, mix, produce, and polish your musical creations using Apple's professional audio software; the DVD includes a 30-day trial version of Logic Express 7.

Apple Pro Training Series: Advanced Logic Pro 7
0-321-25607-7

Composer David Dvorin takes you through Logic's powerful advanced features, covering everything from production, editing, and mixing to notation and scoring to picture.

Apple Pro Training Series: DVD Studio Pro 3
0-321-25610-7

Learn to author professional, interactive DVDs with this best-selling guide, fully compatible with DVD Studio Pro 4. You'll master everything from motion menus to advanced scripting as you design and create four complete DVDs.

Apple Pro Training Series: Final Cut Express 2
0-321-25615-8

The only Apple-authorized guide to Final Cut Express 2, this book delivers the techniques you need to make movie magic from the comfort of your Mac. Fully compatible with Final Cut Express HD.

Apple Pro Training Series: Color Management with Mac OS X
0-321-24576-8

Graphics profession-als will welcome this unique project-based guide that shows, step by step, how to set up a real-world Mac OS X-based color management workflow.

Apple Pro Training Series: Xsan Quick Reference Guide
0-321-36900-9

Apple's exciting new enterprise-class file system offers high-speed access to centralized shared data. This handy booklet provides invaluable setup, configuration, and troubleshooting tips.